D1126354

LAROUSSE
POCKET
ENCYCLOPEDIA
OF
WINE

General Editor
Christopher Foulkes

LAROUSSE

LAROUSSE POCKET ENCYCLOPEDIA OF WINE
First published in 1995 by Larousse

Managing Editors: CLAUDE NAUDIN, LAURE FLAVIGNY
Art Directors: FRÉDÉRIQUE LONGUÉPÉE, SUSAN JONES
Map Director: RENÉ OIZON
Maps: EUROPEAN MAP GRAPHICS, PALIMPSESTE, MARIE-THÉRÉSE MÉNAGER
Production: ANNIE BOTREL

Edited and Produced by SEGRAVE FOULKES PUBLISHERS
8 King's Road, Kingston upon Thames KT2 5HR, United Kingdom

General Editor: CHRISTOPHER FOULKES
Managing Editor: CARRIE SEGRAVE
Art Editor: NIGEL O'GORMAN
Editors: ALISON FRANKS, MAGGIE RAMSAY, GABRIELLE SHAW MW
Typesetting and Page Makeup: MACGURU
Illustrations: TREVOR LAWRENCE

ACKNOWLEDGMENTS

*This book draws upon the resources of the Larousse Encyclopedia of Wine,
produced by the same team, which covers the wine world in much greater detail and
with a more thoughtful tone. Renewed thanks to the worldwide team of contributors
and experts who worked to shape the Encyclopedia, with particular gratitude to
those who helped create this book: Alison Franks, John Gilbert, Nigel O'Gorman,
Maggie Ramsay, Gabrielle Shaw MW and Carrie Segrave.*

ISBN 2 03 507 202 6
Sales United Kingdom: Larousse International, 2 Albion Court, Galena Road,
Hammersmith, London W6 0LT
A CIP catalogue record for this book is available from the British Library

ISBN 2 03 507 201 8
Sales USA: Larousse Kingfisher Chambers Inc., 95 Madison Avenue,
New York, NY 10016

Library of Congress Catalog Card Number: 95-80465

ISBN 203 507 203 4
Larousse, Paris

Printed in France

CONTENTS

INTRODUCTION

THE LAROUSSE POCKET ENCYCLOPEDIA OF WINE is just that: a directory of wine names, places, people and terms. The aim is to aid wine choice and enjoyment by offering facts and guidance on as many wines and winemakers as possible.

It is not a compendium of personal tasting notes, with their inevitable quirks of opinion and prejudice. Nor does it reflect the competitive streak in the wine world whereby winemakers vie for medals or awards. This book aims at a balanced picture of what's what in wine, and where possible how wines taste, with the stress on those we are most likely to find in stores, on restaurant lists and when travelling.

The main part of the book is the A–Z, starting on page 33. However, other sections will aid wine choice and enjoyment: there's news from the world of wine; a chapter on Wine and Food discusses wine styles and which food they best go with; an Atlas of Wine Countries has maps showing where the main wine zones are; and at the end of the book are a chapter on Tasting Wine, Vintage Charts, and our list of Value for Money Wines which highlights affordable alternatives to the big names: *rapport qualité : prix*, as the French say.

Future editions will be much improved by feedback from readers: have we missed your favourite wine? Is there a producer of some minor wine who offers the best in quality and value? Let us know!

Christopher Foulkes, General Editor

HOW TO USE THIS BOOK

THE ALPHABET IS CHOSEN as the key access route. Look up what appears on a label – be it a region, grape name, producer or château – and this will lead to some information about the wine. There is no real need even to know which country the wine comes from. Once an entry is found, cross-references (in SMALL CAPITALS) may take you further.

The range covers the world's top wines – Bordeaux classed growths, Burgundy *Grands Crus* and the like – and it also deals with everyday wines: French *vins de pays*, fresh sources of value such as South America and Portugal, Hungary and southern Italy. There are definitions of label terms, summaries of wine rules, and brief sketches of key wine estates and producers.

Each entry in the A–Z starts with a key word in **BOLD CAPITALS.** This is the name, or the part of the name that is easiest to look up. Prefixes such as "de" and "du" in French, and "von" in German, and terms such as Château and Domaine, follow, not precede, the alphabetized word: Château de Fieuzal is listed as **FIEUZAL, CH DE.** *Italics* show the country and region the entry belongs to, and the style of wine (red, white, etc).

ABBREVIATIONS AND CONVENTIONS

Ch	Château	R	Red (wine)
Dom	Domaine	W	White (wine)
NV	Non-vintage	P	Rosé, or pink, wine
VDN	Vin doux naturel	Sp	Sparkling wine

Various official classifications of wine areas are used, and defined in the A–Z, their abbreviations being:

AOC *France*	Appellation d'Origine Contrôlée
DO *Spain*	Denominación de Origen
DOC *Italy*	Denominazione di Origine Controllata
DOC *Portugal*	Denominação de Origem Controlada
DOC *Spain*	Denominación de Origen Calificada
DOCG *Italy*	Denominazione di Origine Controllata e Garantita
QbA *Germany*	Qualitätswein eines bestimmten Anbaugebietes
QmP *Germany*	Qualitätswein mit Prädikat
VDQS *France*	Vin Délimité de Qualité Supérieure
WO *South Africa*	Wine of Origin
VA *USA*	Viticultural Area

Measurements

Wine production is measured in hectolitres, or 100 litres. A hectolitre (abbreviated to hl) is equal to just over 11 cases, or 133 75cl bottles, of wine. Area is measured in hectares, abbreviated to ha. One hectare equals 2.47 acres.

CHOOSING
WINES

WINE NEWS

A PARTIAL – IN BOTH SENSES – tip-sheet: what's new, what's good, what is causing comment and making waves.

BORDEAUX AND NAPA BACK ON FORM

The 1994 vintage saw a decent Bordeaux crop at last: the best vintage since 1990 – which, considering the sad state of '91, '92 and '93, is not saying much. The year was marred by September rain (a recurring pattern this decade), but the wines have turned out well. Caution is needed as Bordeaux *needs* a good vintage, and wish-fulfilment is a well-honed local skill, but independent experts rate the wines fairly high: 1988 is the best parallel.

In California, too, Napa made excellent '94 Cabernets in a cool summer – as good as those of the last good year, 1991.

ORGANIC BEGINS TO MATTER

From a fad to a theory to common sense: that's the progress of organic viticulture and winemaking. Today even respected domaines such as Leroy in Burgundy, Coulée de Serrant in the Loire, and others are to be found practising the extreme form called biodynamism (invoking the moon and stars as well as eschewing chemicals).

An official European Union (EU) definition of "organic wine" is awaited – but broadly, chemicals to combat pests and diseases must have been banned from the vineyard for at least three years. Artificial fertilizers are out. In the winery, additives are avoided: in some cases, egg-white or fish fining is not used, to allow the wine to be truly "vegetarian". The real test is in the taste: organic but horrible is a blind alley. Thankfully, most organic producers take enormous care – and that in any case is the way to make good wine.

ABC: ANYTHING BUT CHARDONNAY...

Look for a resurgence of other white-wine tastes, as wine-makers, and some drinkers, tire of Chardonnay: the greatest white-wine success story since Liebfraumilch. Everyone took to Chardonnay – it's an easy name to say, and the consensus New World style (imitated in eastern Europe and southern France) offers attractive fruity, creamy, slightly sweet tastes, spiced with a touch of oak. Now eyes turn to other grapes: Sémillon can age well, as Australia proves. But Riesling is the chief alternative – better on an absolute scale, some say, than the vaunted Chardonnay. Riesling makes interesting wine where it is given the chance, and deserves better than the sugar-and-water reputation of cheap German exports. Good Germans (QmP wines from classy growers: *see* A-Z section), wines from Alsace, Australia, Austria, New Zealand – Rieslings all – are all worth trying. And keeping, too, for no white wine ages better.

Watch, too, for red-wine developments: ABC can also stand for Anything But Cabernet.

APPELLATIONS EVERYWHERE

The European Union (EU) has been engaged in appellation diplomacy. If you want to sell us your wines, it tells upstart nations like Australia, New Zealand and Chile, think up a wine law that says where the wine comes from. Like Europe's. Thus the Australian bottles with "Produce of South-East Australia" on them, and the more local names such as Coonawarra and Hunter Valley. Chile has come up with a sensible system of five levels, while New Zealand is still working on it. The USA's system of Viticultural Areas is now mature. The A-Z has details: what the new laws mean is that wine behind a label will come from the place stated. That does not guarantee that it will be good wine, any more than wine from the European countries is good because it has an *appellation* or *denominazione*.

WHAT'S NEW

Tokay, wine of emperors, is being re-born. Foreign investors, French, Italian, British and Danish, are reviving the techniques of the pre-communist era and Hungary's great sweet wine is again as good as its reputation. The "classed growths" are back on the map and single-vineyard wines are on their way through the maturing process.

Flying winemakers – often Australians or Australian-trained – have been making waves, and wine, everywhere from Canada to Brazil, from southern France to Hungary. On the plus side: these wines are fresh, free from faults, true to their variety. Debit points are the charge of sameness: dozens of oak-tinged Chardonnays and light, catty Sauvignons. What the footloose winemakers do is raise the standards of everyday wine. Hopefully they will nurture, not submerge, local traditions where these are worth saving.

The magical Midi is "perhaps the most exciting vineyard in Europe" says an American expert. Australian, American and Bordeaux money is funding investment in the South of France, and names like Corbières, Faugères, Minervois and the various *vins de pays* are found on some fabulous (mostly red) wines. There is no hierarchy of quality, only a sprinkling of good producers amid a sea of *ordinaires*. But once found, what character and value…

WINE STYLES

MANY OF THE GRAPE VARIETIES used for wine, and techniques involved, are defined in the A-Z section. These are the main styles of wine, with some notes on how they are achieved.

ORDINARY WINE AND FINE WINE

There is good wine of every sort – and some bad wine too. But there is another question: is the wine ordinary – for everyday drinking, and thus inexpensive; or fine – with special taste qualities, designed for ageing in bottle, and special occasions? Some wines are *always* ordinary: the vineyards, grapes and climates see to that. In other cases – and increasingly – the winemaker has a choice: make ordinary wine, and lots of it, or a small amount of fine wine. Not all quality wine is made to be kept: it can be made to drink young, stressing fruit, freshness and crispness – still good wine, but in a different style.

RED WINES

Reds can be soft, fruity and early-maturing – Beaujolais, many *vins de pays*, ordinary Côtes du Rhône and Bordeaux, Australian branded wines – or more solid and austere in style – higher-level Rhône reds, Médoc, New World Cabernets. Such wines can age in bottle, and develop subtle and interesting flavours: for this they need "structure" in the form of tannin and acidity. The maker will accept a smaller yield of better grapes from his land in return for the extra concentration of taste.

Grapes to make fruity, easy-to-drink, fast-maturing reds: Gamay, Merlot (though it can be made to age), Grenache, Barbera. Grapes which can make long-maturing, fine wines: Cabernet Sauvignon, Nebbiolo, Pinot Noir, Syrah.

Techniques which lead to fruity, drink-young red wines: carbonic maceration; brief, cool fermentation; stainless steel vats rather than wooden casks for storage; filtering; early bottling. Techniques for long-maturing wines: long, warm fermentation; cask-ageing, perhaps in new oak; minimal filtering, bottling at perhaps 1–2 years old.

WHITE WINES: DRY

Most whites are more or less dry. Dry wine results when all natural grape sugar (plus any which may be added) is converted to alcohol (*see* Fermentation). Modern drinkers like freshness, gentle acidity, fruit aromas and flavours, rather than bone-dry, hard whites. Makers use aromatic grape varieties (Sauvignon, Muscats), skin contact, cold and malolactic fermentations to get this style: some leave a little natural sweetness in, by stopping fermentation; some rely on the sweet flavour of ripe grapes. Drink such wines young: the latest vintage is the best. Fewer whites than reds are made to age: examples are Chardonnays and Graves-type whites, where ageing on lees and/or in cask adds structure (*see* Reds); and Rieslings (Germany, Alsace) where bottle-age alters and improves flavour. However, most Chardonnays and Rieslings – and other dry whites – are made to be drunk young. Oak-derived tastes – nuts, butter, vanilla – add to white-wine character, but can also mask the wine's true flavour. Oak chips, even oak essence, are used in cheaper wines instead of costly new casks.

SWEET WHITES

A wide spectrum of styles stems from several ways of making white wine sweet. Simplest, in technique and taste, are those where fermentation is stopped to leave some sugar, and/or some sweetness is added. These include many German wines, Italian Abbocato wines, simple Vouvray from the Loire.

Sweetness gained from over-ripe grapes, including those with noble rot, makes more complex, subtle sweet wines. Here fermentation stops naturally. Examples are Sauternes, German Auslese, Tokaji, New World late-harvest wines. Muscat grapes, strong in aroma and sweetness, make characteristic sweet wines.

SPARKLING WINES

The many ways of putting bubbles into, or keeping them in, a bottle lead to different qualities of sparkling wine. Champagne's method (*see* Méthode Champenoise) is the best: wines improve in bottle, gaining subtlety; the bubbles are prolific, persistent. Tank-method (Charmat) sparklers can be good. Other ways make less subtle, less fizzy wine – but can be good value. Labels will say if the classic method is used, sometimes using terms like "fermented in this bottle". Sparkling wines do not have to be white: Champagne's rosé, pink wines from other areas, and even red fizz (Burgundy and Australia) have their fans.

FORTIFIED WINES

Adding spirit – brandy or a neutral, non-grape spirit – strengthens the wine and made it safer to ship in pre-scientific days. Now, fortification is part of the style. In port and *vins doux naturel*, it is done before the wine stops fermenting, thereby keeping some natural sugar in the wine. Sherry is fortified later in the process; after fermentation and some ageing.

MATCHING
FOOD AND WINE

THE IDEAL FOOD AND WINE partnership is an equal one, in which each enhances the flavours of the other. However, even a very specific recommendation may prove difficult to replicate: wines may taste different from one producer to another, from vintage to vintage, and at various stages of maturity; foods vary in their seasoning, spicing and ripeness. What ultimately counts is personal taste.

Eclectic experimentation may lead you to some fascinating food and wine discoveries, but the following basic principles can act as a starting point.

COLOUR

The old rule of white wine with fish, red with meat is based on sound sense: a tannic red wine can make fish and shellfish taste metallic, while strongly flavoured meat and game overpower most white wine. Some cheeses are much better with white wine than with red.

WEIGHT

The alcoholic strength and depth of flavour of a wine should reflect that of the dish: delicate foods deserve subtle wines, hearty dishes require sturdier wines.

FLAVOUR

Sometimes a contrast in flavours works well – a lemony-scented wine with fried fish – on other occasions a parallel can be drawn: oak-aged wine with smoked food; spicy wine with spicy (but not too spicy) food.

REGION

Many traditional European dishes have a natural affinity with the wine produced in their region of origin: think of Italian wine and pasta; Swiss wine and cheese fondue; Muscadet with shellfish; Cahors with cassoulet.

OCCASION

An everyday supper calls for a simple wine; an elaborate dinner is a chance to show off better wines. But a great wine, worth serious attention, demands fine but simple food. Some foods are difficult: very salty and acidic foods (especially vinegar) leave their taste in the mouth; eggs can clog the taste buds; chillies numb the palate; very sweet puddings make all but the richest dessert wines seem lean.

The following partnerships have all been enjoyed by tasters, but the list is not definitive: use it as a starting point and see page 8 for suggested wines in similar styles.

AIOLI Provence rosé; Australian Chardonnay.

APPLES In savoury cream sauce White Graves, Australian Chardonnay.

Pies, tarts, strudel Sweet German or Austrian *Auslese, Beerenauslese*, Tokaji, sweet Vouvray, Quarts-de-Chaume.

ARTICHOKES Vinaigrette Acidic white, eg Muscadet, Sauvignon de Touraine; oaked Chilean Sauvignon Blanc.

Hollandaise Full-bodied dry or medium-dry white, eg Australian or California Chardonnay.

ASPARAGUS Aromatic dry or off-dry white, eg Sauvignon Blanc-based wine or German Riesling.

AUBERGINES Grilled or fried Mediterranean (Sardinian, Valencian, Greek, north African) red or rosé.

Stuffed Red Corbières, Dão, Zinfandel, Barbera.

AVOCADO with shellfish California Riesling or Sauvignon Blanc, South African Chenin Blanc, Sancerre.

Vinaigrette Fino sherry.

Guacamole Mexican Cabernet Sauvignon or California Chardonnay.

BARBECUED FOOD Australian Cabernet/Shiraz, California Cabernet Sauvignon or Zinfandel, Fitou; full-bodied dry rosé, eg Tavel, Rioja, Côtes de Provence; retsina.

BEAN STEW *See* Cassoulet.

BEEF roast St-Emilion, Pomerol, Côte de Beaune *Premier Cru*, Châteauneuf-du-Pape, red Mercurey, Côtes du Rhône.

Grilled steak, hamburger Beaujolais-Villages, Margaux, St-Julien, Chianti, Portuguese country wine, young California or Australian Cabernet Sauvignon, Gamay, Zinfandel.

Casserole Sturdy reds, eg Beaujolais, Mâcon, Côtes du

Chef's Eye View: Phil Vickery

"I do a lot of boiled meats, such as silverside of beef and collar of bacon," says Phil Vickery. "I serve the bacon with split peas and mash, but there's a strong madeira sauce, and although most people would choose a light red with bacon, I think a big red – a Rioja, for example – would go equally well with the powerful flavours in the sauce."

Vinegar is said to be the kiss of death to wine, yet a balanced menu often includes it in a dressing for salads, hot vegetables or fish. "There's a little vinegar in my starter of deep-fried skate with beetroot and saffron mayonnaise, and it's hard to make an objective choice beyond recommending a really crisp dry white."

His egg custard tart with nutmeg ice cream has been singled out for praise by restaurant reviewers, and is seldom off the menu: "I don't want to disappoint people who travel a long way to try it. The obvious accompaniment would be a Muscat de Beaumes-de-Venise, but I'd say champagne would be good too."

Phil Vickery, chef at the Castle Hotel in Taunton, Somerset, produces some of Britain's finest food. Mediterranean and Oriental influences are minimal; instead, he uses the West Country's wealth of ingredients to create immaculate interpretations of traditional English dishes such as spiced potted duck, braised lamb and fish cakes.

Rhône, Châteauneuf-du-Pape, Barbaresco, Chianti, Dão, California Cabernet, Zinfandel, Australian Shiraz blends.

CABBAGE, STUFFED Light but earthy or herb-scented red, eg Beaujolais *crus*, Roumanian Pinot Noir, South African Pinotage.

CAKES Sweet white, sparkling or fortified wine. *See also* Chocolate.

CASSOULET Cahors, Côtes du Frontonnais, Minervois, young red Rioja or Navarra, Zinfandel.

CHEESE Soft cheeses can be difficult to match: their creaminess coats the tongue and any hint of ammonia in a ripe cheese "kills" wine.

Brie (mild) Fine, mature red or white.

Camembert, Brie (ripe) Corbières, St-Emilion, Beaujolais-Villages.

Cheddar Fruity red, eg ruby port, St-Emilion; dry oloroso sherry or vintage port.

Goat's cheese; herbed cheese Dry, fruity white with some acidity, eg Sancerre; dry Languedoc or Provence rosé; light red, eg Saumur, Corbières, Hungarian Merlot.

Gorgonzola, strong blue cheeses Barbera, Dolcetto or Nebbiolo d'Alba, Recioto della Valpolicella, Zinfandel; tawny port, sercial madeira.

Gruyère (young) Swiss white or lively red, eg Beaujolais, Zinfandel; **(mature)** full-bodied dry white or mature red.

Maroilles, pungent cheeses Fragrant red, eg St-Emilion, Côte Rôtie; or aromatic white eg Alsace Gewürztraminer.

Parmesan Barolo, Barbaresco, dry Lambrusco, tawny port.

Port-du-Salut, monastery cheeses Light fruity red burgundy or Bergerac.

Roquefort, soft blue cheeses Sauternes or Monbazillac; Muscat de Rivesaltes; young local red, eg Faugères.

Stilton Vintage or tawny port; dry oloroso sherry;

Monbazillac.

Fondue Swiss dry white, Grüner Veltliner, Sauvignon Blanc wines.

CHICKEN Roast Medium-bodied fruity red, eg burgundy, St-Chinian, Gigondas, Côtes du Ventoux, Chianti, young California Cabernet Sauvignon, Merlot, Zinfandel; dry rosé; crisp white.

Kiev Oaky Chardonnay from Australia or Chile, Alsace Riesling; red Bergerac.

With cream Dry Vouvray, medium-dry Gaillac, Alsace Riesling, white Graves or burgundy; Oregon Pinot Noir.

With tarragon California Chardonnay.

With tomatoes and/or garlic Red Bandol, Crozes-Hermitage; California or South African Chardonnay.

CHILLI CON CARNE Rioja, Argentinian or Chilean Cabernet Sauvignon.

CHINESE FOOD Dry or medium rosé, dry sparkling white; aromatic dry white.

Fish/shellfish with ginger and spring onions *Demi-sec* Vouvray, Gewürztraminer, oaky white Rioja, Australian Chardonnay or Sémillon.

Sweet and sour sauce California or Australian Sauvignon Blanc with good acidity, New Zealand Sémillon/Sauvignon blend.

Peking duck St-Emilion, oaky red or white Rioja, Gewürztraminer.

CHOCOLATE Banyuls, málaga, malmsey madeira, Mavrodaphne, California Black or Orange Muscat, Australian Orange Muscat.

CREAMS, CRÈME BRÛLÉE, FOOLS, TRIFLE, SYLLABUB Sauternes, Monbazillac, Moscatel de Valencia, *Beerenauslese*, Tokaji, sweet oloroso sherry, madeira or marsala, Vin Santo.

DUCK Roast St-Emilion, red burgundy, Côte Rôtie,

Châteauneuf-du-Pape, Cahors, red Côtes de St-Mont, Zinfandel; Riesling *Spätlese*.

With oranges or cherries Loire red, Rosso Conero, Zinfandel, Australian Shiraz.

EGGS Scrambled with smoked salmon Unoaked Chablis or other Chardonnay, non-vintage champagne.

Omelette Beaujolais, Chianti or southern French red or white with tomato or ham; Pinot Noir with mushroom; lightly oaked Australian Chardonnay with smoked fish and cheese; fino sherry with cold Spanish omelette/tortilla.

Quiche Dry, medium-full white, eg Graves, Alsace,

Rheingau *Trocken*; light young red, eg Beaujolais, Chinon, Chilean Cabernet Sauvignon; rosé *vin de pays*.

FISH Generally, the finer the fish, the finer the white wine to accompany it, either crisp and lemony or buttery, oaked styles. Avoid tannic reds; lighter wines based on Cabernet Franc, Gamay and Pinot Noir often work well.

Fish pie Mâcon Blanc, Bianco di Custoza, German *trocken*, Napa Chardonnay.

Freshwater fish White Graves, Anjou, Mosel.

Fried fish Sauvignon Blanc, Muscadet, Alsace Riesling, Pinot Grigio, Verdicchio, Frascati,

Chef's Eye View: Antony Worrall Thompson

"The regional approach seems best with Mediterranean flavours," says Antony Worrall Thompson. *"With roast mullet, served with a stew of white beans and duck confit, I would choose Provençal wine, perhaps Bandol rosé from Domaine de Pibarnon, or a light red like Domaine de Trévallon."*

But in wine, as in cooking, inspiration comes from around the world. With a main dish of duck confit he suggests Barolo, a Barbera, or a Malbec from Mendoza in Argentina: *"Malbec is the same grape used in Cahors, but it's streets ahead of anything you get in France."*

When garlic and chillies are to the forefront, for example as a dressing for char-grilled squid, a powerful Primitivo – or a Zinfandel – springs to mind. *"I'm keen on big reds with these spices; they tend to kick white wine in the teeth."*

Rich desserts like sticky toffee pudding normally demand ultra-sweet wine. After suggesting an Orange or Black Muscat, or a Pedro Ximénez sherry, *"to match syrup against syrup"*, Worrall Thompson had another idea: *"An eau-de-vie such as Mirabelle or Quetsch would provide a strong contrast – and they'd help the digestion of a dish like that."*

Antony Worrall Thompson is one of only five chefs who have been awarded the title Meilleur Ouvrier de Grande Bretagne, yet his London restaurants – Bistrot 190, dell'Ugo, Zoë, Palio – are funky, fun, and light-years away from the solemnity and silver usually linked with highly-acclaimed chefs. Drawing on the peasant cooking of Italy, France, Britain and Ireland, with chillies, Oriental herbs and spices turning up in surprising places, his food is truly eclectic.

English wine; chilled Beaujolais, Chinon.

Mediterranean-style (with olive oil, herbs, garlic, tomatoes, saffron) Southern French rosé or white, Muscadet, Italian Pinot Grigio; retsina; light Beaujolais or other Gamay-based red.

Oily fish (herring, mackerel, sardine, swordfish, tuna) Rich Australian Sémillon or Chardonnay; white Dão, Vinho Verde, Muscadet, Gros Plant, New Zealand Sauvignon Blanc; spicy young Côtes du Rhône.

Salmon, poached White burgundy, Sancerre, Alsace Riesling, Condrieu, California or Australian Chardonnay; Beaujolais, Chinon, Bourgueil; Pinot Noir from Alsace, California, Oregon.

White fish, steamed or grilled Steely, elegant Alsace Riesling; tart, appley Loire Chenin Blanc; lemony Soave.

White fish in creamy/buttery sauce Champagne, Vouvray, Chardonnay-based wine, Muscadet *sur lie*; Mosel. *See also* shellfish, smoked fish.

FRUIT PUDDINGS Sweet white, sparkling or fortified wine.

GAME Lightly hung game, plainly cooked, deserves fine red bordeaux or burgundy (classed-growth Médoc or Graves, *Grand* or *Premier Cru* Côte d'Or, Côte Chalonnaise from a good vintage), or Napa Cabernet Sauvignon.

Well-hung game needs the powerful accompaniment of Hermitage, Côte Rôtie, Châteauneuf-du-Pape, Cornas, Rioja *reserva*, Barolo, Australian Shiraz.

Casserole St-Emilion, Pomerol, Barbaresco, Brunello di Montalcino, Valpolicella Amarone, Dão, California Zinfandel, Australian Shiraz/Cabernet Sauvignon. *See also* Pigeon, Quail, Venison.

GOOSE Assertive red, or sweet white with good acidity, eg German *Spätlese*, Alsace *réserve exceptionelle*.

HAM Red burgundy or Mâcon, Beaujolais and other Gamays, Dolcetto; Riesling *Spätlese*.

Raw Pinot Grigio dell'Alto Adige, Soave Classico; fino or manzanilla sherry; young Spanish or Italian red.

Smoked German *Spätlese*.

INDIAN FOOD Mildly spiced Alsace Gewürztraminer, Australian Chardonnay, Orvieto *abboccato*.

Tandoori dishes California Cabernet Sauvignon, Australian Cabernet/Shiraz.

KIDNEYS Pomerol, St-Emilion, Zinfandel.

In mustard sauce Morgon or St-Amour.

LAMB Plainly cooked lamb sets off the finest Médoc (especially Pauillac, St-Estèphe) or Graves red, Rioja *reserva*, Ribera del Duero, New World Cabernet Sauvignon. With more herbs, garlic or other flavours, less expensive examples of the above, or try Châteauneuf-du-Pape or Beaujolais.

LIVER Chianti Classico, Chilean or Bulgarian Reserve Cabernet Sauvignon.

With bacon California or Oregon Pinot Noir.

With sage Flowery Nahe Riesling *Spätlese*; Chinon.

MUSHROOMS Pomerol, most Pinot Noir-based wine, South African Pinotage, Merlot.

OXTAIL STEW Spicy red from southern France or Greece.

PAELLA White, rosé or red Rioja, Penedès.

PASTA Almost any Italian red; white with pesto, seafood or creamy sauce.

PÂTÉ, TERRINE Mâcon Blanc, dry Vouvray, Jurançon, Pinot Grigio dell'Alto Adige, California Fumé Blanc; Côtes de Provence rosé; young fruity red.

Chicken liver Dry amontillado sherry.

PEPPERS Pungent Sauvignon Blanc, Alsace Gewürztraminer; Cabernet Sauvignon or Shiraz blend from California or Australia.

PIGEON Good red burgundy, Pomerol, Chianti Classico, Italian Merlot, Sardinian red.

PIZZA Chianti, Sicilian red, Barbera, Zinfandel, Coteaux d'Aix-en-Provence red or rosé.

PORK Medium-bodied red or white, eg Côtes du Rhône, Mâcon, Anjou, Barbera, Douro red, Bulgarian Mavrud; Alsace *Grand Cru* Riesling, Gewürztraminer, Rheingau or Pfalz *Auslese* or *Spätlese*, New World Chardonnay.

QUAIL Pinot Noir from Alsace, Roumania, Oregon.

QUICHE See Eggs.

RISOTTO Bianco di Custoza, Trebbiano d'Abruzzo, Pinot Grigio, Grüner Veltliner; young red, eg Dolcetto, Bardolino, Valpolicella.

SALAD White or red with good acidity, eg Loire or New Zealand Chenin Blanc.

SALAMI Barbera, Chianti, dry Lambrusco, Valpolicella, red Beaujolais, Provence red or rosé, Tavel or Corsican rosé, Tempranillo or Garnacha-based wines, eg Rioja, Navarra, Penedès.

SAUSAGES Spicy chorizo Fino or manzanilla sherry.

Grilled Châteauneuf-du-Pape, Cahors, Rioja, Dolcetto, Portuguese red, Merlot from anywhere.

SHELLFISH Wines made from

Chef's Eye View: Michael Romano

One of Michael Romano's signature dishes is a filet mignon of tuna; a 3-inch cube of fish marinaded with soy sauce, ginger, garlic and sherry, then grilled so it is sweetish outside, rare in the centre. "It outsells all other food on the menu, so we've had plenty of chance to experiment – and in New York there's a great selection of wines from all over the world. My two favourites are very different: Cornas, the Rhône red, or Tokay Pinot Gris from Alsace."

A truly memorable food and wine partnership, also based on tuna, is a dish he created to accompany Oregon Pinot Noir. The fish was roasted and served with a spicy, lightly creamy, green peppercorn sauce, and the combination was "so perfect it was almost supernatural".

Michael Romano admits to being excited about the honesty and simplicity of Mediterranean cooking. "Right now on the menu we have a filet mignon of beef with a tomato and anchovy sauce made quickly in the pan. To partner it I would bring in a young, lighter red from southern Italy, perhaps from Friuli in northern Italy, or from Provence, ideally a Bandol."

Michael Romano, of New York City's Union Square Cafe, aims to help Americans become more relaxed about food. "In France and Italy people feel comfortable about food, but here they have an adversarial relationship with it: they worry about health and fitness and slimming. The idea of the restaurant is to present seemingly simple, seasonal food in a casual atmosphere, but with really good, knowlegeable service."

Chardonnay, whether crisply dry or rich and buttery, are good with most shellfish.

Crab, lobster, scallops Champagne; white burgundy (the richer the dish, the better the wine), white Hermitage; Alsace Riesling.

Clams, mussels, oysters Muscadet, Gros Plant, Chablis, red or white Vinho Verde, Verdicchio, Australian Hunter Valley Sémillon.

Prawns, shrimps Muscadet, crisp Sauvignon Blanc; fino or manzanilla sherry.

SMOKED FISH Alsace Gewürztraminer, Rheingau *Spätlese*, oak-aged Spanish whites, manzanilla sherry, Chilean Chardonnay.

Salmon Champagne.

SOUFFLÉS Cheese Fine red burgundy or bordeaux; Alsace Pinot Gris; champagne;

Dornfelder *Trocken*.

Fish Dry white burgundy or bordeaux; Napa Fumé Blanc; South Australian Chardonnay.

TURKEY Light red burgundy, Médoc, Napa Cabernet Sauvignon, Zinfandel.

VEAL Roast Medium-bodied red or white.

With cream sauce A rich Chardonnay.

Osso bucco Barbera, Barbaresco, Valpolicella, Chianti.

VEGETABLES Casseroles Beaujolais-Villages, Rhône and Midi reds, Chianti, Bulls Blood, Zinfandel; Provence white.

Raw Crisp Sauvignon Blanc, rosé or light red, eg Beaujolais, Bardolino.

VENISON Top burgundy; Cahors, Gigondas, Barolo, Australian Shiraz, Zinfandel; late-harvest Tokay d'Alsace, Pfalz *Spätlese*.

Chef's Eye View: Cindy Pawlcyn

Some of the most exciting cooking on the USA's West Coast, with California wines to match, comes from Cindy Pawlcyn.

So close to the heart of America's top wine region, the enthusiasm for matching food and wine should not be unexpected. Even the informally named Buckeye Roadhouse has a "Zinfandel challenge", where half glasses of three different Zinfandels accompany selected dishes. Among several highly successful combinations have been a plate of ribs, smoked duck and smoked chicken, cooked in the restaurant's woodburning stoves. "The fruity but rich wines go really well with the smoky flavours of the food." Equally rewarding with Zinfandel was "100 almond curry duck", based on a traditional Indian spicy almond sauce: the sauce and the wine are apparently even better with squab .

A homely-sounding baked lemon pudding is taken to new heights with the Sauternes-style Dolce, made by Far Niente, but Cindy Pawlcyn also loves the luxury of champagne with dessert. "One of my favourites is Billecart-Salmon's Brut Rosé, which I'd be happy to drink with even a very rich butterscotch crème brûlée."

Cindy Pawlcyn's California restaurants range from the Fog City Diner on San Francisco's Embarcadero and Tra'vigna, an Italian-inspired trattoria in the Napa Valley wine country, to Mustard's Grill, "the American truckstop, deluxe", also in Napa, and the Buckeye Roadhouse on Highway 101 north of San Francisco.

ATLAS
OF WINE
COUNTRIES

FRANCE & BELGIUM

THE WINE REGIONS OF FRANCE extend from cool,
northern Champagne, Alsace and the Loire Valley
to the Mediterranean climates of Provence and the Midi.
Bordeaux and the South-West have Atlantic climates,
while Burgundy's is closer to Champagne. Belgium's
vineyards are mostly in the south,
while Luxembourg's line
the Moselle river.

ANJOU
SAUMUR
Nantes
PAYS
NANTAIS

Angers
Loire

Poitiers

la Rochelle

*Atlantic
Ocean*

Bastia

CORSICA

Ajaccio

MÉDOC
BORDEAUX
Bordeaux
GRAVES
ENTRE-DEUX-MERS
SAUTERNES

BLAYE
BOURG
POMEROL
SAINT-EMILION
BERGERAC

Garonne

SOUTH-WEST

Pau
PYRÉNÉES

N

| 0 | 100 | 200 km |
| 0 | 50 | 100 miles |

North Sea

NETHERLANDS

Bruges ○
○ Antwerp
Brussels ○ ○ Maastricht
Escaut
BELGIUM
Mons ○ ○ Liège
Meuse
Sambre
Meuse

LUXEMBOURG
○ Luxembourg

○ Reims
CHAMPAGNE
Moselle
Seine
Paris ○
○ Nancy
F R A N C E
Strasbourg ○
CHAMPAGNE
Rhin
Seine
ALSACE
○ Orléans
Auxerre ○ CHABLIS
TOURAINE
SANCERRE Dijon ○
POUILLY CÔTE DE NUITS
○ Bourges Beaune ○
CÔTE DE BEAUNE JURA
BURGUNDY CÔTE *Lake Geneva*
CHALONNAISE
MÂCONNAIS
○ Mâcon
Clermont-○ BEAUJOLAIS
Ferrand Lyons ○ *Rhône* SAVOIE

CÔTES-DU-RHÔNE
○ Grenoble

Rhône
CAHORS
CÔTES-DU-RHÔNE
GAILLAC ○ Avignon
Nîmes ○
COTEAUX DU COTEAUX D'AIX -
Toulouse LANGUEDOC EN-PROVENCE Nice ○
Montpellier ○ ○ Marseilles
MINERVOIS CÔTES DE PROVENCE

CORBIÈRES
Perpignan ○
CÔTES DU ROUSSILLON

Mediterranean Sea

GERMANY

River valleys shape Germany's pattern of wine regions: the Mosel, Ahr and the eastern regions, being far north, need the shelter of valley slopes to ripen grapes. The Rhein and its tributaries shape the other regions, though the southernmost and warmest, Baden, has vines beside Lake Constance.

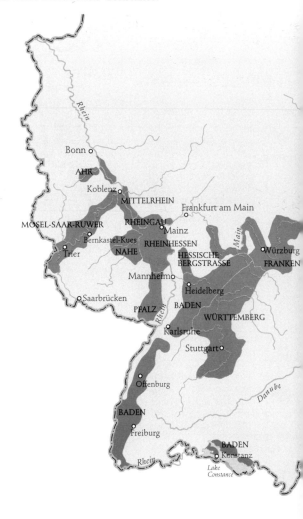

SACHSEN

SAALE-UNSTRUT

Elbe

Halle
Leipzig
Dresden

Nürnberg

Regensburg

Munich

GERMANY

N

| 0 | 50 | 100 km |
| 0 | 25 | 50 miles |

ITALY, SWITZERLAND & AUSTRIA

ITALY HAS VINES FROM the northern Alps right down its Apennine backbone to close to Africa. The north-west (Piedmont) and centre (Tuscany) are the best zones. Switzerland's wine mostly comes from the Vaud and Valais in the west, Austria's from the Danube valley and Burgenland in the east.

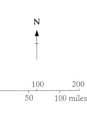

LIECHTENSTEIN

WEINVIERTEL
WACHAU
Danube
DONAULAND
Vienna
CARNUNTUM
Salzburg
THERMENREGION
NEUSIEDLERSEE
AUSTRIA
Innsbruck
SÜD-OSTSTEIERMARK
SÜDBURGENLAND
WESTSTEIERMARK

Bolzano
Adige
Trento
Piave
Trieste
Verona
Venice
Po

Bologna
Ravenna
ALBANA DI
ROMAGNA
CARMIGNANO
Arno
Pisa
Florence
Ancona
CHIANTI
BRUNELLO DI
VINO NOBILE DI
MONTALCINO
MONTE PULCIANO

TORGIANO

Tiber
Pescara

Rome
Adriatic
Sea

ITALY

TAURASI
Bari
Naples

Tyrrhenian
Sea

Ionian
Sea

Palermo
Messina
Reggio di Calabria
SICILY
Catania

SPAIN & PORTUGAL

SPAIN'S QUALITY WINE ZONES are mostly in the cooler
north: the Catalonia zones inland from Barcelona,
the Rioja zone, and the Ribera del Duero. Jerez in the far
south makes sherry. Portugal's Douro river, in the north,
is the home of port. Vinho Verde comes from the north,
good reds and whites from Bairrada and Dão.

San Sebastián

Bilbao TXAKOLI
(CHACOLI)

Vitoria

Logroño

NAVARRA

RIOJA

oPamplona

Huesca

SOMONTANO

AMPURDAN-
COSTA BRAVA

CAMPO
DE BORJA

Ebro Zaragoza

COSTERS
DEL SEGRE

CONCA DE
BARBERA

ALELLA

Lérida

PRIORATO

PENEDES Barcelona

CALATAYUD

CARINENA

Tarragona

TERRA ALTA

TARRAGONA

TARRAGONA

Tajo

VINOS DE
MADRID

UTIEL
REQUENA

Valencia

A MANCHA

Mediterranean

Sea

ALMANSA

VALENCIA

JUMILLA

ALICANTE

YECLA

Alicante

Murcia

BINISSALEM
Palma Majorca

BALEARIC ISLANDS

N

0   100   200 km

0   50   100 miles

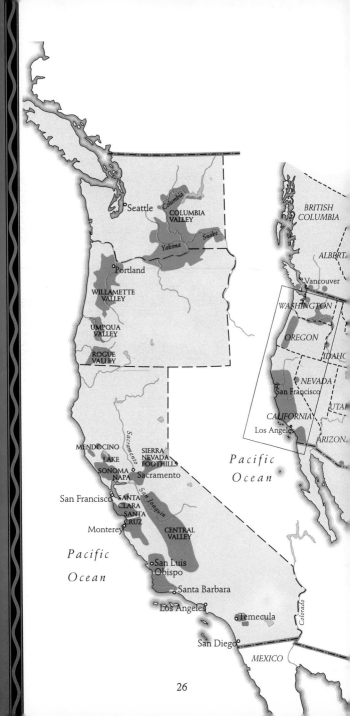

Seattle

COLUMBIA VALLEY

Columbia

Yakima

Snake

Portland

WILLAMETTE VALLEY

UMPQUA VALLEY

ROGUE VALLEY

BRITISH COLUMBIA

ALBERTA

Vancouver

WASHINGTON

OREGON

IDAHO

NEVADA

San Francisco

UTAH

CALIFORNIA

Los Angeles

ARIZONA

Pacific Ocean

MENDOCINO

LAKE

SONOMA

NAPA

SIERRA NEVADA FOOTHILLS

Sacramento

San Francisco

SANTA CLARA

SANTA CRUZ

Monterey

Pacific Ocean

CENTRAL VALLEY

Sacramento

San Joaquin

San Luis Obispo

Santa Barbara

Los Angeles

Temecula

Colorado

San Diego

MEXICO

26

NORTH AMERICA

FEW STATES IN THE USA are without vineyards,
but California, Washington, Oregon and New York
State are the biggest producers. The detail map shows
the West Coast states and their key wine zones.
Canada's vineyards are in southern Ontario,
near the Great Lakes and in western
British Columbia.

Pacific

Ocean

CENTRAL & SOUTH AMERICA

CHILE AND ARGENTINA are the leading wine countries
here, though Mexico has the oldest vineyards, and Brazil,
Uruguay and Peru make wine. The detail map shows
the wine zones of Chile, of which Maipo, Casablanca
and Maule are important; and Argentina,
led by Mendoza.

AUSTRALIA

WINE IS MADE IN THE SOUTHEAST of the country, and in Western Australia. The quality zones are in the hilly districts of New South Wales, in Victoria and in South Australia. Inland, the Murray River zone makes large amounts of good everyday wine. In the west, cool coastal zones are showing promise.

Indian Ocean

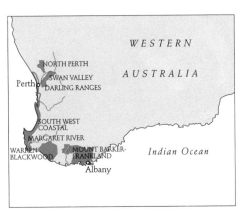

Indian Ocean

QUEENSLAND

Brisbane

GRANITE BELT
INVERELL

Darling

Barwon

NEW   SOUTH   WALES

Macquarie

Port
Macquarie

MUDGEE

UPPER HUNTER VALLEY
LOWER HUNTER VALLEY

Hunter

Lachlan

Newcastle

MURRUMBIDGEE

Orange

Murrumbidgee

COWRA

Sydney

Canberra

AUSTRALIAN
CAPITAL
TERRITORY

BENDIGO

Murray

RUTHERGLEN

PYRENEES

VICTORIA

MACEDON

GOULBURN VALLEY

BALLARAT

Melbourne

YARRA VALLEY

Bass Strait

Pacific Ocean

N

Launceston

TASMANIA

Hobart

| 0 | 100 | 200 | 300 | 400 | 500 km |

| 0 | 100 | 200 | 300 miles |

NEW ZEALAND

THE SOUTH ISLAND VINEYARDS of Marlborough
are the most noted for quality, though Hawke's Bay,
Bay of Plenty and Gisborne in the North run them
close. Most of the vineyards are very new,
and experiments are still going on to find
the best zones: witness the far-south
vineyard of Central Otago.

A-Z
WINES OF
THE WORLD

A

ABBOCCATO *Italy* A gently sweet style of wine.

ABELÉ, HENRI *France, Champagne* One of Champagne's oldest houses, owned by the Spanish Freixenet group. Its traditional style, seen in both vintage and NV *cuvées*, is quite rich and full-bodied.

ABRUZZO *Italy* Mountainous area in central Italy where bears can still be found. Mainly R wine from the Montepulciano grape and W from Trebbiano.

AC *France* See APPELLATION D'ORIGINE CONTRÔLÉE.

ACCAD, GUY Consultant winemaker and oenologist, active in Burgundy since the 1980s, who believes in macerating whole bunches of very ripe (red-wine) grapes before fermentation, leading to deep, dark sweet-tasting wines. No-one knows yet if they will age well.

ACKERMAN-LAURANCE *France, Loire, Saumur, Sp; W, P* The first firm to make sparkling Saumur, in 1811. Linked today with the larger firm of Remy-Pannier, it makes a full range of this wine and a Crémant de Loire (Sp; W, P).

ADEGA *Portugal* Winery.

ADELAIDE HILLS *Australia, South Australia* With its high altitude, this cool-climate area makes wines of great elegance and finesse. Leading producers include: Grand Cru Estate, Petaluma.

ADELSHEIM *USA, Oregon, R, W* This estate on the slopes of Chehalem Mountain has Pinot Noir, Pinot Gris, Chardonnay, Pinot Blanc and White Riesling. Ripe black cherry, mushrooms and truffles scent the Pinot Noir; Pinot Gris is a flinty dry W.

AFFENTAL *Germany, Baden, R* Red wine from Spätburgunder, popular in Germany, comes from this valley in North Baden. (The name means "monkey valley".)

AGE, BODEGAS *Spain, Rioja, R, W, P* One of Rioja's main exporters, producing reliable quality wines. Much of their production appears under the Siglo label, although their best wines are the Marqués del Romeral *reservas*.

AGLIANICO DEL VULTURE *Italy, Basilicata, DOC, R* The southern region Basilicata's only DOC and one of Italy's greatest wines. The R Aglianico grape is grown in the volcanic heights of Monte Vulture. Can age very well. Leading producers include: Fratelli D'Angelo, Paternoster.

AHR *Germany, Anbaugebiet, R, W* The Ahr, a tributary of the Rhine near Bonn, is lined by red-wine vineyards, much visited by tourists. Most wine is soft and slightly sweet, made to enjoy on a summer day; but some growers now make more structured, dry wines. Among these are Kloster Marienthal, Weingut Meyer-Näkel, Weingut Brogsitters.

AIRÉN Low-quality white grape; the most widely planted in Spain (and in the world). With careful, modern vinification it produces large quantities of cheap and cheerful wine – sometimes surprisingly good, especially in DO La Mancha.

AJACCIO *France, Corsica, AOC, R, P, W* One of Corsica's top appellations. Its small production is of Rs from the native Sciaccarello grape, plus Grenache, Cinsaut, Carignan. Some Ps and Ws. Leading producers include: Clos Capitoro, Dom Peraldi.

ALABAMA *USA* Hurricanes and humidity try the patience of a few growers, mostly of Scuppernong and other native grapes.

ALBANA DI ROMAGNA *Italy, Emilia-Romagna, DOCG, W* Italy's first DOCG for W wine. From the relatively neutral Albana grape. At its best, it has soft, peachy perfumes. May be dry, *amabile* or *passito*. Grander status than it deserves. Leading producers include: Fattoria Paradiso, Zerbina.

ALBARIÑO/ALVARINHO Quality white grape from north-west Spain and Portugal. In Galicia it makes some of Spain's best whites in the Rías Baixas DO; in Portugal, as Alvarinho, it becomes the best, appley, Vinhos Verdes.

ALCOHOL An important element in wine, but not the only one. Produced during fermentation when yeasts change the sugar content of the grape juice into alcohol, carbon dioxide and heat. The alcohol content of wine varies from around 8° to around 15°.

ALEATICO Red grape with intense perfume, making wine with deep colour, often sweet and strong. Grown in several regions of Italy, and now in Chile (there are also small plantings in Australia and California).

ALELLA *Spain, Catalonia, DO, W, P, R* Wine zone in the northeast near Barcelona, producing all colours of wine but mostly W: fresh wines for drinking young. Experiments with Chardonnay, especially in the hilly, cooler inland areas, are doing well. Leading producers include: Alta Alella, Bodegas Parxet.

ALENTEJO *Portugal, R, W* New wine zone in southern Portugal: full-flavoured R wines from blends of native grapes show more promise than the rather fat, blowzy Ws. Leading producers include: Adega Cooperativa de Borba, Quinta do Carmo, Esporão.

ALEXANDER VALLEY *USA, California, VA* Wine zone in the north of Sonoma, with deep, rich valley soils for good Ws from Riesling and Gewürztraminer and Chardonnay, while Rs from

Cabernet Sauvignon on lighter soils are soft and light. Leading producers include: Clos du Bois, Jordan, Johnson's, Ch Souverain.

ALEXIS BAILLY WINERY *USA, Minnesota, R, W* In the 1970s David Bailly planted some vines on his farm south-east of Minneapolis; a small winery followed. The R vines are the hybrids Maréchal Foch and Léon Millot; produced as varietals, they are dark in colour and in most vintages balanced and flavourful.

ALGERIA *North Africa, R, W, P* Algeria has had a well-developed quality wine system since colonial days, but less wine is made today than hitherto. All vineyards are concentrated in the provinces of Oran and Alger, in the western half of the country. In Oran the best areas are the Coteaux de Tlemcen, making R, W and P wines of fair quality, powerful yet quite soft and the Coteaux de Mascara, producing big, rustic Rs. In Alger, Médéa is a high-altitude zone, making R wines of some finesse.

ALICANTE *Spain, Levante, DO, W, P, R* Hilly wine zone in the region of Valencia with a variety of grapes and wines in all colours. Leading producers include: Eval.

ALIGOTÉ White grape from Burgundy, making dry, fairly acidic wine of varying quality. The best is the Bourgogne Aligoté de Bouzeron, from the Côte Chalonnaise, which has its own AOC. Also grown in Bulgaria, Romania, Moldova, Russia, California.

ALMACENISTA *Spain, Jerez* Term used in Jerez, the sherry country, for wines matured by small wholesalers (also called Almacenistas). These sherries are usually blended, but sometimes sold in bottle: especially by the firm of LUSTAU.

ALMANSA *Spain, Castilla-La Mancha, DO, R, P* Easternmost of four wine zones of Castilla-La Mancha, with vineyards on flatter lowlands. Essentially R wines but also some *rosado*. Leading producers include: Bodegas Piqueras.

ALOXE-CORTON *France, Burgundy, AOC, R, W* Côte de Beaune village and environs dominated by the Corton hill with its two *Grands Crus:* CORTON (R) and CORTON-CHARLEMAGNE (W). The lower slopes produce the R *Premiers Crus* (less long-lived than the *Grands Crus*) and R village wines (lighter; good value). Leading producers include: Capitain-Gagnerot, Michel Mallard, Prince Florent de Mérode.

ALSACE *France, AOC, W, R, P, Sp* Though northerly, a warm, dry climate produces full-tasting yet dry Ws (most labelled by grape variety) from Riesling, Pinot Blanc, Gewürztraminer, Sylvaner, Pinot Gris, Muscat (Rs and Ps from Pinot Noir). Top vineyards can use village or vineyard names as AOC Alsace *Grand Cru*. Crémant d'Alsace is quality Sp wine, usually Pinot Blanc. Leading producers include: Jean Becker, Hugel, Trimbach, Dom Weinbach, Zind Humbrecht.

ALVARINHO See ALBARIÑO.

AMABILE *Italy* A sweeter style of wine than *abboccato*.

AMIOT, PIERRE & FILS *France, Burgundy, Côte d'Or, R, W* This Côte des Nuits estate makes elegant wines for drinking relatively young, from vines in Morey St-Denis and Gevrey Chambertin.

AMIRAL DE BEYCHEVELLE *France, Bordeaux, Médoc, St-Julien, R* Second wine of Ch Beychevelle.

AMITY *USA, Oregon, R, W* Half of Myron Redford's small vineyard is Pinot Noir, some made in the *nouveau* style: light and fruity, ready just months after harvest. Cinnamon-spiced W Gewürztraminer and the rarely made, peppery R Gamay Noir are noteworthy.

AMMERSCHWIHR *France, Alsace, Haut-Rhin* One of the best villages in Alsace, known for Riesling and Gewürztraminer: particularly from Kaefferkopf, a well-known *terroir*, now a *Grand Cru*. Also includes *Grand Cru* Wineck-Schlossberg. Leading producers include: J B Adam, Sparr.

AMONTILLADO *Spain* Sherry that has matured beyond the fino stage, developing an amber colour, depth and nutty flavour.

AMOUREUSES, LES *France, Burgundy, 1er Cru, Côte de Nuits, R* One of the most attractive Chambolle-Musigny wines. Supremely elegant, with breeding and lovely supple fruit. Leading producers include: Ch de Chambolle-Musigny, Robert Groffier, Georges Roumier, de Vogüé.

AMPEAU, ROBERT *France, Burgundy, Côte d'Or, R, W* Skilled W burgundy specialist based in Meursault. Also fine Rs from Volnay and Pommard.

AMPURDÁN-COSTA BRAVA *Spain, Catalonia, DO, W, P, R* Catalonia's northernmost wine zone, in the province of Girona on the French border. Vineyards rise from sea level to the Pyrenean foothills. Most wine is *rosado*; also old-style dessert wines. Leading producers include: Cavas del Ampurdán.

ANBAUGEBIET *Germany* Wine region: there are 13, such as Pfalz, Baden, Rheingau.

ANCIENNE CURÉ, DOM DE L' *France, South-West, Bergerac, R, W* Good R and W Bergerac, plus sweet W Monbazillac and higher-quality R from the Pécharmant zone.

ANDERSON VALLEY *USA, California, VA* Zone in Mendocino with a cool climate, good for Chardonnay, Sp wines, Zinfandel (R) and Cabernet Sauvignon. Leading producers include: Navarro, Roederer (Sp), Scharffenberger (Sp).

ANDERSON VALLEY VINEYARDS *USA, New Mexico, R, W* In the northern Rio Grande Valley, Anderson, founded in 1973, was the first quality producer in the state, with vineyards around the city of Albuquerque. It has a name for Cabernet Sauvignon, Sauvignon Blanc and other wines.

ANDRÉ, PIERRE *France, Burgundy, Côte d'Or, R, W* Substantial vineyard owner and *négociant* (using the name LA REINE PEDAUQUE): a wide range of wines of varying quality. The best are the Cortons.

ANDRON-BLANQUET, CH *France, Bordeaux, St-Estèphe, Cru Bourgeois, R* Well-sited close to Cos d'Estournel, making strong, rich wines which need time in bottle.

ANGÉLUS, CH L' *France, Bordeaux, St-Emilion, Grand Cru Classé, R* Among the largest of St-Emilion's top properties, with 12,000 cases a year. Recent investment produced a vast improvement in quality. Worth watching.

ANGES, DOM DES *France, Rhône, Côtes du Ventoux, R* Leading estate of the appellation, making complex and tasty wine.

ANGLUDET, CH D' *France, Bordeaux, Margaux, Cru Bourgeois, R* Consistently classed-growth-quality wine: perfumed and elegant, with increasing structure as the vines age. Good value.

ANGERVILLE, DOM MARQUIS D' *France, Burgundy, Côte d'Or, R, W* Top domaine making extremely elegant wines for the medium term from Volnay, Pommard and Meursault. Sole proprietor of the Volnay Clos des Ducs *Premier Cru,* which yields a very classy wine.

ANHEUSER, AUGUST E *Germany, Nahe W* Family estate with four centuries of fine wine behind it: the current list includes wines as old as 1921. Well-structured, long-lived Rieslings from some of the best Nahe vineyards.

ANHEUSER, PAUL *Germany, Nahe, W* Just a century old, another branch of the Anheuser family (*see* above) makes equally good Rieslings but in a lighter, fresher style.

ANJOU *France, Loire, AOC, P, W, R* Within the general Anjou appellation (mostly Rs and dry Ws) are several more specific AOCs. Anjou Villages (R), from Cabernet (Franc and Sauvignon): higher quality than basic Anjou Rouge. Anjou Gamay: light Rs. Anjou Coteaux de la Loire: dry and medium-sweet W wines from Chenin Blanc. Region is best known for simple, slightly sweet, pale pink Rosé d'Anjou, from Groslot grapes; better Ps come from Cabernet Franc grapes, eg CABERNET D'ANJOU. Leading producers include: Aubert Frères, Ch du Breuil, Ch de Fesles, Hervé Papin, Dom de Ste-Anne, Pierre et Yves Soulez, Les Vins Touchais.

ANNEREAUX, CH DES *France, Bordeaux, Lalande-de-Pomerol, R* Good quantities of well-made wine, worth ageing.

ANTINORI *Italy, Tuscany, Chianti, R, W, P, Sp* This famous, top-quality producer makes some of Italy's most innovative wines.

The two main Chianti Classicos, Villa Antinori and Peppoli, are complemented by Cabernet Sauvignon/Sangiovese-based R *vini da tavola* like Solaia and Tignanello. Others include Bolgheri (DOC, P), Galestro (*vino da tavola*, W) and Sp wines.

AOC   *France*   See APPELLATION D'ORIGINE CONTRÔLÉE.

APPELLATION D'ORIGINE CONTRÔLÉE (AOC)   *France*   The top grade of French quality wine. The term created by French authorities (the INAO) to guarantee the origin of wines (also cheeses, etc). AOC rules define the specific area of production, grape varieties, minimum levels of sugar in the juice and of alcohol in the wine, maximum yield per hectare, pruning practices, and cultivation and vinification methods.

APULIA   *Italy*   Huge wine output from Italy's heel. The region has a vast number of DOCs and a bewildering array of grape varieties. Castel del Monte R, W and P is the most famous wine. Locorotondo is one of the best W wines.

AQUÉRIA, CH D'   *France, Rhône, Tavel, P*   Reliable specialist in this powerful rosé, best drunk young.

ARBOIS   *France, Jura, AOC, R, P, W*   Jura's main R-wine appellation, using Trousseau, Poulsard and Pinot Noir grapes. Ws are from Chardonnay, with some Savagnin; this local grape also makes VIN JAUNE. Leading producers include: Fruitière Vinicole d'Arbois, Henri Maire, Rolet Père et Fils.

ARBOIS, FRUITIÈRE VINICOLE D'   *France, Jura, R, W, P*   This major co-op is a leading maker of Arbois wines of all colours, plus VIN JAUNE, using modern facilities: good quality.

ARBOR CREST   *USA, Washington State, W, R*   Having first gained attention through its creamy, richly-fruited Chardonnays, the Mielke family's south-facing vineyard in the Columbia Valley produces an austere Sauvignon W and a generously fruity, currant-and-berry Merlot R.

ARCHAMBEAU, CH D'   *France, Bordeaux, Graves, W, R*   In the commune of Illats, a source of impeccably-made, fresh Ws, and soft delicate Rs.

ARCHE, CH D'   *France, Bordeaux, Sauternes, 2ème Cru Classé, W*   Careful management results in a rich, sweet unctuous Sauternes that, being less well-known than many others, is reasonably priced.

ARGENTINA   *South America*   Major wine-producing country, ranking fifth in the world, with 208,000ha under vine. Wine has been made here since 1557 and today most is drunk locally, although the export market is expanding. Export wines are from the usual European classic varieties, plus Malbec, which makes dark, characterful Rs and may be blended with Cabernet Sauvignon or Barbera. Main vineyard area is MENDOZA province; quality zones are MAIPU and LUJAN DE CUYO (good Cabernet and Malbec Rs),

Tupungato (Pinot Noir, Merlot, Chardonnay, Gewürztraminer), RIO NEGRO (grapes for Sp wines). Leading producers include: Etchart, Bodegas Flichman, Peñaflor, Bodegas San Telmo, Bodegas Weinert.

ARGILLIÈRES, CLOS DES *France, Burgundy, 1er Cru, Côte de Nuits, R* Produces highly-coloured Nuits-St-Georges wines, with a powerful bouquet and a good tannic backbone. Leading producers include: Daniel Rion.

ARIZONA *USA* In one corner of a mostly-desert state, south of Tucson, a handful of wineries exploit the high-altitude. conditions. Wines from Sonoita (VA and vineyard) and others can be good: Cabernet Sauvignon, Sauvignon Blanc, Pinot Noir.

ARKANSAS *USA* Tough climate conditions hinder growers, but some good Ws from Riesling and Chardonnay have joined the mostly hybrid-grape wines made along the Arkansas River. Leading producer: WIEDERKEHR.

ARLAY, CH D' *France, Jura, R, W, P* Old family estate making Côtes de Jura wines, including a Chardonnay/Savagnin W, Pinot Noir R and Corail, a light R from all five local grapes. Also VIN JAUNE and MACVIN.

ARLOT, DOM DE L' *France, Burgundy, Côte d'Or, R, W* Nuits-St-Georges estate using clever, modern winemaking techniques to make top-class red and white wines.

ARMAILHAC, CH D' *France, Bordeaux, Médoc, Pauillac, 5ème Cru Classé, R* Owned by the Rothschilds of Mouton, and called Mouton-Baronne-Philippe until 1989, this once formed part of the Mouton estate. The wine is classic Pauillac, though with less potential to age than its First-Growth neighbour. A particularly good 1993.

ARROSÉE, CH L' *France, Bordeaux, St-Emilion, Grand Cru Classé, R* To the south-west of St-Emilion village, this is one of the less well-known of the *Grands Crus Classés*. A fleshy style, with great concentration: top quality.

ASSMANSHAUSEN *Germany, Rheingau, R* Rhine village making R wine from Spätburgunder, both in traditional sweet style (up to EISWEIN) from the State Domaine; and *barrique*-aged dry style from Weingut Kesseler and others.

ATLAS PEAK *USA, California, VA* Wine zone in the hills east of Napa Valley, with Rs from ANTINORI's Italian-accented Atlas Peak Winery.

AU BON CLIMAT *USA, California, Santa Barbara & Southern California, W, R* This winery in Los Alamos in the Santa Maria Valley buys grapes from some of the best and coolest vineyards in the area, producing stunning, ageable Chardonnays and succulently rich cherry-fruit Pinot Noirs.

AUCKLAND *New Zealand, North Island* New Zealand's oldest wine region, but with a less suitable climate than newer zones further south in North Island and in South Island, which have eclipsed it. Auckland still has some important growing areas like Henderon, Kumeu, Huapai and Waiheke Island. Production is mainly Rs, especially Cabernet Sauvignon.

AUDE, DE L' *France, Vin de Pays, R, W* This *vin de pays* name is mostly used for Rs, from the Aude department in the Midi, using traditional grapes plus some Syrah and Cabernet Sauvignon.

AUSLESE *Germany* German or Austrian wine made from selected bunches of very ripe grapes. Usually a naturally sweet wine, although dry *Auslese* is made. In good vintages, the selection may be of grapes with noble rot (*botrytis cinerea*).

AUSONE, CH *France, Bordeaux, St-Emilion, 1er Grand Cru Classé (A), R* Named after the Roman poet-consul Ausonius, this vies with CHEVAL BLANC as the best St-Emilion. Noticeable in youth for its tannic structure: it can take a decade to soften. Production is tiny.

AUSTRIA Wine is made in the east of the country, with the best quality zones being WACHAU and NEUSEIDLERSEE. Most wines are W, with increasing interest in Rs. The W wines are frequently sweet on the German pattern, but good dry Ws are also made from Riesling and the local Grüner Veltliner grapes.

AUXEY-DURESSES *France, Burgundy, AOC, R, W* Côte de Beaune village and appellation (*see also* **ALOXE-CORTON**); fine, raspberry-fruited R wines, and deliciously toasty and nutty Ws that bear comparison with Meursault. Leading producers include: Jean-Pierre Diconne, Dom Leroy, Jean-Pierre Prunier, Michel Prunier, Pascal Prunier.

AVA *USA* American Viticultural Area, often abbreviated to VA: an approved vineyard zone which can be as large as a state or as small as a single vineyard: many, but not all, delineate a micro-climate and/or soil zone. US law insists that if a VA is named on a label, 85% of the grapes must originate from there.

AVELEDA, QUINTA DA *Portugal, W* Large producer, with two famous W Vinhos Verdes: Castel Garcia and Aveleda. Grinalda is the top-of-the-range W wine.

AVIGNONESI *Italy, Tuscany, Vino Nobile de Montepulciano, R, W* Pacesetter producer of Montepulciano wines. *Vini da tavola* include Il Marzocco (W) Terre di Cortona (W), and Grifi (R). The Vin Santo is highly regarded, but their star is still the Vino Nobile.

AYALA *France, Champagne* One of the lesser GRANDES MARQUES, based in Ay. The Grande Cuvée vintage is better than the light, biscuity NV.

AZIENDA AGRICOLA *Italy* Wine estate.

B

BACCHUS, CAVEAU DU   *France, Jura, R, W, P*   Traditional attitudes and methods make authentic Jura wines. Rs are from the local Tousseau grape, but Ws use Chardonnay as well as Savagnin.

BACH, MASIA   *Spain, Catalonia, Penedès, R, W, P*   Part of Codorníu (Cava) since 1975, this bodega uses the Extrísimo label for its main wines, both R and W.

BAD DÜRKHEIM   *Germany, Pfalz, W, R*   Wine town making good wine (mostly W, from Riesling, Scheurebe and others) and known for its September wine fair. Leading producers include: Fitz-Ritter, Karst.

BAD KREUZNACH   *Germany, Nahe, W*   The centre of the Nahe vineyards, making good W wine; also the HQ of leading Nahe producers, including the Staatsweingut (State Domaine), August Anheuser, von Plettenberg, Finkenauer.

BAD KREUZNACH, STAATSWEINGUT   *Germany, Nahe, W*   Maker of fine W wines from the best Nahe vineyards, combined with a research centre.

BADEN   *Germany, Anbaugebiet, R, W, P*   Germany's southernmost wine region, made up of several districts (including KAISER-STUHL/TUNIBERG, Ortenau) along the upper Rhine valley and further east. Wines are mostly W, with good amounts of R and Weissherbst, the local rosé. Baden Ws are fuller, often drier, than other German wines; Rs can be good in a "French" style (dry and structured). Producers for the whole region are led by the giant BADISCHER WINZERKELLER (cooperative).

BADIA A COLTIBUONO   *Italy, Tuscany, Chianti, R, W*   The Chianti Classico is a fine wine designed for ageing. The *vino da tavola*, Sangioveto (R), comes from the oldest vines: also a light R, Coltibuono Rosso, and a W wine.

BADISCHER WINZERKELLER   *Germany, Baden, W, R*   Enormous in scale, highly competent in quality: hundreds of wines from thousands of growers. Most are good everyday wines, though a premium range matches Baden's best.

BADISCHES BERGSTRASSE/KRAICHGAU   *Germany, Baden, Bereich, R, W, P*   Zone around Heidelberg, making good light Ws and some modern Rs.

BAHANS HAUT-BRION, CH   *France, Bordeaux, Graves*   Second wine of Ch Haut-Brion.

42

BAILLY, JEAN-FRANCOIS *France, Loire, Sancerre, W, R, P* Bailly is linked via marriage with the Reverdy family, joining two important Sancerre names. The Ws from the 12-ha vineyard are excellent, but Bailly is best known for powerful Rs and light Ps.

BAIRRADA *Portugal, DOC, R, W, Sp* Awarded demarcated status in 1979, R Barraida now rivals Dão as one of Portugal's best-known wines. The tannic Baga grape makes a big, ripe fruity wine, traditionally needing time to soften. Modern versions from larger producers are made for younger drinking. Some W also, plus a little Sp. Leading producers include: Caves Aliança, Luís Pato, Caves São João.

BAJA CALIFORNIA *Mexico, Central America* Region where Mexico's greatest vineyard expansion is taking place. More than 10,000ha are currently under vine, with most grapes grown in the Guadalupe Valley and near Ensenada. Very promising Cabernet Sauvignon and Chardonnay.

BALATON *Hungary* Wine region south-west of Budapest, around Lake Balaton, Europe's biggest lake, whose tempering effect on viticulture cannot be overstated. On the south shore is the Dél-Balaton area, making still and Sp Ws from Olaszrizling, Sauvignon Blanc and Chardonnay, plus R from Cabernet Sauvignon. Also home to the huge Balatonboglár winery and research station, source of much good W wine under various labels, including Chapel Hill. The Badacsony area makes W wines from Kéknyelü, Szürkebarát and Olaszrizling, among others. Other areas around the lake are Balatonfüred-Csopak and Batalonmellék.

BALBACH, BÜRGERMEISTER ANTON ERBEN WEINGUT *Germany, Rheinhessen, W* Top maker of NIERSTEIN wine from the best vineyards of this famous town. Specialist in Rieslings, especially late-harvest ones.

BALESTARD-LA-TONNELLE, CH *France, Bordeaux, St-Emilion, Grand Cru Classé, R* This site on the plateau to the east of St-Emilion village produces a richly-coloured Merlot-based wine with lots of body. Needs a good five years in bottle before it begins to mature.

BALLARAT *Australia, Victoria* One of the state's cool-climate areas, ideal for Pinot Noir and Chardonnay.

BANDOL *France, Provence, AOC, R, P, W* Most Bandol is R, with strong perfume, flavour and colour, from at least 50% Mourvèdre grapes, with Syrah and Grenache. Can age for 20 years. Leading producers include: La Bastide Blanche, Dom de l'Hermitage, Mas de la Rouvière, Moulin des Costes, Ch de Pibarnon.

BANNOCKBURN *Australia, Victoria, Geelong, R, W* Producer whose low-yielding, fully mature vineyards and strongly French-influenced winemaking produce superb, complex Sauvignon and Chardonnay Ws, and even more complex Pinot Noir (the estate's speciality) and Shiraz Rs.

BANYULS *France, Midi, AOC, R, P, W, VDN* Sweet, lightly fortified wine (*vin doux naturel*), from Roussillon, mainly from
Grenache Noir: R, W and P wines all become tawny with age,
with rich, raisiny, nutty flavours. Leading producer: Dom du Mas
Blanc.

BANYULS, GROUPEMENT INTERPRODUCTEURS DU CRU *France,
Midi, Banyuls & Collioure, R, VDN* By far the largest maker of
the R Collioure; also a leader of *vin doux naturel* production.

BARANCOURT *France, Champagne* This relatively new house
was founded by three young growers. They produce a wide
range of champagnes, but their best wine is the rare (still, R)
Bouzy Rouge.

BARBADILLO, ANTONIO *Spain, sherry* The largest and most
important producer in Sanlúcar, founded 1821 and still headed by
a Barbadillo. Also a big landowner in Jerez, jointly with **HARVEYS**,
for whom it makes a lot of sherry. Most familiar of Barbadillo's
huge range are the manzanillas (Eva, Sirena, Solear, Pastora and
Don Benigno brands) and a Jerez fino, Balbaina. It has also pioneered a W table wine, Castillo de San Diego, made from
Palomino grapes in a modern, crisp style.

BARBARESCO *Italy, Piedmont, DOCG, R* From the Nebbiolo
grape, one of Italy's greatest R wines, grown in hilly vineyards
east of Alba. Aged for two years, of which one in wood, it has
high acidity and tannin, balanced by lush fruit, with a hint of
violets. Not quite as massive as neighbouring Barolo, but it ages
extremely well. Leading producers include: Ceretto, Pio Cesare,
Fratelli Cigliuti, Gaja, Bruno Giacosa, Giuseppe Mascarello &
Figlio, Alfredo Prunotto.

BARBE BLANCHE, CH *France, Bordeaux, Lussac St-Emilion, R* Historic château making well-received wines, including an all-Merlot
cuvée.

BARBE, CH DE *France, Bordeaux, Côtes de Bourg, R* Large estate
making steadily good wine in the soft, earthy Bourg style.

BARBÉ, CH *France, Bordeaux, 1er Côtes de Blaye, R* Not to be confused with Ch **DE BARBE**: this is a well-known Blaye property
making straightforward, reliable Rs.

BARBERA D'ALBA *Italy, Piedmont, DOC, R* Italy's most widely
planted R grape is regaining prestige in its native Piedmont, producing lively, succulent wine with a perfume of blackberries,
raspberries and licorice. Best drunk 2–4 years after the vintage.
Leading producers include: Aldo Conterno, Giacomo Conterno,
Giuseppe Contratto, Bruno Giacosa.

BARBERA Red grape from Piedmont, now widely planted in Italy
and California. Versatile, with good acidity, making a range of
styles. Best are the silky-textured **BARBERA D'ALBA** and Barbera
d'Asti DOCs.

BARBIER, BODEGAS RENÉ *Spain, Catalonia, Penedès, R, W, P*
Now part of the Freixenet group, Barbier is a reliable producer of
attractive, easy-drinking still wines.

BARDOLINO *Italy, Veneto, DOC, R* Local grape varieties Corvina,
Rondinella, Molinara and others grown near Verona make wine
that is pale in colour, with a cherry perfume and crisp acidity. For
early drinking. Leading producers include: Masi.

BAROLO *Italy, Piedmont, DOCG, R* One of Italy's very greatest R
wines. From the Nebbiolo grape, aged for at least three years, of
which two in wood, before release. Tarry in youth, with high
acidity and tannin, takes on flavours of violets, chocolate, prunes,
tobacco, truffles and autumn smoke. Can age for up to 20 years in
bottle. Leading producers include: Elio Altare, Ceretto, Aldo Conterno, Bruno Giacosa, Giuseppe Mascarello & Figlio, Paolo Scav-
ino, Vietti, Roberto Voerzio.

BAROSSA *Australia, South Australia* Australia's top wine region,
base for many big concerns. Full-bodied dry Rs and Riesling Ws
are perhaps the best wines. Leading producers include: Charles
Melton, Leo Buring, Peter Lehmann.

BARR *France, Alsace, Bas-Rhin* This Alsace village makes good
Sylvaner, with Gewürztraminer and Riesling from the *Grand Cru*
Kirchberg de Barr. Leading producers include: Klipfel, Willm.

BARRELS Wooden barrels (or casks) can be used for fermenting
and/or ageing. Fine reds (and some whites) merit the cost of new
oak to age in: these add tannins and vanilla flavour.

BARRIQUE *France* Barrel mainly associated with Bordeaux, used
for ageing wine, holding 225 litres (24 cases of 12 bottles). The
capacity varies: Muscadet *barriques* hold 228 litres; in Anjou and
Touraine 232 litres. The Burgundy PIÈCE is 228 litres. Barrique-
ageing means the use of new or newish wood: *see* BARRELS.

BARSAC *France, Bordeaux, AOC, W* World-class, luscious, sweet
W wine from a commune within AOC SAUTERNES. Leading
producers include: Ch'x Climens, Coutet, Doisy-Daëne, Doisy-
Dubroca, Doisy-Védrines, Liot, Nairac.

BARTOLI, DE *Italy, Sicily, W, R* Leading Marsala producer whose
range includes old-style, unfortified 20-year-old Vecchio Samperi
and Joséphine Doré, dry, non-DOC wines; exemplary fortified
Vigna La Miccia and 20-year-old Marsala Superiore. Bukkuram is
a sweet Pantelleria.

BASILICATA *Italy* Area between the heel and
toe of southern Italy, that produces one of the
South's greatest Rs, AGLIANICO DEL VULTURE
DOC. Also some good sweet W Moscato.

BASSERMANN-JORDAN *Germany, Pfalz, W* One of the great
estates of the central Pfalz, making Rieslings in classic, elegant
long-lived style.

BATAILLEY, CH *France, Bordeaux, Médoc, Pauillac, 5ème Cru Classé, R* Long-lived wine in the old-fashioned style from this estate on the south-west, inland, side of the commune.

BÂTARD-MONTRACHET *France, Burgundy, AOC, W* Côte de Beaune *Grand Cru*, between Chassagne and Puligny villages and abutting the *Grands Crus* of MONTRACHET, Bienvenues-Bâtard-Montrachet, Les Criots-Bâtard-Montrachet: all are superbly sited for making great W wine. Leading producers include: Dom Leflaive, Dom André Ramonet, Dom Etienne Sauzet.

BAUDRY, BERNARD *France, Loire, Chinon, R* Experimenting with wood and separation of wines by soil type, Baudry is a serious producer of Chinon, stressing fruit balanced with oak and ability to age. He has 25ha at Cravant-les-Coteaux, east of Chinon.

BAY OF PLENTY *New Zealand, North Island* Area south of Auckland, noted for Müller-Thurgau, Sauvignon and Chardonnay Ws.

BÉARN *France, South-West, AOC, R, P, W* Fairly rustic wines from the Pyrenees. Rs and Ps are from Tannat, with Cabernets Franc and Sauvignon. Ws, usually labelled Béarn-Bellocq, are from Raffiat de Moncade, a local variety. Leading producer: Les Vignerons de Bellocq.

BEAU-SÉJOUR-BÉCOT, CH *France, Bordeaux, St-Emilion, Grand Cru Classé, R* One of the *1ers Grands Crus Classés* before its demotion in the 1985 classification, but quality has certainly improved since. Mainly Merlot: the overall style is quite soft and silky, but with enough structure to age well.

BEAU-SITE, CH *France, Bordeaux, St-Estèphe, Cru Bourgeois, R* This is a finely-sited vineyard indeed, with the view of the river that locals say good wine demands. The wines are well-made, fleshy and long-lived.

BEAUCASTEL, CH DE *France, Rhône, Châteauneuf-du-Pape, R, W* Leading estate in Châteauneuf, making long-lived R and good W. Also makers of a top Côtes du Rhône, Coudoulet de Beaucastel, from vineyards adjoining their Châteauneuf land.

BEAUJOLAIS *France, Burgundy, AOC, R, W* Nearly all Beaujolais is R, from Gamay grapes; a little Chardonnay W is made where the St-Véran AOC overlaps with Beaujolais. Famous for Beaujolais Nouveau, or Primeur: newly-made wine sold in November to be drunk within a month or three. Normal Beaujolais is enjoyed at about a year old: fresh, fruity, an appetizing partner to country cuisine. Beaujolais Supérieur has a little more alcohol. Beaujolais-Villages is the best zone: a group of 39 villages; among them are 10 (the *crus*) that can use their own name: ST-AMOUR, JULIÉNAS, CHÉNAS, MOULIN-À-VENT, FLEURIE, CHIROUBLES, MORGON, RÉGNIÉ, CÔTE DE BROUILLY, BROUILLY. The rest produce a range of different styles, though none have the keeping power of the *crus* and are made to be drunk at 1–2 years. Leading producers of Beaujolais and -Villages include: Trenel et Fils, Loron et Fils, Pasquier-Desvignes, Georges Duboeuf, Eventail de Vignerons Producteurs, Henry Fessy, Sylvian Fessy, Pierre Feraud.

BEAULIEU *USA, California, Napa, R* This venerable Rutherford house is famed for Georges de Latour Private Reserve Cabernet Sauvignon, which was perfected by winemaker extraordinaire André Tchelistcheff. One of California's world-class Rs, it is 100% Cabernet Sauvignon, matured only in American oak.

BEAULIEU, CH DE *France, Provence, Coteaux d'Aix-en-Provence, W, R, P* This large estate of 300ha makes easy-drinking wines with a herby, southern character. R is from Grenache, Cabernet Sauvignon, Mourvèdre and Syrah; P from Cinsaut and Carignan, W from Ugni Blanc, Clairette, Sauvignon Blanc and Sémillon.

BEAUMES-DE-VENISE *France, Rhône, AOC, R; W, VDN* France's best-known *vin doux naturel* is the sweet W Muscat from this village. It also makes traditional Grenache-based R wine as one of the Côtes du Rhône-Villages. Leading producers include: Dom de Durban, Dom Coyeux.

BEAUMET *France, Champagne* Based in Epernay, this house produces a wide range of champagnes including Cuvée Malakoff, an outstanding *blanc de blancs*.

BEAUMONT DES CRAYÈRES *France, Champagne* This Epernay cooperative has some 210 grower-members with 75ha of vines. It enjoys a very good reputation, in particular for its Cuvée Nostalgie.

BEAUMONT, CH *France, Bordeaux, Médoc, Cru Bourgeois, R* Large, modern and well-placed château in Cussac making solid, good-value wine to keep for five years.

BEAUNE *France, Burgundy, AOC, R, W* Large production and high standards make Beaune a benchmark for good-value R burgundy with elegant perfume and fine, fruity, spicy flavour, best at 6–10 years old. W wines are less distinguished; to be drunk younger. The appellation, named after the medieval centre of Burgundy's wine trade, has no *Grands Crus*, but the largest area of *Premiers Crus* vineyards on the CÔTE DE BEAUNE. Leading producers include: Besancenot-Mathouillet, Dom Machard de Gramont, Dom du Château de Meursault, Daniel Sénard.

BEAUSÉJOUR (DUFFAU-LAGAROSSE), CH *France, Bordeaux, St-Emilion, 1er Grand Cru Classé, R* Perhaps the least well-known of the *1ers Grands Crus*, currently undergoing a revival and worth watching. Innovations include less Cabernet Sauvignon and late harvesting.

BECKER, J B *Germany, Rheingau, R, W* Fine vineyards in the central Rheingau yield good Rs (from Spätburgunder) as well as Riesling Ws in both classic and dry styles.

BECKER, JEAN *France, Alsace, W, R* Old (1610) family firm making all major Alsace wines. The best are Muscat (including a superb botrytized one), Pinot Noir, Gewürztraminer (from *Grand Cru* Froehn) and Riesling.

BEDELL CELLARS   *USA, New York, Long Island, R*   The first few vintages of Merlot and Cabernet Sauvignon in the early 1980s were so rich and seemingly long-lived that they placed this small winery among the best outside the West Coast.

BEERENAUSLESE   *Germany*   German or Austrian wine made from individually selected grapes that are always overripe (probably affected by noble rot), and thus very sweet.

BELAIR, CH   *France, Bordeaux, St-Emilion, 1er Grand Cru Classé, R*   The Dubois-Challon family also own AUSONE next door. Belair is similarly concentrated and quite tannic, but matures sooner.

BEL-AIR, CH   *France, Bordeaux, Lalande-de-Pomerol, R*   Consistent and long-lived wine, approaching Pomerol in stature.

BELGIUM   Wine producer on a small scale, mainly in the Meuse and Sambre valleys, with around 100 growers and a total of 30ha of vineyard. Most wines are Müller-Thurgau whites, with some Pinot Noir reds.

BELGRAVE, CH   *France, Bordeaux, Haut-Médoc, 5ème Cru Classé, R*   Deservedly obscure till recently, this estate has well-placed land west of St-Julien. Decades of neglect ended in the 1980s with new owners, advice and investment. Results now show.

BELINGARD, CH   *France, South-West, Bergerac, R, W*   Exciting modern wines from an innovative estate: crisp, dry W Bergerac and substantial R Côtes de Bergerac, sweet W Monbazillac, and top wines under the Blanche de Bosredon label.

BELLAND, DOM ADRIEN   *France, Burgundy, Côte d'Or, R, W*   Based in Santenay with vineyards throughout the region, including Corton, Puligny and Chambertin. Good, traditional wines.

BELLE-GRAVES, CH   *France, Bordeaux, Lalande-de-Pomerol, R*   This respected small estate is close to Pomerol in quality.

BELLET   *France, Provence, AOC, R, P, W*   Tiny zone; wines rarely seen outside Nice. Producers: Ch de Crémat, Ch de Bellet.

BELLEVUE LA FORÊT, CH   *France, South-West, Côtes du Frontonnais, R*   Leading private estate of the appellation, with good fresh well-made R plus a prestige *cuvée* aged a year in oak.

BENDIGO   *Australia, Victoria*   This is R-wine country, especially deeply coloured, full-bodied single-variety Shiraz and Cabernet Sauvignon, plus blends of these two grapes. Leading producers include: Jasper Hill, Mount Ida, Passing Clouds, Yellowglen.

BENNWIHR-MITTELWIHR   *France, Alsace, Haut-Rhin*   These two adjacent villages produce Gewürztraminer and Muscat. *Grands Crus*: Marckrain (Bennwihr) and Mandelberg (Mittelwihr). Leading producers include: Deiss.

BERBERANA, BODEGAS *Spain, Rioja, R, W, P* Established in 1877, this is now one of the largest and most impressive wineries in Rioja. Main labels include Carta de Oro and Carta de Plata, as well as Berberana.

BERCHER, WEINGUT *Germany, Baden, R, W* Modern-minded estate which ages its best Rs and Ws, from Spätburgunder and Grauburgunder, in cask. Most wines are dry.

BEREICH *Germany* Wine district.

BERGER, M *France, Loire, Montlouis, W, Sp* The family's 20ha in St-Martin-le-Beau provides the grapes for this quality-conscious firm. Half their production is Sp, the rest still, ranging from dry to a luscious botrytized *moelleux*.

BERGERAC *France, South-West, AOC, R, W, P* Large area adjoining and east of St-Emilion. Grapes and wine styles are similar to Bordeaux: Cabernet Sauvignon, Cabernet Franc and Merlot for Rs and Ps; Sémillon, Sauvignon Blanc and others for Ws. Modern, crisp dry Ws from Sauvignon Blanc are labelled Bergerac Sec. Côtes de Bergerac Rs have higher alcohol, Ws are medium-sweet, or *moelleux*. PÉCHARMANT is a small zone for good Rs, SAUSSIGNAC for Ws. Leading producers include: Dom de l'Ancienne Curé, Ch Belingard, Ch La Jaubertie, Cave Coopérative de Montravel et Sigoulès.

BERGHEIM *France, Alsace* Bergheim village, and its *Grand Cru* Altenberg de Bergheim, are famous for Gewürztraminer from limestone soils. Leading producers include: Deiss, Lorentz, Gassmann, Sipp.

BERGKELDER *South Africa, Stellenbosch, R, W* Unique to South Africa, the Bergkelder fulfils several roles, which include selling estate wines and producing various ranges of its own (Stellenryck, Fleur du Cap).

BERGSTRASSE, STAATSWEINGUT *Germany, Hessiche Bergstrasse, W* Most important estate in this small region, specializing in EISWEIN, but making a full range of typical soft, generous Ws.

BERLIQUET, CH *France, Bordeaux, St-Emilion, Grand Cru Classé, R* Raised to *Grand Cru Classé* in the 1985 classification, this wine is made under the guidance of the local co-op. Densely structured: best years need about a decade in bottle.

BERLUCCHI, GUIDO *Italy, Lombardy, Franciacorta, W, R, Sp* Italy's largest *metodo classico* producer of Sp wines: Cuvée Impériale Berlucchi Brut, Grand Crémant, Pas Dosé and Max Rosé. Still wines include Bianco Impériale.

BERNKASTEL *Germany, Mosel-Saar-Ruwer, Bereich, W* Zone covering the central, and best, vineyards of the Mosel. Also called the Mittel (middle) Mosel. While several villages – Bernkastel itself, WEHLEN, PIESPORT – have top-class vineyards, there is much poor land within the Bereich. For leading producers see above-named villages and GRAACH, TRABEN-TRARBACH etc. Bernkastel the village has top vineyards including the famous Doctor, a steep hill above the rooftops making fabulous sweet wine in good vintages; Graben, next to and almost as good as Doctor; Alte Badstube am Doktorberg, ditto. Bernkasteler Badstube is a high-quality *grosslage*; Bernkasteler Kurfürstlay a larger and lesser one. Leading growers in Bernkastel include: Friedrich-Wilhelm-Gymnasium, Lauerburg, Dr Thanisch (both concerns of that name), Wegeler Erben, Loosen, J J Prüm.

BERTAGNA, DOM *France, Burgundy, Côte d'Or, R, W* German-owned domaine with several top vineyards, notably in the Côte de Nuits *Grands Crus* of Chambertin, Clos St-Denis and Clos de Vougeot, that produce elegant, reliable wines.

BERTAUD-BELIEU, CH *France, Provence, Côtes de Provence, W, R, P* Three ranges are produced from this new 50-ha estate near St-Tropez: Cuvée Tradition and Cuvée Prestige, both in R, W and P; and the top R, Ch Villa de Belieu.

BERTINEAU ST-VINCENT, CH *France, Bordeaux, Lalande-de-Pomerol, R* Small estate which is owned by oenologist Michel Rolland's family: excellent winemaking, worth 6-8 years' ageing in good vintages, such as 1990.

BESSAN, CH *France, Bordeaux, 1er Côtes de Bordeaux, R* Family links to Ch BRETHOUS; attractive Rs for fairly early drinking.

BESSERAT DE BELLEFON *France, Champagne* Now owned by giant MARNE ET CHAMPAGNE. Somewhat light in style, the best wine is the Grande Cuvée Blanc de Blancs.

BEYCHEVELLE, CH *France, Bordeaux, Médoc, St-Julien, 4ème Cru Classé, R* Grand 18th-century château, with large, well-situated vineyard along the edge of the riverside plateau. Lush and delicious, in good vintages it ages well. 2nd wine: Amiral de Beychevelle.

BEYER, LEON *France, Alsace, W* Wine merchants since the 16th century, and producers since the mid-19th, Beyer is known for its dry wine style – particularly Riesling, Gewürztraminer (Cuvée des Comtes d'Eguisheim) and Muscat. Beyer does not produce *Grand Cru* wines.

BIANCO DI CUSTOZA *Italy, Veneto, DOC, W, Sp* From the southern tip of Lake Garda, this wine has a mellow fruitiness often compared to greengages and peaches. Best drunk young.

BIENVENUES-BÂTARD-MONTRACHET See BÂTARD-MONTRACHET.

BIERZO *Spain, Castilla-León, DO, W, R* Fifth and newest wine zone of Castilla-León, owing much in style to neighbouring Galicia. It produces light, fresh, basic wines, made with increasingly modern equipment and methods. Leading producers include: Prada a Tope.

BIGI *Italy, Central Italy, Umbria, W, R* Large-scale producer with many single-vineyard wines. Top Orvietos include dry Torricella and sweet Orzalume. Marrano is a dry barrel-aged Grechetto (W). Est! Est!! Est!!! and Aleatico di Gradoli come from Lazio.

BILLECART-SALMON *France, Champagne* Small family-owned GRANDE MARQUE at Mareuil-sur-Ay producing superb quality wines which age extremely well. Outstanding.

BILTMORE, CH *USA, North Carolina, R, W, Sp* This Ashville winery is part of the historic Vanderbilt estate and mansion built in 1880. Cabernet Sauvignon, Chardonnay and a sparkling Blanc de Blancs are made.

BINGEN *Germany, Rheinhessen, Bereich, W, R* The western half of the Rheinhessen region, with some good vineyards at Bingen itself and Iphofen and wide tracts of ordinary ones. The leading producer in Bingen is Weingut Villa Sachsen.

BINISSALEM *Spain, Majorca, DO, R, W, P* Spain's first offshore DO, in Majorca, north-east of Palma. Mainly R wines, some better-quality ones aged in oak; W and *rosados* made only as *jovenes*. Leading producers include: Franja Roja.

BIODYNAMIC A thoroughgoing form of organic viticulture: growing vines according to the cycles of the moon and stars, using balanced plant communities to combat diseases and pests, etc. Some superb wines are made on biodynamic estates: Coulée de Serrant from the Loire, Frick in Alsace, Bize-Leroy in Burgundy, but there is more faith than science in the explanations: sceptics suggest that taking great care of one's vines will bear fruit, whatever the philosophy that inspires the care.

BIONDI-SANTI *Italy, Tuscany, Brunello di Montalcino, R, W* Vineyards date back 400 years. Two estates produce Brunello blended wine. Vigna del Fiore is a *riserva*. The Brusco dei Barbi (R) is big and more rustic than the Brunello. Expensive.

BISCHÖFLICHEN WEINGÜTER *Germany, Mosel-Saar-Ruwer, W* Charitable estate (like the HOSPICES DE BEAUNE) owning many top vineyards in the Mosel Valley and making fine, elegant Riesling wines.

BIZE, DOM SIMON ET FILS *France, Burgundy, Côte d'Or, R, W* Based in Savigny-lès-Beaune, this highly-regarded family-owned and run estate makes mostly R wine in a fruity, elegant style.

BLAGNY *France, Burgundy, AOC, R, W* Positive, slightly earthy R from a Côte de Beaune hamlet between Meursault and Puligny; it uses those names for its W wines.

BLANC DE BLANCS *France* White wine made from only white grapes. This term is most commonly used for champagne made entirely from Chardonnay.

BLANC DE NOIRS   *France*   White wine made from black grapes.

BLANC FUMÉ DE POUILLY   See POUILLY-FUMÉ.

BLANCHOTS   *France, Burgundy, Chablis, Grand Cru*   The lightest, most accessible and earliest-maturing of the Chablis *Grands Crus*.

BLANDY BROS   *Portugal, Madeira*   Best-known madeira in the UK. The "Duke of" range: Sussex sercial, Cambridge verdelho, Cumberland bual and Clarence malmsey are all 5-year-old wines. Blandy's 10-year-old special reserve wines are among the best. The historic lodges at Funchal are a must for any visitor to the island.

BLANQUETTE DE LIMOUX   *France, Midi, AOC, W*   This Sp W wine is usually made by the method used in Champagne, from local Mauzac grapes (which confer firm acidity and a taste of quince) with some Chardonnay and Chenin Blanc. Crémant de Limoux has more of these two classics. Leading producers include: Cave Coopérative de Limoux, Dom de Martinolles.

BLAYE   *France, Bordeaux, AOC, R, W*   Large appellation (also known as Blayais) on the right bank of the Gironde. Shared a historical reputation for robust, dark, long-lived Rs with neighbour CÔTES DE BOURG (or Bourgeais). Today, these are from Merlot and Cabernet Franc (plus some Malbec and Cabernet Sauvignon), with good fruit and structure. The Ws, from Sémillon, Sauvignon Blanc and Colombard, are akin to Entre-Deux-Mers. Leading producers include: Blaye R, Ch'x Barbé, Haut-Sociondo, Petraud, Segonzac.

BLIN   *France, Champagne*   This dynamic co-op at Vincelles has 85 growers and makes attractive, light, fruity, uncomplicated wines.

BLUE RIDGE MOUNTAINS   *USA, Virginia, VA*   This well-regarded wine zone in central Virginia makes good Ws from Chardonnay and Riesling, and Rs from Cabernet. MONTICELLO is a sub-zone. Leading producers include: Prince Michel, Montdomaine.

BLUSH WINE   Term for pale rosé, mostly used in America.

BODEGA   *Spain*   Cellar. Can also describe the building where wine is made and matured, or the firm that makes it.

BODEGAS FLICHMAN   *Argentina, R, W*   Reliable exporter, making well-aged, highly scented Cabernet Sauvignon under Caballero de la Cepa label. Also good Chardonnay and Syrah.

BODENSEE   *Germany, Baden, Bereich, R, W, P*   Vineyards on Lake Constance (Bodensee) which yield wines of all colours: light, fruity and (the Rs) sometimes pale.

BOIZEL   *France, Champagne*   An old firm, still family-owned. Extensive exports, especially of the NV *brut*, which is a medium-weight champagne with attractive biscuity overtones.

BOLLA   *Italy, Veneto, W, R*   Verona house making Soave, Soave Classico Castellaro and Vigneti di Frosca; Valpolicella Classico Jago and Amarone Cantina del Nonno; Creso (R) *vino da tavola*.

BOLLINGER   *France, Champagne*   Leading GRANDE MARQUE with a large vineyard holding. Specialities include fermentation in wood, the use of reserve wines and late disgorgement. Once the youthful austerity has worn off these wines become extremely full, rich and biscuity. Bollinger RD is one of the great champagnes, as is their extremely rare Vieilles Vignes Françaises.

BON PASTEUR, CH LE   *France, Bordeaux, Pomerol, R*   Owned by the family of Michel Rolland, the oenologist who defined the late-harvest, long-maceration style of Pomerol. Excellent, good value Pomerol, ready at three years in lesser vintages but lasting much longer in the finest years. *See also* BERTINEAU ST-VINCENT.

BONALGUE, CH   *France, Bordeaux, Pomerol, R*   This is a wine which has to soften before drinking: try it at 5-7 years old.

BONHOMME, DOM ANDRÉ   *France, Burgundy, Mâconnais, W*   Leading producer of rich, concentrated Mâcon-Viré.

BONNAT, CH LE   *France, Bordeaux, Graves W, R*   Serious winemaking for oaky, age-worthy Rs and Ws.

BONNEAU DU MARTRAY, DOM   *France, Burgundy, Côte d'Or, R, W*   Top Corton (R) and delicious, elegant Corton-Charlemagne (W) are made by this Pernand-Vergelesses estate.

BONNES MARES   *France, Burgundy, AOC, R*   Côte de Nuits *Grand Cru* at Chambolle-Musigny: powerful, solid R wines, among Burgundy's greatest. Leading producers include: de Vogüé, Dom des Varoilles.

BONNET, CH   *France, Bordeaux, Entre-Deux-Mers, W, R*   André Lurton's lovely château makes pungent, soft W in the modern style plus good AOC Bordeaux R.

BONNEZEAUX   *France, Loire, AOC, W*   High-class sweet Chenin Blanc Ws from this Coteaux du Layon village. Leading producers include: Ch de Fesles, René Renou.

BONNY DOON   *USA, California, Santa Cruz, R, W*   Randall Grahm's distinctive wines include a tasty Rhône-style red, Le Cigare Volant, full of cranberry and cherry aromas and flavours; an intensely sweet Muscat Canelli in the style of a German EISWEIN, and several other Rhône and Italy-inspired wines.

BOORDY VINEYARDS   *USA, Maryland, R, W*   With grapes from its small estate vineyard and from local growers, this winery makes a range from hybrid vines.

BORDEAUX   *France, Bordeaux, AOC, R, W, P, Sp*   Wine region and appellation. Within the region are 53 appellations in several tiers. Four main groups, MÉDOC, GRAVES/SAUTERNES, ST-EMILION/POMEROL and ENTRE-DEUX-MERS, have sub-divisions of increasingly higher standards. Most of the Gironde *département*, however, is entitled to grow AOC Bordeaux – or Bordeaux Supérieur with slightly higher alcohol. These are mostly R: lively wines showing the personalities of the Cabernet Sauvignon and Merlot grapes. Pale R wine may be labelled Bordeaux Clairet. Sp Ws are sold as Bordeaux *mousseux* and Crémant de Bordeaux. Bordeaux Côtes de Francs, a small appellation east of St-Emilion, makes R and W (dry and sweet) wines.

BORGES & IRMÃO *Portugal, W* Substantial producers and exporters of Vinho Verde W table wines. Gatão is the biggest brand on the home market.

BORTOLI, DE *Australia, New South Wales, Murrumbidgee, R, W* One of the fastest-growing wineries in Australia, producing three million cases a year. Its sweet, luscious botrytized Sémillon W, Noble One, is a great wine and a flagship.

BOSCHENDAL ESTATE *South Africa, Paarl, R, W, Sp* Wide range of wines including a very good blended white, Grand Vin Blanc, and a well-made Sp, Boschendal Brut.

BOSCQ, CH LE *France, Bordeaux, St-Estèphe, Cru Bourgeois, R* An increasingly attractive wine from a château on the northern edge of the area.

BOSSARD, GUY *France, Loire, Muscadet, W, Sp* Organic (since the 1970s) wines of high quality and reputation. His estate wine is Dom de l'Ecu and his top *cuvée* Hermine d'Or. Also **GROS PLANT** and a Sp Muscadet.

BOTRYTIS CINEREA Fungus, known as "noble rot", which shrivels the grapes, concentrating their juice. Botrytized grapes make some of the world's greatest sweet wines: Sauternes, Hungarian Tokaji, *Trockenbeerenauslese*.

BOUCHARD AÎNÉ ET FILS *France, Burgundy, Côte d'Or, R, W* Major Burgundy *négociant*, owning land ranging from *Grand Cru* Chambertin to the Côte Chalonnaise.

BOUCHARD FINLAYSON *South Africa, Walker Bay, R, W* Very small coastal winery recently established in partnership with Burgundy *négociant* **BOUCHARD AÎNÉ ET FILS**. Not surprisingly, their best wine is an elegant, silky Pinot Noir.

BOUCHARD PÈRE ET FILS *France, Burgundy, Côte d'Or, R, W* *Négociant* based in Beaune with world-wide sales. Has major vineyard holdings, with further good land under the name Domaines du Château de Beaune. High and reliable standards, especially in the Côte de Beaune.

BOUCHAUD, HENRI *France, Loire, Muscadet, W, R* The Dom du Bois-Joly in Le Pallet produces classic Muscadets, with all the requisite lightness and freshness; plus **GROS PLANT** and a red **VIN DE PAYS DU JARDIN DE LA FRANCE** from Cabernet Franc.

BOUCHES-DU-RHÔNE, DES *France, Vin de Pays, R, P, W* Wines from the southern Rhône, mostly Rs from Rhône grapes plus some Merlot and Cabernet Sauvignon.

BOUGROS *France, Burgundy, Chablis, Grand Cru* Vineyard yielding firm wines with a certain rustic quality.

BOURDY, CHRISTIAN *France, Jura, R, W, P* Grower and *négociant* making the full range of Jura wines, including Château-Chalon VIN JAUNE, in a traditional style.

BOURG See CÔTES DE BOURG.

BOURGOGNE *France, Burgundy AOC, R, W, P* Burgundy has a complex hierarchy of appellations. At the base are the regional AOCs – wine from approved vineyards anywhere in Burgundy:
Bourgogne R from Pinot Noir, W from Chardonnay or Pinot Blanc, or (rarely) P (the term CLAIRET can be given to Rs, sometimes to Ps); Bourgogne (Grand) Ordinaire also from anywhere in the region, but Gamay (for R and P) and Aligoté (for W) grapes can be used. Bourgogne Aligoté is a brisk W, at its best from BOUZERON in the Chalonnais, where it has its own AOC. Sp wine (Crémant de Bourgogne or Bourgogne *mousseux*) is also made. Some villages (Irancy for Rs, St-Bris for Ws) and some districts (CÔTE CHALONNAISE, HAUTES CÔTES DE BEAUNE, HAUTES CÔTES DE NUITS) may add their name to the Bourgogne label.
Village wines The main villages in the CÔTE D'OR, such as Pommard, Meursault (and a few villages, eg Mercurey in the Côte Chalonnaise and Pouilly-Fuissé in the Mâconnais), which have their own appellations.
Premiers & Crands Crus Certain vineyards within these villages are *Premiers Crus:* these will be mentioned on label, but are not appellations in their own right. The top vineyards or *Grands Crus* are appellations, and use their name alone – for example Chambertin in the Côte de Nuits, Montrachet in the Côte de Beaune.

BOURGUEIL *France, Loire, AOC, R* Good Cabernet Franc Rs from the north bank of the Loire. Akin to CHINON, for drinking young but good vintages age well (up to 10 years). St-Nicolas-de-Bourgueil village has its own appellation. Leading producers include: Pierre-Jacques Druet, Jacques Mabileau, Joël Taluau.

BOUSCASSÉ, CH *France, South-West, Madiran, R* Pioneer of the Madiran revival: keen on oak-ageing, sometimes to excess; these wines need bottle-age too.

BOUSCAUT, CH *France, Bordeaux, Pessac-Léognan, Cru Classé, R, W* Winemaker Lucien Lurton prefers subtlety to flamboyance. The barrel-fermented W is one of the AOC's best; the R is improving.

BOUVET-LADUBAY *France, Loire, Saumur, W, Sp* Most enterprizing and innovative of the sparkling Saumur houses, owned by Taittinger Champagne. Their range includes two top W *cuvées:* Saphir, and Trésor with its high proportion of Chardonnay, partly oak-fermented.

BOUZERON *France, Burgundy, AOC, W* Dry W from Aligoté grape is at its best in Bourgogne Aligoté de Bouzeron, from this Côte Chalonnaise village. Leading producers include: Bouchard Père et Fils, Michel Goubard, A et P de Villaine.

BOYD-CANTENAC, CH *France, Bordeaux, Médoc, Margaux, 3ème Cru Classé, R* Relatively small estate with powerful, long-lasting wine from old vines.

BRACHETTO D'ACQUI *Italy, Piedmont, DOC, R, Sp* Sweet R Sp wine from the Brachetto grape with a distinctive bouquet of roses and sometimes violets. For early drinking. Leading producers include: Ivaldi, Villa Banfi.

BRANAIRE-DUCRU CH *France, Bordeaux, Médoc, St-Julien, 4ème Cru Classé, R* Château is just west of Beychevelle, but its vines are scattered around the commune. The wine does not show the refined "riverside" character of its neighbours, having more body and perfume. A good, elegant 1993.

BRANE-CANTENAC, CH *France, Bordeaux, Médoc, Margaux, 2ème Cru Classé, R* Large well-sited vineyard on the south tip of the Margaux gravel plateau. The Seventies were disappointing, but Prof Peynaud's advice was sought and the decade of the 1980s saw improvement. Wines now show finesse, especially since 1986, and deserve their 2nd-Growth status.

BRANGER, CLAUDE *France, Loire, Muscadet, W* Award-winning, soft yet crisp Dom La Haute Févrie, plus some GROS PLANT. Top *cuvée*, Excellence, is worth ageing: rare for Muscadet.

BRAUNEBERG *Germany, Mosel, W* Village of the Mittel Mosel, close to Bernkastel, with fine Riesling vineyards including the top-class Juffer and Juffer Sonnenuhr. Leading growers include Fritz Haag, Richter, Pauly-Bergweiler, Dr Thanisch.

BRAZIL *South America* After Argentina and Chile, South America's third wine country, in quantity if not quality. Vines were first planted in the 17th century and today it is *labrusca*, rather than classic *vinifera*, which is most widely grown, from the prolific R variety Isabella to Niagara and Dutchess for W. Rio Grande do Sul province in the south is by far the most important. Many international wine companies have been attracted by Brazil's potential wine market. Leading producers include: Vinicola Aurora, Dreher, Marcus James, Riograndense.

BREISGAU *Germany, Baden, Bereich, R, W, P* Light, fresh W wines from the Rhine near Freiburg; the P *weissherbst* is a speciality.

BREJOEIRA, PALÁCIO DE *Portugal, W* Remarkable "first growth" estate producing Vinho Verde, entirely from W Alvarado grapes, typically round and with more body than is customary.

BRENATO'SCHE GUTSWERWALTUNG, BARON VON *Germany, Rheingau, W* Very traditional, a link with the Rheingau's past, making Riesling Ws that stress elegance and fruit.

BRETHOUS, CH *France, Bordeaux, 1er Côtes de Bordeaux* Well-made wine, worth keeping for longer than the appellation would suggest: a good 1990, and a success in '93.

BREUER, BERNARD *Germany, Rheingau, W* Modern pioneer of dry Rheingau Riesling wine under the **CHARTA** label which Breuer helped start. Dry wines, with structure and fruit, designed to go with food.

BREUIL, CH DE *France, Loire, Anjou, W, R, Sp* The Morgats make fine sweet W **COTEAUX DU LAYON-BEAULIEU**, R and W Anjou, Sp **CRÉMANT DE LOIRE** and **VIN DE PAYS DU JARDIN DE LA FRANCE** (R, W). Sweet wines are deep and rich; the dry benefit from modern techniques.

BRIDGEHAMPTON WINERY *USA, New York, Long Island, W, R* This compact, state-of-the-art winery has made a name with Chardonnay, Merlot and an occasional sweet late-harvest Riesling W.

BRITISH COLUMBIA *Canada* The Okanagan Valley, in the south of the province, is technically a desert, with hot days and cool nights. Irrigation allows grapes (mostly German varieties) for good Ws to be grown. Rs are not yet up to the standard of the Ws. About 30 wineries and 4 wine zones, which include Okanagan and Victoria Island, make wine. Leading producers include: Blue Mountain Vineyard, Brights, Cedar Creek, Dom de Chaberton, Gehringer, Hainle, Lang, Le Comte, Mission Hill, Sumac Ridge, Summerhill.

BRL HARDY *Australia, South Australia, McLaren Vale, R, W* The Renmano/Thomas Hardy merger has created one of the country's biggest wine groups, based in McLaren Vale in South Australia but with vineyards across Australia. Brands are many and various: honest rather than exciting, except for the top wines: eg Eileen Hardy.

BROCARD, JEAN-MARC *France, Burgundy, Chablis, W* Medium-sized producer: mainly *Village* Chablis. No oak used to make good, steely Chablis which ages well.

BROUILLY *France, Burgundy, AOC, R* Largest, most productive and most southerly Beaujolais *cru:* much fairly ordinary R, but also some substantial and long-lived ones. Leading producers include: Ch de la Chaize, J-F Gaget, Ch Thivin.

BROUSSEAU, ROBERT *France, Loire, Muscadet, W* The Dom des Mortiers-Gobin in La Haie-Fouassière has belonged to generations of the Brousseaus. Traditional methods, including some wood maturation, produce wines that can age.

BROUSTET, CH *France, Bordeaux, Barsac, 2ème Cru Classé, W* Despite being large and frankly commercial, this estate makes delicious, spicy, stylish and very well balanced wines, among the bargains of Sauternes. Changed hands in 1994.

BROWN BROS *Australia, Victoria, R, W* Old-established, but still experimenting with (among others) new varieties and high-altitude vineyards. They specialize in single-variety wines.

BRÛLÉSCAILLE, CH *France, Bordeaux, Côtes de Bourg, R* Solid and well-made claret, worth cellaring.

BRUN DE NEUVILLE, LE *France, Champagne* Co-op in the little-known Côte de Sézanne with 145 members and 140ha of vines. The Chardonnay-based wines have lots of fruity appeal.

BRÜNDLMAYER, WILLI *Austria, Kamptal, W, R* One of Austria's top producers, whose family has been making wine since the 17th century. Top quality throughout, from fine dry Grüner Veltliner and steely Riesling to a finely-balanced bordeaux blend and rich, chocolatey Blauburgunder-based R wine.

BRUNELLO DI MONTALCINO *Italy, Tuscany, DOCG, R* From the Brunello grape, a clone of Sangiovese, aged in oak for at least three years. Very full-flavoured and tannic, this expensive wine will age in bottle almost indefinitely. Leading producers include: Altesino, Barbi, Biondi-Santi, Lisini, Villa Banfi.

BRUN DE NEUVILLE, LE *France, Champagne* A cooperative in the little-known Côte de Sézanne district, with 145 members with 140ha of vines. The Chardonnay-based wines have lots of fruity appeal.

BRUT *France* Usually the driest style of champagne and, by extension, other sparkling wines.

BRUT NATURE *France* Very dry sparkling wine style – with no *dosage*.

BUCELAS *Portugal, DOC, W* Less than 30km from Lisbon, produces dry W wines from the acidic Arinto and Esgana Cão ("dog strangler") grape varieties. The best are lemon-fresh. The area is showing sure signs of a revival. Leading producers include: Caves Velhas.

BUENA VISTA *USA, California, Sonoma, R, W* Now German-owned, with 360ha in Carneros; winemaker Jill Davis does well with Chardonnay and Rs such as Pinot Noir, soft, silky Merlot and rich, blackcurrant Cabernet Sauvignon.

BUGEY, VIN DU *France, Savoie, AOC, R, P, W, Sp* Often labelled by grape variety: Jacquère, Molette, Roussette and Chardonnay for Ws; Mondeuse, Pinot Noir and Gamay for Rs. Cerdon is the best of several named *crus*. Roussette du Bugey has its own AOC, with several *crus*. Also many Sp Ws and Ps. Leading producers include: Monin, Caveau Bugiste co-op.

BUHL, VON *Germany, Pfalz, W* Serious Rieslings, made to last, with their balance of fruit and steely acidity.

BUITENVERWACHTING *South Africa, Constantia, R, W* Fairly large ultra-modern winery producing a wide range, including award-winning Merlot and good Chardonnay.

BUJANDA, BODEGAS MARTINEZ *Spain, Rioja, R, W, P* Outstanding producer of meticulously-made wines. A modern style, stressing elegance and balance, is much in evidence here, particularly in their Conde de Valdemar (R).

BULGARIA A drive to make and sell good-value, international-standard wine means Bulgaria has been exporting large quantities to the West since the early 1980s. Cabernet Sauvignon led the way and today 75% of the vineyards are planted with classic varieties. Of the R grapes, a massive 75% are either Cabernet Sauvignon or Merlot. The most widely planted W is Rkatsiteli. Native R varieties like Mavrud, Melnik and Gamza can be good. Mavrud from Assenovgrad in the south is very good; dark and spicy, it can age well. The cooler east and north provide good Ws (Chardonnay, Aligoté) and Rs, especially Cabernet Sauvignon.

BURGAUD, BERNARD *France, Rhône, Côte Rôtie, R* Rising star of Côte Rôtie, making reliable, typical wines.

BURGENLAND *Austria* Some R wines (22%) as well as full-bodied dry Ws. There are four regions: both Neusiedlersee-Hügelland and Neusiedlersee are important for sweet botrytized wines, Mittelburgenland is R wine country, notably Blaufränkisch. The fourth region, Südburgenland, is very small.

BÜRGERSPITAL ZUM HEILIGEN GEIST WEINGUT *Germany, Franken, W* Great charitable estate owning superb vineyards and making a full range of Franken wines.

BÜRGSTADT *Germany, Franken, R* Wine town on the River Main known mostly for serious Rs. Leading producers include: Rudolf Fürst and Weingut der Stadt Klingenberg.

BÜRKLIN-WOLF, WEINGUT DR *Germany, Pfalz, W, R* The top wine estate of the central Pfalz, making both traditional sweet wines and superb modern dry ones from Riesling and a range of other grapes.

BUXY, CAVE COOPERATIVE DE *France, Burgundy, Chalonnais, R, W* Large and well-run concern which produces a wide range of good-value lesser burgundies, but which is especially well known for their Montagnys. Quality may vary, but generally very reliable.

BUZET *France, South-West, AOC, R, P, W* Mostly R wine, from Bordeaux varieties: Cabernet Sauvignon, Cabernet Franc, Merlot, Malbec. Leading producer: LES VIGNERONS DE BUZET.

BUZET, LES VIGNERONS DE *France, South-West, Buzet, R* Quality-biased cooperative making good R Buzet: the top wines spend time in new oak, indeed most wines have some oak-ageing. Its top *cuvée* is the excellent Baron d'Ardeuil.

C

CABARDÈS *France, Midi, VDQS, R, P* Worthwhile Rs and Ps from Cabernet Sauvignon, Merlot and Grenache. Leading producers include: Ch'x de Pennautier, de Rayssac, Rivals.

CABERNET D'ANJOU *France, Loire, AOC, P* Rosé, sweet or dry, from Cabernet (Franc and Sauvignon). Better than Rosé d'Anjou.

CABERNET DE SAUMUR As CABERNET D'ANJOU.

CABERNET FRANC Red Bordeaux grape: 12–20% of Médoc and Graves wines, but often 50% or more in St-Emilion. Lacks the tannin and acidity of Cabernet Sauvignon, but adds fresh fruit aromas, soft-fruit and earthy tastes. Dominant in Touraine, central Loire, for wines such as Saumur, Chinon, Bourgueil – light reds, mostly for drinking young. Popular in north-east Italy, in the Veneto and Friuli-Venezia Giulia. Some is grown in California.

CABERNET SAUVIGNON The foundation of red Bordeaux and, although low-yielding, the world's favourite grape for quality red wine. Often blended with Cabernet Franc and Merlot, as 100% Cabernet Sauvignon can prove austere. Wine is dark, tannic, with blackcurrant aromas when young, cedar-wood in mature wines. Reacts well to oak-ageing and well-made wines from a good vintage will improve in bottle for decades.

CÁCERES, BODEGAS MARQUÉS DE *Spain, Rioja, R, W, P* This meticulously-run modern winery boasts a justifiably high reputation. Harmonious wines which age very well.

CADET-PIOLA, CH *France, Bordeaux, St-Emilion, Grand Cru Classé, R* Small estate on one of the highest points of the St-Emilion plateau. The wines, high in Cabernet Sauvignon for St-Emilion, are quite tannic when young, but begin to soften with a few years' bottle-age, and can be good value.

CADILLAC *France, Bordeaux, AOC, W* Near-extinct appellation for sweet W wine made across the river from Sauternes.

CAHORS *France, South-West, AOC, R* Fine, tannic R from the Lot Valley, using Malbec grapes (local name Auxerrois), with Merlot and Tannat. Best are capable of long ageing. Leading producers include: Ch du Cayrou, Les Côtes d'Olt, Clos la Coutale, Clos de Gamot, Ch Triguedina.

CAILLERET, LE *France, Burgundy, Côte de Beaune, 1er Cru, W* Top Chassagne-Montrachet vineyard, producing fat, weighty mouth-filling wines which age well. Leading producers include: Jean-Noël Gagnard, Bernard Morey, André Ramonet.

CAILLOU, CH *France, Bordeaux, Barsac, 2ème Cru Classé, W* This Barsac estate makes pleasant, but not remarkable, wines.

CALABRIA *Italy* Italy's toe, where quality is still relatively foreign. The only wine known outside the region is R, W and P Cirò DOC.

CALATAYUD *Spain, Aragón, DO, W, P, R* Most recent (1990) of Aragón's four wine zones. High vineyards, little rainfall and thus low yields. All colours of wine produced in *joven* style. Leading producers include: Cooperativa del Campo de San Isidro.

CALIFORNIA *USA* The most important American wine state, with 750 wineries making both world-class premium and good-value mass-produced wines. Quality wines are from coastal zones, including the NORTH COAST counties of NAPA, SONOMA, MENDOCINO; plus SANTA CRUZ, SANTA CLARA and SANTA BARBARA further south. Bulk wines come mostly from the vast CENTRAL VALLEY vineyards. For producers see wine zones.

CALITERRA *Chile, R, W* Ultra-modern winery established in 1986 in MAIPO VALLEY, now owned outright by Errázuris Panquehue. Produces 100,000 cases a year of varietal wines under Calitterra label, including Cabernet Sauvignon, Chardonnay and Sauvignon Blanc.

CALLAWAY *USA, California, Santa Barbara & Southern California, W* The winery, in Temecula, north of San Diego, specializes in a buttery, non-oak-aged Chardonnay called Calla-Lees. Also popular are a complex Fumé Blanc (barrel-aged Sauvignon) and a fruity Sauvignon made in stainless steel.

CALON, CH *France, Bordeaux, Montagne & St-Georges St-Emilion, R* Vineyards in both appellations, so two labels; but the wines are equally good: well-made, supple and enjoyable.

CALON-SÉGUR, CH *France, Bordeaux, Médoc, St-Estèphe, 3ème Cru Classé, R* Most northerly of the Médoc *crus classés*, making long-lasting, solid wines, especially good in the late 1980s.

CAMENSAC, CH *France, Bordeaux, Haut-Médoc, 5ème Cru Classé, R* In St-Laurent, the commune inland from St-Julien. Much investment here: not yet top class, but the wines are honest, and enjoyable with moderate bottle-age.

CAMPANIA *Italy* The region around Naples is best known for its white wines, especially Falerno, a favourite of ancient Rome. R, W, P and Sp Lacryma Christi del Vesuvio is also made here, as is DOCG Taurasi (R).

CAMPO DE BORJA *Spain, Aragón, DO, R, P* One of four of Aragón's wine zones. R and *rosado* are main styles, as well as a sweet (non-DO) mixture of grape juice and spirit called *mistela*. Leading producers include: Bodegas Bordeje and Sociedad Cooperativa Agricola de Borja.

CAMPO VIEJO, BODEGAS   *Spain, Rioja, R, W, P*   This is Rioja's biggest firm. The quality of its very wide range of wines is generally reliable and can be very good indeed, especially with the Selección José Bezares and Viña Alcorta.

CANANDAIGUA WINE CO   *USA, New York, Finger Lakes, R, W, P, Sp*   This Orange County wine company is one of America's largest (over 8 million cases a year), and includes its oldest wine label – Virginia Dare. Makes many *labrusca* wines but also some premium varietals, including Muscat.

CANARD-DUCHÊNE   *France, Champagne*   Owned by the LVMH group, this house produces attractive, good-value wines. The NV has medium weight and an elegantly fruity style.

CANEPA, JOSÉ   *Chile, R, W*   Family enterprize founded in 1930, one of the first to ferment W wine in stainless steel. Has a good reputation for Sauvignon Blanc, Cabernet Sauvignon and Merlot.

CANNONAU DI SARDEGNA   *Italy, Sardinia, DOC, R, P*   Elsewhere known as Grenache, the Cannonau grape produces R wines, both dry and sweet, and sometimes Ps. After a year in wood, the wine is high in alcohol, with a soft warm palate. Leading producers include: Giovanni Cherchi, Cantina Sociale di Dorgali.

CANON, CH   *France, Bordeaux, St-Emilion, 1er Grand Cru Classé, R*   Among the top properties, Canon's wines equal AUSONE and CHEVAL BLANC in best years. Quality has improved hugely since 1982. Made to last, often showing a cedary, elegant character with bottle-age. (For the Fronsac ch of the same name *see* below.)

CANON DE BREM, CH   *France, Bordeaux, Canon-Fronsac, R*   The famous Libourne merchants J-P Moueix own three "Canons" in Fronsac: Châteaux de Brem, Canon, Canon-Moueix. Each is good, making wines that help push this appellation up the quality ladder, but de Brem is perhaps the best. It deserves bottle-age.

CANON-FRONSAC   *France, Bordeaux, AOC, R*   Merlot, Cabernet Sauvignon, Cabernet Franc and Malbec grapes make deep-coloured, powerful, supple and long-lasting (10 years or more) wines in this zone on slopes above Fronsac, near Pomerol. Good value. Leading producers include: Ch Canon, Ch Canon de Brem, Ch Canon-Moueix, Ch La Fleur Caileau, Ch Mazeris-Bellevue.

CANON-LA-GAFFELIÈRE, CH   *France, Bordeaux, St-Emilion, Grand Cru Classé, R*   Totally transformed by its relatively new owners, the Comtes de Neipperg, who brilliantly combine tradition and technology to make outstanding wines.

CANON-MOUEIX, CH   *France, Bordeaux, Canon-Fronsac, R*   See CH CANON DE BREM.

CANTEMERLE   *France, Bordeaux, Médoc, Haut-Médoc, 5ème Cru Classé, R*   Very traditional southern Médoc property, modernized in the last decade. High Merlot content gives a soft, early-maturing style. Recent vintages ('88, '89, '90) gained high praise.

CANTENAC-BROWN, CH   *France, Bordeaux, Médoc, Margaux, 3ème Cru Classé, R*   One of several Médoc estates owned by AXA, the insurance giant, and run by Jean-Michel Cazes (*see* Ch LYNCH-BAGES, Pauillac). Vintages since 1988 have improved as modernization and new management take effect. A good 1993.

CANTERBURY-CHRISTCHURCH   *New Zealand, South Island*   Vines were planted in this district in 1840 but current interest dates from the early 1970s. Produces a wide variety. Leading producers include: Giesen, St Helena, Waipara Springs.

CANTINA SOCIALE   *Italy*   Cooperative winery.

CAP CORSE, MUSCAT DU   *France, Corsica, AOC, VDN*   Sweet W *vin doux naturel* from the north of the island.

CAP DE MOURLIN, CH   *France, Bordeaux, St-Emilion, Grand Cru Classé, R*   Until 1982 there were two properties by this name, but they are now united. The wine is quite rich and generous, with lots of fruit. The same owners as BALESTARD-LA-TONNELLE.

CAPBERN-GASQUETON, CH   *France, Bordeaux, St-Estèphe, Cru Bourgeois, R*   Linked through ownership to CALON-SÉGUR; the wines are lighter-style St-Estèphes.

CAPE MENTELLE   *Australia, Western Australia, Margaret River, W, R*   Majority-owned by Veuve Clicquot of Champagne. Margaret River's cool climate produces outstanding wines from a richly fruity Sémillon/Sauvignon Blanc W blend to a very classy Shiraz R – and a voluptuous Zinfandel R.

CAPEZZANA, TENUTA DI   *Italy, Tuscany, R, W*   The leading estate of the small Carmignano DOCG makes fine Rs, including a bordeaux-style blend, Ghiaie della Furba, plus normal and *riserva* Carmignano. Also a Chardonnay, Sp Villa di Capezzana Brut and fine Vin Santo.

CARBONNIEUX, CH   *France, Bordeaux, Pessac-Léognan, Cru Classé, R, W*   Old and beautiful turreted château where white Graves was pioneered. The W improved greatly in the late 1980s under Denis Dubourdieu: at its best rich, toasty, elegant. The R is richly flavoured, firm and often oaky, for medium-term drinking.

CARCAVELOS   *Portugal, DOC*   Near the estuary of the River Tagus and all but swallowed up by Lisbon. Just one vineyard remains (Quinta dos Pesos) making a fortified wine: sweet and raisiny, with a slight nutty flavour, like a tawny port. Very difficult to find, especially a good one.

CARDONNE, CH LA   *France, Bordeaux, Médoc, Cru Bourgeois, R*   Large vineyard and impressive facilities in open landscape of the northern Médoc. The wine has improved recently: the 1993 was in a softer, fruitier style.

CAREMA   *Italy, Piedmont, DOC, R*   Wines here are made from the Nebbiolo grape. Aged for four years, of which at least two are spent in wood. Blackcurrant colour, good acidity, with a fragrance of alpine flowers, mint and tar. Drink at 4 to 6 years old. Leading producers include: Luigi Ferrando.

CARIGNAN, CH *France, Bordeaux, 1er Côtes de Bordeaux, R* Old and handsome château making good fresh R with hints of oak, attractive young.

CARIGNAN/CARIÑENA France's most widely planted red grape, yielding lots of deep-coloured, alcoholic, tannic *vin de table*. New methods produce better wines in the Midi, especially in blends. Grown in North Africa, California, South America and Spain.

CARILLON, DOM LOUIS *France, Burgundy, Côte d'Or, R, W* The emphasis at this domaine, which is based in Puligny-Montrachet, is on elegant, stylish white wines from Puligny and elsewhere.

CARIÑENA *Spain, Aragón, DO, R, W, P, Sp* Most established of Aragón's four wine zones. Young or *crianza* Rs are best-known wines; also young, fresh Ws and *rosados*. The region is also classified for production of CAVA. Leading producers include: Bodega Cooperativa SAN VALERO.

CARMEL *Israel, R, W, P* Biggest Israeli company with 70% of the market, only making kosher wines. A growers' cooperative where overdue modernization has recently taken place. Top of the range is the Rothschild series.

CARNEROS, LOS *USA, California, VA* Wine zone that straddles the southern ends of Napa and Sonoma. A thin-soiled tract cooled by San Francisco Bay, it is famous for Rs from Pinot Noir and Merlot, and Ws from Chardonnay. Leading producers include: Acacia, Dom Carneros, Saintsbury, Sterling (Winery Lake).

CARRUADES, LES *France, Bordeaux, Médoc, Pauillac, R* 2nd wine of Ch Lafite-Rothschild. Formerly called Moulin Les Carruades.

CASABLANCA *Chile, South America, W, R* New region, north-west of Santiago, benefiting from cool breezes from the Pacific. Chardonnay does very well here, achieving delicate concentrated flavours. Other varieties include Merlot and Sauvignon Blanc.

CASK, CASK-AGEING See BARRELS, BARRIQUE.

CASSIS *France, Provence, AOC, R, P, W* Village near Marseilles with a name for herb-scented W wine from Sauvignon Blanc, Marsanne and Ugni Blanc. Leading producers include: Dom du Bagnol, Clos Ste-Magdelaine, Dom de la Ferme Blanche, Ch de Fontcreuse, Mas Calendal.

CASTEL DEL MONTE *Italy, Apulia, DOC, R, W, P* The best-known DOC of Apulia, producing some of its finest wines using a variety of grapes. The P is popular, the R wines can age very well, the W wine is pleasant. Leading producers include: Rivera.

CASTELL   *Germany, Franken, W*   The centre of the Steigerwald district in the east of Franken, dominated by the Fürst Castell-Castell estate with its dry, solid W wines.

CASTELLANE, DE   *France, Champagne*   Owned by Laurent-Perrier, and far better known within France than outside. Styles range from an exotic, almost New World, pure Chardonnay *cuvée* to the more restrained and elegant Cuvées Commodore and Florens de Castellane.

CASTRIS, LEONE DE   *Italy, Apulia, W, R, P, Sp*   Large private producer with a state-of-the-art winery. Famous for the mass-market Five Roses (P). The best of their Salice Salentino DOC wines is Donna Lisa (R). Also Sp wines, Locorotondo (DOC, W) and the sweet, cask-aged Negrino (R).

CATALAN   *France, Vin de Pays, R, P, W*   Wines from the CÔTES DU ROUSSILLON area, mostly R, using local and classic grapes: a wider range of flavours than the equivalent AOC, and some interesting wines are made.

CATALANS, VIGNERONS   *France, Midi, Roussillon, W, R, VDN*   Most of the village cooperatives in the Roussillon AOC are members of this large producers' union, which makes a large proportion of the wines of the Roussillon: *vins de pays*, Rivesaltes *vins doux naturels* and the appellation wine.

CATOCTIN   *USA, Maryland, VA*   Wine zone in the mountains west of Baltimore, showing potential for R and W wines. Leading producers include: Boordy, Catoctin Vineyards.

CATTIN, THÉO & FILS   *France, Alsace, W, R*   Maker of good Gewürztraminer (from *Grand Cru* Hatschbourg and from Bollenberg *lieu dit*) as well as Pinot Gris and a fine Riesling from *Grand Cru* Hatschbourg, which ages beautifully and for which Théo Cattin is famous.

CAUHAPÉ, DOM   *France, South-West, Jurançon, W*   Both dry and *moelleux* (sweet) wines from the leading estate of the appellation. There are three grades of each: Vieilles Vignes is the top dry wine, Quintessence the top *moelleux.*

CAUSSES, DOM DES   *France, Rhône, Lirac, R*   One of the leading makers of this deep R which is made just across the Rhône from Châteauneuf. His 70% Syrah *cuvée* is new-oak-aged; the standard Lirac, also good, is a blend of several grapes. Also owns Dom des Garrigues in the same appellation.

CAVA   *Spain & Greece*   Cellar in Spanish. Also, by inference, a definition of Spanish *méthode champenoise* sparkling wine, which is made in Catalonia (the vast majority) and elsewhere in Spain.The same word is a Greek term for high-quality table wine.

CAVE COOPÉRATIVE   *France*   Cooperative winery.

CAVE   *France*   Cellar, either literally or as a storage place for wine.

CAVE SPRING   *Canada, Ontario, W, R*   This model small winery makes top-flight Chardonnay and Riesling.

CAYMUS   *USA, California, Napa, R, W*   The Wagner family began making wine here in Rutherford in 1972. Their Special Selection Cabernet Sauvignon is stunning. Conundrum is a barrel-fermented dry W blending Muscat, Sauvignon, Chardonnay and Sémillon.

CAZANOVE, CHARLES DE   *France, Champagne*   Large family-run house, very well known in France. Their top wine is the Cuvée Stradivarius, a Chardonnay/Pinot Noir blend.

CENCIBEL   *See* TEMPRANILLO.

CENTRAL COAST   *USA, California, VA*   This name is used on labels for wine, usually mid-priced blends, from the California counties south of San Francisco: most important are SANTA CRUZ, MONTEREY, SAN LUIS OBISPO, SANTA BARBARA.

CENTRAL OTAGO   *New Zealand, South Island*   With a mere 35ha under vine, this is the country's smallest grape-growing area, and also its furthest south, tucked into a cool valley in the mountains-Mainly Ws. Leading producer: Chard Farm.

CENTRAL VALLEY   *South America, Chile, R, W*   The heart of the Chilean wine industry: wide irrigated vineyard and farmland. Extends 80km north of Santiago and more than 240km south of the city, with a range of climates and several sub-regions, notably the MAIPO VALLEY, the most concentrated vineyard area. Also the MAULE VALLEY, a much cooler sub-region developed and expanded in the 1980s.

CÉPAGE   *France*   Grape variety.

CERONS   *France, Bordeaux, AOC, W*   Sweet W, lighter and less sweet than Sauternes, from a small zone next to Barsac. Leading producers include: Ch de Cérons, Grand Enclos du Ch de Cérons.

CERTAN DE MAY, CH   *France, Bordeaux, Pomerol, R*   On the highest and best part of the Pomerol plateau, making consistently brilliant wines which need several years in bottle.

CÉSAR   Grape variety, now in decline, used in the R wines of Irancy in the Yonne district, near Chablis. Normally blended with Pinot Noir, to which more fashionable variety it is losing ground.

CESARE, PIO   *Italy, Piedmont, R*   Internationally-known R-wine specialist. Barolo, Barbaresco, Barbera and Dolcetto are blended from various vineyards; also a single-vineyard Barolo Ornato.

CHABLIS   *France, Burgundy, AOC, W*   These Chardonnay W wines are typically drier and more austere than those of the Côte d'Or. There are four tiers of quality and status: from the top down are *Grand Cru* (seven of these), *Premier Cru*, simple Chablis and

Petit Chablis (little used). Appealing in youth; good examples of *Premier* and *Grand Cru* Chablis are rewarding after 5–10 years in bottle. Leading producers include: La Chablisienne (co-op), Dauvissat, Durup, Fèvre, Laroche, Michel, Moreau, Raveneau.

CHABLISIENNE, LA   *France, Burgundy, Chablis, W*   Cooperative with 200 members, making honest, well-made wines at all levels from *Village* to *Grand Cru*.

CHADDSFORD WINERY   *USA, Pennsylvania, W, R*
This winery in Chester County began in 1982, producing hybrids and blends. Eric Miller buys grapes from the Piedmont region and wins accolades for his barrel-fermented Chardonnays and also makes Cabernet Sauvignon.

CHAIZE, CH DE LA   *France, Burgundy, Beaujolais, R*   One of the top producers of Brouilly, making good, ripe fruity wines with plenty of body and a rounded finish.

CHALK HILL   *USA, California, Sonoma, VA*   This white-wine zone is in a warm part of Sonoma: good for Sauvignon Blanc and Chardonnay.

CHALONE   *USA, California, Monterey, R, W*   The winery, east of Soledad, uses classic Burgundian methods to gain maximum character from Pinot Noir and Chardonnay grapes. Partnered by Ch LAFITE-ROTHSCHILD, Chalone is linked with Edna Valley (San Luis Obispo), Acacia (Napa), Carmenet (Sonoma) and Woodward Canyon (Washington State).

CHALONE   *USA, California, Monterey, VA*   Wine zone with one estate, CHALONE, in Monterey County.

CHAMARD VINEYARDS   *USA, Connecticut, R, W*   Small coastal winery concentrating on classic varieties – Chardonnay, Pinot Noir and Cabernet Sauvignon; also Merlot and Cabernet Franc for blending.

CHAMBERT, CH DE   *France, South-West, Cahors, R*   Good winemaking, using second-hand *barriques* from Ch Margaux, produces a fruity, well-structured concentrated Cahors.

CHAMBERT-MARBUZET, CH   *France, Bordeaux, St-Estèphe, Cru Bourgeois, R*   This château makes enjoyable, approachable claret which is ready quite quickly.

CHAMBERTIN CLOS DE BÈZE   *France, Burgundy, AOC, R   Grand Cru* adjoining CHAMBERTIN; in Clos de Bèze the land is less divided, and the standard is higher. Leading producers include: Dom Bruno Clair, Faiveley.

CHAMBERTIN   *France, Burgundy, AOC, R*   One of nine *Grands Crus* (the others are Chambertin Clos de Bèze, Chapelle-, Charmes-, Griotte-, Latricières-, Mazis-, Mazoyères- and Ruchottes-Chambertin) in the village of Gevrey-Chambertin in the CÔTE DE NUITS.

Quality varies widely, but the greatest have the ability to age for 20 years. Leading producers include: Bouchard Père & Fils, Leroy, Dom Ponsot, Rousseau.

CHAMBOLLE-MUSIGNY *France, Burgundy, AOC, R, W* Powerful, elegant, complex Rs, among Burgundy's greatest, come from the *Grands Crus* (**BONNES MARES** and **MUSIGNY**) of this Côte de Nuits village. It has several *Premiers Crus*, and village wines of a good standard. The W is rare. Leading producers include: Hudelet-Noëllat, Mugnier, Mortet, de Vogüé.

CHAMPAGNE *France, Champagne, AOC, Sp, W, P* The world's supreme Sp wine, made in a variety of styles from dry to very sweet, usually from a blend of three grapes: Pinot Noir, Chardonnay and Pinot Meunier. Most is non-vintage or NV (ie blended from wines from different vintages), although single-vintage champagne is made in good years. Leading producers include: Bollinger, Charles Heidsieck, Krug, Laurent-Perrier, Moët & Chandon, Perrier-Jouët, Pol Roger, Louis Roederer, Veuve Clicquot Ponsardin.

CHAMPAGNON, DOM LOUIS *France, Burgundy, Beaujolais, R* One of the leading producers in the least-known Beaujolais *Cru* of Chénas. Good, rich concentrated wine. Also produces a Moulin-à-Vent.

CHANDON, DOMAINE *Australia, Victoria, Yarra Valley, Sp* Owned by Moët & Chandon of Champagne, this state-of-the-art winery makes Sp wines of extremely high quality, including the Green Point brand.

CHANSON PÈRE ET FILS *France, Burgundy, Côte d'Or, R, W* Vineyard owner and *négociant*. The estate wines, which are mostly R, can be very good.

CHANTEGRIVE, CH DE *France, Bordeaux, Graves, W, R* Large estate in Podensac. *Barrique*-ageing yields impressive results. New oak is used for the W Cuvée Caroline and the R Cuvée Edouard.

CHAPELLE-CHAMBERTIN See CHAMBERTIN.

CHAPELOT *France, Burgundy, Chablis, 1er Cru* See **MONTÉE DE TONNERRE**.

CHAPOUTIER *France, Rhône, R, W* Estate owner and *négociant* based at Tain-l'Hermitage: the largest landowner in Hermitage, making much-improved wines since 1990, including the Le Pavillion and Monier de la Sizeranne *cuvées*. Also a good source of Côte Rôtie and other north Rhône AOCs, R and W, and Châteauneuf-du-Pape.

CHAPTALIZATION Technique of adding sugar to the grape juice before fermentation in order to give the wine a higher alcoholic content. Widely used in Burgundy, Bordeaux, Loire.

CHAPUIS, MAURICE *France, Burgundy, Côte d'Or, R, W* This Corton estate is very seriously run. The Corton Charlemagne (W) in particular is extremely fine.

CHARBAUT *France, Champagne* Family-owned house that is best known for its pink champagnes, especially the elegant, perfumed Certificate Rosé.

CHARDONNAY Profoundly adaptable, easy-to-grow white grape from Burgundy and Champagne, now an international classic. It has strong fruit flavours: in hotter climates the fruits move from the citrus of burgundy to pineapple and banana. White burgundy successfully marries the tastes of Chardonnay and oak, a pairing tried everywhere the grape is grown, although Chardonnay with no oak-ageing is made for early drinking

CHARLES MELTON *Australia, South Australia, Barossa, R, W* Graeme (Charlie) Melton is at the forefront of the Barossa's rebirth, especially with his velvety, liquorice-and-prune R Nine Popes, blended from Shiraz, Grenache and Mourvèdre.

CHARMES, CH DES *Canada, Ontario, W, R* Majestic replica French château with some Burgundian-style Chardonnay, Auxerrois and Gamay, plus good Cabernet in ripe years.

CHARMES, LES *France, Burgundy, Côte de Beaune, 1er Cru, W* At the southern end of Meursault, next to Puligny-Montrachet, this vineyard produces top-quality wine with a certain steeliness, for long ageing. Leading producers include: Robert Ampeau, Michelot-Buisson, Guy Roulot.

CHARMES, LES *France, Burgundy, Côte de Nuits, 1er Cru, R* One of the top vineyards of Chambolle-Musigny, making wines with good colour and body, and supple elegant fruit. Leading producers include: Barthas-Noëllat, Hudelot-Noëllat.

CHARMES-CHAMBERTIN *France, Burgundy, AOC, R* This *Grand Cru* vineyard in the village of Gevrey-Chambertin has a reputation for consistent, early-maturing wines. See also CHAMBERTIN. Leading producers include: Bachelet, Rousseau.

CHARTA *Germany* Association of Rheingau producers committed to making medium-dry and dry Riesling wines, good with food.

CHARTRON & TREBUCHET *France, Burgundy, Côte d'Or, R, W* Both *négociant* and estate (Dom Chartron) with the emphasis on W wines. The estate wines are especially good.

CHASSAGNE-MONTRACHET *France, Burgundy, AOC, R, W* The Côte de Beaune village of Chassagne long ago added the name of the *Grand Cru* vineyard MONTRACHET (which it shares with the village of Puligny) to its own; it also shares BÂTARD-MONTRACHET and has its own *Grand Cru*, Les Criots-Bâtard-Montrachet. The *Grands Crus* produce outstanding, long-lived and very expensive W burgundy. W village Chassagne-Montrachet is made to a high standard; Chassagne also makes R wine: soft, fruity, well-structured and can age 10 years in good vintages, yet often overlooked: these can be good value. Leading producers include: Gagnard, B Morey, Ramonet.

CHASSE-SPLEEN, CH *France, Bordeaux, Moulis, Cru Bourgeois, R* One of the best, and best-known, *crus bourgeois*, whose large vineyard makes wine to classed-growth standard. Enjoyable young, but can age for 10 years or longer.

CHASSELAS White grape grown mainly in Switzerland (where it is known as Fendant or Perlan), for a soft, dry white wine. Also grown in the upper Loire, Alsace, Savoie and Germany (where it is called Gutedel).

CHASSENAY D'ARCE *France, Champagne* This cooperative, based in the AUBE district, has 130 growers and takes the grapes from 303ha. Wines are appealing and fruity and there is a 100% Pinot Noir champagne, Cuvée Sélection.

CHÂTEAU *France* Literally castle or country house; in wine terms a unit of land, with or without a dwelling, which is run as a wine estate. Used elsewhere in the world to convey the same message.

CHÂTEAU GRILLET See GRILLET, Ch.

CHÂTEAU-CHALON *France, Jura, AOC, W* The best VIN JAUNE comes from this Jura village. Leading producers include: Christian Bourdy, Jean Macle.

CHÂTEAUMEILLANT *France, Loire, VDQS, R, P* Small production of Rs and Ps from Gamay, Pinot Noir and Pinot Gris, from an area in the southern Cher *département*.

CHÂTEAUNEUF-DU-PAPE *France, Rhône, AOC, R, W* Thirteen grape varieties are allowed in this renowned R of southern Rhône, but most wine is based on Grenache, with Syrah, Mourvèdre and others. A good example from a hot vintage should last for 20–25 years, but will drink well at 5–6. Minor vintages, and most *négociant* wines, are ready at 3–5 years. The W Châteauneuf is also from a blend of grapes, including Clairette, Grenache Blanc and Roussanne. Leading producers include: Ch de Beaucastel, Chapoutier, Ch Rayas, Dom du Vieux Télégraphe.

CHÂTILLON-EN-DIOIS *France, Rhône, AOC, R, P, W* Remote district east of the Rhône Valley. Rs from Gamay blended with Syrah and Pinot Noir, Ws from Chardonnay or Aligoté.

CHAVE, GÉRARD *France, Rhône, Hermitage, R* The key name in Hermitage today, with wines of elegance and breed. Also small amounts of very good St-Joseph.

CHÉNAS *France, Burgundy, AOC, R* The smallest of the Beaujolais *crus*: next to, and similar to, Moulin-à-Vent. Top Chénas can be quite rich and concentrated. Leading producers include: Guy Braillon, Dom des Brureaux (Daniel Robin), Louis Champagnon, Cave du Ch de Chénas, Dom des Trémont.

CHENIN BLANC   White grape from the Loire with high acidity; can make dry or moderately sweet wine, but the great Chenin-based Loires (Bonnezeaux, Coteaux du Layon, Vouvray) are complex, luscious, long-lived sweet wines. Grown in South Africa, California and New Zealand, for blending or as a medium-dry or dry varietal wine.

CHENONCEAU, CH DE   *France, Loire, Touraine, W, Sp, R*   One of the few historic Touraine châteaux to produce wine. From a 12-ha vineyard on higher ground away from the river, it makes wines with the AOC of Touraine, including dry Ws, Rs and Sp.

CHÉREAU-CARRÉ   *France, Loire, Muscadet, W*   All wines from the four Chéreau-Carré estates that total 74ha are bottled individually *sur lie*. They pioneered wood fermentation and ageing for Muscadet, producing a wine that could easily be mistaken for a white bordeaux.

CHEVAL BLANC, CH   *France, Bordeaux, St-Emilion, 1er Grand Cru Classé (A), R*   Vying with AUSONE as St-Emilion's top property, but with a more consistent record. Relatively large, with 12,000 cases a year. The wine is rich, ripe and intense: often deceptively approachable when young, it can last for 40 years or more.

CHEVALIER, DOM DE   *France, Bordeaux, Pessac-Léognan, Cru Classé, R, W*   Classic R, elegant and long-lived, and a small amount of W which is both very expensive and very fine. Needs 8 years' ageing, but can last for 30.

CHEVALIER-MONTRACHET   See MONTRACHET.

CHEVERNY   *France, Loire, AOC, R, W, P*   Minor zone near Blois, with Ws from Chenin Blanc, Sauvignon Blanc, Chardonnay or the high-acid Romorantin, a grape unique to Touraine; light Rs and Ps from Gamay, Cabernet Franc, Pinot Noir or Cot. Leading producers include: Courtioux, Sauger, Tessier.

CHEVILLON, DOM ROBERT   *France, Burgundy, Côte d'Or, R, W*   This relatively new estate specializes in very good-quality Nuits-St-Georges made in the traditional manner.

CHIANTI   *Italy, Tuscany, DOCG, R*   This broad DOCG currently covers five Tuscan provinces. Sometimes sold in straw-covered flasks, this Sangiovese-based R wine has a fresh cherry aroma and attractive, fruity, sometimes rather light palate. It is best drunk young. Leading producers include: Frescobaldi, Ruffino.

CHIANTI CLASSICO   *Italy, Tuscany, DOCG, R*   The largest of the CHIANTI sub-zones, responsible for some of its best wines, based on the Sangiovese grape. Raspberry and black cherry flavours, combined with dryness and acidity. The best can age well. Leading producers include: Antinori, Badia a Contibuono, Castello di Volpaia, Isole e Olena.

CHIANTI COLLI FIORENTINI   *Italy, Tuscany, DOCG, R*   An important Chianti sub-zone. Not as good as Classico or Rufina, but the wines can be attractive, with supple fruit flavours. Leading producers include: Costello del Trebbio, Il Corno, Parri, Sammastana .

CHIANTI RUFINA *Italy, Tuscany, DOCG, R* The smallest of the Chianti sub-zones and one of the best. Not dissimilar to *classico* but has a higher acidity, often coupled with better fruit and ageing ability. Leading producers include: Frescobaldi, Selvapiana, Villa Vetrice.

CHICAMA VINEYARDS *USA, Massachusetts, R, W, Sp* This estate on the island of Martha's Vineyard grows Chenin Blanc, Chardonnay, Sauvignon Blanc, Gewürztraminer, Cabernet Sauvignon, Merlot and Pinot Noir. The R wines are particularly rated but the Sp Chardonnay, Sea Mist, shows promise.

CHILE *South America* After Argentina, South America's second producer, with 64,530ha. One of the world's few regions with pre-phylloxera vines on their own roots. Two categories of wine are made: for the local market and for export. The former are usually in an old-fashioned style from prolific and low-class varieties, such as País; the latter from French varieties using modern technology. Main region is the **CENTRAL VALLEY**, with its sub-regions the **MAIPO** and **MAULE VALLEYS**. Came to prominence in the 1980s as a source of reasonably-priced, good wines from Cabernet Sauvignon, Merlot and Sauvignon Blanc. 1995 brought a new appellation system, with five viticultural regions made up of sub-regions, zones and areas. Wines exported to Europe will be at least 85% from the appellation. Leading producers include: Caliterra, Concha y Toro, Errázuriz Panquehue, Cousiño Macul, Santa Rita, Mighel Torres, Undurraga, Los Vascos.

CHINA Although growing wine-grapes is not alien to Chinese culture, historically it has been of little importance. Production is in the north-east and the emphasis is on medium dry, consumer-friendly W wines. The more progressive wineries, however, are beginning to work with international firms to make western-style wines from varieties such as Riesling and Chardonnay.

CHINON *France, Loire, AOC, R* Cabernet Franc Rs from the south bank of the Loire, opposite Bourgueil. Young wines have soft fruit and earthy tastes; from warm years they age to attractive truffle and violet flavours. Leading producers include: Bernard Baudry, Couly-Dutheil, Ch de la Grille, Charles Joguet, Les Caves des Vins de Rabelais, Jean-Maurice Raffault.

CHIROUBLES *France, Burgundy, AOC, R* Most balanced and fragrant of the Beaujolais *crus*, light in colour and style, and the first to be ready: drink within two years. Fashionable and expensive. Leading producers include: Dom Desmoures, Ch de Jauvenard, Dom Passot, Maison de Vignerons Chiroubles.

CHIVITE, BODEGAS JULIÁN *Spain, Navarra, R, W, P* This bodega was the pioneer in establishing Navarra on the export market. Chivite consistently produces very well-made wines, including a range under the Gran Feudo label and a top-quality unwooded R wine, Viña Marcos.

CHOREY-LÈS-BEAUNE *France, Burgundy, AOC, R* Village producing good-value burgundy for early drinking. Leading producers include: J Germain, Maillard Père & Fils, Tollot-Beaut.

CHURCHILL GRAHAM *Portugal, port* Founded 1981, by one of the old-established Graham port family. The wines, labelled Churchills, have been acclaimed by critics and include aged tawnies and an **LBV**. Also two single-*quinta* wines, Quinta da Agua Alta and Quinta de Fojo.

CIGALES *Spain, Castilla-León, DO, W, P, R* Newest DO (1991) of Castilla-León, but boasts centuries of winemaking experience. Emphasis on excellent *rosados,* though fine Rs promise well for the future. Leading producers include: Avelino Vegas, Hijos de Frutos Villar.

CINSAUT Red grape of medium quality, low in tannin. Likes heat; much used for blending in southern Rhône, Provence, Midi, Lebanon, North Africa, South Africa (where it was crossed with Pinot Noir to make Pinotage).

CINZANO *Italy, Piedmont, W, R, Sp* The major vermouth company also makes Sp Cinzano Brut and Marone Cinzano Pas Dosé under the Asti DOCG. Other Sp wines include Pinot Chardonnay and Principe di Piemonte Brut.

CIRÒ *Italy, Calabria, DOC, R, W* Probably the only DOC of Calabria known outside the region, whose reputation is greater than it deserves. The R can be quite hefty and, at their best, the W wines are attractively fruity. Leading producers include: Librandi, Fattoria San Francesco.

CISSAC, CH *France, Bordeaux, Haut-Médoc, Cru Bourgeois, R* Reliable, good-value claret, dark and tasty, that can age very well.

CITÉ DE CARCASSONE, DE LA *France, Vin de Pays, R* Light, enjoyable Rs from around the famous medieval city in southern France.

CITRAN, CH *France, Bordeaux, Haut-Médoc, Cru Bourgeois, R* On the edge of Moulis. Recent vintages have seen big improvements.

CLAIR, DOM BRUNO *France, Burgundy, Côte d'Or, R, W, P, Sp* Dynamic estate with diverse vineyard holdings in Côte de Nuits. Go-ahead but with a great respect for tradition: very good quality wines.

CLAIRET *France* Red wine, light in body and colour. The word claret is derived from it. Usually used today for pale red wine from Bordeaux.

CLAIRETTE DE BELLEGARDE *France, Midi, AOC, W* Dry W wine from Clairette grapes, made where the Languedoc vineyards meet the Rhône's. Limited production.

CLAIRETTE DE DIE   *France, Rhône, AOC, W, Sp*   Sparkler from the Clairette grape, with some Muscat. There is a traditional *méthode dioise*, but Champagne's technique is increasingly used for the Crémant de Die. Leading producer: Cave Cooperative.

CLAIRETTE DU LANGUEDOC   *France, Midi, AOC, W*   Flavoury dry W from the Clairette grape, recently revived. Leading producers include: Ch la Condamine Bertrand, Dom St-André.

CLAPE, AUGUSTE   *France, Rhône, Cornas, R*   The top maker of this robust Syrah R, with very old vines: a wine to age 10 years.

CLARE VALLEY   *Australia, South Australia*   District with a number of small, well-run, family wineries. Superb, long-lived Riesling Ws. Leading producers include: Jim Barry, Grosset, Knappstein, Mitchell, Skillogalee, Taylors, Wendouree.

CLARIDGE   *South Africa, Wellington, R, W*   Roger Jorgensen gave up fruit farming in Kent, England, for winemaking in the Cape in 1987. He now produces a superb R blend and very good Chardonnay, both innovatively packaged in 50cl bottles.

CLARKE, CH   *France, Bordeaux, Listrac, Cru Bourgeois, R*   Edmond de Rothschild's money has conjured a virtually new vineyard out of a neglected corner. The style is fresh, fruity and relatively fast to mature, though the latest vintages have increasing structure.

CLASSED GROWTH   Translation of CRU CLASSÉ.

CLASSICO   *Italy*   A restricted zone, usually the heart of a wine area. For example; Chianti Classico, Bardolino Classico.

CLEAR LAKE   *USA, California, VA*   Wine zone in Lake County, northern California, making good Sauvignon Ws and Cabernet Sauvignon Rs. Leading producers include: Beringer, Kendall-Jackson, Louis Martini, Sutter Home.

CLERC-MILON, CH   *France, Bordeaux, Médoc, Pauillac, 5ème Cru Classé, R*   The vines are to the east of Ch'x MOUTON and LAFITE. Owned by the Rothschilds of Mouton since 1970, their investment is slowly producing results, with the duo of 1985 and 1986 attracting praise.

CLIMENS, CH   *France, Bordeaux, Barsac, 1er Cru Classé, W*   One of the few estates that can on occasion challenge Ch d'YQUEM, although the wines are very different. Climens is a Barsac: subtle and understated. But after 10 years in bottle it begins, very slowly, to show the majestic elegance of which it is capable. On very good form since 1983.

CLINET, CH   *France, Bordeaux, Pomerol, R*   Michel Rolland is the adviser here. There used to be a fairly high percentage of Cabernet Sauvignon (very unusual in Pomerol), but this has gradually been reduced. Superb wines in good vintages.

CLINTON VINEYARDS   *USA, New York, Hudson River Valley, W, Sp*   This winery specializes in the Seyval Blanc grape, including a Sp version, and also makes good Chardonnay and Riesling Ws.

CLOS *France* Generally refers to a vineyard surrounded by a wall, in Burgundy particularly. Often they have monastic origins.

CLOS CABRIERE *South Africa, Franschhoek, W, Sp* Achim von Armin makes some of the Cape's top Sp wines in the Franschhoek Valley from Chardonnay and Pinot Noir.

CLOS CAPITORO *France, Corsica, Ajaccio, W, R, P* Jacques Bianchetti makes prestigious wines under this name: Rs and Ps from Sciacarello and Grenache, and Ws from Vermentino. The R, sold with some maturity, is the best.

CLOS DE LA ROCHE *France, Burgundy, AOC, R* This *Grand Cru* in Morey-St-Denis produces, along with Clos St-Denis, some of the greatest, longest-lived R wines in the Côte de Nuits. Leading producers include: Bouchard Père & Fils, Dom Dujac, Dom Lignier, Dom Ponsot.

CLOS DE TART *France, Burgundy, AOC, R* One of Burgundy's original walled, monastic vineyards, this *Grand Cru* in Morey-St-Denis is owned entirely by Mommessin. Rich, dark wine that needs age.

CLOS DE VOUGEOT *France, Burgundy, AOC, R* Famous *Grand Cru* in a large walled vineyard. With 80 owners, the wine varies in style. Leading producers include: Dom Bertagna, Joseph Drouhin, Jean Gros, Dom Mongeard-Mugneret.

CLOS DES CHÊNES *France, Burgundy, Côte de Beaune, 1er Cru, R* At the southern end of Volnay, next to Monthélie. Makes elegant, fairly delicate wines which age very well. Leading producers include: Jean-Marc Bouley, Joseph Drouhin, Michel Lafarge, Comtes Lafon.

CLOS DES JACOBINS, CH *France, Bordeaux, St-Emilion, Grand Cru Classé, R* Owned by Bordeaux *négociant* Cordier, this impeccably-run property consistently makes fine quality wines, with good depth of colour and ripe, plummy fruit.

CLOS DES LAMBRAYS *France, Burgundy, AOC, R* Côte de Nuits *Grand Cru* in Morey-St-Denis, with (unusually for Burgundy) just one owner, Dom des Lambrays. Replanted in 1980, and the wine has yet to return to the heights.

CLOS DES MOUCHES, LE *France, Burgundy, Côte de Beaune, 1er Cru, R, W* One of the top vineyards of the Beaune appellation, situated at its southern end. The Ws are quite soft and broad in flavour and the Rs are densely coloured, with a tannic backbone. Leading producers include: Joseph Drouhin.

CLOS DES PAPES *France, Rhône, Châteauneuf-du-Pape, R* Traditional producer of Châteauneuf, making some of the most elegant and suave wines in the appellation.

CLOS DU BOIS   *USA, California, Sonoma, W, R*   Large-scale winery making creamy, lemony barrel-fermented Chardonnay; also single-vineyard (Flintwood and Calcaire) Chardonnays and (Briarcrest and Marlstone) Cabernet Sauvignons.

CLOS DU MARQUIS   *France, Bordeaux, Médoc, St-Julien, R*   2nd wine of Ch Léoville Las-Cases.

CLOS DU VAL   *France, Burgundy, Côte de Beaune, 1er Cru, R*   In the commune of Auxey-Duresses. One of the top names in the appellation, producing supple, medium-bodied, raspberry fruited wines. Leading producers include: Michel Prunier.

CLOS DU VAL   *USA, California, Napa, R, W*   Bernard Portet brings a French flavour to this Stags Leap winery, notably in a blackberry-like Zinfandel R and an unusual silky, oily, dry Sémillon W.

CLOS FLORIDÈNE   *France, Bordeaux, Graves W, R*   Denis Dubourdieu, master of white winemaking in the Graves and consultant at many Graves estates, owns this small property in Pujols. The results at Floridène are delicious. At present the Ws, aged in new oak, are better than the Rs. *See also* Ch'x REYNON, DU JUGE.

CLOS HAUT-PEYRAGUEY   *France, Bordeaux, Sauternes, 1er Cru Classé, W*   Elegance and finesse rather than power are the declared aims here. The wine is always good, but scarcely as great as its *premier* rank would suggest.

LES CLOS   *France, Burgundy, Chablis, Grand Cru*   The largest *Grand Cru* in Chablis, with the longest-lasting, firmest-structured wines.

CLOS PEGASE   *USA, California, Napa, R, W*   The wines of Clos Pegase, south of Calistoga, are a lean, lemon-pear Chardonnay, a broad, blackcurrant Merlot, a herbaceous Cabernet Sauvignon and a juicy **MERITAGE** red blend of Cabernets Sauvignon and Franc, with Merlot. The property is an architectural showpiece.

CLOS SAINT-JACQUES   *France, Burgundy, Côte de Nuits, 1er Cru, R*   Top Gevrey-Chambertin vineyard whose wines are densely coloured, powerful and masculine and which require long ageing. Leading producers include: Bruno Clair.

CLOS ST-DENIS   See CLOS DE LA ROCHE.

CLOS ST-MARTIN, CH   *France, Bordeaux, St-Emilion, Grand Cru Classé, R*   This miniscule property is quite a well-guarded secret. Difficult to find, but worth seeking out because of the quality.

CLOUDY BAY VINEYARDS   *New Zealand, South Island, W, R, Sp*   In large part responsible for New Zealand's world reputation for Sauvignon Blanc, Cloudy Bay is expensive and hard to find. Now owned by Veuve Clicquot and Australia's Cape Mentelle, they make a Sp wine, Pelorus, which is also excellent. They also make Chardonnay and, more recently, R wines.

COASTAL REGION   *South Africa, WO*   Zone which takes in the best wine areas (WOs)of the Cape: **CONSTANTIA**, Durbanville,

STELLENBOSCH, PAARL, Swartland and Tulbagh.

COCHE-DURY, DOM   *France, Burgundy, Côte d'Or, R, W*   Top estate, making mainly Ws from the Côte de Beaune: excellent Meursault and Corton Charlemagne.

COCHEM   *Germany, Mosel, W*   The centre of one of the better lower Mosel districts, making ripe, attractive Riesling Ws.

COCKBURN SMITHES   *Portugal, port*   Known familiarly as Cockburn's, one of port's most famous names. Wines from its estates Quinta do Tua and Quinta da Eira Velha are occasionally bottled as single-*quinta* vintages. Cockburn's Special Reserve is the UK's leading brand, Fine Ruby almost as popular: both well-made, commercial wines. Aged tawnies are among the best. Cockburn's declares vintages less often than other houses: its 1983 and 1985 releases showed a style which is softer and more velvety than some – although they last as long.

CODORNíU   *Spain, Catalonia, Sp*   Cordoníu, founded in 1872, produced Spain's first Sp wine and is now one of the leading Cava makers, with a wide range that includes a Pinot Noir/Chardonnay blend, Jaume de Codorníu.

COLARES   *Portugal, DOC, R, W*   Three wines may be produced under this DOC, rapidly disappearing because of its proximity to Lisbon. The best is a deeply coloured and austere R, mainly from the Ramisco grape. Also a less good R from a blend of varieties, and a little W from Malvasia which is not worth trying. Leading producers include: António Bernardino, Paulo da Silva.

COLDSTREAM HILLS   *Australia, Victoria, Yarra Valley, R, W*   Founded by author James Halliday, this award-winning winery makes superb Pinot Noir and Chardonnay.

COLLET, JEAN   *France, Burgundy, Chablis, W*   Son Gilles now runs this estate, making rich, stylish oak-aged wines, mainly *Premier* and some *Grand Cru*.

COLLI ORIENTALI DEL FRIULI   *Italy, Friuli-Venezia Giulia, DOC, W, R*   Mainly W wines from the widely-planted Tocai grape, pale in colour with an almond-scented bouquet. Also Pinot Grigio, Chardonnay and many others. R wines from Cabernet Sauvignon and Franc, Merlot, Refosco and Schioppettino. Picolit, the dessert wine, comes from here. Leading producers include: Abbazia di Rosazzo, Livio Felluga, Volpe Pasini.

COLLINES RHODANIENNES, DES   *France, Vin de Pays, R, W*   This zone covers the hinterland of the northern Rhône. Most of the wine is varietal; not only the local Syrah, but also Gamay and Merlot. Can be good value: look for famous Rhône names, estates which use the *vin de pays* name on wine from young vines.

COLLIO GORIZIANO   *Italy, Friuli-Venezia Giulia, DOC, W, R*   Known also as simply "Collio", the wine is similar to neighbouring Colli Orientali, with Tocai dominating but with other good W wines from Pinot Grigio and Pinot Bianco. Leading producers include: Marco Felluga, Gravner, Pra de Pradis, Russiz Superiore.

COLLIOURE *France, Midi, AOC, R*   Solid R wine from Grenache, Mourvèdre and Syrah, sharing with Banyuls VDN the steep coastal vineyards near the Spanish border. Leading producers include: Dom du Mas Blanc, Dom de la Rectorie.

COLOMBARD   White grape from south-west France, making flowery young wines with crisp acidity. Very successful in California and South Africa.

COLOMBO, JEAN-LUC *France, Rhône, Cornas, R*   Maker of good Cornas, plus Vin de Pays and Côtes du Rhône, and a *négociant*. Well-known, too, as a successful consultant oenologist, with radical views (similar to ACCAD's in Burgundy). Bordeaux-trained, he has championed ripe fruit, small-cask, new-oak ageing and an organic regime.

COLORADO *USA*   The Grand Valley provides tolerable growing conditions for Riesling, Gewürztraminer and Syrah.

COLUMBIA *South America*   Very little table wine is made in Columbia. Most production is of fortified wines, vermouth or tropical fruit blends.

COLUMBIA *USA, Washington State, R, W*   This company has some of the Yakima Valley's top vineyards, and makes around 80,000 cases a year, with varietal Rs from Cabernet Sauvignon, Merlot, Syrah and Cabernet Franc, and Ws from Chardonnay, Riesling, Gewürztraminer and Sémillon.

COLUMBIA VALLEY *USA, Washington, VA*   The main wine zone of this north-western state, with good fresh Ws (Chardonnay, Riesling, Sémillon) and fruity Rs (Merlot and Cabernet) plus Sp. YAKIMA VALLEY and Walla Walla Valley are sub-zones. Leading producers: *see* WASHINGTON.

COMBETTES, LES *France, Burgundy, Côte de Beaune, 1er Cru, W*   At the northern end of Puligny-Montrachet, next to Meursault. Yields wines which are slightly broader than some other Pulignys and a little less elegant. Leading producers include: Robert Ampeau, Leflaive, Sauzet.

COMTÉ DE GRIGNAN, DU *France, Vin de Pays, R*   Area on the right bank of the Rhône, around Montélimar. The wines are dominated by southern Rhône grapes such as Grenache. Varietal wines from Gamay, Merlot or Cabernet Sauvignon are allowed.

COMTÉ TOLOSAN, DU *France, Vin de Pays, R, P*   Regional *vins de pays* zone covering most of South-West France: not much used, but offering a name for varietal wines now being developed here.

COMTÉS RHODANIENS, DES *France, Vin de Pays, R, W, P*   Catch-all *vins de pays* for wines from all over the Rhône-Alpes region, including Provence. Relatively new, and so far little used.

CONCA DE BARBERÀ *Spain, Catalonia, DO, W, P, R* Small, hilly wine zone in central Catalonia. A little experimental Cabernet Sauvignon, but production is 80% *joven* W. Leading producers include: Concavins.

CONCANNON *USA, California, Livermore Valley, R* Founded in 1883, the winery is one of the last to make Petite Sirah, a bold, rustic R, full of plummy flavour.

CONCHA Y TORO *Chile, R, W* Founded in 1883, Chile's largest producer. Makes over three million cases a year under a variety of labels, including modestly-priced Casillero del Diablo range and single-vineyard Cabernet Sauvignon, Merlot and Chardonnay under the Marqués de Casa Concha label.

CONDADO DE HUELVA *Spain, Andalucia, DO, W, P, R* Andalucian wine zone near Portuguese border, producing new-style *joven afrutado* (cool-fermented) wines and old-style fortified.

CONDAMINE BERTRAND, CH LA *France, Midi, Coteaux du Languedoc, W* Quality and production of the various styles of white CLAIRETTE DU LANGUEDOC fell until the Jany family of Condamine Bertrand set out to restore the reputation of the appellation. Today the best wine is lighter and fresher: made at 12°, rather than the previous 13° or 14°.

CONDRIEU *France, Rhône, AOC, W* The Viognier grape achieves perfection in this northern Rhône vineyard. Best drunk between 1½ and 4 years old. Leading producers include: Cuilleron, Delas, Dezormeaux, Guigal, Niero et Pinchon, Alain Paret, André Perret, Georges Vernay.

CONFURON-COTETIDOT, DOM *France, Burgundy, Côte d'Or, R* Followers of the ACCAD style of vinification, producing especially good Nuits-St-Georges and Echézeaux.

CONNECTICUT *USA* Vineyards along the coast and in the west, in the Western Connecticut Highlands area – reckoned the best place for classic vines. Producers include CHAMARD, Haight Vineyards (sited in the west, good for Riesling, Chardonnay and Sp).

CONNÉTABLE DE TALBOT *France, Bordeaux, Médoc, St-Julien, R* Second wine of Ch Talbot.

CONSEILLANTE, CH *France, Bordeaux, Pomerol, R* There is a high percentage of Cabernet Franc in this consistently fine wine, which will age for 20 years or more.

CONSTANTIA *South Africa, WO* The Cape's most historic wine zone, source in the 18th century of great sweet wines, a style revived recently by Klein Constantia. Also a source of Chardonnay, Sauvignon Blanc and Riesling Ws and Cabernet Sauvignon and Shiraz Rs. Leading producers include: Buitenverwachting, Groot Constantia, Klein Constantia.

CONSTANTIN, CH *France, Bordeaux, Graves, W* In Portets, a source for rich, oaky Ws in a commercial but very appealing style.

COOKS *New Zealand, North Island* Now owned by **CORBANS**, a very large winery that did much to put New Zealand on the map. A wide range: both inexpensive and consistently well made: especially their Chenin Blanc.

COONAWARRA *Australia, South Australia* At the southernmost tip of the mainland, and famed for its thin strip of "terra rossa" soil and cool climate. Australia's greatest Cabernet Sauvignons and high-quality Shiraz (R). Leading producers include: Bowen, Brands Laira, Lindemanns, Mildara, Redman, Rouge Homme, Wynns, Zema.

COOPERATIVE Union of grape-growers who jointly own wine-making facilities and sometimes bottle and market wines. Some, but not all, are leaders in their appellations.

CORBANS WINES *New Zealand, North Island, W, R* The second-largest wine firm in New Zealand, ranging from 3-litre boxes to fine estate wines. The best are from Stoneleigh Vineyard in Marlborough, South Island.

CORBIÈRES *France, Midi, AOC, R, P, W* Predominantly R, from Carignan improved by Syrah and Mourvèdre. Large area, from the Mediterranean to the Pyrenees, with many soils, micro-climates and winemakers: 11 *terroirs* are recognized. Some good estates emerging as outsiders invest. Leading producers include: Cave d'Embres et Castelmaure, Ch de Lastours, Ch La Voulte-Gasparets.

CORBIN-MICHOTTE, CH *France, Bordeaux, St-Emilion, Grand Cru Classé, R* One of five properties by the Pomerol border with Corbin in its name. A fairly exotic style of wine, with good depth and body.

CORKED Describes wine that has a strong smell of rotten cork. This rather rare occurrence is caused by the development of certain moulds in the cork: the powerful smell makes the wine clearly undrinkable. Nothing to do with pieces of cork in the glass, which are harmless.

CORNAS *France, Rhône, AOC, R,* 100% Syrah wine from south of Hermitage that can start tough and tannic, but be superb after 10 years. Leading producers include: Auguste Clape, Paul Jaboulet Aîné, Robert Michel, Noël Verset.

CORNEILLA, CH DE *France, Midi, Roussillon, W, R, VDN* Here *vin de pays* and Rivesaltes *vin doux naturel* are made as well as the rich, sturdy CÔTES DE ROUSSILLON, R (45% Carignan, 35% Grenache Noir and 20% Syrah), which is made in the classic way.

CORSE, VIN DE *France, Corsica, AOC, R, P, W* General appellation for Corsica, with Rs and Ps from interesting native grapes or imported ones, such as Carignan, Grenache, Cinsaut, Syrah; one bottle in 10 is W, mainly from Vermentino (local name for Malvoisie). Best wines add on the name of a sub-zone: Calvi; Coteaux du Cap-Corse; Figari Porto-Vecchio; Sartène.

CORSIN, DOM *France, Burgundy, Mâconnais, R, W* Elegant, fruity Pouilly-Fuissé and St-Véran.

CORTON *France, Burgundy, AOC, R* The only R *Grand Cru* in the Côte de Beaune. The name is usually linked with a specific vineyard, eg Corton Les Bressandes, Corton Clos du Roi, Corton Les Renardes. Powerfully flavoured, earthy and highly tannic when young; subtlety, perfume and spicy fruit emerge after 6–7 years in bottle. The best wines can last 20 years. Leading producers include: Pierre André, Bonneau du Martray, Capitain-Gagnerot, Dubreuil-Fontaine, Daniel Senard, Tollot-Beaut.

CORTON-CHARLEMAGNE *France, Burgundy, AOC, W* Aloxe-Corton *Grand Cru* for W wines, on the same slope as **CORTON**, yielding some of the world's finest Chardonnays. Their nutty, spicy, sumptuous bouquet and flavour begin to open up after 5 years; will still be great at 15–20. Leading producers include: Bonneau du Martray, Maurice Chapuis, Coche-Dury, Joseph Drouhin, Jaffelin, Louis Latour.

COS D'ESTOURNEL, CH *France, Bordeaux, Médoc, St-Estèphe, 2ème Cru Classé, R* Well-known both for its odd, orientally styled *chai* and for its consistent excellence. There is 40% Merlot, and modern methods are used; but the wines are long-lived and classic in style. Proprietor Bruno Prats is one of the leading winemakers of the Médoc. His wines vie with the region's best. 2nd wine: Ch de Marbuzet.

COS LABORY, CH *France, Bordeaux, Médoc, St-Estèphe, 5ème Cru Classé, R* Next-door to Ch Cos d'Estournel, but different in style: straightforward and early-maturing. Recent vintages have improved.

COSSART GORDON *Portugal, Madeira* Among the major, and oldest, firms: founded in 1745. The style is comparatively light and elegant. Good Company is the basic range, Finest Old the 5-year-old reserve wines, while Duo Centenary is the 15-year-old exceptional reserve range.

COSTERS DEL SEGRE *Spain, Catalonia, DO, W, R, Sp* One of Catalonia's eight wine zones, producing Cava and still wines. Leading producers include: **RAIMAT**, Cellers Castell de Remei.

COSTIÈRES DE NÎMES *France, Midi, AOC, R, P, W* Mainly light R for drinking young (Grenache plus Carignan, Cinsaut, Syrah, Mourvèdre), from Languedoc vineyards by the Rhône. Leading producers include: Dom de l'Amarine, Dom St-Louis la Perdrix, Ch'x de Belle Coste, de Campuget, de Rozier, and de la Tuilerie.

COT See MALBEC.

CÔTE CHALONNAIS *France, Burgundy, R, W, Sp* Area south of the Côte d'Or and making similar but lesser wines. The villages of (N to S) BOUZERON, RULLY, MERCUREY, GIVRY and MONTAGNY offer good-value wines: true Burgundian character at sensible prices.

CÔTE D'OR *France, Burgundy, R, W* The "Golden Slope" of Burgundy, comprising the CÔTE DE NUITS (northern half) and the CÔTE DE BEAUNE (southern). R wines from Pinot Noir, W from Chardonnay. *See* map (Atlas section) for villages. Also the name of the *département* (county) covering these vineyards.

CÔTE DE BEAUNE *France, Burgundy, AOC, R, W* Southern part of the Côte d'Or . Mainly R, but notable exceptions in the W *Grands Crus* of Corton-Charlemagne and Montrachet, the *Premiers Crus* and the village wines from Meursault, Puligny and Chassagne. Simple Côte de Beaune AOC is rarely seen, but Côte de Beaune-Villages may be used for R wine by most of the region's villages and for blends.

CÔTE DE BRÉCHAIN *France, Burgundy, Chablis, 1er Cru* See MONTÉE DE TONNERRE.

CÔTE DE BROUILLY *France, Burgundy, AOC, R* The Mont de Brouilly rises from the vineyards; those on its slopes form this Beaujolais *cru*. On the Côte the grapes ripen well, yielding generally richer, more characterful wines than BROUILLY. Leading producers include: André Large, Ch Thivin, Ch du Grand Vernay, Les Vins Mathelin, Morin, Viornery.

CÔTE DE FONTENAY *France, Burgundy, Chablis, 1er Cru* See FOURCHAUME.

CÔTE DE NUITS *France, Burgundy, R, W* Name for the northern half of the Côte d'Or: mostly red-wine vineyards, including famous villages such as Nuits St-Georges and Gevry-Chambertin. The name Côte de Nuits is only seen on labels when used of the AOC below.

CÔTE DE NUITS-VILLAGES *France, Burgundy, AOC, R, W* Mainly R wine chanelled from five villages on the north and south edges of this northern part of Burgundy's Côte d'Or. Leading producers include: Dom Allexant, Dom Robert Jayer, Dom de la Poulette, Reine Pedaque, Dom Daniel Rion.

CÔTE, LA *Switzerland, Vaud* To the west of Lausanne, a wine-producing district where most of the crop is handled by cooperatives and merchants' cellars. Stylish W wines from the Chasselas grape and Pinot Noir for gentle, drinkable R.

CÔTE ROANNAISE *France, Loire, AOC, R, P* Gamay Rs and Ps from Roanne, near the source of the Loire. Best producers: Paul Lapandéry, Félix Vial.

CÔTE RÔTIE *France, Rhône, AOC, R* One of the world's great Rs, long-lived and rich. The most elegant expression of the Syrah grape, plus up to 20% of the aromatic W Viognier, from the most northern Rhône vineyards. Leading producers include: Bernard Burgaud, Chapoutier, Marcel Guigal, Joseph Jamet, René Rostaing, Vidal-Fleury.

COTEAUX CHAMPENOIS *France, Champagne, AOC, R, W* Rare still wines from Champagne: the best Rs are from the villages of Ay, Bouzy and Cumières. Both R and (rarer) W wines are like light burgundies. Leading producers include: Barancourt, Bollinger, Gosset, Jacquesson & Fils, Lanson Père & Fils, Laurent-Perrier, Moët et Chandon, Ruinart Père & Fils.

COTEAUX D'AIX-EN-PROVENCE *France, Provence, AOC, R, P, W* Local grapes are now stiffened by Cabernet Sauvignon and Syrah for a modern profile and some interesting R wines are now being made. Leading producers include: Commanderie de la Bargemone, Ch Fonscolombe, Ch Vignelaure.
Les Baux-de-Provence, a sub-zone, has cool, hilly vineyards, welcoming to Cabernet Sauvignon. Leading producers include: Mas de la Dame, Mas de Gourgonnier, Dom des Terres Blanches, Dom de Trévallon.

COTEAUX D'ANCENIS *France, Loire, VDQS, R, P, W* Mainly R wine, from Gamay or Cabernet (Franc or Sauvignon), made around Ancenis in western Loire. Limited production.

COTEAUX DE DIE *France, Loire, AOC, W* Still W wine from Clairette grape, from the same region as the more interesting Sp Clairette de Die.

COTEAUX DE L'ARDÈCHE, DES *France, Vin de Pays, R, W, P* Successful for R from Cabernet, Merlot or Gamay; P, including pure Syrah ones; and W from Chardonnay and Viognier. Growers include several local co-ops and Burgundy *négociant* Louis Latour, whose whites have been especially successful.

COTEAUX DE L'AUBANCE *France, Loire, AOC, W* Medium-sweet to sweet W wines from Chenin Blanc, made in small and declining amounts in the Auibance valley in the Anjou Villages area. Leading producer: Hervé Papin.

COTEAUX DE PEYRIAC *France, Vin de Pays, R, P* Overlapping with the Minervois AOC zone, these wines are Rs from traditional grapes plus imported classic varieties and (increasingly) Ps from Grenache and Cinsaut.

COTEAUX DE PIERREVERT *France, Rhône, VDQS, R, P, W* Large zone along the Durance river; R, W and P wines are closer to Provence than Rhône in style.

COTEAUX DES BARONNIES, DES *France, Vin de Pays, R, W* This zone is east of the Côtes du Rhône region. Rs are from a range of grapes including Merlot and Cabernet Sauvignon, with Ws from Chardonnay and Viognier, alongside the local Clairette and Grenache Blanc.

COTEAUX DU GIENNOIS *France, Loire, VDQS, R, P, W* Gien, between Sancerre and Orléans, makes Ws from Sauvignon Blanc and Chenin Blanc, Rs and Ps from Gamay and Pinot Noir. Limited production.

COTEAUX DU LANGUEDOC *France, Midi, AOC, R, P, W* Large AOC: nearly 100 villages, 14 of them quality *crus*: Quatourze, La Clape (good W wine from limestone hills), St-Chinian (large area, some good Rs), Faugères (increasingly good Rs, worth 4-5 years' ageing, some from Syrah and Mourvèdre), Picpoul de Pinet (W from the local Picpoul grape), Cabrières (P and Rs), St-Saturnin, Montpeyroux, St-Georges d'Orques (good Rs), Pic St-Loup, Méjanelle, St-Drézéry, St-Christol, Coteaux de Vérargues. Leading producers include: Dom d'Aupilhac, Ch Coujan, Ch Grézan, Dom des Jougla, Ch de la Liquière, Ch Rouquette-sur-Mer.

COTEAUX DU LAYON *France, Loire, AOC, W* Luscious sweet Ws made from Chenin Blanc (ideally super-ripe, botrytized grapes). Finest vintages show astonishing depth and richness. Certain villages (eg Chaumes) can add their name to the general appellation. BONNEZEAUX and QUARTS-DE-CHAUME have their own AOCs. Leading producers include: Dom des Baumard, Ch du Breuil, Ch de Fesles, Ch de Belle-Rive, René Renou.

COTEAUX DU LOIR *France, Loire, AOC, R, P, W* Area of diminishing importance, on the Loir (not Loire) river, north of Tours.

COTEAUX DU LYONNAIS *France, Burgundy, AOC, R, P, W* Zone south of Beaujolais making Rs from Gamay plus a very little W (from Chardonnay and Aligoté). Leading producers include: Cave Coopérative de Sain Bel.

COTEAUX DU TRICASTIN *France, Rhône, AOC, R, P, W* Mostly Grenache-based Rs, from southern Rhône. Leading producer: Dom de Grangeneuve.

COTEAUX DU VENDÔMOIS *France, Loire, VDQS, R, P, W* Zone on Loir (not Loire) river, west of Vendôme. Small production, almost all drunk locally.

COTEAUX FLAVIENS, DES *France, Vin de Pays, R, P* Some interesting Rs from non-traditional grapes (Cabernet Sauvignon, Merlot) come from this zone south of Nîmes.

COTEAUX VAROIS *France, Provence, AOC, R, P, W* Wide zone making R wines for drinking young, and reasonable Ps. Leading producers: Dom du Deffends, Dom de Garbelle.

CÔTES D'AUVERGNE *France, Loire, VDQS, R, P, W* Wines from this district around Clermont-Ferrand are similar to Beaujolais: Gamay for R and P, Chardonnay for W. Limited production: most of the wine is drunk locally. Leading producers: Rougeyron, Cave St-Vernay.

CÔTES DE BERGERAC See BERGERAC.

CÔTES DE BLAYE *France, Bordeaux, AOC, W* Dry W wine from the same area as BLAYE. Premières Côtes de Blaye covers better Rs and Ws from the same area.

CÔTES DE BORDEAUX ST-MACAIRE *France, Bordeaux, AOC, W* Seldom-seen medium-sweet or sweet W wine from the south of Entre-Deux-Mers.

CÔTES DE BOURG *France, Bordeaux, AOC, R, W* Best part of the Bourg zone, mostly R, from slopes above the Dordogne. The AOC Bourg has fallen out of use. A little W is also made. Leading producers include: Ch'x de Barbe, Eyquem, Roc des Cambes, Tayac.

CÔTES DE CANON-FRONSAC See CANON-FRONSAC.

CÔTES DE CASTILLON *France, Bordeaux, AOC, R* Rising source of good-value clarets, east of St-Emilion. Leading producers include: Ch Pitray, Ch Thibaud-Bellevue.

CÔTES DE DURAS *France, South-West, AOC, R, W, P* Light, early-maturing Rs, and dry and medium-sweet (*moelleux*) W wine from Bordeaux grape varieties. Leading producers include: Duras co-op, Dom de Ferrant, Dom de Laulan.

CÔTES DE FRANCS *See* BORDEAUX CÔTES DE FRANCS.

CÔTES DE GASCOGNE, DES *France, Vin de Pays, W, R* Mostly Ws from the Armagnac country in South-West France: fresh, well-made wines. Most is from the UNION PLAIMONT cooperative, but some private estates are making good wines.

CÔTES DE LA MALEPÈRE *France, Midi, VDQS, R, P* Merlot, Cot and Cinsaut grapes, plus Cabernets Franc and Sauvignon, Grenache and Syrah, make wines combining sound structure with Mediterranean warmth. Leading producers include: Ch de Malviès, Ch de Routier.

CÔTES DE MELITON *Greece, North, R, W* Wine zone on a penin-sula on the north-eastern coast of Greece. The Ws are made from native varieties blended with Sauvignon Blanc and Ugni Blanc; Rs from Limnio and Cabernet Sauvignon. Leading producers include: Ch Carras.

CÔTES DE MILLAU *France, South-West, AOC, R, W, P* Small zone in the Tarn valley for Rs, Ws and Ps.

CÔTES DE MONTRAVEL See MONTRAVEL.

CÔTES DE PROVENCE *France, Provence, AOC, P, R, W* The largest AOC of Provence. Two-thirds of the wine is P, made from Grenache, Carignan, Cinsaut, Syrah, Mourvèdre and other grapes, and increasingly Cabernet Sauvignon. Some good Rs from the same grapes from individual estates. Leading producers include: Ch Bertraud-Belieu, Dom Gavoty, Les Maîtres Vignerons de La Presqu'île de St-Tropez, Doms Ott, Commanderie de Peyrassol, Dom Richeaume.

CÔTES DE ST-MONT *France, South-West, VDQS R, W, P* Well-made, good-value country wines come from the same grapes as Madiran (Rs) and Pacherenc du Vic-Bilh (Ws). Leading producer: Plaimont Co-op.

CÔTES DE TOUL *France, Alsace, VDQS, R, P, W* Some of France's most northerly vineyards, in Lorraine, make R and P (Gris de Toul) wine from Gamay and Pinot Noir; small amount of W.

CÔTES DU BRULHOIS *France, South-West, AOC, R, P* Rustic R from the Garonne valley. Little is made.

CÔTES DU FOREZ *France, Loire, VDQS, R, P* Good Rs and Ps from Gamay, made just across the mountains from Beaujolais. Leading producer: Les Vignerons Foréziens co-op.

CÔTES DU FRONTONNAIS *France, South-West, AOC, R, P* This supple, fruity wine is based on the low-tannin Négrette grape, with Cabernet Franc and others. Two sub-areas: Fronton and Villaudric. Leading producers include: Ch Baudare, Ch Bellevue la Forêt, Ch Flotis, Fronton co-op, Ch Montaurio.

CÔTES DU JURA *France, Jura & Savoie, R, P, W, Sp* Mostly W, using Savignan and Chardonnay grapes, from 72 villages. Some R (Pinot Noir and others) and P. Also **VIN JAUNE**. Leading producers include: Ch d'Arlay, Chalandard, Pignier.

CÔTES DU LUBÉRON *France, Rhône, AOC, R, P, W* Mountain area to the east of the southern Rhône: mostly soft, enjoyable Rs, using Syrah and Grenache. W from Clairette grapes can be good. Leading producers include: Dom de Mayol, Ch Val Joanis.

CÔTES DU MARMANDAIS *France, South-West, AOC, R, P, W* Mainly R wines from Merlot, Cabernets Franc and Sauvignon, with Cot, Gamay, Syrah and local Fer Servadou and Abouriou. Leading producer: Cocumont co-op.

CÔTES DU RHÔNE *France, Rhône, AOC, R, P, W* Very varied wines from a huge area of the southern Rhône. Rs are Grenache with Cinsaut, Syrah and others; Ws from Clairette, Roussanne and Marsanne. Leading producers include: Chapoutier, Ch de Fonsalette, Ch du Grand Moulas, Guigal, Jaboulet, Vidal-Fleury.

CÔTES DU RHÔNE-VILLAGES *France, Rhône, AOC, R, W* This AOC is for better wines from 16 communes within the Côtes du Rhône area, which can add their name to the labels:
Beaumes-de-Venise: traditional Rs as well as the famous Muscat dessert wine;
Cairanne: Rs; leading producers include: Dom Rabasse-Charavin;
Laudun: Rs and Ws;
Rasteau: hearty Rs as well as *vins doux naturels*; leading producers include: Dom de la Soumade;
St-Gervais: good Rs and luscious Viognier Ws; leading producers include: Dom Ste-Anne;
Sablet: leading producers include: Dom des Gourbets;

Séguret: some good Rs from close to Gigondas; leading producers include: Dom de Cabasse;

Valréas: leading producers include: Dom des Grands Devers; plus Chusclan, Roaix; Rousset-les-Vignes; Rochegude; St-Maurice-sur-Eygues; St-Pantaléon-les-Vignes; Vinsobres; Visan.

CÔTES DU ROUSSILLON *France, Midi, AOC, R, P, W* Sturdy, full-bodied Rs from Grenache, Cinsaut, Syrah and Mourvèdre and a decreasing amount of Carignan. Some Ps, and fairly neutral Ws from Macabeo and Malvoisie. The superior appellation Côtes du Roussillon Villages can only be R; two villages – Caramany and Latour de France – can add their names to the appellation's. Leading producers include: Ch de Cazenove, Dom Cazes, Ch de Corneilla, Ch de Jau, Dom Piquemal.

CÔTES DU TARN, DES *France, Vin de Pays, R, W, P* This zone around Gaillac makes robust Rs, some good Ps from Gamay and Syrah, and fresh fruity Ws.

CÔTES DU VENTOUX *France, Rhône, AOC, R, W, P* Southern Rhône Rs and Ps (from Grenache, Syrah and many others) and Ws (Clairette and others). Can be good value. Leading producers include: Dom des Anges, Jaboulet, Vieille Ferme.

CÔTES DU VIVARAIS *France, Rhône, VDQS, R, P, W* Decent but rather light southern Rhône Rs, Ps and Ws (based on Clairette, Marsanne and Bourboulenc). Leading producer: Dom de Vigier.

COTNARI *Romania* Area in the north-east, and well known for its pale, honeyed sweet W wine, similar to Hungary's famous Tokaji. Grapes are left to shrivel on the vine, but noble rot is rare. Made from a blend of varieties, large oak barrels are used for both its fermentation and maturation, and the wine is bottled after a couple of years. Can age very well.

COUHINS-LURTON, CH *France, Bordeaux, Pessac-Léognan, Cru Classé, W* Small vineyard, solely Sauvignon Blanc. Fermented and aged in new oak, the wine is distinctive and successful.

COULÉE DE SERRANT, CLOS DE LA *France, Loire, Anjou, W* Nicolas Joly combines biodynamic farming and a belief in astrological influence to make a great wine, designed for an immense life, from a single-vineyard appellation in SAVENNIÈRES. The steep vineyard is worked by horsepower.

COULY-DUTHEIL *France, Loire, Chinon, R* This is the largest producer of Chinon wines actually based in Chinon, with 65ha of vines, plus grapes from local growers. The top wine is Clos de l'Echo, from a single vineyard that once belonged to Rabelais.

COURANÇONNE, CH DE *France, Rhône, Côtes du Rhône-Villages, R* Gabriel Meffre's estate uses mostly Grenache grapes to make an excellent, solid R.

COURCEL, DOM DE *France, Burgundy, Côte d'Or, R* Pommard specialist making wonderful, richly coloured, dense, long-lived wines.

COUSINO MACUL *Chile, R, W* On the outskirts of Santiago, a family estate long known for its Cabernet Sauvignon. Since 1990 R wines have been aged in French *barriques*. New additions include Merlot and Chardonnay.

COUTET, CH *France, Bordeaux, Barsac, 1er Cru Classé, W* In the late 1980s Coutet once again found its form, producing tangy wines with the Barsac delicacy behind a great richness of fruit. In great years a special *cuvée* of this sweet wine, Cuvée Madame, is produced.

COUVENT-DES-JACOBINS, CH *France, Bordeaux, St-Emilion, Grand Cru Classé, R* Consistent quality is now ensured by using the lesser vats for a 2nd label. Beautifully perfumed, with lovely, supple fruit. The underground cellars are well worth a visit.

COVEY RUN *USA, Washington State, R, W* This Zillah (Yakima Valley) winery produces Lemberger, an unusual, fragrant, stainless-steel-fermented R, White Riesling and Chardonnay. La Caille de Fumé is a dry W Sauvignon Blanc/Sémillon blend.

COWRA *Australia, New South Wales* This small, high-up, region of New South Wales is emerging as an important producer of fleshy, buttery Chardonnay. Leading producers include: Cowra Estate, Rothbury.

CRÉMANT *France* Describes gently sparkling wine in Champagne; elsewhere in France a wine made by the *méthode champenoise*.

CRÉMANT DE DIE See CLAIRETTE DE DIE.

CRÉMANT DE LIMOUX See BLANQUETTE DE LIMOUX

CRÉPY *France, Savoie, AOC, W* Delicate dry W wine from Chasselas grapes. Leading producers include: Fichard, Mercier.

CRIOTS-BÂTARD-MONTRACHET, LES See BÂTARD-MONTRACHET

CRIANZA *Spain* See VINO DE CRIANZA.

CROCHET, LUCIEN *France, Loire, Sancerre, W, R* Family firm with 30ha in some of the best Sancerre *crus*: Chêne Marchand and Grand Chemarin for Ws, Clos du Roi for Rs.

CROCK, CH LE *France, Bordeaux, St-Estèphe, Cru Bourgeois, R* Lavish modern equipment and the best advice combine to make increasingly impressive wine at this handsome château.

CROFT *Portugal, port; Spain, sherry* One of the oldest (1678) port shippers. A full range of ports, from Distinction Finest Reserve (sound, commercial quality), up to aged tawnies and vintage wines (including single-*quinta* Quinta da Roeda) that are among the best. Its sister sherry company revolutionized the sherry market in the 1960s with Croft Original Pale Cream, a pale sherry that looked dry, but tasted sweet. Other brands include Delicado fino, Croft Particular medium amontillado and Brandy Croft.

CROIZET-BAGES, CH *France, Bordeaux, Médoc, Pauillac, 5ème Cru Classé, R* Unusually for Pauillac, Cabernet Sauvignon is not the main variety here: it is overtaken by Merlot and Cabernet Franc. Style is thus softer and more open, and wines mature quite quickly.

CROQUE-MICHOTTE, CH *France, Bordeaux, St-Emilion, Grand Cru Classé, R* Near the Pomerol border; this wine is very approachable young. The seductive fruit and soft, supple palate are best enjoyed within a decade.

CROZES-HERMITAGE *France, Rhône, AOC, R, W* Perhaps the best *rapport qualité/prix* of the northern Rhône, with recent dramatic improvements. As in HERMITAGE, Rs are from Syrah, Ws from Marsanne and Roussanne. Leading producers include: Belle, Alain Graillot, Jaboulet/Dom de Thalabert, Etienne Pochon.

CRU *France* Literally meaning growth: an area that reflects a particular soil and climate. In Bordeaux, a wine from a specific estate or château, and from this, the various ranks of wine estates; see below: CRU BOURGEOIS and CRU CLASSÉ

CRU BOURGEOIS *France* The category of château below classed growths in the Médoc.

CRU CLASSÉ Classed growth: in the Médoc, a château placed in one of five ranks by the 1855 Classification (*Premier Cru, Deuxième Cru*, etc).

CRUSIUS, WEINGUT HANS & PETER *Germany, Nahe, W* Small, high-quality estate making long-lived wines from some of the top Nahe vineyards.

CRUZEAU, CH DE *France, Bordeaux, Pessac-Léognan, R, W* Straightforward unoaked W, mostly Sauvignon Blanc, and an austere but stylish oak-aged R.

CUILLERON *France, Rhône, Condrieu, W* Top maker of this rare W, with a standard wine for early drinking and Les Chaillets, a *cuvée* for ageing.

CUMBERLAND VALLEY *USA, Maryland & Pennsylvania, VA* High-quality wine zone, fast expanding, which grows hybrid and classic grapes. Leading producers include: Basignani, Boordy.

CURÉ-BON-LA-MADELEINE, CH *France, Bordeaux, St-Emilion, Grand Cru Classé, R* Relatively unknown property making a wine that is essentially Merlot, backed up with a little Cabernets Sauvignon and Franc. Highly regarded by those who know it well.

CUVE *France* Vat or cask to hold the fermenting grape juice, or to store wine; an alternative for ageing to *barriques*. Can be made of cement or (increasingly) stainless steel.

CUVÉE *France* Signifies a selection of wine that may or may not have been blended. Also describes a batch of wine with the same characteristics.

CVNE (COMPAÑÍA VINÍCOLA DEL NORTE DE ESPAÑA) *Spain, Rioja, R, W, P* One of Rioja's oldest and finest houses, producing good-quality wines throughout their extensive range. Top-of-the-range Imperial and Vina Real (Rs) rank among the finest in the region.

CYPRUS Quality potential as yet is far from realized. Most wine is R, from the alcoholic, tannic, unexciting Mavron grape. W mainly from Xynisteri. The famous dessert wine, Commandaria, can be excellent but is usually simple commercial stuff.

CZECH REPUBLIC The two Czech regions of Bohemia and Moravia make wines, mainly W, of roughly equal quality. A wide range of varieties includes the native, aromatic Irsay Oliver (W). Close in style to those of Austria and Hungary: dry, ripe and crisp, with good fruit. R wines from Pinot Noir can be very good, Sp wine, both W and R, is mader on a large scale and is acceptable. Fine future potential.

D

DAGUENEAU, DIDIER *France, Loire, Pouilly-Fumé, W* Burgundy-trained Dagueneau ferments in new wood as well as stainless steel, for wines (from various – labelled – *terroirs*) that age well. His top *cuvée*, Silex (the name of a type of stony soil), is one of the finest made in Pouilly today.

DAMBACH-LA-VILLE *France, Alsace,* Considered the best wine village in the Bas-Rhin. *Grand Cru* Frankstein is good for Riesling and Gewürztraminer. Leading producers include: Gisselbricht.

DÃO *Portugal, DOC, R, W* Mainly R wine, from one of Portugal's most famous wine areas, from anything up to nine grape varieties. Should be firm, but can taste hard and austere due to old-fashioned winemaking. W wines are also old-fashioned. Modern wineries are beginning to produce better wines: Caves São João, Vinicola do Vale do Dão.

DASSAULT, CH *France, Bordeaux, St-Emilion, Grand Cru Classé, R* This fairly large property makes wine with few hidden depths, but with lots of obvious appeal.

DAUVISSAT, RENÉ *France, Burgundy, Chablis, W* Small, high-quality estate owned by René and son Vincent. Some wines are still vinified in oak and all enjoy some oak ageing. With bottle-age they acquire the flinty mineral taste of the *terroir*.

DAUZAC, CH *France, Bordeaux, Médoc, Margaux, 3ème Cru Classé R* Estate in Labarde, close to the Gironde, making wine that has improved over the last decade but does not yet scale the heights. A new winery, a new *chai* and replanting in the vineyards represent hope for the future.

DEIDESHEIM *Germany, Pfalz, W, R* Top wine village in the Mittelhaardt, the best part of the Pfalz, making serious and long-lived Ws. Top vineyards are Hohenmorgen, Grainhübel and Hergottsackert. Leading producers include: Basserman-Jordan, von Buhl.

DEINHARD, WEINGUT DR *Germany, Pfalz, W* Quality estate based at DEIDESHEIM making good Pfalz W wines, mostly Riesling, in a traditional style

DEISS, MARCEL, DOM *France, Alsace, W, R* One of the region's best winemakers, making concentrated wines of only the highest quality in many varieties and styles, including *vendange tardive* and *sélections des grains nobles*.

DELAFORCE *Portugal, port* The Delaforces are still involved, though the firm is now part of the IDV combine. His Eminence's Choice, an old tawny, is well regarded. Their vintage wines are based on Quinta da Corte: elegant wines, with delicacy and less longevity than some of the blockbusters of the trade.

DELAMOTTE *France, Champagne* Owned by Laurent-Perrier, based in the Côte des Blancs. Quality and elegance are hallmarks, especially in both the vintage *blanc de blancs* and the prestige *cuvée* Nicolas-Louis Delamotte.

DELAPORTE, VINCENT *France, Loire, Sancerre, W, R* Small but top-quality family estate in Chavignol: mainly Ws, small amount of R. The steep slopes, above the village, are worked by hand. Wines are sold around the world, and served in smart Paris restaurants.

DÉLAS FRÈRES *France, Rhône, R, W* Major vineyard owner in the Northern Rhône, with land in Hermitage, Côte Rôtie, St-Joseph and in Condrieu. Wines are correct, not exciting – but they are improving.

DELBECK *France, Champagne* Now owned by François d'Aulun, who used to own Piper-Heidsieck, this house has undergone many changes. Best known for its NV Brut Héritage and a fine rosé.

DELORME, ANDRÉ *France, Burgundy, Chalonnais, R, W, Sp* Good-quality Rully estate producing both R and W wines, especially from Dom de la Renarde.

DEMI-SEC *France* Medium-dry; however in Champagne the term means medium-sweet.

DENOMINAÇÃO DE ORIGEM CONTROLADA (DOC) *Portugal* The top tier of Portugal's appellation system.

DENOMINACIÓN DE ORIGEN (DO) *Spain* The most common grade of Spanish quality wine.

DENOMINACIÓN DE ORIGEN CALIFICADA (DOC) *Spain* A "super-category" for Spanish quality wines meeting special criteria of quality and consistency.

DENOMINAZIONE DI ORIGINE CONTROLLATA (DOC) *Italy* Italian quality wine.

DENOMINAZIONE DI ORIGINE CONTROLLATA E GARANTITA (DOCG) *Italy* Higher grade of Italian quality wine, above DOC. The guarantee is a signal of tighter quality control.

DESCOMBES, DOM JEAN *France, Burgundy, Beaujolais, R* Leading producer of Morgon, the richest and most long-lived of the Beaujolais *Crus*.

DESMIRAIL, CH *France, Bordeaux, Médoc, Margaux, 3ème Cru Classé, R* Recently revived: the land was for many years owned by other châteaux. Results awaited.

DEUTZ *France, Champagne* Family-owned **GRANDE MARQUE**, at Ay. Overall style quite fruity and forward, although the prestige *cuveé* William Deutz is particularly good.

DEUX ROCHE, DOM DES *France, Burgundy, Mâconnais, R, W* Estate which produces a range of good-quality R and W Mâconnais. The St-Véran in particular is very good.

DEVAUX *France, Champagne* The flagship wine of the dynamic Union Auboise, a group of co-ops in the **AUBE** district, with 750 growers and 1,400ha of vines. Mainly Pinot Noir, very good value, well-made champagne.

DEZALEY *Switzerland, Vaud, Lavaux, W, R* To the east of Lausanne, a leading wine-producing village making attractive W wine from the Chasselas grape and agreeable but not very complex R from Pinot Noir.

DIAMOND CREEK *USA, California, Napa, R* Estate specializing in R wines with four tiny vineyard plots on Diamond Mountain which yield four distinctive Cabernet Sauvignons: Volcanic Hill, Red Rock Terrace, Gravelly Meadow and Lake – the last released only in top years.

DIAMOND MOUNTAIN *USA, California, VA* Steep hillside vineyards above the Napa Valley form a wine zone making austere, classy Chardonnay and Cabernet Sauvignon. Leading producers include: Diamond Creek, Sterling, Stonegate.

DO *Spain* See DENOMINACIÓN DE ORIGEN.

DOC *Italy* See DENOMINAZIONE DI ORIGINE CONTROLLATA.

DOC *Portugal* See DENOMINAÇÃO DE ORIGEM CONTROLADA.

DOC *Spain* See DENOMINACIÓN DE ORIGEN CALIFICADA.

DOCG *Italy* See DENOMINAZIONE DI ORIGINE CONTROLLATA E GARANTITA.

DOISY-DAËNE, CH *France, Bordeaux, Barsac, 2ème Cru Classé, W* Sauternes in a light and delicate style (except in 1989), with charm rather than power. Can be disappointing in light years, but in good years quintessential Barsac. Also makes a dry white Graves.

DOISY-DUBROCA, CH *France, Bordeaux, Barsac, 2ème Cru Classé, W* Same owners as **CH CLIMENS**, and the techniques are the same. *Terroir* will out, however, and Dubroca does not have the distinction of Climens; but it is nonetheless classic Barsac that needs bottle-age.

DOISY-VÉDRINES, CH *France, Bordeaux, Barsac, 2ème Cru Classé, W* An outstanding source of fine, complex sweet wine in a relatively full-bodied style.

DOLCETTO Red grape used in seven DOCs in Italy's Piedmont (such as **DOLCETTO D'ALBA**, Dolcetto d'Acqui), usually meant to be drunk within two or three years of the vintage. Prized for easy drinkability, crisp and well structured, with plenty of fruit.

DOLCETTO D'ALBA   *Italy, Piedmont, DOC, R*   The Dolcetto grape produces wines for which are easy to drink. Mulberry-hued, with bright pink highlights, crisp in taste, with luscious fruit flavours and a rich perfume. Leading producers include: Elio Altare, Ceretto, Giacomo Conterno, Vietti.

DOMAINE   *France*   Equivalent to château; a wine estate. The inference is that the wine is made, and bottled, by the landowner. Also used in New World countries to convey the same sense.

DOMECQ, BODEGAS   *Spain, Rioja, R, W, P*   Offshoot of the famous sherry firm, producing soft, agreeable wines. Viña Eguia (R) is good, but the Marqués de Arienzo R, W and P are best.

DOMECQ, PEDRO   *Spain, sherry*   Famous equally for its flagship La Ina fino sherry and for Fundador and Carlos I brandies. The firm dominates the sherry trade from its spectacular *bodegas* and palace in Jerez. Top of the range, along with La Ina fino, are Rio Viejo dry oloroso, Sibarita Palo Cortado and Venerable Oloroso. The more commercial Double Century range is well regarded.

DOMERGUE, DANIEL   *France, Midi, Minervois, R*   A newcomer to the Minervois but among the appellation's leaders, Daniel Domergue replanted his land in Le Petit Causse, near Siran, with quality vines: Syrah, Cinsaut, Grenache and Mourvèdre. He makes two wines: Clos Centeilles, destined for long life, and Campagne de Centeilles, for earlier drinking.

DOMEYNE, CH   *France, Bordeaux, St-Estèphe, Cru Bourgeois, R*   Small, but modern-minded, estate with well-made wine.

DOMINIQUE, CH LA   *France, Bordeaux, St-Emilion, Grand Cru Classé, R*   On the Pomerol border, and recently a rising star. The wine, which has a very high percentage of Merlot, is outstanding: concentrated but not overly tannic, with a certain opulence.

DON ZOILO   *Spain, sherry*   The Very Old Fino is the star of the respected Don Zoilo range of Jerez sherries.

DONATIEN BAHUAUD   *France, Loire, Muscadet, W*   Wine made and bottled *sur lie* at historic Ch de la Cassemichère. This firm of growers and *négociants* also has cellars in La Chapelle-Heulin. Most famous Muscadet is Le Master de Donatien, selected at yearly tastings.

DONNAFUGATA   *Italy, Sicily, W, R, P*   Their deliciously fresh W wine is entitled to the new Contessa Entellina DOC. Also a P, a rich, barrel-aged R, a Marsala and an apéritif-style Pantelleria.

DOPFF & IRION   *France, Alsace, W*   Grower and *négociant*: its list includes Riesling Les Murailles (from *Grand Cru* Schoenenberg); Gewürztraminer Muscat Les Sorcières, a powerful, long-lived wine; Muscat Les Amandiers; and Pinot Gris Les Maquisards.

Having distanced itself from the system for years, the company is now marketing *Grand Cru* wines.

DOPFF AU MOULIN *France, Alsace, W* This 400-year-old company continues at the forefront of Crémant d'Alsace production, with Cuvée Julien, Cuvée Bartholdi, Blanc de Noirs and Brut Sauvage among the best. Also some fine still wines under the Domaines Dopff label.

DOUDET-NAUDIN *France, Burgundy, Côte d'Or, R, W* Vineyard owner and *négociant* in Corton and Beaune. Old-fashioned wines for long maturing.

DOURO *Portugal, DOC, R, W* Valley (also the source of PORT) and DOC ,where the production of mainly R and some W table wines is currently undergoing a revival. A wide range of grapes is permitted, with the best producers using Portugal's distinctive native varieties, notably Tinta Roriz and Touriga Nacional for the Rs. Leading producers include: Quinta da Cismeira, Cockburn Smithies, Quinta do Côtto, Ferreira.

DOUX *France* Sweet; applies to wines with a sugar content of over 45 grams per litre.

DOW *Portugal, port* Dow, based at Quinta de Bomfim, is known for its dry style of vintage ports. Owned (since 1912) by SYMINGTON.

DRAPPIER *France, Champagne* Family-run house based in the AUBE district. Wines are rich and biscuity, especially the single-vineyard Grande Sendrée, from old vines.

DROIN, JEAN-PAUL *France, Burgundy, Chablis, W* Young, dynamic producer of *Premier* and *Grand Cru* Chablis: leading exponent of new oak. Some superb wines, others atypically rich and over-oaked.

DROMANA ESTATE *Australia, Victoria, Mornington Peninsula, W, R* The cool Mornington Peninsula climate produces wonderful Chardonnay and Cabernet Sauvignon at this leading estate. Their 2nd label, Shinus, is for wines from bought-in grapes.

DRÔME, DE LA *France, Vin de Pays, R, W* Wines from the Rhône, between Valence and Montélimar. Nearly all R, principally from Grenache, Cinsaut and Syrah. Gamay, Cabernet Sauvignon or Merlot are used for varietal wines. Gamay, in particular, has been successful.

DROUHIN, JOSEPH *France, Burgundy, Côte d'Or & Chablis, R, W* Respected *négociant* and important vineyard owner in the Côte d'Or and Chablis. Strikingly well-made, reliable wines, especially Beaune Clos des Mouches, both R and W.

DRUET, PIERRE-JACQUES *France, Loire, Bourgueil, W, R* Innovative Bourgueil producer, with wines made for ageing but which can also be enjoyed young. The best of the *cuvées,* from the superior

Coteaux zone, is Vaumoureau; the Beauvais and Grand-Mont *cuvées* are also very good.

DRY CREEK VALLEY   *USA, California, Sonoma, VA*   Sonoma Valley wine zone with good conditions for Bordeaux varieties (Cabernets and Merlot for Rs, Sauvignon for Ws), and for Zinfandel Rs. Leading producers include: Dry Creek, Preston, Ridge (especially for Zinfandel).

DUBOEUF, GEORGES   *France, Burgundy, Beaujolais, R, W*   The leading *négociant* of Beaujolais and Mâconnais, who has done more than anyone to raise the profile and quality standards of the region. Duboeuf wines appear both under his own label and those of individual properties and his name, in large print or small, is a surefire guarantee of quality.

DUBREUIL-FONTAINE, DOM   *France, Burgundy, Côte d'Or, R, W*   Top-quality domaine, based in Pernand-Vergelesses, making very serious wines from Corton and Pernand.

DUC DE MAGENTA, DOM DU   *France, Burgundy, Côte d'Or, R, W*   Chassagne-Montrachet domaine whose high-class wines are made by Jadot of Beaune. The Puligny-Montrachets are especially good.

DUCRU-BEAUCAILLOU, CH   *France, Bordeaux, Médoc, St-Julien, 2ème Cru Classé, R*   Well-placed vineyard on the riverside rim of the St-Julien gravel banks. Consistent quality, especially since 1985, is its hallmark; wines, though made in the old-fashioned way, are elegant. A very good 1993. 2nd wine: La Croix.

DUFF GORDON   *Spain, sherry*   Famous sherry house, founded in 1768. Brands include fino Feria and Club Dry amontillado.

DUHART-MILON-ROTHSCHILD, CH   *France, Bordeaux, Médoc, Pauillac, 4ème Cru Classé, R*   Part of the Rothschild jigsaw puzzle on Pauillac's northern plateau, this vineyard (which has no actual château) is owned by the Lafite Rothschilds. Vintages since 1981 have begun to fulfil the site's potential.

DUJAC, DOM   *France, Burgundy, Côte d'Or, R*   Jacques Seysses of Dujac is one of Burgundy's top winemakers: his incredibly elegant wines range from a delicious Morey-St-Denis to great Clos de la Roche.

DULCE   *Italy & Spain*   Term meaning sweet.

DURBACH   *Germany, Baden, W, R*   Village with a good name for Riesling Ws: solid, full of flavour, from steep and spectacular vineyards. Leading producers include: von Nevau, Wolf Metternich, Schloss Staufenberg.

DURFORT-VIVENS, CH   *France, Bordeaux, Médoc, Margaux, 2ème Cru Classé, R*   Very high proportion of Cabernet Sauvignon makes for tough, long-maturing wine. Older vintages are patchy.

DURUP, JEAN *France, Burgundy, Chablis, W* Durup's Dom de l'Eglantière is Chablis's largest estate, mainly *Village* and *Premier Cru* wines, plus some Petit Chablis. Firmly of the anti-oak school, he believes it distorts the true flavour of Chablis.

DUTRUCH-GRAND-POUJEAUX, CH *France, Bordeaux, Moulis, Cru Bourgeois, R* One of a series of châteaux with "Poujeaux" in their name, this structured wine ages well.

DUVAL-LEROY *France, Champagne* Large and dynamic house in the Côte des Blancs which owns 140ha of vines. It sells under many different labels, but under the Duval-Leroy name produces an elegant P and impressive NV.

E

ECHÉZEAUX *France, Burgundy, AOC, R* This *Grand Cru* on the Côte de Nuits above Vougeot makes powerful, scented R wines, maturing in about 10 years. Leading producers include: Drouhin, H Jayer, Mongeard-Mugnerat, Romanée-Conti.

EDEN VALLEY *Australia, South Australia* Wine zone between BAROSSA and the ADELAIDE HILLS. Riesling does particularly well here. Leading producers include: Heggies, Henschke, Hill-Smith, Mountadam, Pewsey Vale.

EDNA VALLEY *USA, California, VA* Wine zone in San Luis Obispo county, known for elegant Chardonnays. Leading producers include: Edna Valley Vineyard, Corbett Canyon.

EGER *Hungary* District in the northern part of Hungary, most famous for the R Bulls Blood (Egri Bikavér) mainly from the Kék-frankos grape. A legendary wine, but today's version is a commercial blend, somewhat light in style. Some good new Rs are appearing under the Eger district name.

EGLISE CLINET, CH L' *France, Bordeaux, Pomerol, R* Very small, mainly Merlot estate making a rare wine but one of Pomerol's finest: full-bodied and generous yet with great finesse.

EGUISHEIM *France, Alsace* This village has *Grands Crus* Eichberg and Pfersigberg, famous for Gewürztraminer. Leading producers include: Léon Beyer, Kuentz-Bas.

EISWEIN *Germany* Literally, "ice-wine". Made from grapes that have frozen on the vine. When the grapes are pressed, still frozen, the water in the grapes remains as ice and the concentrated juice flows out.

ELAN, CH *USA, Georgia, W, R* This winery, restaurant and museum complex, north of Atlanta, attracts over 250,000 visitors a year. The 80-ha vineyard is mainly Chardonnay, Sauvignon Blanc, Riesling, Cabernet Sauvignon and two hybrids, Chambourcin and Seyval Blanc.

ELTVILLE *Germany, Rheingau, W* Leading village of the Rheingau, famous as the HQ of the State Domaine (Staatsweingut). Mostly Riesling Ws, with Sonnenberg rated the top vineyard. Leading producers include: Knyphausen, Schönborn, von Simmern.

EMBRES ET CASTELMAURE, CAVE D' *France, Midi, Corbières, R, W* Cooperative in the forefront of new developments. It has done some wood-ageing since 1980, and in 1992 tried using new barrels for its top wine, Cuvée de Pompadour.

EMILIA-ROMAGNA *Italy* The gastronomic capital of Italy, centred on Bologna, is also home to its most infamous wine, LAMBRUSCO. Other popular varietals include Albana, Sangiovese and Trebbiano.

EN PRIMEUR *France* Wine sold before it has even been bottled. Common in Bordeaux when classed growths are sold in the year after they are made. In America, to buy futures means the same thing.

ENCLOS, CH L' *France, Bordeaux, Pomerol, R* Delicious wines that are relatively inexpensive (for Pomerol) and early-maturing.

ENGLAND Over 1,000ha of vineyards in the south and east make wine, mainly W, on a commercial scale; most is dry, flowery and crisp, though late-harvest Ws and some Rs are appearing. Leading producers include: Adgestone, Barkham Manor, Biddenden, Car Taylor, Denbies, Lamberhurst, Nutbourne, Pilton, Tenterden, Three Choirs, Wootton.

ENTRAYGUES ET DU FEL, VIN D' *France, South-West, VDQS, R, P, W* Rustic Ws from Chenin Blanc; Rs and Ps from local Fer Servadou and Cabernets Sauvignon and Franc, from a tiny zone in the Aveyron *département*.

ENTRE-DEUX-MERS *France, Bordeaux, AOC, W* Dry W wine from Sauvignon Blanc and Sémillon. The Haut-Benauge sub-zone stresses the perfumed Sémillon grape. Leading producers include: Ch Bonnet, Ch le Bos, Ch Grossombre, Ch Haut-Reygnac, Ch Roquefort, Dom de la Serizière, Ch Tour de Mirambeau, Ch la Tuilerie.

EPENOTTES, LES *France, Burgundy, Côte de Beaune, 1er Cru, R* Lying parallel to the N74 highway at the southern end of the Beaune commune, this vineyard produces wines which are densely coloured and perfumed, and with a good tannic structure. Leading producers include: Pierre Bourée & Fils, Michel Bouzereau, Michel Gaunoux, Parent.

ERBACH *Germany, Rheingau, W* Famous wine village with superb, full Riesling Ws from vineyards such as Marcobrunn, beside the Rhine. Leading producers include: the Staatsweingut Eltville, von Simmern, Schönborn.

ERDEN *Germany, Mosel, W* Village on the Mosel, north of Bernkastel, which (like several of its neighbours) has vineyards on the opposite bank: the south-facing Treppchen and Prälat are among the best in the region. Leading producers include: Loosen.

ERMITAGE DE CHASSE-SPLEEN *France, Bordeaux, Médoc, Moulis* 2nd wine of Ch Chasse-Spleen.

ESCHENDORFER LUMP *Germany, Franken, W* Famous Franken vineyard, above the River Main, noted for Silvaner. Leading growers include Juliusspital.

ESER, AUGUST *Germany, Rheingau, W, R* Mostly Rieslings in the classic, long-lasting Rheingau style, with a little R.

EST! EST!! EST!!! *Italy, Lazio, DOC, W* Fairly innocuous dry W wine based on Trebbiano, sometimes with the addition of Malvasia to increase aroma. Leading producers include: Falesco, Mazziotti.

ESTAING, VIN D' *France, South-West, VDQS, R, P, W* France's smallest VDQS zone makes pleasant Ws from Chenin Blanc and Mauzac, fruity P and R (which can be astringent) from Gamay, Cabernet Franc and local Fer Servadou.

ETCHART *Argentina, R, W* Partly owned by Pernod-Ricard, this concern produces many good wines. Their Torrontes, sometimes using the brand Cafayate, is flowery and delicious. The range also includes a good-value Malbec.

ETOILE, CH L' *France, Bordeaux, Graves, W, R* Well-known Langon estate making structured Rs and fresh, clean Ws.

ÉTOILE, L' *France, Jura, AOC, W* Still and Sp W wine from Chardonnay, Savagnin and Poulsard grapes; VIN JAUNE from Savagnin. Leading producers include: Christian Bourdy.

EVANGILE, CH L' *France, Bordeaux, Pomerol, R* The Rothschilds of Lafite control this property, always regarded as one of Pomerol's greatest.

EYQUEM, CH *France, Bordeaux, Côtes de Bourg, R* Not to be confused with Ch YQUEM , this is a solid R in the Bourg manner.

EYRIE *USA, Oregon, W, R* Pioneers of fine wine in Oregon, David and Diana Letts make legendary Pinot Noirs modelled on, and challenging in quality, the best of Burgundy; plus good Ws from Chardonnay and Pinot Gris.

FABAS, CH *France, Midi, Minervois, R* Jean-Pierre Ormières of Ch Fabas was one of the first exponents of *barrique*-matured Minervois, participating in the initial experiments with oak conducted by the *appellation's* oenologist.

FAIVELEY, JOSEPH *France, Burgundy, Côte d'Or, R, W* Very important Burgundy *négociant* and vineyard owner using modern techniques. Good, reliable quality.

FALFAS, CH *France, Bordeaux, Côtes de Bourg, R* Ambitious new owners are following organic techniques and making increasingly good claret.

FALL CREEK VINEYARDS *USA, Texas, W, R* With vines on the shores of Lake Buchanan in Llano County, the Aulers have built a replica of a French château and produce Chardonnay, Cabernet Sauvignon and Sauvignon. A limited amount of Reserve Chardonnay is made and has been impressive.

FARGUES, CH DE *France, Bordeaux, Sauternes, W* Very small amounts of rich and luscious wine made by the same team as Ch YQUEM (qv). Although half the price of Yquem, Fargues remains the second most expensive wine of the appellation.

FATTORIA *Italy* Wine estate.

FAUGÈRES *France, Midi, AOC, R* Appellation within the Coteaux du Languedoc: quite rich, mouthfilling R from Grenache, improved by Syrah and Mourvèdre, gaining from 4–5 years in bottle. Leading producers include: Gilbert Alquier, Ch'x Grézan, Haut Fabregues, de la Liquière.

FAZI-BATTAGLIA *Italy, Central Italy, Marches, W, R* The single-vineyard Le Moie is one of best wines in the Verdicchio dei Castelli di Jesi Classico zone. Also makes Rosso Conèro and Rosso Piceno.

FENDANT See CHASSELAS.

FERMENTATION, ALCOHOLIC AND MALOLACTIC Conversion of the sugar in grape juice into alcohol and carbon dioxide, prompted by yeasts. Malolactic fermentation follows in some wines: malic acid is converted into lactic acid and carbon dioxide. The wine becomes softer and less acidic.

FERNÁNDEZ, ALEJANDRO *Spain, Castilla-León, Ribera del Duero, R* Former village blacksmith Alejandro Fernández makes long-lived Pesquera (R) from grapes from his own vineyards and matured in new oak casks.

FERRARI   *Italy, Trentino, Sp*   Large Trento producer of *metodo classico* Sp wine: reliable.

FERREIRA   *Portugal, port*   Producer best known for aged tawnies: Duque de Bragança is among the finest 20-year-olds; the Quinta do Porto 10-year-old, rich and fruity, is also respected. Vintage wines are quite sweet, Portuguese-style.

FERRIÈRE, CH   *France, Bordeaux, Médoc, Margaux, 3ème Cru Classé, R*   Small classed-growth leased to CH LASCOMBES, where the wine is made. Though hard to find, it can be very good.

FETZER   *USA, California, Mendocino, R, W*   Sizeable yet good producer: Barrel Select Cabernet Sauvignon and Chardonnay are much admired. Sundial Chardonnay, fresh with pear and apple flavours, is good value for money. Bel Arbors is a 2nd label.

FEUILLATTE, NICOLAS   *France, Champagne*   Epernay house owned by 85 co-ops with some 4,000 members and 1,600ha of vines. Their best wine is the prestige *cuvée*, Palmes d'Or.

FÈVRE, WILLIAM   *France, Burgundy, Chablis, W*   With Dom de la Maladière, Fèvre is the most important owner of *Grand Cru* vineyards. The wines, made and aged in new oak, are austere in youth but with age gain wonderfully rich mineral flavours.

FIEFS DE LAGRANGE   *France, Bordeaux, Médoc, St-Julien, R*   2nd wine of Ch Lagrange.

FIEFS VENDÉENS   *France, Loire, VDQS, R, W*   Vineyards near the Atlantic, south of the Loire, produce R wine from Gamay and Pinot Noir (at least 50%), plus Cabernet Franc and Cabernet Sauvignon. Also some W.

FIEUZAL, CH DE   *France, Bordeaux, Pessac-Léognan, Cru Classé, R, W*   Star estate in Léognan: the W sensational, though needing bottle-age. The burly R, with its black-cherry flavours and dense structure, can be superb.

FIGEAC, CH   *France, Bordeaux, St-Emilion, 1er Grand Cru Classé, R*   Among the area's most beautiful estates, lying towards the Pomerol border. Cabernet Sauvignon is approximately one-third of the blend: the wines are generally quite concentrated, yet supple and apppealing. Some vintages lack staying-power.

FILHOT, CH   *France, Bordeaux, Sauternes, 2ème Cru Classé, W*   Large estate which does well in favourable years, but lesser vintages can lack flair and excitement.

FILLIATREAU, PAUL   *France, Loire, Saumur, R, W*   Largest producer of Saumur-Champigny Rs. They include a Jeunes Vignes (vines under 50 years old), a Vieilles Vignes, and a special *cuvée*, Lena Filliatreau, from old vines on *silex* soil. Filliatreau also makes Saumur Blanc.

FINGER LAKES   *USA, New York State, VA*   Largest New York State wine zone, with 40 wineries and vineyards along the shores of the lakes. Good hybrid wines; and increasingly, classic-grape ones too: Chardonnay and Riesling Ws are good. Leading producers include: Canandaigua, Glenora, Knapp, Wagner.

FINKENAUER, WEINGUT CARL   *Germany, Nahe, W, R*   Dry wines with flavour and character, worth bottle-age, from one of the best estates in the Nahe, mostly Riesling.

FINO   *Spain*   A pale, dry sherry aged under *flor*.

FIRELANDS WINERY   *USA, Ohio, W, R*   The winery, on the Isle St George (VA) in Lake Erie, is enormously popular with tourists, focusing on Chardonnay, Cabernet Sauvignon and Gewürztraminer.

FIRESTONE   *USA, California, Santa Barbara and Southern California, R, W*   At his winery in the Santa Ynez Valley, Brooks Firestone focuses on apricoty Johannisberg Rieslings Ws (dry and sweet), a rose-perfumed Pinot Noir and a silky, lingering Merlot.

FITOU   *France, Midi, AOC, R*   Earliest appellation of the Midi, R only, made from Carignan, Grenache, Cinsaut, Syrah and Mourvèdre. Fitou has two zones: coastal Fitou-Maritime for lighter, less tannic wines, using a higher proportion of Mourvèdre; Fitou des Hautes Corbières has higher, drier vineyards with more Syrah – wines are sturdier and fuller-bodied. Leading producers include: Mont Tauch co-op, Ch de Nouvelles.

FITZ-RITTER, WEINGUT   *Germany, Pfalz, W, R*   Specialist in dry wines, typical of the Pfalz in their full-flavoured style.

FIXIN   *France, Burgundy, AOC, R*   Village at the north of the Côte de Nuits, with five *Premiers Crus*: powerful burgundies that can age well. Leading producers include: Dom Bart, Bruno Clair, Gelin, Juliet, Morion.

FLEUR CAILEAU, CH LA   *France, Bordeaux, Canon-Fronsac, R*   Small production but elegant and "correct" wine.

FLEUR-DE-GAY, CH LA   *France, Bordeaux, Pomerol, R*   Rare, expensive and superb all-Merlot wine made by Michel Rolland since 1982.

FLEUR-PÉTRUS, CH LA   *France, Bordeaux, Pomerol, R*   Pomerol's most perfumed, elegant wine, which begins to reach maturity in 5-6 years but in a really fine vintage will easily last for 20 years or more.

FLEURIE   *France, Burgundy, AOC, R*   Hilltop village at the heart of the Beaujolais *crus:* attractive, popular and expensive wines. Full of fruit and easy to drink when young, even better after two years. Leading producers include: Fleurie co-op, Dom de Fontabons, Dom de la Grand'Cour, Ch des Labourons, André Metrat, Dom du Pont du Jour.

FLOR   *Spain*   A particular type of yeast that develops on the surface of FINO sherry, protecting it from oxidation and giving it its distinctive flavour.

FLORIDA   *USA*   The climate is considered too warm for classic (vinifera) vines, but a handful of wineries make hybrid wines.

FOLIE, DOM DE LA   *France, Burgundy, Chalonnais, R, W*   One of the top producers of Rully, especially the white Premier Cru, Clos-St-Jacques.

FOLLE BLANCHE   High-yielding, highly acidic white grape used for Gros Plant in Muscadet, and in blends in California.

FONPLÉGADE, CH   *France, Bordeaux, St-Emilion, Grand Cru Classé, R*   This relatively unknown *Grand Cru Classé* deserves greater recognition. Owned by Armand Moueix.

FONROQUE, CH   *France, Bordeaux, St-Emilion, Grand Cru Classé, R*   Not very well known, but Fonroque consistently produces very attractive, medium-term wines that are reasonably priced.

FONSALETTE, CH DE   *France, Rhône, Côtes du Rhône R*   Sharing the same owners as Ch RAYAS, this wine is made to the same high standards: possibly the best Côtes du Rhône of all.

FONSCOLOMBE, CH   *France, Provence, Coteaux d'Aix-en-Provence, W, R*   This 160-ha estate makes good-value, early-drinking wines, predominantly Rs, with a top-range Cuvée Spéciale made from Carignan with Cabernet Sauvignon, Grenache and Cinsaut, oak-matured.

FONSECA GUIMARAENS   *Portugal, port*   Some of the finest vintage ports, rich, plummy and generally quite sweet: quite different in style from parent company TAYLOR'S. There is also a single-quinta vintage, Quinta do Panascal. Best-known is the vintage-character Bin 27.

FONSECA INTERNACIONAL, J M DA   *Portugal, P, Sp*   Part of the Grand Metropolitan group, based in Setúbal, producing Lancers medium-dry, slightly sparkling P and the Sp Lancers Brut.

FONSECA SUCCESSORES, JOSÉ MARIA DA   *Portugal, R*   This Setúbal family firm, dating from 1834, makes Periquita, one of the country's most famous R wines. In the Dão, they select R and W wines from local cooperatives, which are then bottled under the Terras Altas label.

FONTANA CANDIDA   *Italy, Southern Italy, Lazio, W*   The biggest producer in the region, making predominantly Frascati. Part of the same group as BIGI of Orvieto. The basic Frascati Superiore is consistent, while the single-vineyard Casal Morena and Santa Teresa are among the best of the DOC.

FONTANAFREDDA   *Italy, Piedmont, W, R, Sp*   Large winery making *metodo classico* Sp wines, such as Contessa Rosa and Gattinera

Brut. Also top-quality, powerful Barolos from nine *crus*, with great ageing potential.

FONTENIL, CH *France, Bordeaux, Canon-Fronsac, R* Michel Rolland's winemaking has made this 90% Merlot wine a star: the 1989 is good, tasting of plums and spice, the 1990 better.

FOPPIANO *USA, California, Sonoma, R, W* Top-quality Cabernet Sauvignon and Chardonnay are sold under the Fox Mountain label, reasonably priced R and W are dubbed Foppiano Vineyards, and the lowest-priced varietals are labelled Riverside Farm.

FORST *Germany, Pfalz, W, R* One of the centres of the Pfalz region, with a name for Riesling Ws, steely and firm in character. Top vineyards include Jesuitengarten and Kirchenstück; leading growers include BASSERMAN-JORDAN, VON BUHL, BÜRKLIN-WOLF, FORSTER WINZERVEREIN (co-op).

FORSTER WINZERVEREIN *Germany, Pfalz, W* Top-quality, good-value wines, mostly Rieslings, come from this growers' co-op at Forst, a leading Pfalz village.

FORTIA, CH *France, Rhône, Châteauneuf-du-Pape, R, W* Highly traditional estate, known for its quality in poor vintages. It has recently been inherited: methods are changing, and the wine style may become more modern.

FORTIFIED WINES Wines to which brandy is added, usually before fermentation is complete. This preserves grape sugar, thus sweetness, in the wine, and adds to the alcohol level. Examples are PORT, SHERRY and VINS DOUX NATURELS.

FORTS DE LATOUR, LES *France, Bordeaux, Médoc, Pauillac, R* 2nd wine of Ch Latour.

FOURCAS-DUPRÉ, CH *France, Bordeaux, Listrac, Cru Bourgeois, R* Rich, gamey claret from the woods of Listrac.

FOURCAS-HOSTEN, CH *France, Bordeaux, Listrac, Cru Bourgeois, R* Serious wine from 40% Merlot. Deserves ageing to bring out the richness.

FOURCHAUME *France, Burgundy, Chablis, 1er Cru* Leading *Premier Cru* Chablis vineyard, facing southwest on the right bank of the River Serein, and thus next to the *Grands Crus*. Refined, charming wines. Vaupulent, Côte de Fontenay, L'Homme Mort and Vaulorent are plots within Fourchaume.

FOURMONE, DOM LA *France, Rhône, Vacqueyras, Gigondas, Côtes du Rhône, R* Roger Combe makes excellent, structured traditional wine in both appellations; also L'Oustau Fauquet, a Gigondas.

FRANCE, CH DE *France, Bordeaux, Pessac-Léognan R, W* Large Léognan estate, recently modernized, with simple though direct and fruity W and velvety, charming R.

FRANCIACORTA *Italy, Lombardy, DOC, R, W, Sp* This DOC blends Cabernet Franc, Barbera, Nebbiolo and Merlot for Rs; Ws are from Pinot Bianco and Chardonnay. The highly-regarded Sp includes some Pinot Nero. Leading producers include: Bellavista, Ca' del Bosco, Cavalleri.

FRANCO-ESPAÑOLAS, BODEGAS *Spain, Rioja, R, W, P* Part of the same group as Federico Paternina, this bodega makes a wide range of wines: some overtly fruity, others along more traditional, wood-aged lines.

FRANCS, CH DE *France, Bordeaux, Côtes de Francs, R* Investment from St-Emilion in an old estate is yielding delicious, fruity but well-structured wines.

FRANKEN *Germany, Anbaugebeit, W, R* Region at the heart of Germany, east of the Rhine, along the River Main. Cold winters and springs affect yields, but in warm years the W wines are characterful, intense and long-lasting. Traditionally, Silvaner is the local vine, but many others have been planted. Rs are in a minority. Franken uses a special, squat bottle: the *bocksbeutel*. Leading producers: *see* MAINDREIECK, WÜRZBURG.

FRANSCHHOEK *South Africa, WO* Settled by Huguenots three centuries ago and still retaining a distinctly French character, noticeable in its oak-aged wines and the country's best *Cap Classique* (traditional-method) Sp wine at Clos Cabrière. Leading producers include: Clos Cabrière, La Motte.

FRASCATI *Italy, Lazio, DOC, W* From the hills around Rome. Main varieties are Malvasia and Trebbiano. Can be very dull but the best are fresh with ripe fruit and a softly rounded palate. Leading producers include: Colli di Catone, Fontana Candida, Villa Simone, Conte Zandotti.

FREEMARK ABBEY *USA, California, Napa, R, W* Focuses on Chardonnay and Cabernet Sauvignon; the former makes floral, fruity, fresh Ws, the latter Rs that tend towards cedar, tobacco, cherry and tar, which in good years age remarkably well.

FREIXENET *Spain, Catalonia, Sp* This powerful Cava producer also owns a champagne house, Henri Abelé, and makes Sp wine in California. Quality is very high and their best-selling wine, Cordon Negro Brut, very good.

FRESCOBALDI *Italy, Tuscany, Chianti, W, R, Sp* Large producer with 500ha of vineyards in Chianti Rufina and Pomino areas. The Pomino Il Beneficio (W) is notable. Other wines include a reliable basic Chianti, Predicato *vini da tavola*, Sp wines and a Brunello di Montalcino.

FRIEDRICH-WILHELM-GYMNASIUM *Germany, Mosel, W* Old charitable estate at Trier with a good clutch of well-placed Riesling vineyards which yield traditional flowery, elegant Mosel wines.

FRIULI-VENEZIA GIULIA   *Italy*   In the north-eastern corner of Italy, a mountainous region enjoying a good reputation for crisp dry W wines and fresh, highly-scented Rs.

FRIZZANTE   *Italy*   Term meaning lightly sparkling.

FRONSAC   *France, Bordeaux, AOC, R*   Lighter in style than those from adjoining CANON-FRONSAC, these Rs are made in an area near Pomerol from Merlot, Cabernets Sauvignon and Franc and Malbec. Can be drunk from about two years after the vintage. Leading producers include: Ch'x Fontenil, Moulin Haut-Laroque, de la Rivière, Villars.

FRONTIGNAN, MUSCAT DE   *France, Midi, AOC, VDN*   Aromatic, golden, sweet *vin doux naturel* made entirely from Muscat Blanc à Petits Grains, the best Muscat grape, grown around the town of Frontignan in Languedoc. Leading producer: Ch de la Peyrade.

FUISSÉ, CH DE   *France, Burgundy, Mâconnais, W*   The leading producer of Pouilly-Fuissé. In quality terms more akin to a Côte d'Or wine than a more modest Mâconnais. Good ageing potential.

FUMÉ BLANC   Sauvignon Blanc synonym in California, New Zealand, Australia, South Africa.

FÜRST LÖWENSTEIN   *Germany, Franken, W, R*   Top Franken estate making Silvaner in the classic intense, earthy style, plus Rs.

FÜRSTLICHE CASTELL'SCHES WEINGUT   *Germany, Franken, W*   The largest private estate in Franken, making mostly dry wines, but also late-picked sweet ones when vintages allow.

G

GABILLIÈRE, DOM DE LA   *France, Loire, Touraine, W, R, P, Sp*   The experimental wine school in Amboise makes commercial quantities of high-quality wines from its 16ha of vineyards, notably a concentrated Sauvignon Blanc and a Crémant de Loire (W, Sp).

GAFFELIÈRE, CH LA   *France, Bordeaux, St-Emilion, 1er Grand Cru Classé, R*   The past history of this château was somewhat chequered, but things seem to be on track now. Medium-bodied wines with a good depth of fruit.

GAGNARD, DOM JEAN-NOEL   *France, Burgundy, Côte d'Or, R, W*   Extremely good producer with excellent Chassagne-Montrachets (W); the Rs are very good too.

GAILLAC   *France, South-West, AOC, R, P, W*   One of the most diverse appellations in South-West France. R Gaillac is usually based on the local Duras grape, blended either with local Fer Servadou and Syrah, or with Merlot and Cabernet; generally ready young. W Gaillac can be dry, sweet or *moelleux* (rich and soft); still, Sp (*mousseux*) or *perlé* (very slightly Sp). Sp wine is sometimes made as in Champagne and sometimes by traditional local methods. For Ws, Gaillac's oldest grape variety, Mauzac, can be blended with Loin de l'Oeil (Len de l'El), or with the standard Bordeaux varieties Sémillon and Sauvignon Blanc. A few villages have the appellation Gaillac Premières Côtes for rich, aromatic, sweet W wines. Leading producers include: Ch Clément-Termes, Dom de Labarthe, Cave de Labastide de Lévis co-op, Ch Larroze, Ch de Lastours, Mas Pignou, Técou co-op, Dom des Très Cantous.

GAJA   *Italy, Piedmont, R, W*   Leading Barbaresco producer, with wines including *crus* Sorì Tildìn, Sorì San Lorenzo and Costa Russi, Barolo and Barbera Vignarey. Also a wide range of R and W *vini da tavola*.

GALIL   *Israel, R, W*   This cool-climate area, rising from the Sea of Galilee to the Golan Heights, has been responsible for some very fine quality R and W wines from French varieties. Leading producers include: Golan Heights Winery.

GALISSONNIÈRE, CH DE LA   *France, Loire, Muscadet, W*   The Lusseauds' 30-ha vineyard produces Cuvée Philippe and Cuvée Anne. A GROS PLANT is called Cuvée Valérie. They also own Ch de la Jannière.

GALLANTIN, DOM LE   *France, Provence, Bandol, W, R, P*   Achille Pascal's speciality is his R wines. They are fermented at high temperature, bringing out the colour in the Mourvèdre grapes, and are both long-lived and among the richest in Bandol. A fresh, lively W and a P are also made.

GALLO *USA, California, Central Valley, W, R, P, Sp* The world's largest winery, selling 65 million cases a year, ranging from "pop" wines to oak-aged Chardonnay. Most wines are inexpensive but soundly made, though Sauvignon W has star quality.

GAMAY The red Beaujolais grape, making light red wines with a simple ripe fruit character, mostly for drinking young. Also grown in central France, the Loire and California.

GAMOT, CLOS DE *France, South-West, Cahors, R* Old family estate with 100% Auxerrois vines (*see* **CAHORS**) making solid, tannic wines.

GANDINES, DOM DES *France, Burgundy, Mâconnais, W* Delicious fresh fruity Mâcon-Clessé, with some potential to age.

GARD, DU *France, Vin de Pays, R, P* The *vin de pays* name of the southern *département* of the Gard, used mostly for Rs.

GARDE, CH LA *France, Bordeaux, Pessac-Léognan R, W* Ancient estate recently renovated. Its top Rs, labelled Réserve, are aged in new oak: rich and silky, they can be drunk young but will age. Quality is impressive and prices sensible. Small amount of elegant W from pure Sauvignon Blanc.

GARNACHA/GRENACHE Spain's (and the world's) most widely planted red-wine grape, Garnacha Tinta/Grenache Noir grows well in hot, dry climates, and is used for blending and for good, fruity P. R wine can be good with careful winemaking. Found in the southern Rhône, Provence, Corsica, Midi, California, Australia, South Africa.

GARRAFEIRA *Portugal* Wine (R) from an exceptional vintage that has been matured for at least two years before bottling, with a further year in bottle prior to sale.

GASSMANN, ROLLY *France, Alsace, W, R* Well-known winemaker: his wines are rich, with high levels of residual sugar. They include an excellent Muscat Moenchreben (from a single vineyard in Rorschwihr, not the *Grand Cru* in Eichhoffen), a well-regarded Auxerrois, and some good *cuvées*, such as Réserve Rolly Gassmann, from the classic varieties.

GATINOIS *France, Champagne* Tiny, quality-conscious firm with 7ha of vineyard at Ay, all of which is *Grand Cru*.

GATTINARA *Italy, Piedmont, DOCG, R* Principally made from Nebbiolo, this robust R wine, not dissimilar to Barolo, needs a long time in bottle. Leading producers include: Antoniolo, Luigi Dessilani, Luigi & Italo Nervi.

GAUNOUX, DOM MICHEL *France, Burgundy, Côte d'Or, R* Very traditional domaine, specializing in long-lived Pommards.

GAVI   *Italy, Piedmont, DOC, W, Sp*   From the Cortese grape, crisp and fruity, with hints of lime. Still wines can be quite full, with a silky texture. Best consumed within two years of the vintage, although the finest can last longer. Sp wines are also made. Leading producers include: Michele Chiarlo, La Scolca.

GEELONG   *Australia, Victoria*   This region of plains and gentle slopes is well suited to fragrant Pinot Noir and Chardonnay. Leading producers include: Bannockburn, Clyde Park, Idyll, Prince Albert, Scotchmans Hill.

GEISENHEIM   *Germany, Rheingau, W*   Wine village and home of the famous Geisenheim research and teaching college, which has influenced winemaking in Germany and around the world. Also a source of good Riesling Ws from (among others) the Kläuserweg and Rothenberg vineyards.

GENEVA   *Switzerland*   This Swiss canton has 1,500ha under vine. Half the production is W, mainly from the Chasselas grape (local name Perlan) but also some Aligoté and Chardonnay and light R from the Gamay grape.

GENEVRIÈRES, LES   *France, Burgundy, Côte de Beaune, 1er Cru, R*   Meursault vineyard which produces highly attractive wines with elegance and finesse. Leading producers include: Louis Latour, Michelot-Buisson.

GENTILE, DOM   *France, Corsica, Patrimonio, W, R*   This is a new estate reviving old local traditions: R, P and both dry and Muscat-based sweet Ws are made.

GEORGIA   *USA*   Nearly all the vines grown here are natives or hybrids, but some ambitious experiments may raise the profile of wines from classic *vinifera* vines.

GERMAIN, DOM JACQUES   *France, Burgundy, Côte d'Or, R, W*   Vineyards in both Chorey-lès-Beaune and Beaune. Very classy, elegant wines.

GERMAIN, HENRI & FILS   *France, Champagne*   Linked with Bricout and based at Rilly-la-Montagne, with 90ha of vines. Good value, well-made champagne.

GEVREY-CHAMBERTIN   *France, Burgundy, AOC, R*   Côte de Nuits village with 9 *Grands Crus* (see **CHAMBERTIN**) and 28 *Premiers Crus*. The best Gevrey-Chambertin is powerful, fruity and tannic in character, but not all the wine is worthy of the village name. Leading producers include: Bachelet, Bruno Clair, Drouhin, Dujac, Faiveley, Labouré-Roi, Rousseau.

GEWÜRZTRAMINER   In German, "*gewürz*" means spicy, which describes this grape's distinctive aroma; when well made, from ripe fruit, akin to lychees, mangoes or ripe grapefruit. Good examples are fround in Alsace and Baden; the variety is also grown in northern Italy, Austria, eastern Europe, California and New Zealand (sometimes as Traminer).

GEYSER PEAK *USA, California, Sonoma, W, R* Australian wine-maker Daryl Groom makes a brisk, delightful dry W Sémillon/Chardonnay blend at this Geyserville winery. Reserve Alexandre is a complex Meritage R.

GIESEN ESTATE *New Zealand, South Island, W* Canterbury's largest wine estate. The botrytized, late-harvest Rieslings are top quality; also good Chardonnay and Sauvignon Blanc.

GIGONDAS *France, Rhône, AOC, R, P* Some very good R and P wines are made in this southern Rhône area, mainly from Grenache, with Syrah and Mourvèdre. Leading producers include: Dom's des Goubert, des Pallières, Raspail-Ay, St-Gayan.

GIPPSLAND *Australia, Victoria* Flat, often parched, landscape, dotted with small vineyards. Low yields help the production of fine Chardonnay and a few magnificent Pinot Noirs. Leading producers include: Bass Phillip, Briagolong, McAlister, Nicholson River.

GISBORNE *New Zealand, North Island* Historically a bulk wine zone but now regarded as a W wine area with Müller-Thurgau the main variety. Currently promoted as the "Chardonnay capital of New Zealand".

GISCOURS, CH *France, Bordeaux, Médoc, Margaux, 3ème Cru Classé, R* One of the success stories of Margaux, a big estate rescued from dereliction, modernized, extended and replanted. Excellent in the 1970s but less consistent since, apart from the fine 1986 and good 1988, 1989. Style is forward, fruity and attractive.

GITTON PÈRE ET FILS *France, Loire, Sancerre & Pouilly-Fumé, W, R* Vineyard differences are emphasized in this firm's bottlings of ten Sancerres and five Pouilly-Fumés. Its cellars are in Sancerre. Barrel fermentation of the whites gives them strong characters.

GIVRY *France, Burgundy, AOC, R, W* Côte Chalonnaise village noted for its Pinot Noir wine – a powerful, somewhat rustic R, but capable of improvement in bottle for 4–6 years. Leading producers include: Jean-François Delorme, Dom du Gardin-Clos Salomon, Dom Joblot, Louis Latour, Dom Ragot, Dom Thénard.

GLEN ELLEN *USA, California, Sonoma, R, W* The winery made a splash with its affordable Proprietor's Reserve Chardonnay and Cabernet Sauvignon, and makes a quality Sauvignon Blanc. Inventive treatments of unusual R grapes such as Aleatico, Trousseau, Syrah and Cabernet Franc.

GLENORA WINE CELLARS *USA, New York, Finger Lakes, W, R, Sp* The winery emphasizes classic varieties, with grapes from its own vineyard and from local growers. Wines include fine, balanced Riesling; rich, barrel-fermented Reserve Chardonnay; and outstanding *méthode champenoise* Sp (blends of the classic Champagne varities Chardonnay and Pinot Noir).

GLENROWAN *Australia, Victoria* In north-eastern Victoria, better known as Milawa. Glenrowan has an excellent reputation for dessert wines. Leading producers include: Brown Brothers.

GLORIA, CH *France, Bordeaux, St-Julien, Cru Bourgeois, R* One of the success stories of the Médoc, this 48-ha vineyard did not exist until the 1940s. The late Henri Martin assembled the land from small plots bought all around the commune. Despite this the wine gained, and has kept, a fine reputation. Not for long keeping, though the great vintages can be superb.

GOLAN HEIGHTS WINERY *Israel, Galil, R, W* Collectively owned by eight local settlements, this cool-climate winery produces good-quality R and W wines from French varieties. Has three ranges which, in increasing order of quality, are named Gamla, Golan, Yarden. All wines are kosher.

GONZALEZ BYASS *Spain, sherry* Formidable-quality sherries. From spectacular *bodegas* (the shell-shaped La Concha was designed by Eiffel) come the top-of-the-range fino, Tio Pepe, and La Concha amontillado, from 100-year-old *soleras*. Its very old wines – Amontillado del Duque, the dry oloroso Apostoles and the Matusalem sweet oloroso – are some of the finest sherries made.

GOSSET *France, Champagne* An old firm, but a GRANDE MARQUE only since 1992. Family-owned, with an excellent name for wines which age very well in bottle and are not released until several years old. Both the Grande Réserve and Grand Millésime are excellent.

GOULAINE, MARQUIS DE *France, Loire, Muscadet, W* The Ch de Goulaine was founded over 1,000 years ago. The 31-ha vineyard, plus some bought-in wine, produces a prestige Cuvée du Millénaire and a GROS PLANT. Around one-third is bottled *sur lie*.

GOULBURN VALLEY *Australia, Victoria* Centred around the town of Tabilk. Best wines include Shiraz (R), long-lived Cabernet Sauvignon and powerful Riesling. Leading producers include: Mitchelton, Château Tahbilk.

GOURBERTS, DOM DES *France, Rhône, W, R* Family estate making good Gigondas R, an unusual Côtes du Rhône W from Viognier, and Côtes du Rhône-Villages (R and W). All Rs are made with structure to age.

GOURGAZAUD, CH DE *France, Midi, Minervois, R* Roger Piquet, former MD of the *négociant* company Chantovent, experiments with different grape varieties. He first planted Syrah here in the Midi village of La Livinière as far back as 1974.

GRAACH *Germany, Mosel, W* Famous village of the middle Mosel, with vineyards on the great southwest-facing slope upon which also lie ZELTINGEN and WEHLEN. Graach's top vineyards are Domprobst and Himmelreich; leading growers include J A Prüm, S A Prüm, Richter and Wegeler.

GRAF ADELMANN, WEINGUT *Germany, Württemberg, R, W* Top estate of this little-known region, making good Rs in an international style with *barrique*-ageing.

GRAF VON SCHÖNBORN, WEINGUT *Germany, Franken, W* This estate makes typical, traditional Franken Ws with plenty of concentration and flavour.

GRÄFLICH WOLFF-METTERNICH'SCHES WEINGUT *Germany, Baden, W, R* Dry wines in the flavourful Baden style, both Ws (from Grauburgunder and Weissburgunder) and also Rs.

GRAHAM, W & J *Portugal, port* Graham's, based at Quinta de Malvedos, is part of the SYMINGTON group. Rich, sweet wines.

GRAILLOT, ALAIN *France, Rhône, Crozes-Hermitage, R, W* Excellent wines from a patchy appellation: the W is especially good, the R ages well, especially the La Guirande *cuvée*.

GRAMONT, DOM MACHARD DE *France, Burgundy, Côte d'Or, R* Domaine at Nuits-St-Georges using traditional methods, with the emphasis on retaining the individual style of each *cru*.

GRAMPIANS *Australia, Victoria* This area is noted mainly for high-quality Shiraz (R), fleshy Cabernet Sauvignon and peachy Chardonnay. Leading producers include: Best's, Montara, Mount Langi Ghiran, Seppelt Great Western.

GRAN RESERVA *Spain* Red wines, made only in particularly good vintages, that must have spent at least two years in *barricas* (BARRIQUES) and three in bottle.

GRAND CHAMPAGNE NAPOLEON *France, Champagne* This family-owned house is the least known of the GRANDES MARQUES and one of the smallest. Produces top-quality wines, especially the vintages.

GRAND CRU *France* Top-quality French wine: the term is used differently in Bordeaux, Burgundy, Champagne and Alsace.

GRAND MOULAS, CH DU *France, Rhône, Côtes du Rhône, R* Lighter, modern style of R with freshness, fruit and no need to age. The Cuvée de l'Ecu is Syrah.

GRAND ROUSSILLON *France, Midi, AOC, VDN, R, P, W* Rarely-seen *vin doux naturel*, similar to RIVESALTES.

GRAND TINEL, DOM DU *France, Rhône, Châteauneuf-du-Pape, R* Fine R Châteauneuf comes from Elie Jeune's reticent estate.

GRAND VIN *France* The best, or first, wine of a château.

GRAND-MAYNE, CH *France, Bordeaux, St-Emilion, Grand Cru Classé, R* Bought by French insurance giant AXA in the late 1980s, this property should do well under the careful guidance of Jean-Michel Cazes of LYNCH-BAGES.

GRAND-PUY-DUCASSE, CH   *France, Bordeaux, Médoc, Pauillac, 5ème Cru Classé, R*   New owners have bought more land and have renovated the château, which is in the town of Pauillac, away from the vineyard. Consistent and classic Pauillac, often good value.

GRAND-PUY-LACOSTE, CH   *France, Bordeaux, Médoc, Pauillac, 5ème Cru Classé, R*   The Borie family, owners of DUCRU-BEAUCAILLOU (St-Julien), took over in 1980 to modernize, improve, and conjure still better wine from the excellent vineyard on the Bages plateau. Style is fruity yet well-structured. A good 1993. 2nd wine: Lacoste-Borie.

GRANDE MARQUE   *France*   One of the champagne-producing firms belonging to the Institut de Grandes Marques de Champagne. Most – but not all – of the 28 members are the leading champagne houses of today.

GRANDE RUE, LA   *France, Burgundy, AOC, R*   Côte de Nuits *Grand Cru*, newly-promoted, in Vosne-Romanée.

GRANDS ECHÉZEAUX   *France, Burgundy, AOC, R*   This *Grand Cru* is smaller than, and reckoned superior to, ECHÉZEAUX. Its wines take even longer to mature. Leading producers include: Joseph Drouhin, Dom de la Romanée-Conti.

GRANDS ÉPENOTS, LES   *France, Burgundy, Côte de Beaune, 1er Cru, R*   Top Pommard vineyard producing wines of great concentration and structure which age very well. Leading producers include: Michel Gaunoux.

GRANGENEUVE, DOM DE   *France, Rhône, Coteaux De Tricastin, R*   Elegant and interesting Rs are made here: Grangeneuve is the leading maker of this AOC.

GRATIEN MEYER SEYDOUX   *France, Loire, Saumur, Sp: W, P*   One of the largest producers of sparkling Saumur, and the only one founded by a Champagne house, Alfred Gratien. Its top wine, Cuvée Flamme (P, W) is a blend of older wines, usually given some bottle-age before release.

GRATIEN, ALFRED   *France, Champagne*   Traditional house where some wood is still used. Their NV special *cuvée* is mainly Pinot Meunier: quite full-bodied with youthful appeal. Vintage wines last remarkably well.

GRAUBÜNDEN   *Switzerland*   This canton has 376ha under vine, almost all Blauburgunder (Pinot Noir) which, in a good year, produces full, soft wines, ideal for drinking within two years or so of the vintage.

GRAUBURGUNDER   See PINOT GRIS.

GRAVES DE VAYRES *France, Bordeaux, AOC, R, W* From gravel sites beside the Dordogne, in the north of the Entre-Deux-Mers zone.

GRAVES *France, Bordeaux, AOC, R, W* Huge region and appellation south of the city of Bordeaux, with a sub-zone, PESSAC-LÉOGNAN, for fine R and dry W wine. Sauternes, the celebrated sweet W wine, is an enclave within Graves. Graves AOC is for R and dry W wines. The R wines are earthy, supple and appealing, with in richer years hints of black cherries, tobacco or chocolate. Cabernet Sauvignon is the dominant R-wine variety, although in the southern Graves, Merlot is more plentiful, giving wines that evolve more rapidly. W Graves, from Sauvignon Blanc and Sémillon, can be rich, oaky, well-structured wine, delicious in youth but improving in bottle for 10 years or more. Graves Supérieures is W – dry, medium or sweet – with slightly higher alcohol. Leading AOC Graves producers include: Ch d'Archambeau, Clos Bourgelat, Ch de Chantegrive, Ch L'Etoile, Clos Floridène, Dom La Grave, Ch Landiras, Ch Magence, Ch Montalivet, Ch Rahoul.

GREATER CANBERRA *Australia, New South Wales* Australia's Capital Territory enjoys a continental climate, so vineyards are at high altitudes. Cabernet Sauvignon, Riesling and Chardonnay are the best wines. Leading producers include: Brindabella, Doonkuna, Helm's, Lark Hill.

GREEN VALLEY SONOMA COUNTY *USA, California, VA* One of the two sub-zones within Russian River, on the cooler, ocean side of the VA a mere 10 miles from the Pacific. Mainly Chardonnay and Pinot Noir.

GRENACHE See GARNACHA.

GRENOUILLES *France, Burgundy, Chablis, Grand Cru* The smallest *Grand Cru*, making solid, perfumed wines. The vineyard is shared by LOUIS MICHEL, JEAN-PAUL DROIN and LA CHABLISIENNE cooperative.

GRES ST-PAUL, CH DU *France, Midi, Coteaux du Languedoc R; Lunel VDN* The principal independent producer in Lunel takes immense care to retain the freshness and grapiness which is the hallmark of fine Muscat de Lunel. Also known for their R Coteaux de Languedoc: warm and fruity, for early drinking.

GRESSER, DOM ANDRÉ & RÉMY *France, Alsace, W, R* Old-established (1667) company with a young, vibrant image. Reputation founded on *Grands Crus* Rieslings, Brandhof Pinot Noir and Andlau Gewürztraminer.

GRESSIER-GRAND-POUJEAUX, CH *France, Bordeaux, Moulis, Cru Bourgeois, R* Here the good gravel soil yields traditional wines that need plenty of time.

GRESY, MARCHESI DI *Italy, Piedmont, R* Maker of modern-style single-vineyard Barbarescos: Martinenga, Camp Gros and Gaiun.

GRÈVES, LES *France, Burgundy, Côte de Beaune, 1er Cru, R* Vineyard in the northern half of the Beaune appellation, producing elegant wines with good structure and length. Leading producers include: Bouchard Père & Fils, Michel Lafarge, Louis Latour, Tollot-Beaut.

GREYSAC, CH *France, Bordeaux, Médoc, Cru Bourgeois, R* Large, well-run, recently-developed estate: sound, enjoyable wine.

GRGICH HILLS *USA, California, Napa, W, R* Miljenko "Mike" Grgich is noted for his generous, well-proportioned Chardonnays. Also Cabernet Sauvignon and Zinfandel Rs, and Sauvignon and Johannisberg Riesling Ws.

GRILLET, CH *France, Rhône, AOC, W* Small, single-château AOC amid the **CONDRIEU** vineyards of the Northern Rhône. Viognier grapes make serious, concentrated W: however, some Condrieus are better and much cheaper.

GRIÑÓN, MARQUÉS DE *Spain, Castilla-León, Rueda, R, W* The personable Carlos Falco, Marqués de Griñón, makes an outstanding Cabernet Sauvignon-based R wine under his own name. Also an attractive W wine.

GRIOTTE-CHAMBERTIN See CHAMBERTIN.

GRIPA, BERNARD *France, Rhône, St-Joseph R, W; St-Péray W* Maker of reliable R St-Joseph, and Ws from both St-Joseph and from the little zone of St-Péray.

GRIPPAT, JEAN-LOUIS *France, Rhône, St-Joseph R, W; Hermitage R* One of the best R St-Josephs is Grippat's Hospices *cuvée*: both this and his standard wine need bottle-age.

GRIVOT, DOM JEAN *France, Burgundy, Côte d'Or, R* Devotee of the ACCAD method, with wines that age well but are not too austere in youth. Very fine *Grands* and *Premiers Crus*.

GROENESTEYN, SCHLOSS *Germany, Rheingau, W, R* One of the grand old estates of the Rheingau, 600 years old, today making wood-aged Rieslings in the traditional style that stress natural sweetness, in contrast to the CHARTA dry wines.

GROOT CONSTANTIA *South Africa, Constantia, R, W* Established in 1685, this is the Cape's most historic winery. Until 1993 it was Government-owned and run but is now in the hands of a Trust. Their best wine is a bordeaux blend, Gouverneurs Réserve.

GROS PLANT *France, Loire, VDQS, W* Dry W from the Muscadet region, made from Folle Blanche grapes: very acidic; good (if the vintage was warm) with local seafood. Sometimes called Gros Plant du Pays Nantais. Leading producer: Les Vignerons de la Noëlle co-op.

GRUAUD-LAROSE, CH *France, Bordeaux, Médoc, St-Julien, 2ème Cru Classé, R* This large vineyard has made fashionable and consistent wine for 250 years. In 1815 the Bordeaux *négociant* Lawton described Larose as "substantial, yet fragrant and mellow" – this is still true. The wine needs time to mature. 2nd wine: Sarget de Gruaud-Larose.

GRÜNER VELTLINER   White grape from Austria, making light, peppery wines with firm acidity. Nearly always for drinking young, though in the Wachau region they can be as powerful and long-lived as Rieslings. Also found in the Czech Republic.

GUEBERSCHWIHR   *France, Alsace*   Village producing good Muscat and Riesling. *Grand Cru* Goldert is known for Gewürztraminer as well. Leading producers include: Zind Humbrecht.

GUEBWILLER   *France, Alsace*   With more *Grands Crus* (Kessler, Kitterlé, Saering and Spiegel) than any other village, Guebwiller is famous for Gewürztraminer, Pinot Gris and Riesling. Leading producers include: Schlumberger.

GUENOC   *USA, California, Lake, W, R*   Vineyard overlapping Lake and Napa counties. Langtry Red is a MERITAGE blend of blackcurrant suppleness; Langtry White is oily with olive and licorice. Distinctive Reserve Chardonnay, with rich yet restrained creamy lemon fruit.

GUFFENS-HEYNEN, DOM   *France, Burgundy, Mâconnais, R, W*   Produces top quality Pouilly-Fuissé and Mâcon, which improve with some bottle-age.

GUIGAL, MARCEL   *France, Rhône, R*   Top producer of Côte Rôtie, including the highly expensive special *cuvées* Mouline, Landonne and Turque. His Syrah-dominated Côtes du Rhône is excellent value.

GUIRAUD, CH   *France, Bordeaux, Sauternes, 1er Cru Classé, W*   Restored in the 1980s, this large estate makes Sauternes in a rich, ample style, a creamy confection of peaches and oak.

GUNDERLOCH, WEINGUT   *Germany, Rheinhessen, W, R*   Quality-conscious estate at Nackenheim on the famous, and favoured, Rheinterrasse hillside. Their Riesling wines are full of flavour and local character.

GUNTRUM, WEINGUT LOUIS   *Germany, Rheinhessen, W*   Powerful, fruity, good-value wines with real varietal character from Riesling, Silvaner, Scheurebe etc.

GURGUE, CH LA   *France, Bordeaux, Margaux, Cru Bourgeois, R*   Small vineyard sited just west of Ch Margaux. In the same ownership as Ch CHASSE-SPLEEN and much improved as a result.

GUTEDEL   See CHASSELAS.

H

HAAG, FRITZ *Germany, Mosel, W* Small but top-quality estate making fine, typical Rieslings including a good-value QBA blended from several vineyards.

HAIGHT VINEYARDS *USA, Connecticut, W, Sp* This small hillside vineyard makes Chardonnay, a blend under the Recolte label and a little Sp Blanc de Blancs by the *méthode champenoise*.

HALBTROCKEN *Germany* Term for medium-dry wine.

HAMILTON RUSSELL *South Africa, Walker Bay, R, W* Top-quality Pinot Noir is produced at this coastal winery established over a decade ago by Tim Hamilton Russell. Ws include a good Chardonnay, and an unusual Chardonnay/Sauvignon Blanc blend.

HARGRAVE VINEYARDS *USA, New York, Long Island, R, W* Founded in 1973, this north-coast winery enjoys most success with Rs, notably Cabernet Sauvignon, a good Merlot and Cabernet Franc; its best W, Chardonnay, is slightly inconsistent. Also Sauvignon, Johannisberg Riesling, Gewürztraminer and Pinot Noir.

HARVEY, JOHN *Spain, sherry* The biggest sherry producer. Major brands include all the Harvey sherries (among them the world's biggest seller, Bristol Cream), and the top-quality 1796 range (including a good PALO CORTADO).

HATTENHEIM *Germany, Rheingau, W* Town and vineyard centre on the Rhine, with vines in some of the best Rheingau sites. Up the hill is the STEINBERG, the famous vineyard of the State Domain, and Kloster Eberbach, the ancient monastery and centre of German wine studies. Leading producers include: Schloss Reinhartshausen, von Simmern, Schönborn.

HAULLER, J, & FILS *France, Alsace, W, R* Relatively large producer of good-value wines from all the Alsace varieties. It stresses Sylvaner, but the best wines include Gewürztraminer *Grand Cru* Frankstein and several Rieslings.

HAUNER, CARLO *Italy, Sicily, W* Painter, architect, designer and winemaker Carlo Hauner makes amber-coloured, aromatic Malvasia delle Lipari and a Catarratto-based dry W wine.

HAUT-BAGES LIBÉRAL, CH *France, Bordeaux, Médoc, Pauillac, 5ème Cru Classé, R* The vineyard is well-placed, with a parcel next to Latour. Modernization and replanting are bringing results: this is now classic Cabernet Sauvignon-flavoured Pauillac. Good vintages (such as 1985, 1986) are long keepers.

HAUT-BAGES-AVÉROUS *France, Bordeaux, Médoc, Pauillac, R* 2nd wine of Ch Lynch-Bages.

HAUT-BAILLY, CH *France, Bordeaux, Pessac-Léognan, Cru Classé, R* Firm and elegant, with discreet oak, this R can be enjoyed early but can age well. Often successful in lesser vintages.

HAUT-BATAILLEY, CH *France, Bordeaux, Médoc, 5ème Cru Classé, R* Run by the Borie family (*see* Ch **GRAND-PUY-LACOSTE**), a modest-sized property with no château but with a growing name for good wine that matures quickly.

HAUT-BRION, CH *France, Bordeaux, Pessac-Léognan, 1er Grand Cru Classé (1855), R, W* In the commune of Pessac, the sole red *Premier Grand Cru* of the Graves. A wine of breed and consistency, it became more forward and voluptuous by the mid-1980s. Even in modest years (eg 1987, 1991) it produces perfumed, elegant wines. Small quantities of excellent W are made, but are released only in top years. Their Bahans-Haut-Brion (R) is one of the best 2nd wines in Bordeaux.

HAUT-MACO, CH *France, Bordeaux, Côtes de Bourg, R* Reliable quality Rs from a vineyard with (unusually) mostly Cabernet Franc.

HAUT-MARBUZET, CH *France, Bordeaux, St-Estèphe, Cru Bourgeois, R* Well-placed vines, new oak and competent winemaking produce well-regarded deep-coloured and high-flavoured wines.

HAUT-MÉDOC *France, Bordeaux, AOC, R* Southern Médoc appellation covering most vineyards outside Listrac, Moulis, and the more famous communes of St-Estèphe, Pauillac, St-Julien and Margaux; the wines represent good value. Leading producers include: Ch'x Belgrave, de Camensac, Cantemerle, Cissac, Citran, La Lagune, La Tour-Carnet.

HAUT-MONTRAVEL See MONTRAVEL.

HAUT POITOU *France, Loire, VDQS, R, P, W* Gamay, Cabernet Franc and Cabernet Sauvignon Rs and Ps, Sauvignon Blanc and Chardonnay Ws, produced in a zone to the south of the main Loire vineyards. Leading producer: Haut Poitou co-op.

HAUT-SERRE,CHDE *France,South-West,Cahors,R* See VIGOUROUX.

HAUX, CH *France, Bordeaux, 1er Côtes de Bordeaux, R* The large vineyard and new facilities, combined with *barrique*-ageing and modern methods, make prize-winning and attractive claret.

HAWKE'S BAY *New Zealand, North Island* On the east coast of the North Island, a pioneering area. Chardonnay is widely planted, then Müller-Thurgau and Sauvignon. Also top quality Rs. Leading producers include: Esk Valley, Mills Reef, Pask, Te Mata, Vidal, Waimarama.

HEGER, WEINGUT DR *Germany, Baden, W, R* Top Baden estate, with a range of fine and age-worthy wines, all dry, including Spätburgunder Rs, Weissburgunder and Riesling Ws and others. Cheaper, good-value wines are sold under the Joachim Heger label.

HEIDSIECK MONOPOLE *France, Champagne* This house is a GRANDE MARQUE, but is not among the leaders. The NV is called Dry Monopole; their best is the fruity Diamant Bleu.

HEIDSIECK, CHARLES *France, Champagne* Bought by Rémy Cointreau in the mid-1980s and completely transformed by winemaker Daniel Thibault. The NV *brut réserve* is one of the best on the market: rich, weighty, with a lot of Pinot Meunier plus some reserve wines.

HEITLINGER, WEINGUT ALBERT *Germany, Baden, W, R* One of the leaders in Baden of the "burgundy style", with oak-aged, dry wines, both R and W, from Spätburgunder, Weissburgunder and Grauburgunder.

HEITZ CELLARS *USA, California, Napa, R* Joe Heitz's winery south-east of St Helena, where his son David handles the wine-making, is famous for one of California's most revered red wines: Martha's Vineyard Cabernet Sauvignon, identified by its euca-lyptus scent and classic structure.

HENRIOT *France, Champagne* GRANDE MARQUE owned by the LVMH group. Unusually, almost entirely supplied from its own vineyards. The NV Souverain Brut is a Chardonnay-dominated, richly fruity medium-weight wine.

HENRIQUES & HENRIQUES *Portugal, Madeira* This is the largest firm outside the MADEIRA WINE COMPANY, and a considerable (for Madeira) landowner. As well as its own wines, it makes HARVEYS' own-label madeiras, and ranges for other wine merchants. It also owns other brands: Belem and Casa dos Vinhos de Madeira.

HENSCHKE *Australia, South Australia, Eden Valley, R, W* One of the country's greatest small wineries. Founded in 1868, it makes a wide range of outstanding wines, led by the velvety Hill of Grace Shiraz (R), from 120-year-old vines.

HÉRAULT, DE L' *France, Vin de Pays, R, P, W* Wines from the prolific vineyards of the south: most is attractive, good-value R, but some seri-ous estates (such as DAUMAS GASSAC) use the name on their wines, as do modern-minded large-scale producers such as Dom de la Baume.

HERMITAGE/ERMITAGE *France, Rhône, AOC, R, W* Both R and W wines have been famous since the 17th century. Syrah is the sole permitted grape for Rs; at first the wines can be tough, but after 8 years in bottle they begin to reveal a sublimely sensuous fruit. The Ws, from Marsanne or Roussanne or both, are astonishingly long-lived. Leading producers include: Chapoutier, Gérard Chave, Delas Frères, Guigal, Jaboulet.

HERTZ, ALBERT *France, Alsace, W, R* Relative newcomer, but already considered to be among the best Pinot Noir producers in the region. The wine is elegant and well-balanced. Gewürztraminer and Riesling Ws are also top quality.

HESSEN, WEINGUT PRINZ VON *Germany, Rheingau, R, W* This reliable Riesling specialist, with good vineyards in the Rheingau, stresses late-picked and sweet (rather than Charta-style dry) wines.

HESSISCHE BERGSTRASSE *Germany, Anbaugebiet, W* Small wine region specializing in Riesling Ws with flavour and charm, though they are not wines to age. Leading producers: Weingut der Stadt Bensheim, Bergsträsser cooperative, Staatsweingut Bergstrasse.

HEYL ZU HERRNSHEIM, WEINGUT *Germany, Rheinhessen, W* One of the top Riesling estates in Germany, with land in the best vineyards of Nierstein. Most wines are dry; all (including the Silvaners and Weissburgunders) show real breed and character, balancing acidity and fruit.

HEYMAN-LÖWENSTEIN *Germany, Mosel, W* Small estate at Winningen making spicy, fruity Rieslings.

HIDALGO, VINICOLA *Spain, sherry* Manzanilla La Gitana is the most famous wine from this family-owned Sanlúcar *bodega*. Even the amontillados and olorosos have a light, Sanlúcar character, though they also make a heavier Jerez fino.

HOCHHEIM *Germany, Rheingau, W* Set apart from the rest of the Rheingau, a village which gave its name to "hock" – the English word for Rhine wine. Today's Hochheim wine is solid, long-lasting yet full Riesling. The top vineyard is Domdechaney. Leading producers include: Aschrott'sche Erben, Ress, Staatsweingut, Werner.

HOFSTÄTTER, J *Italy, Alto Adige, W, R* Fine Alto Adige Pinot Nero, notable Gewürztraminer and excellent *vini da tavola*: Yngram Rosso and Yngram Bianco, from this estate.

HOGUE CELLARS *USA, Washington State, W, R* The Hogues run a large mixed farm and a 240,000-case winery near Prosser (Yakima Valley), producing a silky W Sémillon, some minty R Merlots, and Rs from Cabernet Sauvignon and Cabernet Franc.

HOMME MORT, L' *France, Burgundy, Chablis, 1er Cru* See FOUR-CHAUME.

HOSPICES DE BEAUNE *France, Burgundy, Côte d'Or, R, W* The Hospice charity dates from 1443. Now an important vineyard owner whose wines are sold annually at a dramatic auction in

November: this event sets benchmark prices for the Burgundy vintage as a whole. Wines, from named *cuvées* throughout the CÔTE DE BEAUNE, are reliable, if expensive.

HOSPICES DE NUITS-ST-GEORGES, DOM DES   *France, Burgundy, Côte d'Or, R, W*   Small brother of the HOSPICES DE BEAUNE, with top vineyard sites in Nuits.

HOSTENS-PICANT, CH   *France, Bordeaux, Ste-Foy-Bordeaux, R, Entre-Deux-Mers, W*   Newly-revived estate in the eastern corner of Bordeaux region, making good-value, well-constructed R and W.

HÖVEL, WEINGUT VON   *Germany, Saar, W*   Traditional Saar estate, making Riesling wines which (in warm years) reach Auslese levels and above.

HOWELL MOUNTAIN   *USA, California, Napa, VA*   Hill vineyards above Napa Valley which yield fine Zinfandel and Cabernet Sauvignon (Dunn's).

HUDSON RIVER VALLEY   *USA, New York State, VA*   Wine zone north of New York City with 20 wineries, growing hybrid wines plus (increasingly) Chardonnay and Cabernet. Leading producers include: Benmarl, Clinton, Millbrook, Rivendell.

HUET, GASTON   *France, Loire, Vouvray, W, Sp*   The Le Mont vineyard has been recognized as a top Vouvray since the 1600s. Its wines, together with those from Le Haut-Lieu and Clos de Bourg, are made and sold separately. Huet makes Sp and sweet wines, with only a little still dry wine.

HUGEL & FILS   *France, Alsace, W, R*   The 13th generation since 1639 now runs this, the most famous Alsace house. Reliability is the keynote. Gewürztraminer and Pinot Blanc de Blancs are good in the basic range; Cuvée Tradition and Jubilée Réserve Personnelle are superior qualities. Hugel virtually invented, and leads in, *vendange tardive* wines; in its *sélections des grains nobles* the Pinot Gris and Riesling stand out. Wines from their Sporen and Schoenenbourg vineyards are at *Grand Cru* level.

HUNAWIHR   *France, Alsace*   This village produces good Gewürztraminer, but its reputation is for Riesling from Clos Ste-Hune (part of *Grand Cru* Rosacker): possibly the best wine of Alsace. Leading producers include: Sipp-Mack, Trimbach, Zind Humbrecht.

HUNGARY   Bereft of its major export markets after the collapse of communism, Hungary found itself with a massive glut of wine. This potential disaster has been averted by bringing in western (often Australian) expertize to produce clean, well-made Ws from Sauvignon Blanc and Chardonnay, eminently saleable to thirsty hard-currency markets. The most widely planted variety is the Olaszrisling (Laski Rizling or Welschriesling), but the Hungarians are rediscovering native varieties like Furmint. R varieties showing promise include Kadarka. Hungary's most famous wine is

TOKAJI (Tokay), an extraordinary dessert wine made by adding *botrytis*-affected grapes to dry W wine. Incredibly long-lived, it is one of the world's great wines.

HUNTER VALLEY *Australia, New South Wales* The state's best-known region divides into Lower and Upper. In spite of poor weather the Lower Hunter manages to produce Sémillon (W) and Shiraz (R) of outstanding quality. The Upper Hunter offers early-maturing Chardonnay and Cabernet Sauvignon. Leading producers include: *Upper Hunter*: Allandale, Allanmere, Broke, Brokenwood, Drayton's, Evans, Lake's Folly, Lindemans, McGuigan, McWilliams, Murray Robson, Richmond Grove, Rothbury, Tulloch, Tyrrells, Wyndham; *Lower Hunter*: Arrowfield, Reynolds Yarraman, Rosemount.

HYBRID Vines cross-bred from *vitis vinifera* (the classic European grape vine) and another species, usually *vitis labrusca* or *vitis amurensis,* which confers resistance to cold weather. Hybrid vines are grown in the USA and Canada, where their wine can be good, and in England. New plantings of hybrid vines are forbidden for quality wine in EU countries.

I

IDAHO *USA* East of **WASHINGTON**, and with similar conditions, the state has a handful of wineries making mostly Ws, with Riesling and Chardonnay among the best grapes. Leading producers include: Ste Chapelle, Hell's Canyon.

IHRINGEN *Germany, Baden, W, R* Village in the **KAISERSTUHL** district, the best area of Baden, with good Ws from Silvaner and Rs from Spätburgunder. The Winklerberg is the best vineyard. Leading producers include: Heger, Stigler and the local Kaiserstuhler co-op.

ILE DE BEAUTÉ, DE L' *France, Vin de Pays, R, P, W* Wines from Corsica, using both traditional Corsican and classic grapes for R and P wines. Ws from Chardonnay and Chenin Blanc, made in a modern way, are successful: investment from mainland France has rejuvenated mass-production vineyards.

ILLINOIS *USA* A small clutch of wineries keep up a long wine tradition here.

INDIA Wine has been made here for 2,000 years, but even today less than 1% out of the country's 50,000ha of grapes are used for wine. However, western investment and new-wave winemakers are using European varieties such as Chardonnay, Ugni Blanc, Pinot Noir and Merlot. Indian Sp wine, made by the champagne method, can be very good.

INDIANA *USA* The Ohio River Valley was a wine zone a century ago, and today several wineries make good Ws from cool-climate grapes such as Riesling and Chenin Blanc.

INDICAÇÃO DE PROVENIENCIA REGULAMENTADA (IPR) *Portugal* Wines on the second tier of Portugal's appellation system.

INGELHEIM *Germany, Rheinhessen, R, W* Town famous for R wines since Charlemagne's palace stood on this south bank of the Rhine. Also now known for good Riesling Ws.

INGLENOOK *USA, California, Napa, R, W* The winery is known for Cabernet Sauvignons that show their Rutherford origins with cedar, eucalyptus and tobacco flavours. Gravion is a dry W bordeaux-style blend of Sauvignon and Sémillon.

INNISKILLIN *Canada, Ontario, W, R* Estate known for its vineyard-designated Chardonnays from around Niagara, and for its award-winning Icewine (*see* **EISWEIN**).

IOWA   *USA*   A small and often struggling clutch of wineries today where, pre-Prohibition, there was a flourishing industry.

IPHOFEN   *Germany, Franken, Bereich, W*   Village with a large area of vineyards, the best being the Julius-Echter-Berg. Good, typical Franken W wines. Leading producers include: Johann Ruck, Wirsching.

IPR   *Portugal*   See INDICAÇÃO DE PROVENIENCIA REGULAMENTADA.

IRACHE, BODEGAS   *Spain, Navarra, R, W, P*   Large family-owned business, the quality of whose wines have been somewhat hit-and-miss in the past. Things have improved though, and the wines are attractively fruity.

IRON HORSE   *USA, California, Sonoma, W, R, Sp*   The chilly climes of Green Valley are ideal for Pinot Noir and Chardonnay, used by this Sebastopol winery both for Sp (notably Brut Rosé and Wedding Cuvée) and still wines. Cabernet Sauvignon comes from winemaker Forrest Tancer's vines in Alexander Valley.

IROULÉGUY   *France, South-West, AOC, R, P, W*   Tannat grapes, grown in mountainous terrain in the Pyrenees, give these R and P wines vivid colours, fragrance and richness, although Cabernets Franc and Sauvignon are also important. W Irouléguy is rare. Leading producer: Irouléguy co-op.

ISOLE E OLENA   *Italy, Tuscany, Chianti, R, W*   One of the best Chianti Classicos; the estate also makes Cepparello, an outstanding R *vino da tavola*, a R from (unusually for Italy) the Rhône grape Syrah, and a W from Chardonnay.

ISSAN, CH D'   *France, Bordeaux, Médoc, Margaux, 3ème Cru Classé, R*   Romantic, moated château, with vines on the best east-facing slopes of the Margaux plateau. The wine is approachable quite young but is still long-lived. Smooth, with Margaux sweetness; it is one of the best of the commune and the Médoc. A good 1993.

J

JABOULET, PAUL AINÉ *France, Rhône, R, W*
Reliable *négociant*/grower for all Rhône wines,
especially Hermitage, where La Chapelle is a
top R. Their style is more elegant than some.
Crozes-Hermitage Domaine de Thalabert is a
good buy, as is Parallèle 45 Côtes du Rhône.

JABOULET-VERCHERRE *France, Burgundy, Côte d'Or, R, W* Important Beaune-based *négociant* and estate owners. Reliable wines, especially the Rs.

JACQUART *France, Champagne* Co-op based at Reims calling upon the production of 1,000ha of vineyards. This reliable and very successful brand is especially well-known in France.

JACQUESSON *France, Champagne* Small, 200-year-old firm making an attractive NV and bigger, more austere *cuvée*, Signature, fermented and aged in wood.

JADOT, LOUIS *France, Burgundy, Côte d'Or, R, W Négociant* and important vineyard owner based in Beaune. Good Rs and even better Ws, especially those from its own vineyards, though the *négociant* wines are also delicious.

JAFFELIN *France, Burgundy, Côte d'Or, R, W Négociant* business with good, reliable wines made for relatively early drinking.

JAMET, JOSEPH *France, Rhône, Côte Rôtie, R* Wines are made here in a wonderfully traditional way by the two young Jamet brothers from their vineyards on the Côte Brune. Their wines are remarkably supple and aromatic, but they take time to reveal their great character.

JAPAN The 1970s saw far-reaching developments here, with European vines and foreign expertize being imported as Japan's interest in wine grew. The Suntory, Mann and Sanraku companies opened wineries, but wine imports are growing and are now more affordable. Today the most widely-planted vines are American hybrids which, together with Japan's native *vinifera*, Koshu, account for 85% of plantings. Some excellent if expensive wines are made in the French style, with the Ch'x Lumière and Mercian labels to the fore. Ch Lion, a Sauternes-style botrytized wine, is also very good.

JARDIN DE LA FRANCE, DU *France, Vin de Pays, R, W, P* This *vin de pays* zone covers the entire Loire Valley, and is used for mainly varietal wines including Chardonnay and Sauvignon Ws, and Gamay, Cabernet Franc and Cabernet Sauvignon Rs.

JASMIN *France, Rhône, Côte Rôtie, R* More elegant than assertive, the Côte Rôtie from here is made in the traditional style and offers good value.

JASNIÈRES *France, Loire, AOC, W* Small AOC for dry Ws from Chenin Blanc, within the larger Coteaux du Loir appellation. Leading producer: Joël Gigou.

JAU, CH DE *France, Midi, Roussillon, W, R, P, VDN* This innovative estate west of Rivesaltes makes a spicy, plummy Côtes de Roussillon (R) and a very aromatic W, as well as a P and a *vin doux naturel*.

JAUBERTIE, CH LA *France, South-West, Bergerac, R, W, P* New World influence and well-placed vineyards offer crisp, fresh W and soft R Bergeracs.

JERMANN *Italy, Friuli-Venezia Giulia, Collio and Colli Orientali, W, R* Superb varietal and blended wines include opulent dry Vintage Tunina (W), a Chardonnay named "Where the Dreams have no End", Engelwhite and Vinnae (both Ws) and the sweet cherry-coloured Vigna Bellina.

JOGUET, CHARLES *France, Loire, Chinon, R* Producer offering several *crus* made from different parts of his vineyard at Sazilly: notably Jeunes Vignes, from vines under 10 years, Clos de la Cure, Varennes du Grand Clos and Clos de Chêne Vert; and the finest, Clos de la Dioterie, which receives considerable wood-ageing.

JOHANNISBERG *Germany, Franken, W* Wine town above the River Main, making good Silvaner and other Ws. Leading producers include: Johann Ruck and Wirsching.

JOHANNISBERG *Germany, Rheingau, Bereich, W, R, Sp* Town in the Rheingau, and also the name for the sole *bereich* or zone of the Rheingau, a label used chiefly for blended and Sp wines. Johannisberg's own vineyards, which include the Hasensprung and Hölle, and the estate of **SCHLOSS JOHANNISBERG**, make top-class Riesling Ws.

JOHANNISBERG RIESLING *USA* Synonym used in America for the "classic" Riesling of the Rhine, as opposed to various lesser grapes with Riesling in their name.

JOHANNISBERG, SCHLOSS *Germany, Rheingau, W* One of the great names in German wine, owning a splendid Riesling vineyard yielding a range of fine, structured wines that (from good vintages) will age for decades.

JOHNER, WEINGUT KARL HEINZ *Germany, Baden, R, W* Johner spent some time running a leading English vineyard, Lamberhurst, and now manages his family estate at Bischoffingen, making excellent R and W Baden wines in the modern style. All are aged in *barriques*; the Rs and the Weissburgunder and Chardonnay Ws in new oak.

JOLYS, CH *France, South-West, Jurançon, W*   The largest estate in the AOC, making dry (but unoaked) W, a *moelleux* or sweet W and, in great vintages, the rich W Cuvée Jean.

JORDAN *USA, California, Sonoma, R, W, Sp*   Tom Jordan's château-style winery at Healdsburg makes a soft, blackcurranty Cabernet Sauvignon and a Chardonnay oily with licorice and anise; also a small amount of a botrytized, sweet W Sémillon/Sauvignon Blanc and a toasty, apple-fruited, classic-method Sp called "J".

JOVEN *Spain*   Term which means young, or un-aged, wine, as opposed to matured wine or VINO DE CRIANZA.

JUGE, CH DU *France, Bordeaux, 1er Côtes de Bordeaux, R, W*   Prof Denis Dubourdieu (*see* Ch REYNON) has family links here so the quality of the wine is no surprise: a good R and an attractive W (AOC Bordeaux).

JULIÉNAS *France, Burgundy, AOC, R*   Beaujolais *cru* making Rs from Gamay grapes; wines develop plenty of body after 2–4 years. Leading producers include: Benon, Descombes, Ch de Juliénas.

JULIÉNAS, CH DE *France, Burgundy, Beaujolais, R*   François Condemine's estate makes consistently good, perfumed Juliénas with plenty of concentration.

JULIUSSPITAL-WEINGUT *Germany, Franken, W*   This large charitable estate makes classic Franken wines: the winemaking stresses the taste that comes from each vineyard and variety.

JUMILLA *Spain, Levante, DO, W, R*   One of two Murcia wine zones, in semi-arid country inland from Alicante. Vineyards have been replanted since phylloxera in the 1980s. There is a trend towards *joven* wines, with experiments in cask-ageing. Leading producers include: Bodegas Vitivino.

JURANÇON *France, South-West, AOC, W*   Fine, sweet W wines – and dry Ws with the AOC Jurançon Sec – from Gros Manseng, Petit Manseng and Courbu grapes grown in the foothills of the Pyrenees. Leading producers include: Dom Cauhapé, Gan co-op/Ch les Astous, Ch Jolys.

JUSTICES, CH LES *France, Bordeaux, Sauternes, W*   Estate making soundly crafted, reliable and affordable Sauternes.

K

KABINETT *Germany* The basic, QMP, level of German and Austrian wines: usually medium-dry to medium-sweet, depending upon the vintage.

KADARKA Red grape native to Hungary; difficult to grow but promising in quality.

KAISERSTUHL TUNIBERG *Germany, Baden, Bereich, R, W, P* Zone of south Baden, taking in the dramatic Kaiserstuhl hill and the adjacent, lower, Tuniberg. The volcanic soil and warm climate of the Kaiserstuhl makes the best wines: flavoursome, even powerful, Ws from Riesling and Grauburgunder; structured Rs from Spätburgunder. Tuniberg wines are less distinguished. Leading producers include: Badischer Winzerkeller, Weinguts Bercher, Dr Heger, Salwey and Stigler.

KAMPTAL *Austria, Niederösterreich* Wine zone north of Langenlois on either side of the River Kamp. W wine dominates, but an increasing number of producers are turning out promising Rs. Leading producers include: Willi Bründlmayer, Jurtschitsch.

KANONKOP ESTATE *South Africa, Stellenbosch, R* South Africa's indigenous grape, Pinotage, is given prominence at this R-only estate, and they show just how good it can be when handled in the right way. Their bordeaux-style blend, Paul Sauer, is amongst the best produced in the Cape.

KARTHÄUSERHOF, WEINGUT *Germany, Ruwer, W* Estate making top-class Rieslings in the elegant, restrained but long-lived style of the Ruwer Valley.

KENDALL-JACKSON *USA, California, Lake, R, W* The original Lakeport winery has grown into a vinous empire producing nearly a million cases a year. The Chardonnay is slightly sweet and pineapply. The Cardinale (R), an expensive **MERITAGE** blend, is big and bold, with cassis, iodine and tobacco fruit.

KENWOOD *USA, California, Sonoma, R, W* The 200,000 or so cases of good, interesting wines made here include pepper-spiced Zinfandel R, refined Artist Series Cabernet Sauvignon, herballemon Sauvignon W, supple Pinot Noir R, crisp, melon-fruited Chenin Blanc and creamy Chardonnay.

KESSELSTATT, WEINGUT REICHSGRAF VON *Germany, Mosel, W* Large estate, all Riesling, with good vineyards in the Middle Mosel, Saar and Ruwer Valleys, making wines which though dry retain fruit and character.

KIENTZHEIM *France, Alsace* This village had the first *Grand Cru* (Schlossberg) to be officially recognized. It is famous for Gewürztraminer, but Riesling is also impressive. Leading producers include: Dom Weinbach, Dopff & Irion, Dopff Au Moulin.

KIRWAN, CH *France, Bordeaux, Margaux, 3ème Cru Classé, R* The well-placed Kirwan vineyard on the gravel plateau east of Brane-Cantenac, with its high proportion of Merlot and Cabernet Franc, yields Margaux in the softer style, gaining finesse with age.

KLEIN CONSTANTIA ESTATE *South Africa, Constantia, R, W* Duggie Jooste makes some of the Cape's finest wines, from the crisp, gooseberry-tinged Sauvignon Blanc to the delicious Muscat dessert wine, Vin de Constance: a modern version of the historic Constantia.

KLÜSSERATH *Germany, Mosel, W* Riesling Ws from this village's Brüderschaft vineyard are well regarded.

KNIGHT'S VALLEY *USA, California, Sonoma, VA* Warm-climate zone north of (and with similar conditions to) Napa, though within Sonoma county. Good for Cabernet Sauvignon and Merlot (R) and Sauvignon (W). Leading producers include: Beringer.

KNUDSEN ERATH *USA, Oregon, R, W, P* Oregon's largest estate winery. Half the production is a mint-spiced, black-cherry-filled Pinot Noir. A honeysuckle-scented Riesling is made both dry and in a Mosel semi-sweet style. Pinot Gris, fermented in French oak and lees-aged, is new; some Pinot Noir is made as a fruity, dry Vin Gris (P).

KOCHER-JAGST-TAUBER *Germany, Württemberg, Bereich, W* Small zone of northern Württemberg making mostly W wine.

KOEHLER-RUPPRECHT, WEINGUT *Germany, Pfalz, W, R* Long-lived, traditionally-made wines, dry but full, from Riesling, Spätburgunder and other varieties.

KREMSTAL *Austria, Niederösterreich* Region which extends on either side of the Danube and its tributary the Krems. Mainly W grapes, including Riesling and Grüner Veltliner, producing very elegant wines. Leading producers include: Malat-Bründlmayer, Mantlerhof, Josef Nigl, Fritz Salomon.

KREUZNACH *Germany, Nahe, Bereich, W* The northern part of the Nahe region, making W wine in the Nahe style: earthy, able to age well, showing good acidity. The town of **BAD KREUZNACH** is the centre. Leading producers include: August Anheuser, von Plettenberg, Staatsweingut Bad Kreuznach.

KRUG *France, Champagne* Perhaps the greatest name in Champagne. Big, rich, traditional wines needing years in bottle before they even begin to show of their best. All wines are prestige *cuvées*, using only first pressings and fermenting in wood. Krug NV Grande Cuvée, the most consistently great wine in Champagne, has a high percentage of reserve wine and Pinot Meunier.

KRUG, CHARLES *USA, California, Napa, R, W* Founded in 1861 by Charles Krug, this winery, north of St Helena, is now owned by Peter Mondavi and his sons. It is known for its fine Vintage Selection Cabernet Sauvignons and silky, sweet grass- and hay-scented Chenin Blanc.

KUENTZ-BAS *France, Alsace, W, R* Kuentz began in 1795, and joined André Bas in 1918. Wines of great quality, in particular the *vendange tardive* versions. The top wines are Gewürztraminer, Pinot Gris, Muscat and, increasingly, Pinot Noir. They also make Crémant d'Alsace.

KWV *South Africa, Paarl, R, W* Founded in 1918, the KWV dominates the South African wine scene. It is a huge cooperative producing a wide range of reliable, good-value wines under a variety of labels.

L

LABASTIDE DE LÉVIS, CAVE DE *France, South-West, Gaillac, W, R, P, Sp* This large cooperative makes the full, diverse range of Gaillac styles, each of them to a good standard.

LABÉGORCE, CH *France, Bordeaux, Margaux, Cru Bourgeois, R* Big improvements over recent vintages make this a château to try.

LABÉGORCE-ZÉDÉ, CH *France, Bordeaux, Margaux, Cru Bourgeois, R* Reliable, good-quality, traditionally made wine.

LABOURÉ-ROI *France, Burgundy, Côte d'Or, R, W* This well-known *négociant* specializes in W wines from all over the Burgundy region. Quality is reliable. Also a range of varietal *vins de pays* from the Languedoc – and a Pinot Noir *vin de pays* from the Aude.

LABRUSCA Vines of the species *vitis labrusca* are grown for wine in the eastern USA. Their wine is reckoned inferior to that of VINIFERA vines, having a strong taste described as "foxy".

LACLAVERIE, CH *France, Bordeaux, Côtes de Francs, R* Owned by the Thienponts of Pomerol, this 50/50 Merlot/Cabernet wine is good, dark, juicy claret. *See also* Ch PUYGUERAUD.

LACOSTE-BORIE *France, Bordeaux, Médoc, St-Julien, R* 2nd wine of Ch Grand-Puy-Lacoste.

LADOIX *France, Burgundy, AOC, R, W* Northernmost Côte de Beaune village; its best vineyards are on the Corton hill and are entitled to be sold as *Grands Crus* or as *Premier Cru* Aloxe-Corton. Wine labelled Ladoix is thus of village status: it can be good value. Leading producers include: Capitain-Gagnerot, Michel Mallard, Prince Florent de Mérode.

LAFAURIE-PEYRAGUEY, CH *France, Bordeaux, Sauternes, 1er Cru Classé, W* With the 1983 vintage new winemaking policies were applied, and since then the wine, aged in 50% new oak, is superb: silky in texture, oaky, elegant: copybook Sauternes. In modest years it can be among the best wines of the vintage.

LAFITE-ROTHSCHILD, CH *France, Bordeaux, Médoc, Pauillac, 1er Cru Classé, R* The large vineyard is superbly placed on the rim of the northern Pauillac plateau. The soil is gravel, the drainage good. Lafite was bought by the famous Paris banking family the Rothschilds in 1868, and is still owned by them. Lafite was the wine to match in the great vintages of the 1980s. It has 70% Cabernet Sauvignon, compared to neigbouring MOUTON-ROTHSCHILD's 85%; and its 15% Merlot (Mouton has only 8%) shows in its lighter style. Lafite is the most graceful, refined, even delicate of the First Growths, though it has the concentration and structure to age for decades.

LAFLEUR, CH *France, Bordeaux, Pomerol, R* Tiny amounts of fabulous – and expensive – pure Merlot wine.

LAFON, DOM DES COMTES *France, Burgundy, Côte d'Or, R, W* Exceptional domaine specializing in Meursault – but their Montrachet is also brilliant.

LAFON-ROCHET, CH *France, Bordeaux, Médoc, St-Estèphe, 4ème Cru Classé, R* The fine vineyard faces south towards Lafite, with old vines, but the wines do not quite reach the heights. There is 80% Cabernet Sauvignon, so most years need keeping. A good 1993.

LAGAROSSE, CH *France, Bordeaux, 1er Côtes de Bordeaux, R, W* Mostly Merlot, the R is solid and structured, ageing in 3 years to elegance; the W (70% Sémillon) is fruity but dry.

LAGEDER, ALOIS *Italy, Alto Adige, W, R* Leading producer of single-vineyard wines from steep sub-Alpine slopes including Alto Adige Chardonnay Löwengang and Erlehof, Cabernet Sauvignon Löwengang and Romigberg, Lagrein Dunkel Lindenburg and Terlano Sauvignon Blanc Lehenhof.

LAGRANGE, CH *France, Bordeaux, Médoc, St-Julien, 3ème Cru Classé, R* The Japanese group Suntory bought the property in 1983 and have spent millions on it, with the vineyards replanted and expanded, new air-conditioned *chai*, etc. Results are now impressive, with enthusiastic notes from critics on the wines from 1985 onwards. 2nd wine: Fiefs de Lagrange.

LAGUNE, LA *France, Bordeaux, Haut-Médoc, 3ème Cru Classé, R* Being outside the famous communes (it is south of Margaux, near Bordeaux) has hidden Lagune's true standing. Excellent wine in the scented, silky Margaux style.

LAKE *USA, California* County in cool-climate northern California with vineyards around the **CLEAR LAKE** VA and Guenoc.

LALANDE-DE-POMEROL *France, Bordeaux, AOC, R* North of Pomerol two communes, Lalande de Pomerol and Néac, produce Merlot-based Rs which mature faster than most Pomerols and offer a slightly lighter version of the same rich, plummy taste. Leading producers include: Ch'x des Annereaux, Bel-Air, Belle-Graves, Bertineau St-Vincent, Siaurac, Tournefeuille.

LALANNE, JACQUES *France, Loire, Quarts-de-Chaume, W* Lalanne's Ch de Belle Rive estate is dedicated to quality regardless of expense. Yields are low and only botrytized grapes go into this sweet wine, which is fermented in wood before bottling in April/May. The wines, although attractive when young, repay ageing.

LAMBRUSCO   *Italy, Emilia-Romagna, R, W, P, Sp*   The adaptable Lambrusco grape is usually reserved for R wines which are lightly Sp, sweet and easily quaffable: the best is Lambrusco di Sorbara. It can, however, be vinified dry (and is better for it), though most Lambrusco made for export is medium-sweet. Lambrusco should always be drunk young. Leading producers include: Cavvicchioli, Chiarli, Giacobazzi, Riunite, Villa Barbieri.

LAMOTHE, CH   *France, Bordeaux, Sauternes, 2ème Cru Classé, W*   There is a new generation taking over here, so quality is likely to improve, but in the past Lamothe has been disappointing.

LAMOTHE-GUIGNARD, CH   *France, Bordeaux, Sauternes, 2ème Cru Classé, W*   Since new owners took over in the early 1980s the improvement has been spectacular. Since 1986 the wine has been delicious: rich and sweet, lightly oaky, elegant and complex, getting better with every vintage. Now represents one of the few bargains of Sauternes.

LANDIRAS, CH DE   *France, Bordeaux, Graves, W, R*   Look for Sémillon-dominated Ws in a rich, oaky style from this estate. Rs are impressive too.

LANDWEIN   *Germany*   Literally country wine; this is a superior sub-category of *Tafelwein*, equivalent to *vin de pays*.

LANGOA BARTON, CH   *France, Bordeaux, Médoc, St-Julien, 3ème Cru Classé R*   The Barton family has owned and run Langoa- and LÉOVILLE-BARTON for 170 years. The winemaking is traditional, as are the prices, making Langoa a byword for value. The vineyard is quite small: 15ha.

LANGUEDOC   *France*   This enormous wine region, known generally as the Midi, is strung between the Mediterranean and the inland hills, west of the Rhône. One of the most exciting places in wine today, with many new wines under the various AOC names (MINERVOIS, COTEAUX DU LANGUEDOC, CORBIÈRES etc) and the many *vins de pays*, including the overall VIN DE PAYS D'OC. The most innovative growers often label their wines as simple *vins de pays*, since this frees them from the restrictions the AOC rules put on choice of grape varieties.

LANSON   *France, Champagne*   Sold in 1990 to giant Marne et Champagne, Lanson's Black Label is one of the world's best-known champagnes. Fresh, citrussy, perhaps a little on the lean side. Vintage wines are better, and can age very well.

LAPATENA   *Spain, Ribeiro, W, R, Sp*   New winery on a spectacular bend of the River Miño. Production is mainly W, and their best is the Fin de Siglo. R wines include Rectoral de Amandi and Teliro.

LAPORTE, DOMS   *France, Loire, Sancerre, W*   This 15-ha estate has modern cellars, making high-quality wines. Top *cuvée* is Domaine du Rochoy, from low-yielding vines, left *sur lie* until bottling. Others are Clos la Comtesse and Grand Domaine.

LARMANDE, CH *France, Bordeaux, St-Emilion, Grand Cru Classé, R*
This old estate to the north of St-Emilion village is planted with
two-thirds Merlot. Very reliable, high-quality wines.

LAROCHE, DOM *France, Burgundy, Chablis, Corsica, Midi, W* A
leading (100ha) Chablis estate, also *négociant*, with holdings in
both *Premiers* and *Grands Crus*. Top-quality wines which age well.
Recent ventures in Corsica and LANGUEDOC yield good-value
varietal *vins de pays*.

LAROSE-TINTAUDON, CH *France, Bordeaux, Médoc, Cru Bourgeois,
R* Well placed château just inland from Pauillac; a good source
of reliable claret.

LAROZE, CH *France, Bordeaux, St-Emilion, Grand Cru Classé, R*
This good-sized property, with almost 50% Cabernet Franc, produces attractive, easy wines that mature fairly quickly.

LARRIVET-HAUT-BRION, CH *France, Bordeaux, Pessac-Léognan, R, W*
Investment in new cellars has brought impressive results: the W
rich and spicy, the R firm and oaky.

LASCOMBES, CH *France, Bordeaux, Médoc, Margaux, 2ème Cru
Classé, R* Big vineyard on a grand estate that was restored by
the Franco-American wine merchant and writer, the late Alexis
Lichine, and sold by him to an English brewer. Formerly unexciting wine, but much better in the late 1980s.

LASKI RIZLING See WELSCHRIESLING.

LASTOURS, CH DE *France, Midi, Corbières, R* Estate of international repute, employing handicapped people in the cellar and
vineyard. Classic methods produce several *cuvées* with the
emphasis on the *terroir*, mostly designed for fairly early drinking.

LATOUR À POMEROL, CH *France, Bordeaux, Pomerol, R* Very
dense, compact wines from an estate run by the Jean-Pierre
MOUEIX firm.

LATOUR, CH *France, Bordeaux, Médoc, Pauillac, 1er Cru Classé, R*
The wines of Latour have been sought after since the Middle
Ages. Its old-fashioned Cabernet Sauvignon-based style made it a
legend for longevity. Modernization (it was the first Médoc estate
to install stainless steel vats) has tamed the wine a little, but
hardly changed its deep, dark, sturdy character. The excellence of
the *terroir* allows Latour to make good wines in poor years, and its
microclimate often spares it the region's damaging spring frosts.
In good years it offers up a dark, chewy monster of a wine that
demands patience measured in decades. 2nd wine: Les Forts de
Latour. A 3rd wine, labelled AOC Pauillac, is made in some years.
A very fine 1994, both the *Grand Vin* and Les Forts.

LATOUR, LOUIS *France, Burgundy, Côte d'Or, R, W* Major *négociant*
and vineyard owner in Burgundy whose name is known around
the world. The Ws are excellent: their R wines are not quite so
reliable.

LATRICIÈRES-CHAMBERTIN   See CHAMBERTIN.

LAUGEL, MAISON MICHEL   *France, Alsace, W, R*   This large producer is now owned by Rémy-Pannier of the Loire region. Wines are good value, and certain *cuvées* of Gewürztraminer, Pinot Noir, Riesling and Muscat can excel. The Crémant d'Alsace is consistent and good.

LAUREL GLEN   *USA, California, Sonoma, R*   Source of one of the finest Cabernet Sauvignons in the USA, plush with fruit, firmly structured for age.

LAURENT-PERRIER   *France, Champagne*   This leading GRANDE MARQUE is one of Champagne's largest houses. Extremely elegant wines, from bone-dry Ultra Brut to the superb prestige *cuvée* Grand Siècle. The flowery NV is Chardonnay-based.

LAVAUX   *Switzerland, Vaud*   District within the Vaud canton, with steep vineyards overlooking the lake east of Lausanne. Chasseles (W) and Pinot Noir (R) are specialities.

LAVIÈRES, LES   *France, Burgundy, Côte de Beaune, 1er Cru, R*   In the commune of Savigny-lès-Beaune, this vineyard produces wines which are quite light in colour, sport an elegant bouquet and have a supple, soft palate. Leading producers include: Pierre Bitouzet, BOUCHARD PÈRE & FILS, Jean Grivot.

LAVILLE-HAUT-BRION, CH   *France, Bordeaux, Pessac-Léognan, Cru Classé, W*   This is, in effect, the W wine of Ch LA MISSION-HAUT-BRION. Perhaps a little less sumptuous than Ch HAUT-BRION, made by the same team, but an opulent wine by any standards. It needs a decade in bottle.

LAVILLEDIEU, VIN DE   *France, South-West, VDQS, R, P*   Minor country wine of the Tarn valley near Fronton, made from a blend of Négrette, Gamay, Cabernet Franc, Syrah and Tannat grapes.

LAVILLOTTE, CH   *France, Bordeaux, St-Estèphe, Cru Bourgeois, R*   Good, old-fashioned, long-keeping wine that wins prizes in prestigious tastings.

LAZIO   *Italy*   Also called Latium, this region of central Italy is unusual in that the vast majority (90%) of its production is W. Frascati, from the hills south of Rome called the Castelli Romani, is its best-known W wine, though the neighbouring DOCs of Colli Albini and Marino are also good.

LEBANON   Lebanon's name has become synonymous in wine terms with one winery, Ch MUSAR, but there are other vineyards, including the recent Ch Kefraya.

LECCIA, DOM   *France, Corsica, Patrimonio, W, R*   Modern techniques and equipment give the Rs a good fruit flavour with some structure. It also produces a good sweet Muscat.

LEEUWIN ESTATE   *Australia, South Australia, Margaret River, R, W*   Flamboyant promotion and excellent quality made Leeuwin's reputation. Long-lived Chardonnay and classic Cabernet Sauvignon lead the way, though the wine range is wide.

LEFLAIVE, DOM *France, Burgundy, Côte d'Or, W* Together with Domaine Sauzet, Leflaive is the top producer in Puligny-Montrachet: an impressive array of *Premiers* and *Grands Crus* are made, showing elegance and finesse with tremendous staying power.

LEFLAIVE, OLIVIER FRÈRES *France, Burgundy, Côte d'Or, R, W* As *négociant*, and increasingly as a grower, Olivier produces white wines very much in the elegant style of the family estate, DOMAINE LEFLAIVE.

LEITZ, WEINGUT JOSEPH *Germany, Rheingau, W* Young producer of elegant, racy Riesling from good, low-yielding Rüdesheim vineyards.

LEMOINE *France, Champagne* Marque owned by Laurent-Perrier. The main brand, Cuvée Royale, is an extremely well made, good value champagne with an attractive lively palate.

LEO BURING *Australia, South Australia, Barossa, W* Long regarded as the maker of Australia's greatest Rieslings: these are W wines that evolve magnificently for 20 years or more, from citrus and lime in youth to mature toasted aromas and flavours.

LEÓN, JEAN *Spain, Catalonia, Penedès, R, W, P* Pioneer of "new-wave" winemaking in Catalonia, the *bodega* specializes in using classic French grapes and oak fermentation. Their Chardonnay is full-bodied, and the Cabernet Sauvignon-based R ages well.

LÉOVILLE BARTON, CH *France, Bordeaux, Médoc, St-Julien, 2ème Cru Classé, R* Léoville was a large estate on the best vineyard land in St-Julien. It eventually split in three (see below). Barton's 45-ha portion of that original estate is reckoned to make slightly better, more concentrated wine than its sister LANGOA-BARTON.

LÉOVILLE LAS-CASES, CH *France, Bordeaux, Médoc, St-Julien, 2ème Cru Classé, R* This large estate, which includes the original walled Léoville *clos*, is owned and run by Michel Delon, one of Bordeaux's best winemakers. Powerful, concentrated, long in taste and long-lived in bottle, this is one of the great red wines. Comparisons are often made with its 1st-Growth neighbour Latour, across the Pauillac border. 2nd wine: Clos du Marquis.

LÉOVILLE POYFERRÉ, CH *France, Bordeaux, Médoc, St-Julien, 2ème Cru Classé, R* The third portion of the great Léoville property, much improved during the 1980s when Didier Cuvelier took charge and introduced a more rigorous selection. 2nd wine: Moulin-Riche.

LEROY, DOM *France, Burgundy, Côte d'Or, R, W* Proprietior Lalou Bize-Leroy, *négociant* and vineyard owner, is also part-owner of Dom de la ROMANÉE-CONTI. Recently much enlarged, the Leroy estate makes fine, long-lasting wines.

LEY, BODEGAS BARÓN DE   *Spain, Rioja, R*   New *bodega* where modern technology is intelligently combined with tradition: some experimentation with Cabernet Sauvignon is under way.

LIEBFRAUMILCH   *Germany, Rhine, W*   German wine, blended by a merchant or cooperative, from at least 70% Riesling, Müller-Thurgau, Silvaner or Kerner grapes grown anywhere in the Rheingau, Pfalz, Nahe or Rheinhessen (usually in the last), of QBA standard. Usually medium-sweet.

LIGURIA   *Italy*   Cupped around the Gulf of Genoa and bordering Provence in France, most wine from these hilly coastal vineyards is consumed locally. Easy-quaffing W wines and a few long-lived R are made under four DOCs.

LILIAN LADOUYS, CH   *France, Bordeaux, St-Estèphe, Cru Bourgeois, R* Impressive wine from this newly restored château. Its hilltop site and apricot walls form a local landmark.

LIMOUX   *France, Midi, AOC, W*   Appellation for still wines made, like **BLANQUETTE DE LIMOUX**, from the Mauzac grape plus some Chenin Blanc and Chardonnay. The Chardonnay varietals can be particularly good: the local *cave cooperative* (see below) has identified four different *terroirs* and offers wines from each. Leading producers include: Cave Coopérative de Limoux.

LIMOUX, CAVE COOPÉRATIVE DE   *France, Midi, Limoux, W, Sp*   Of the annual 666,600 cases of Sp Blanquette de Limoux, 75% comes from this modern, well-run co-op. Its variety of *cuvées* includes Aimery, Cuvée Aldéric and Sieur d'Arques. Also good still Ws from Chardonnay.

LINDEMANS   *Australia, New South Wales, Hunter Valley, R, W*   Founded in 1870, Lindemans produce good Shiraz (R) plus some Sémillon-based Ws and sophisticated Chardonnays. Production centres also in other parts of Australia, and a wide and reliable range of wines.

LINGENFELDER, WEINGUT K & H   *Germany, Pfalz, W, R*   Rainer Lingenfelder, who has made wine in Bordeaux and Australia, now runs the family estate and is a leader of modern German R-winemaking, using *barriques* with great success. Noted maker of dry, well-structured Spätburgunder Rs and dry, full-flavoured Riesling Ws.

LIONNET, JEAN   *France, Rhône, St-Péray W; Cornas R* Maker of solid, wood-aged Cornas Rs which needs time in bottle to soften, and also excellent St-Péray Ws.

LIOT, CH   *France, Bordeaux, Barsac, W*   Popular Barsac in a light style, sometimes lacking in *botrytis*, and aged in a mixture of tanks and *barriques*, of which 15% are new. Relatively inexpensive, it makes a sound apéritif Sauternes.

LIQUOROSO   *Italy*   Fortified dessert wine.

LIRAC *France, Rhône, AOC, R, P, W* The best R and W Liracs aspire to the quality of Châteauneuf-du-Pape; the best Ps to that of Tavel. Leading producers include: Jean-Claude Assémat, Dom Duseigneur, Dom Maby, Dom Roger Sabon.

LISTRAC-MÉDOC *France, Bordeaux, AOC, R* Solid Haut-Médoc wines that repay keeping. Leading producers include: Ch'x Clarke, Fourcas-Dupré, Fourcas-Hosten.

LIVERMORE VALLEY *USA, California, VA* Wine zone south of San Francisco with gravel soils growing Bordeaux varieties: Cabernets, Merlot, Sauvignon. Leading producers include: Concannon, Wente.

LJUTOMER-ORMOZ *Slovenia, Podravski* This wine zone has the country's best-quality vineyards and two huge cellars, Ljutomer and Ormoz. Famous for light, pleasant Laski Rizling. Ormoz has the edge over Ljutomer in quality. Wines exported under the Lutomer label come from both. The full potential of the excellent *terroir* has yet to be reached.

LLANO ESTACADO *USA, Texas, W* Among the leaders in the Texas wine renaissance, this Lubbock winery averages 75,000 cases a year, producing acceptable Chardonnay, Chenin Blanc and Sauvignon Ws. Cabernet Sauvignon is its next challenge.

LLANOS, BODEGAS LOS *Spain, Valdepeñas, R, W* Large producer with 1,200ha of vines. Los Llanos has invested heavily in oak casks, and the best wines include impressive *gran reservas* such as Pata Negra, which is 100% Tempranillo. Also doing good work with Ws from the Airén grape.

LOIRE *France, Loire, AOC, W, P, Sp* Most Loire wines go under local names (*see* ANJOU, SAUMUR, MUSCADET, etc), but Crémant de Loire, Sp W or P wine, can be made throughout the vast Loire Valley. Controls for Crémant are stricter than for the straightforward Sp (*mousseux* or *pétillant*) Saumur and Vouvray. Rosé de Loire, a dry P from a minimum 30% Cabernet grapes, can also be made throughout the region. Leading Crémant de Loire producers include: Ackerman-Laurance, Ch du Breuil, Dom de la Gabillière, Langlois-Château.

LOMBARDY *Italy* To the east of Piedmont in northern Italy. Wine is less important here than in Piedmont. Oltrepò Pavese is the best-known DOC, though the Valtellina wines – mountain Rs – can be good in warm years.

LONG-DEPAQUIT *France, Burgundy, Chablis, W* Unoaked Chablis made to give a true expression of the *terroir*. The flagship wine is from the tiny La Moutonne vineyard.

LONG ISLAND, NORTH FORK OF *USA, New York State, VA* Wine zone on a sandy, mild-climate peninsula at the eastern end of the Island, recently burgeoning as a source of good wines: elegant Rs from Merlot and Cabernet; Ws from Sauvignon and

Chardonnay. Leading producers include: Bedel, Bridgehampton, Hargrave, Palmer, Pindar.

LOOSEN, WEINGUT OEKONOMIERAT DR *Germany, Mosel-Saar-Ruwer, W* Ernst Loosen is a modern-minded maker of Mosel Rieslings, using low yields and the latest techniques including experiments with *barriques*. His wines are piquant, spicy and full of taste. The Riesling Trocken (dry) is good value.

LORCH, LORCHHAUSEN *Germany, Rheingau, W* Twin villages officially in the Rheingau wine region, but geographically in the Rhine gorge and thus closer in wine style to the **MITTELRHEIN**: light, elegant Riesling Ws.

LOUBENS, CH *France, Bordeaux, St-Croix-Du-Mont, W; Bordeaux, R* The leading estate in this sweet-white zone, offering good-value wines akin to minor Sauternes. Also an AOC Bordeaux R.

LOUDENNE, CH *France, Bordeaux, Médoc, Cru Bourgeois, R* Reliable English-owned estate beautifully placed by the Gironde. A light, relatively early-maturing R – and a good W, rare in the Médoc. Also a museum and a respected wine school.

LOUPIAC *France, Bordeaux, AOC, W* Sweet W from a small zone across the Garonne from Barsac. Leading producers include: Ch'x du Cros, Loupiac-Gaudiet, de Ricaud.

LOUPIAC-GAUDIET, CH *France, Bordeaux, Loupiac, W, Bordeaux, R* Old estate making good, light, sweet Ws and a good, fruity AOC Bordeaux R.

LOUVIÈRE, CH LA *France, Bordeaux, Pessac-Léognan, W, R* The W, dominated by Sauvignon Blanc, is a sound oaky wine of some distinction. The R is well structured and ages well. Also made here is Ch Coucheroy: simple but well-made R and W Graves, very good value.

LUGNY, CAVE COOPERATIVE DE *France, Burgundy, Mâconnais, R, W* Very well made lesser burgundies, both R and W – but particularly well known for their good-quality W Mâconnais.

LUJAN DE CUYO *South America, Argentina, R* South of the city of Mendoza, this high-elevation area has a cool microclimate. Cabernet Sauvignon and Malbec do well here.

LUNEL, MUSCAT DE *France, Midi, AOC, VDN* This *vin doux naturel*, from 100% Muscat Blanc à Petits Grains (the best Muscat grape), is made on the eastern edge of the Hérault *département*. Leading producers include: Dom des Aires, Clos Bellevue, Ch du Grès St-Paul.

LUNGAROTTI, CANTINE *Italy, Central Italy, Umbria, W, R* Giorgio Lungarotti is the patriarch of Umbrian wines. The Torgiano DOC, which he instigated, is almost entirely dominated by Lungarotti. His Torgiano (R) is named Rubesco, his W Torre di Giano.

Torgiano *riserva* is a DOCG wine. Miralduolo is the name for R and W *vini da tavola* from Cabernet Sauvignon and Chardonnay. Also has a splendid wine museum.

LUSSAC ST-EMILION   *France, Bordeaux, AOC, R*   North of St-Emilion are several "satellite" villages, of which this is one, whose wines can represent excellent value. Leading producers include: Ch'x Barbe Blanche, Bel-Air, Haut-Piquat, de Lussac, Lyonnat, de Tabuteau, Tour de Grenet; Vieux Ch Chambeau.

LUSTAU, EMILIO   *Spain, sherry*   Innovative firm that launched the ALMACENISTA idea onto the world market, and then followed that with the Landed Age concept (sherries bottled in the country of export and aged in bottle before sale). Also has a growing range of commercial sherries.

LUXEMBOURG   Nearly 2,000ha of vineyards in the upper Moselle valley make crisp, dry W and Sp wines. The quality rating *marque nationale* is equivalent to French AOC.

LYNCH-BAGES, CH   *France, Bordeaux, Médoc, Pauillac, 5ème Cru Classé, R*   Traditional wine from modern equipment is the Cazes family's philosophy. The style is supple and accessible, yet with the concentration and depth of a truly good Pauillac. The large and superbly sited vineyard means that it is in ample supply. A good 1993. 2nd wine: Haut-Bages-Avérous.

LYNCH-MOUSSAS, CH   *France, Bordeaux, Médoc, Pauillac, 5ème Cru Classé, R*   Yet another Médoc château starting to show form after a major renewal programme. The vineyard has 30% Merlot, producing wines in the lighter style which are good value.

M

MABILEAU, JACQUES *France, Loire, Bourgueil, R* Based in St-Nicolas-de-Bourgueil, Jacques Mabileau makes two wines from 13ha on the western edge of the Coteaux zone: a standard *cuvée*, Domaine Jacques Mabileau, and a blend from older vines, Vieilles Vignes, which, for a St-Nicolas, ages well.

MACAY, CH *France, Bordeaux, Côtes de Bourg, R* This recent star of the appellation offers balanced and fruity wines.

MACEDON *Australia, Victoria* This cool-climate area makes Cabernet Sauvignon and Shiraz (R) of note, plus a good range of other single-variety wines. Leading producers include: Hanging Rock, Virgin Hills.

MACÉRATION CARBONIQUE *France* Winemaking technique (used, for example, in Beaujolais) in which R-wine grapes are put into sealed vats without being crushed. Carbon dioxide is pumped in, and fermentation takes place naturally inside the grapes, which split under their own weight. This extracts aroma and colour. After pressing, fermentation is then completed in the normal way.

MACLE, HENRI *France, Jura, W* Specialist in the rare VIN JAUNE of the Château-Chalon AOC: Macle's meticulous winemaking produces long-lived wines.

MÂCON *France, Burgundy, AOC, R, W, P* Wide area in southern Burgundy making mostly modest wines. The Rs are from Gamay or Pinot Noir, Ws from Chardonnay; most wines achieve the extra degree of alcohol needed to qualify for the AOC Mâcon-Supérieur. Both Rs and Ws are best drunk young and fresh. Leading producers include: Cave Coopérative de Lugny, Cave Coopérative de Viré, Trenel & Fils.
Mâcon-Villages AOC for W wines from one of 43 "superior" villages; the village name can be attached, as in Mâcon-Lugny or Mâcon-Viré. Leading producers include: Dom André Bonhomme, Dom des Gandines, Dom Guillemot-Michel, Dom Manciat-Poncet, Dom Jean Thévenet.

MACULAN *Italy, Veneto, R, W* Star Breganze producer, making Cabernet, oak-aged Tocai (W) and Torcolato, a sweet W from dried grapes aged in new oak.

MADEIRA *Portugal, DOC* Island in the Atlantic, 600km west of Casablanca. Its fortified W wine gains uniqueness from the cooking process (*estufagem*) giving the wine its slightly burnt character, together with high acid. Four main styles of Madeira exist, from very dry to very sweet, named after grape varieties used: Sercial, Verdelho, Bual, Malmsey. Basic Madeira (3-year-old) from Tinta Negra Mole is essentially cooking wine. 5-year-old and up can be extremely good and ages very well. Leading producers include: Blandy Brothers, Cossart Gordon, Henriques & Henriques.

MADEIRA WINE CO *Portugal, Madeira* Many of the great madeira names are united in the Madeira Wine Co, formerly an association of shippers but now owned by the BLANDY and SYMINGTON families. Today it is moving to emphasize the differences between the various companies' wines.

MADIRAN *France, South-West, AOC, R* Wines from the tannic Tannat grape, blended with Cabernet Franc and Cabernet Sauvignon, grown on varied soils in the Pyrenean foothills. Leading producers include: Ch d'Aydie, Ch Bouscassé, Dom du Crampilh, Dom Laffitte-Teston, Ch Montus, Dom Moureou.

MAGDELAINE, CH *France, Bordeaux, St-Emilion, 1er Grand Cru Classé, R* Owned by the Moueix family, Pomerol's leading producers, this beautiful property is among the top *1ers Grands Crus*. The high percentage of Merlot contributes to the wine's opulence and richness.

MAGENCE, CH *France, Bordeaux, Graves, W, R* Well-known estate in St-Pierre-de-Mons in the southern Graves, producing sound Rs and Ws.

MAINDREIECK *Germany, Franken, Bereich, W* The heart of the Franken region, vineyards along the Main, particularly around WÜRZBURG and Escherndorf. Leading producers: *see* WÜRZBURG.

MAINE, CH DU *France, Bordeaux, Graves, R* Langon estate making a fine example of traditional R Graves, with ample structure and a hint of austerity, clearly fashioned for a long life.

MAIPO VALLEY *South America, Chile, R, W* Sub-region of the Central Valley, Chile's most important wine-producing area. Maipo was the first sub-region to be developed and still remains its most concentrated vineyard area. Much Cabernet Sauvignon and Merlot is grown for Rs.

MAIPU *South America, Argentina, R* To the south of the city of Mendoza, a high-elevation area with a cool micro-climate. Good Cabernet Sauvignon and Malbec are grown here.

MAIRE, HENRI *France, Jura, R, W, P, Sp* Large-scale *négociant* and grower (with four estates), making over half of all Jura wine. They make good Arbois R and VIN JAUNE, though their Vin Fou (Sp W) is not a Jura wine, but a brand drawing upon wine from all over France.

MÁLAGA *Spain, Andalucia, DO, W, R* The few remaining vineyards inland from the city of Málaga furnish grapes for the celebrated fortified wine, which is made sweet, medium-sweet and dry. Lágrima is a sweet version made from free-run juice.

Leading producers include: Hijos de Antonio Barcelo, Lopez Hermanos, Scholtz Hermanos.

MALARTIC-LAGRAVIÈRE, CH *France, Bordeaux, Pessac-Léognan, Cru Classé, R, W* The W, made entirely from Sauvignon Blanc, at its best is rich and aromatic, but can be inconsistent. The Rs are supple with ripe tannins. Both gain from a few years in bottle.

MALBEC Red grape grown for dark, tannic, long-lived wine in Cahors (where it is known as Auxerrois). It is excellent in Argentina, where the wines are deeply aromatic (blackcurrants and spices). Used, in small proportions, in the classic red Bordeaux blend, especially in the Médoc. Malbec is also grown (under the name Cot) in the Loire and Chile.

MALCONSORTS, AUX *France, Burgundy, Côte de Nuits, 1er Cru, R* One of the larger vineyards of Vosne-Romanée, abutting Nuits-St-Georges. Aromatic, supple, elegant wines, needing bottle-age to show their best. Leading producers include: Hudelot-Noëllat, Lamarche, Moillard-Grivot.

MALECASSE, CH *France, Bordeaux, Haut-Médoc, Cru Bourgeois, R* Well-placed estate between Margaux and St-Julien, subject to much investment and recently making very good-value claret. A good 1993.

MALESCOT-ST-EXUPÉRY, CH *France, Bordeaux, Médoc, Margaux, 3ème Cru Classé, R* Known for its tannic, backward youth, this wine blossoms with maturity. It is often rated among the top Margaux.

MALLE, CH DE *France, Bordeaux, Sauternes, 2ème Cru Classé, W* One of the lighter Sauternes, easy and rounded, it usually has attractive fruit. More richness is evident in the 1989 and 1990 vintages, as indeed it should be. 1991 also showed improvement.

MALVASIA/MALVOISIE Good-quality aromatic white grape, producing deep-coloured, full W wines, and in some cases Ps, and adding its character to blends. Grown in Italy, Spain and Portugal. Malvasia gave its name to the sweetest style of madeira, malmsey. (The Malvoisie of Switzerland and some parts of France is actually Pinot Gris.)

MANCHA, LA *Spain, Castilla-La Mancha, DO, W, P, R* This is Spain's largest wine zone. In the southern part of the central plateau or Meseta, its high, dry vineyards produce mainly *jovenes* in all three colours, representing good-value everyday wines. Leading producers include: Rodríguez y Berger, Vinícola de Castilla.

MANZANILLA *Spain* The driest and lightest style of sherry, akin to FINO but made only at the coastal town of Sanlúcar de Barrameda, where (makers say) it gains a salty tang from the sea.

MARANGES *France, Burgundy, AOC, R, W* Rather tough and earthy style of (mostly R) wine from three villages, Cheilly-les-Maranges, Dezizies-les-Maranges and Sampigny-les-Maranges, at the southern end of the Côte de Beaune. These are solid but enjoyable Rs for drinking at 5–8 years old. Leading producers include: Mestre Père & Fils.

MARBUZET, CH DE *France, Bordeaux, Médoc, St-Estèphe, R* 2nd wine of Ch Cos d'Estournel.

MARCHES *Italy* Region of central Italy. Quality has much improved here since the mid-1980s. Best known for the lemony W DOC Verdicchio dei Castelli de Jesi and a promising R, Rosso Conerò DOC.

MARCILLAC *France, South-West, AOC, R, P* Spicy, blackcurrant Rs, mostly for drinking young, from Fer Servadou (Mansois) grapes grown in the Aveyron *département*.

MARCONNETS, LES *France, Burgundy, Côte de Beaune, 1er Cru, R* Vineyard at the northernmost end of the commune of Beaune, visible from the A6 *autoroute*. The wines have good colour, are well-structured and are at their best after a few years in bottle. Leading producers include: Bouchard Père & Fils.

MARCUS JAMES *Brazil, R, W* Brand owned by the Canadaigua Wine Company of the USA, producing almost one million cases of varietal wines including Chardonnay, Cabernet Sauvignon, Merlot and white Zinfandel.

MARGARET RIVER *Australia, Western Australia* Top-quality wines are produced in this cool-climate area, ranging from delicious Sémillon (W), Sauvignon Blanc and Chardonnay to powerful Cabernet Sauvignon which matures gracefully. Leading producers include: Brookland, Cullens, Leeuwin, Cape Mentelle, Moss Wood, Pierro, Vasse Felix, Ch Xanadu.

MARGAUX *France, Bordeaux, AOC, R* The southernmost AOC of the Haut-Médoc, with 22 classed growths. Long-lived R wines with a softer, more opulent and perfumed style than those of Pauillac. Leading producers include: Ch'x Brane-Cantenac, d'Issan, Lascombes, Margaux, Palmer, Prieuré Lichine, Rausan-Ségla.

MARGAUX, CH *France, Bordeaux, Médoc, Margaux, 1er Cru Classé, R, W* The beautiful mansion and some of the best vineyard land in the Médoc make this a true 1st Growth, and since 1978 the wine has matched the status. Bottles a century old attest to Margaux's quality. There is also a W, Pavillon Blanc, (good but expensive) from a vineyard of Sauvignon Blanc west of the main estate. 2nd wine: Pavillon Rouge.

MARGRÄFLERLAND *Germany, Baden, Bereich, R, W, P* Baden's southern, and thus warmest, corner, making soft, enjoyable Ws from Gutedel (the local name for Chasselas) and equivalent Rs from Spätburgunder. Leading producer: Schloss Istein.

MARLBOROUGH   *New Zealand, South Island*   Now the largest grape-growing area of New Zealand. Marlborough enjoys a dry, sunny climate especially suited to Ws from Müller-Thurgau, Sauvignon Blanc, Chardonnay and Riesling. Rs, from Cabernet Sauvignon, tend to be herbaceous. Leading producers include: Cloudy Bay, Le Brun, Hunter's, Jackson, Montana.

MARNE ET CHAMPAGNE   *France, Champagne*   One of the region's giants, owning no vineyards but selling 10 million bottles annually. The name is rarely seen, though: it sells mainly as the buyer's own brand, or under a range of labels including Eugène Clicquot, Gauthier, Gieslier and Alfred Rothschild.

MARQUIS D'ALESME BECKER, CH   *France, Bordeaux, Médoc, Margaux, 3ème Cru Classé, R*   This small estate is typical of the Soussans commune in both size and in the solid, earthy quality of its wine.

MARQUIS DE SÉGUR   *France, Bordeaux, Médoc, St-Estèphe, R*   2nd wine of Ch Calon-Ségur.

MARQUIS DE TERME, CH   *France, Bordeaux, Médoc, Margaux, 4ème Cru Classé R*   New ownership a decade ago brought welcome changes in winemaking, which now more closely matches the quality of the well-placed vineyard.

MARSALA   *Italy, Sicily, DOC, W*   One of the world's great fortified wines. Made from local grapes including Catarratto and Inzolia, it can be dry or sweet. The dry version – "Vergine" – must have 18% alcohol and five years' wood ageing. Leading producers include: De Bartoli, Florio, Carlo Pellegrino.

MARSANNAY   *France, Burgundy, AOC, R, P, W*   In the north of the CÔTE DE NUITS, the village of Marsannay-la-Côte has an AOC for solid and well-coloured R burgundies, and one of the best Ps in France: long-lived, dry and intense. Leading producers include: René & Regis Bouvier, Marc Brocot, Dom Charlopin-Parizot, Bruno Clair, Dom Fougeray de Beauclair, Jean-Pierre Guyard, Louis Jadot.

MARSANNE   White grape (often blended with ROUSSANNE) making dry W wines in the northern Rhône; also grown in the Languedoc for *vins de pays*, Switzerland and Australia.

MARTEAU, JACKY   *France, Loire, Touraine, W, R*   Low yields and high quality are the policy at Marteau's small vineyard south of the River Cher. The usual Touraine grapes are grown for varietal wines: Ws from Sauvignon Blanc, Pineau d'Aunis and Chardonnay; Rs from Gamay and Cabernet Franc.

MARTIN BROTHERS   *USA, California, San Luis Obispo, R, W*   American wines with Italian flavours: the prime Piedmontese grape Nebbiolo is a popular R, with its tar, violet and pomegranate fruit. A supple dry W from Chenin Blanc is distinctive, and a rare Vin Santo is made from Malvasia Bianca grapes.

MARTINENS, CH   *France, Bordeaux, Margaux, Cru Bourgeois, R*   This is a Merlot-dominated vineyard: recent investment has improved an already good, consistent Margaux.

MARTÍNEZ, BODEGAS FAUSTINO   *Spain, Rioja, R, W, P*   Good-quality wines come from this family-owned *bodega*. Both their R and W wines make attractive early drinking, and their *reservas* and *gran reservas* age very well.

MARTINI & ROSSI   *Italy, Piedmont, W, R, Sp*   Largest producer of Asti *spumante* and vermouth; also Sp Riesling and Riserva Montelera Brut by the *metodo classico*.

MARTINI, LOUIS M   *USA, California, Napa, R, W, Sp*   Family-run winery known for Cabernet Sauvignons of finesse and ageability. Martini's Muscato Amabile is a treat: a low-alcohol, fresh, floral, grape-tasting sweet Sp W.

MARTINOLLES, DOM DE   *France, Midi, Limoux, W, Sp*   Owned by the Vergnes family, this is the best of the local private producers of this up-and-coming Sp wine. They have 65ha from which to make stylish Crémant de Limoux and Blanquette de Limoux, and some still W *vin de pays*.

MARYLAND   *USA*   Boordy, founded by Phillip Wagner in 1945, led the way in modern winemaking here: now the state's eastern corner, near Virginia, has several good wineries. The best zone so far is CATOCIN (a VA), in the mountains west of Baltimore. Leading producers include: BOORDY, Catocin Vineyards (Chardonnay and Cabernet Sauvignon), Montbray.

MAS AMIEL   *France, Midi, VDN*   Large estate at Maury planted with 90% Grenache Noir. This *vin doux naturel* is sold in three versions: 6-, 10- and 15-year-old. The last is best, with its flavour of fruit, nuts and prunes, not unlike an old tawny port.

MAS BLANC, DOM DE   *France, Midi, Banyuls, VDN*   The best producer of Banyuls *vins doux naturels*, in three styles. A vintage wine made in top years is aged for a year in 5-hl barrels; a second style has 6 years in 40-hl casks, topped up every 6 months. The third style is made in a kind of *solera* system and is bottled after 6 years.

MAS DE DAUMAS GASSAC   *France, Midi, Languedoc, R, W, Sp*   Estate near Montpellier which produces *vins de pays* at *Grand Cru* quality (and price) levels: some of the most interesting wines in France. Daumas Gassac's success has boosted the quality image of the LANGUEDOC as a whole. A cool microclimate and unusual red glacial powder and limestone soils combine to create unique *terroirs*. Grapes are mainly Cabernet Sauvignon for R and Chardonnay for W, but with a wide selection of others such as Merlot, Syrah, Pinot Noir, Viognier and Gros Manseng. The Rs need bottle-age: up to a decade in good vintages. The Ws are ready sooner. There is also a Sp P wine and a fluctuating list of other wines.

MAS DE LA DAME *France, Provence, Coteaux d'Aix-en-Provence Les Baux, R, P* The 55-ha vineyard here has a high proportion of Grenache, but the wines also have a good backbone of Syrah and Cabernet Sauvignon. There are two Rs: Cuvée Réserve and Cuvée Gourmande, and the Rosé du Mas is very fruity.

MASI *Italy, Veneto, W, R* Top estate for R wines from Valpolicello. Valpolicellas include Amarone Mazzano, Amarone Campolongo de Torbe and Recioto Mezzanella. *Vini da tavola* include Toar and Campo Fiorin.

MASSACHUSETTS *USA* State with a dozen wineries, most close to the ocean, growing classic and native grapes. Leading producer: Chicama Vineyards.

MASTROBERARDINO *Italy, Southern Italy, Campania, W, R, P* High-standard wines from near Naples include the finest Fiano di Avellino (W), Greco di Tufo (W) and Taurasi (R). An elegant Lachryma Christi del Vesuvio DOC is made in R, W and P versions.

MATANZAS CREEK *USA, California, Sonoma, W, R* There is a wide range here, but the focus is on Chardonnay, rich with butterscotch and vanilla, accented by clove, apple and licorice notes. Also a lean, lasting Merlot R and a Sauvignon, its W equivalent.

MATARO See MOURVÈDRE.

MÁTRAALJA *Hungary* Large and diverse district in the northern part of Hungary. Mostly W wines of all styles from Olaszrisling, Rizlingszilváni and Tramini grapes among others. Also the location of the Gyöngyös estate, where Australian-trained pioneer winemaker Hugh Ryman oversees the making of clean, crisp Ws from Sauvignon Blanc and Chardonnay.

MATUA VALLEY WINES *New Zealand, North Island, W, R, Sp* One of the country's most innovative wineries. Wide range includes a good Sp called "M". The top-of-the-range Ararimu wines include Chardonnay and Cabernet Sauvignon.

MAUCAILLOU, CH *France, Bordeaux, Moulis, Cru Bourgeois, R* Source of elegant, modern-style wine from a modern *chai* and lots of new oak. Lavish facilities for visitors.

MAUFOUX, PROSPER *France, Burgundy, Côte d'Or, R, W* This Santenay *négociant* firm ages all its wines, R and W, in oak, with good results.

MAULE VALLEY *Chile, South America, W, R* Sub-region of the Central Valley, Chile's major wine-producing area. Developed and expanded in the 1980s, when it was found that Sauvignon Blanc, Merlot and Chardonnay are well suited to the cool climate.

MAURY *France, Midi, AOC, VDN* Mainly R *vin doux naturel* from Grenache Noir grapes, from a tiny AOC within Rivesaltes. It is aged for at least two years, and up to 15, before sale. Some is made in the *rancio* (oxidized) style. Leading producer: Mas Amiel.

MAUVEZIN, CH *France, Bordeaux, St-Emilion, Grand Cru Classé, R* This very small estate has, unusually for St-Emilion, almost 50% Cabernet Franc in the blend. New oak is very important here. A perfumed, elegant wine with supple fruit.

MAVRUD Red grape native to Bulgaria; it is difficult to grow, low-yielding and late-ripening, but when fully ripe and well made it gives dense, tannic and long-lasting wine that can be compared to that from MOURVÈDRE.

MAZIS-CHAMBERTIN See CHAMBERTIN.

MAZOYÈRES-CHAMBERTIN See CHAMBERTIN.

MAZUELO A Spanish name for CARIGNAN.

MCLAREN VALE *Australia, Victoria* To the south of Adelaide, the Vale's name was originally for R wines. While it still yields distinctive Shiraz and Cabernet Sauvignon Rs, many of its vineyards now make very good W wines, too. Leading producers include: Chapel Hill, D'Arenberg, Garrett, Ingoldby, Geoff Merrill, Normans, Wirra Wirra.

MCWILLIAM'S MOUNT PLEASANT *Australia, New South Wales, Hunter Valley R, W* Family-run firm producing top-quality wines, including Elizabeth Sémillon (W), only released when it is 6 years old.

MÉDOC *France, Bordeaux, AOC, R* Clarets from the Left Bank of the Gironde and Garonne rivers, made with a high proportion of Cabernet Sauvignon: refined, austere but appetizing, and long-lived. Within the Médoc peninsula, there is a hierarchy of appellations:
Haut-Médoc (which see) is the southern (better) half of the Médoc. Within Haut-Médoc are MOULIS, LISTRAC and the four renowned riverside appellations: ST-ESTÈPHE, PAUILLAC, ST-JULIEN and MARGAUX.
AOC Médoc covers the northern part of the peninsula. Here there is less of the vital well-drained gravel soil found in the Haut-Médoc. Wines from AOC Médoc typically have less Cabernets and more Merlot, do not need such long keeping (2–5 years) and are good value. Leading AOC Médoc producers include: Ch'x la Cardonne, Greysac, Loudenne, Les Ormes Sorbet, Patache d'Aux, Potensac, La Tour de By, La Tour St-Bonnet.

MEERLUST ESTATE *South Africa, Stellenbosch, R* A beautiful, R-wine only estate where Italian winemaker Giorgio Dalle Cia produces a superbly rich Merlot and a delicious bordeaux blend, Rubicon.

MELINI *Italy, Tuscany, Chianti, R* The third-largest Chianti producer after Ruffino and Antinori. Single-vineyard Chianti Classicos include La Selvanella and Terrarossa.

MELON DE BOURGOGNE/MUSCADET   White grape grown for the light, dry wine of the western Loire, also called Muscadet. Sometimes (erroneously) called Pinot Blanc in California.

MENDOCINO   *USA, California*   County on the north coast of California, with vineyards in **ANDERSON VALLEY** and Ukiah Valley. Rs do well: Zinfandels, Cabernet Sauvignon, Merlot. Anderson Valley is becoming a Sp wine centre.

MENDOZA   *Argentina, South America, R, W, P*   Argentina's winemaking centre is here in the province of Mendoza, some 960km west of Buenos Aires. Responsible for 70% of Argentina's wine.

MENETOU-SALON   *France, Loire, AOC, R, P, W*   Small upper-Loire wine district around villages west of Sancerre, making mainly Sauvignon Blanc W, but also Pinot Noir Rs and Ps. Can be good value. Leading producers include: Chavet, Pelle, Teiller.

MÉNTRIDA   *Spain, Castilla-La Mancha, DO, P, R*   One of four Castilla-La Mancha wine zones, south-west of Madrid, Méntrida is now a mass-production zone – but with scope for great potential. Leading producers include: Bodegas Valdeoro.

MERCIER   *France, Champagne*   The LVMH group owns this maker of good, reliable, medium-bodied champagne: particularly popular in France.

MERCIER, CH   *France, Bordeaux, Côtes de Bourg, R*   Perfumed and interesting claret from old vines.

MERCREDIÈRE   *France, Loire, Muscadet, W*   The Futeul family, who are also *négociants*, produce full and powerful Muscadets from 36ha complete with an ancient castle on the banks of the River Sèvre.

MERCUREY   *France, Burgundy, AOC, R, W*   One of the main villages of the **CÔTE CHALONNAISE**, Mercurey makes predominantly R wine from Pinot Noir (and some W from Chardonnay). Good Mercurey can be well-priced and interesting burgundy at 4–6 years. Leading producers include: Dom de Chamerose, Chartron & Trébuchet, Faiveley, Michel Juillot, Mercurey co-op, Antonin Rodet/Ch de Chamirey, Hugues de Suremain.

MEREDYTH VINEYARDS   *USA, Virginia, W, R*   The state's oldest winery, in Middleburg, skilfully produces wines from hybrids and classic grapes. Decent Merlot R recently joined the consistently fine Seyval Blanc.

MERIDIAN   *USA, California, San Luis Obispo, W, R*   This large winery concentrates on a creamy, melon and vanilla Santa Barbara Chardonnay. Cabernet Sauvignon, Syrah and Zinfandel Rs are also made from the Home Vineyard.

MERITAGE   *USA*   Made-up term for a bordeaux-style wine from a blend of the same grapes used in Bordeaux, particularly Cabernet Sauvignon and Merlot for Rs.

MERLOT   The classic red grape of St-Emilion and Pomerol, also used in Médoc blends – and now in southern French *vins de pays*. Unblended, Merlot has a rich colour, a direct aroma and soft, earthy, fruity taste, appreciated in Switzerland, north Italy and increasingly in eastern European and New World vineyards.

METAIREAU, LOUIS   *France, Loire, Muscadet, W*   Nine producers, with 100ha, market their top-quality wines under Metaireau's label. The wines undergo rigorous tastings during vinification and before bottling (*sur lie* in the growers' cellars). Metaireau's own estate is Dom du Grand Mouton.

MÉTHODE CHAMPENOISE   *France*   The method of making sparkling wine that was developed in Champagne in France and has been copied the world over. A secondary fermentation in the bottle results in bubbles of carbon dioxide becoming trapped in the wine. Following an EU directive, the term may no longer appear on the label of any wine from outside the region, although the technique is in use world-wide. Alternative terms include classic method and traditional method.

MÉTHODE RURALE   *France*   Sparkling wine method: the wine is bottled before fermentation is over, producing a sparkle.

METODO CLASSICO, METODO TRADIZIONALE   *Italy*   Terms used in Italy for the MÉTHODE CHAMPENOISE technique for production of sparkling wines.

MEURSAULT   *France, Burgundy, AOC, W, R*   Côte de Beaune village famous for W wines of powerful, persistent flavour and good ability to age. There are no *Grands Crus*, but a large number of *Premiers Crus*. Leading producers include: Bouchard Père & Fils, Comte Lafon, Michelot, Prieur, Ropiteau.

MEXICO   *Central America*   Although Mexico boasts the New World's oldest vineyards, today its climate is considered too hot to be hospitable to wine grapes and the top priority is growing grapes for brandy. There are more than 70,000ha of vines and close to 80% of the wine-grape harvest goes directly into brandy or vermouth production, although table wine production has been on the increase since 1980.

MEYNEY, CH   *France, Bordeaux, St-Estèphe, Cru Bourgeois, R*   The Cordier firm of *négociants* own Meyney and ensure its high standards and wide distribution. One of the best *Crus Bourgeois*, and one of the classic St-Estèphes.

MICHEL, LOUIS   *France, Burgundy, Chablis, W*   The great exponent of unoaked Chablis. Mainly *Premiers Crus*: quintessential Chablis with the classic nerve, steeliness and mineral quality. Michel also uses the label Domaine de la Tour Vaubourg.

MICHIGAN   *USA*   Lake shores provide warm conditions in this Mid-West state for good classic-variety wines. Leading producers include: Ch Grand Traverse, St Julian.

MIGUEL TORRES *Chile, R, W, Sp* Highly innovative venture begun in 1979 by Spain's Torres family: a key stage in Chile's wine renaissance. Miguel Torres concentrates on Sauvignon Blanc and Cabernet Sauvignon, in addition to a Sp wine, Brut Nature. Wines are mainly destined for export.

MILDARA-BLASS *Australia, R, W* Mildara's merger with Wolf Blass unites two of Australia's best-known names. Production, centred in South Australia, includes a wide range of multi-regional, multi-varietal blends such as the succulent R Jamieson's Run. Quality wines are made in Coonawarra and other areas.

MILLBROOK VINEYARDS *USA, New York, Hudson River Valley, W, R* At Millbrook, east of the Hudson, John Dyson grows only classic varieties. Half the production is Chardonnay, a barrel-fermented Reserve. He also features Cabernet Franc and Pinot Noir Rs, and is experimenting with Rhône and Italian varieties.

MILLERIOUX, PAUL *France, Loire, Sancerre, W, R* Clos de Roy (W) and Côte de Champtin (R) are the top wines from Millerioux's well-regarded estate in Crézancy-en-Sancerre. Both are matured in wood.

MILLÉSIME *France* Term meaning year; vintage.

MILLET, CH *France, Bordeaux, Graves, R* This large Portets estate is best known for its fruity if not especially complex Rs, which are best drunk young.

MINERVOIS *France, Midi, AOC, R, P, W* Mostly R-wine appellation: a large and varied area with an improving reputation thanks to better vinification and grapes: eg Grenache, Syrah and Mourvèdre for Rs. W Minervois is being improved by Marsanne and Roussane in addition to Macabeo and Bourboulenc. Leading producers include: Daniel Domergue, Ch Fabas, Ch de Gourgazaud, La Livinière co-op, Dom Ste-Eulalie.

MINNESOTA *USA* Cold winters hamper vine-growing, but ALEXIS BAILLY and a cooperative of small growers keep trying (with some success) with hybrids.

MIREVAL, MUSCAT DE *France, Midi, AOC, VDN* This *vin doux naturel* zone adjoins better-known Frontignan. Very similar wine.

MISSION The name of this R-wine grape variety tells its story: it was grown at the Catholic mission stations of California when the Mexicans ruled. Until the late 19th century it made most California wine, but it is now in decline. Its wine is unimpressive.

MISSION-HAUT-BRION, CH LA *France, Bordeaux, Pessac-Léognan, Cru Classé, R* The same owners as Ch HAUT-BRION, yet the two wines are very different. Rich and tannic, La Mission stresses power and depth of flavour. Sold at 1st-growth prices, it is often worth what is asked.

MISSION HILL   *Canada, British Columbia, W, R*   New Zealand winemaker John Simes makes rich New World-style Chardonnay and some interesting W blends.

MISSISSIPPI   *USA*   Native American grapes are the ones to thrive here, making wine with a Southern accent.

MISSOURI   *USA*   Four VAs and 30 wineries represent the revival of a century-old tradition. Most vines are hybrids, though quality can be good, with a few classic *vinifera* vines. Leading producers include: Hermannhof, Mount Pleasant, Stone Hill.

MITTELHAARDT/DEUTSCHE WEINSTRASSE   *Germany, Pfalz, Bereich, W, R*   The district which forms the heart of the Pfalz, making good, even great Ws, and some good Rs, in villages such as FORST and DEIDESHEIM. East-facing slopes and a dry climate give conditions comparable to Alsace. Riesling is joined for Ws by Silvaner, Gewürztraminer, Rulander and other grapes. Leading producers include: Basserman-Jordan, Von Buhl, Bürklin-Wolf, Weingut Dr Deinhard, Weingut Pfeffingen.

MITTELRHEIN   *Germany, Anbaugebiet, W*   The Rhein valley vineyards north of the Rheingau, lining the Rhine Gorge and side-valleys. W wines, the best from Riesling, are made in scenic but often inaccessible sites. Good, if a touch earthy, wines.

MOELLEUX   *France*   Describes sweet white wines, particularly those of Vouvray and other Loire vineyards.

MOET & CHANDON   *France, Champagne*   The largest vineyard owner in Champagne, with 558ha. The NV is the biggest-selling champagne worldwide, although quality has been variable. The vintage wine is consistently fine and Moët also produce one of Champagne's most prestigious wines, the luxury *cuvée* Dom Pérignon.

MOILLARD-GRIVOT   *France, Burgundy, Côte d'Or, R, W*   Reliable *négociant* and vineyard owner based in Nuits-St-Georges.

MOLDOVA   The most western-influenced of the former USSR's winegrowing republics. Its 160,000–200,000ha of vineyards have more European varieties than any other republic, with huge tracts planted to Chardonnay, Cabernet Sauvignon, Sauvignon Blanc, Aligoté and the Pinot family. Native varieties include the rich and spicy Saperavi (R) and the somewhat neutral Rkatsiteli (W). The best wines come from the centre of the country and along the Dniester River. Enormous potential, particularly for Rs. Names to look for include the long-lived Cabernet-dominated Negru de Purkar R.

MOLISE   *Italy*   In central Italy, one of the smallest and least important wine regions. The main grapes grown are Montepulciano for R and Trebbiano for W. The local DOC, Biferno, is for R, P and W wines.

MOLLEX, MAISON   *France, Savoie, Seyssel, W, R, Sp*   The appellation's leading grower, with vineyards which include the noted Clos de la Péclatte. Makers of still W from Roussette, R (AOC Savoie), and Sp Seyssel. Methods are traditional, results good.

MOMMESSIN   *France, Burgundy, Côte d'Or, R, W*   Large *négociant* based at Mâcon, with a range of Beaujolais, Mâconnais and other wines; also sole owner of the Côte de Nuits *Grand Cru* Clos de LAMBRAYS.

MONBAZILLAC   *France, South-West, AOC, W*   Great sweet W wine of the Dordogne; like Sauternes, it is made from Sémillon, Sauvignon Blanc and Muscadelle. True quality comes from NOBLE ROT. Leading producers include: Ch de Monbazillac, Ch du Treuil de Nailhac.

MONBRISON, CH   *France, Bordeaux, Margaux, Cru Bourgeois, R*   A small vineyard in Arsac with a good name for solid, elegant wines which repay ageing.

MONDAVI, ROBERT   *USA, California, Napa, W, R*   Both company and eponymous founder are among the vital forces in the American wine industry. Famed for its Fumé Blanc (oak-aged Sauvignon Blanc); the Oakville winery also makes structured Cabernet Sauvignon, fruity Chardonnays and supple Pinot Noirs. Reserve wines are among the best made in California. Affordable table wines come from the Woodbridge winery and Mondavi also owns Vichon and Byron.

MONGEARD-MUGNERET, DOM   *France, Burgundy, AOC, R, W*   Expanding domain with holdings of *Grand* and *Premier Cru* vineyards, producing concentrated R wines of quality.

MONIN   *France, Savoie, Bugey, R, W, Sp*   Most important maker of the wines of this VDQS zone: W Roussette de Bugey with a good amount of Chardonnay, R from Mondeuse, and Sp W. Good wines, but most are drunk locally.

MONNIER, DOM JEAN & FILS   *France, Burgundy, Côte d'Or, R, W*   Top-quality R and W wine using traditional methods, from Meursault, Pommard and Puligny.

MONT BOUQUET, DU   *France, Vin de Pays, R*   Zone in the Gard, southern France, making Rs from traditional grapes, often with some added Syrah for spice and interest.

MONT DE MILIEU   *France, Burgundy, Chablis, 1er Cru*   This south-facing vineyard is tucked into a side-valley, earning its *1er Cru* status with powerful, age-worthy Chablis.

MONT-REDON, DOM DE   *France, Rhône, Châteauneuf-du-Pape, R, W*   Reliable producer of R and W Châteauneuf; the R ages well, the W is among the best made.

MONT TAUCH, COOPERATIVE DES PRODUCTEURS DU   *France, Midi, Fitou, R*   The most important of the appellation's co-ops, in the village of Tuchan. It makes six qualities of Fitou, including a selection of the best *terroir* and oldest vines, and wines from various individual domaines.

MONTAGNE ST-EMILION *France, Bordeaux, AOC, R* The largest and probably best of the St-Emilion satellite appellations, sited close to the border with Pomerol. The wines, from varying proportions of Cabernet Sauvignon, Cabernet Franc, Merlot, Malbec and Carmenère, can be supple and fruity with some finesse and good ageing potential. Leading producers include: Ch'x Calon, Croix-Beauséjour, Laroze-Bayard, des Laurets, Maison Blanche, Roudier, La Tour Mont d'Or, Tour-Musset, des Tours, Vernay Bonfort.

MONTAGNY *France, Burgundy, AOC, W, R* Southern village of the CÔTE CHALONNAISE, producing good and sometimes age-worthy Chardonnay Ws. All wines that achieve 11.5° can be labelled *Premier Cru*. Leading producers include: Buxy co-op, Louis Latour, Antonin Rodet, Ch da la Saule, Jean Vachet.

MONTALIVET, CH *France, Bordeaux, Graves W, R* Wines of great consistency: Sémillon-dominated, oaky Ws and juicy Rs. Both should be enjoyed when quite young.

MONTANA WINES *New Zealand, North Island W, R, Sp* The country's largest wine group is also one of the most innovative, and was the first to plant Sauvignon Blanc in Marlborough. Working with Deutz champagne they make the top-quality Sp, Deutz Marlborough Cuvée.

MONTÉE DE TONNERRE *France, Burgundy, Chablis, 1er Cru* Hill of vines next to the *Grands Crus* of Chablis, making wine almost as good and worth bottle-age. Chapelot, Pied d'Aloue and Côte de Bréchain are plots within Montée de Tonnerre.

MONTELENA, CH *USA, California, Napa, W, R* The old stone château, north of Calistoga, excels in richly textured Chardonnays, firm blackberry and blackcurrant Cabernet Sauvignons, zingy, raspberry and peppercorn Zinfandels, and velvety, apricot-laden off-dry Johannisberg Rieslings.

MONTEPULCIANO D'ABRUZZO *Italy, Abruzzo, DOC, R* The best of these good-value Rs are very full-flavoured with lots of warm, ripe fruit. Leading producers include: Barone Cornacchia, Illuminati, Emidio Pepe, Valentini.

MONTEREY *USA, California* County of California's central coast, sunny but dry, yielding good everyday wines from irrigated vineyards in the Salinas Valley, and quality ones from Arroyo Seco, Carmel Valley, CHALONE and Santa Lucia Highlands.

MONTES *Chile, R, W* Estate formed by four partners in 1988, set in the MAIPO VALLEY. The vineyards grow mainly Cabernet

Sauvignon and Merlot for Rs, followed by Sauvignon Blanc and Chardonnay for Ws. Nogales is the label for lower-priced wines, Villa Montes the top-of-the-range export brand.

MONTEVIÑA *USA, California, Sierra Foothills, R* This Amador County winery focuses on Italian-style Rs, including California's most reliable Barbera. New plantings of Nebbiolo share space with trials of Sangiovese, Refosco and Aleatico.

MONTHÉLIE *France, Burgundy, AOC, R, W* Mainly R wines come from this village between Volnay and Meursault in the Côte de Beaune. Increasingly good-value, fragrant, well-structured wines are made from Pinot Noir grapes. Leading producers include: Paul Garaudet, Comte Lafon, Ch de Monthélie.

MONTICELLO *USA, Virginia, VA* Wine zone named after Jefferson's estate, where vines were planted two centuries ago (but without great success). Today, Chardonnay and bordeaux-style Rs are being made. Leading producers include: Montdomaine.

MONTILLA-MORILES *Spain, Andalucia, DO, W* Andalucian wine zone in province of Córdoba, producing *jovenes*, fortified and unfortified wines. The fortifieds, which can be sweet or dry, are similar in style to sherry. Leading producers include: Alvear, Pérez Barquero.

MONTLOUIS *France, Loire, AOC, W, Sp* Still and Sp (*mousseux* and *pétillant*) Ws, from medium-dry to sweet, made across the River Loire from Vouvray. Leading producers include: M Berger, Deletang Père et Fils.

MONTRACHET *France, Burgundy, AOC, W* Côte de Beaune *Grand Cru* which makes the most expensive and often the best W wine in all of Burgundy. Dense, buttery and rich, with a backbone of acidity that means it reaches its potential after 10 years and allows it to last in bottle for 20 years or more. On the slope above Montrachet is the *Grand Cru* of CHEVALIER-MONTRACHET, below it the *Grand Cru* of BÂTARD-MONTRACHET. Leading producers include: Bouchard Père & Fils, Dom de la Romanée-Conti, Drouhin, Leflaive, Jacques Prieur.

MONTRAVEL *France, South-West, AOC, W* Little-known appellation near Bergerac for dry W wine, with sub-zones Côtes de Montravel for medium-sweet and Haut-Montravel for sweet W wines.

MONTROSE, CH *France, Bordeaux, Médoc, St-Estèphe, 2ème Cru Classé, R* The solid, long-lasting wines of this château suggest a St-Estèphe version of Latour, as does the site – though the style has softened since the 1989. In good vintages, among the Médoc's best wines.

MORAVIA *Czech Republic* One of the two Czech regions, the other being Bohemia. Moravia enjoys a slightly warmer climate and has a greater area under vine. R varieties include Frankovka

(Germany's Limberger) and St-Laurent, plus a little Pinot. Ws, which can be good, include Pinot Blanc, Traminer, Laski Riesling and the native, aromatic Irsay Oliver; good Sp wine is also made.

MOREAU, J-J *France, Burgundy, Chablis, W* The largest *négociant* house in Chablis, making sound wines, although not always very exciting ones.

MOREY-ST-DENIS *France, Burgundy, AOC, R* Long-lived R burgundies in the classic, solid Côte de Nuits style. Those from the five *Grands Crus* (CLOS DE TART, CLOS ST-DENIS, CLOS DE LA ROCHE, CLOS DES LAMBRAYS, BONNES MARES) can be great, while the *Premiers Crus* and village wines offer comparatively good value. Leading producers include: Dujac, G Lignier, Roumier, Rousseau.

MORGEOT *France, Burgundy, Côte de Beaune, 1er Cru, R, W* Located in Chassagne-Montrachet around the Abbaye de Morgeot, this vineyard produces fine, full-bodied Ws and deeply-coloured, well-structured Rs. Leading producers include: Blanc-Gagnard, Jean-Noël Gagnard, Olivier Leflaive.

MORGON *France, Burgundy, AOC, R* Beaujolais *cru* whose best vineyards share distinctive slate soil, making particularly rich and full, deep-coloured, long-lived wines that develop exotic fruit flavours in age. However, Morgons from less favoured sites can be unsubtle and heavy. Leading producers include: Jonchet, Passot, Savoye, Dom de Thizy.

MORNINGTON PENINSULA *Australia, Victoria* Sited south of Melbourne, the cool maritime climate here is proving ideal for winemaking. Results include delicate, elegant W Chardonnays, and Rs from Pinot Noir, Shiraz, Merlot and Cabernet Sauvignon. Leading producers include: Dromana, Elgee Park, Stoniers Merricks.

MOROCCO *North Africa, R, P* Wine here is made with a more commercial approach than in neighbouring Algeria. Morocco has 12 wine regions in all, the best and biggest of which is Meknès and Fèz, a high-altitude area beneath the Atlas Mountains, specializing in rich and chewy R wine. Lighter R wines are produced around Rabat, and P wine is made in the regions of Gharb and Semmour.

MOSEL-SAAR-RUWER *Germany, Anbaugebiet, W* The wine region taking in the Mosel valley plus its tributaries the SAAR and RUWER. The main valley is divided into (north to south) the Bereichs ZELL, BERNKASTEL, Obermosel and Moseltor. The latter two are of limited interest. Most Mosel wines are W; the best are from Riesling, but many wines at the cheaper end are made from Müller-Thurgau.

MOSELLAND *Germany, Mosel, W* The enormous cooperative of the central Mosel, representing many small growers, makes reliable wine at every quality and price level.

MOSELLE, VIN DE   *France, Alsace, VDQS, W, R*   Mainly W wines from France's most northerly vineyards, along the upper Moselle valley. Main grapes are Rivaner (Müller-Thurgau) and Auxerrois for Ws; and Pinot Noir for Rs.

MOUEIX, J-P   *France, Bordeaux, St-Emilion & Pomerol*   Well-known firm of *négociants* in Libourne, Bordeaux, owning or part-owning several châteaux in Pomerol, St-Emilion and adjoining districts. They produce reliable blended wines from all these AOCs. Pioneers of the revival of Fronsac, they are now active, too, in the Côtes de Castillon.

MOULIN DE DUHART   *France, Bordeaux, Médoc, Pauillac, R*   2nd wine of Ch Duhart-Milon-Rothschild.

MOULIN DES COSTES   *France, Provence, Bandol, R, W*   The Bunan family own 75ha of vineyards, making this one of the appellation's leading domaines. Rs, blended from different estates, are 65% Mourvèdre, 14% Grenache and 6% Syrah. Cuvée Spéciale, which is made only in the best years, has a higher proportion of Mourvèdre. Also a Cabernet Sauvignon made as Vin de Pays de Mont-Caume.

MOULIN DU CADET, CH   *France, Bordeaux, St-Emilion, Grand Cru Classé, R*   This estate is now managed by Ets Jean-Pierre **MOUEIX**. The once fairly delicate style of wine is becoming richer, with more body and staying-power.

MOULIN-À-VENT   *France, Burgundy, AOC, R*   Most serious, most expensive, most age-worthy of the Beaujolais *crus*: deep ruby-R, powerful, well-structured wines that can still impress after 10 years. Leading producers include: Dom la Chevalière, Jean George, Hubert Lapierre, Hospices de Romanèche-Thorins, Dom des Vignes de Tremblay.

MOULIN-À-VENT, CH   *France, Bordeaux, Moulis, Cru Bourgeois, R*   Good, long-maturing wine in the Moulis style.

MOULIS   *France, Bordeaux, AOC, R*   Solid, dark, long-lived Médoc Rs from an inland commune, neighbour to **LISTRAC**. Leading producers include: Ch'x Chasse-Spleen, Dutruch-Grand-Poujeaux, Gressier-Grand-Poujeaux, Maucaillou, Moulin-à-Vent, Poujeaux.

MOUNT BARKER-FRANKLAND   *Australia, Western Australia*   Beautiful cool-climate area which has recently gained a fine reputation for its wines, ranging from Ws from Chardonnay, Sauvignon Blanc and Riesling to Rs from Pinot Noir, Shiraz, Cabernet Sauvignon and Malbec. Leading producers include: Alkoomi, Goundrey, Plantagenet.

MOUNT LANGI GHIRAN   *Australia, Victoria, Grampians, R*   Trevor Mast is the maker here of long-lived Shiraz Rs which bear comparison with the best of the Rhône.

MOUNT PLEASANT VINEYARD *USA, Missouri, W, R* Historic winery founded in 1881, revived in 1968, now producing up to 20,000 cases of varietals and sparkling wines. The Vidal Blanc is often top-notch, along with Seyval Blanc, a delicate Riesling W and port-style fortified wine.

MOUNT VEEDER *USA, California, VA* Area of hill vineyards to the west of Napa Valley, with well-drained volcanic soils yielding good Cabernet Sauvignons and Chardonnays. Leading producers include: Hess Collection, Mayacamas, Mount Veeder, Ch Potelle.

MOURVÈDRE Sturdy, dark, aromatic red grape, usually blended with Syrah, Grenache and Cinsaut in the southern Rhône, Provence and Midi. Known as Mataro in California and Australia. Spanish in origin, but unknown there now.

MOUTON-ROTHSCHILD, CH *France, Bordeaux, Médoc, Pauillac, 1er Cru Classé, R* The late Baron Philippe de Rothschild and (since his death) his daughter Philippine have made Mouton the 1st Growth the Baron always believed it to be (he attained its promotion from 2nd in 1973). Cabernet Sauvignon dominates in the vineyard, and the wine style is full, even opulent. A superb museum of works of art showing wine is housed at the estate.

MOUTONNE, LA *France, Burgundy, Chablis* See VAUDÉSIR.

MUDGEE *Australia, New South Wales* Not as well known as the Hunter Valley, this region also produces good Sémillon (W) and Shiraz (R), plus Chardonnay and Cabernet Sauvignon. Leading producers include: Botobolar, Craigmoor, Huntington, Stein.

MUGA, BODEGAS *Spain, Rioja, R, W, P, Sp* Absolutely top quality wines are made along very traditional lines at this leading Rioja *bodega*. The emphasis is on Rs, although W, P and Sp wines are also produced.

MULDERBOSCH VINEYARDS *South Africa, Stellenbosch, R, W* Larry Jacobs produced his first wines in 1991 but has already achieved international status for both his Ws: a richly exotic Sauvignon Blanc and mouthwatering, buttery Chardonnay.

MULLER, DE *Spain, Catalonia, Priorato, R, W, P* Established in 1851, De Muller makes hefty, long-lived R wines. A wide range of other wines includes a delicate Moscatel Seco, and the rare but delectable *solera*-aged Priorato wines.

MÜLLER-CATOIR *Germany, Pfalz, W* Grower whose wide range of grapes, including Gewürztraminer and Grauburgunder, and very traditional techniques make individual, powerful wines.

MÜLLER-SCHARZHOF, EGON *Germany, Saar, W* Superb, long-lived and expensive Riesling wine (in warm vintages), hand-crafted from the fruit of great vineyards including the noble Scharzhofberg hill at Wiltingen.

MÜLLER-THURGAU   Germany's most-planted grape (a crossing: Riesling x Silvaner), producing fairly neutral sweet or dry white wine. Makes ordinary wine in Hungary; better, floral-scented examples in New Zealand, northern Italy, Austria, England and Luxembourg.

MUMM   *France, Champagne*   The largest **GRANDE MARQUE**, though not the top. Its best-known wine, the NV Cordon Rouge, which has gone through some rough patches, is widely exported. At its best it is attractive, with a delicately fruity palate. The prestige *cuvée*, René Lalou, is very fine.

MURRAY RIVER VALLEY   *Australia, Victoria*   Region yielding more than 80% of Victoria's grapes. Everyday Ws are its life blood.

MURRIETA, BODEGAS MARQUÉS DE   *Spain, Rioja, R, W*   Established in 1870, this Rioja pioneer uses wholly traditional methods. The Rs are oaky, sturdy but capable of ageing to finesse; the Ws are deep and golden but dry in the traditional Rioja style. A small range includes Marqués de Murrieta (R, W) and the expensive, memorable *reserva* Castillo Ygay (R, W), which is only released when mature.

MURRUMBIDGEE   *Australia, New South Wales*   Production in this large, irrigated semi-desert region is mainly bulk Ws, with Sémillon the dominant grape. The only R of significance is Shiraz. Sweet W botrytized Sémillon is a speciality.

MUSAR, CH   *Lebanon, R, W*   Owned by Serge Hochar, who trained in France. Produces top-quality, opulent, long-lived R wine from Cabernet Sauvignon, Cinsaut and Syrah and fine Ws from Chardonnay and Sauvignon Blanc. Despite being in a war zone, 1984 was the only year he did not succeed in making wine.

MUSCADELLE   Aromatic white grape used blended in some white bordeaux, and for rich dessert Liqueur Tokays in Australia.

MUSCADET   *France, Loire, AOC, W*   From the mouth of the Loire, near Nantes. Good Muscadet is fresh, crisp and dry: poor ones are very acidic. With a very few exceptions, these are wines to drink young: the year after they are made. The grape is Melon de Bourgogne, now usually known simply as Muscadet. The region divides into three AOCs:
Muscadet is made mainly in the west, in fairly small quantities.
Muscadet des Coteaux de la Loire comes from east of Nantes.
Muscadet de Sèvre-et-Maine is by far the largest, and best, appellation, from areas around two valleys south-east of Nantes. It is best, fresh and with a hint of bubbles, when it is bottled *sur lie*: straight from the cask, without first racking it off its lees. This gives a rich yeasty flavour as well as a slight natural sparkle. *Sur lie* wines will say so on the label. Leading producers include: Chéreau-Carré, Donatien Bahuaud, Ch de la Galissonnière, Marquis de Goulaine, Louis Metaireau, Ch la Noë, Marcel Sautejeau, Sauvion.

MUSCAT   Family of at least 200 grapes; most white, all making distinctively grapey wines. Styles range from light and sparkling Moscato d'Asti and dry Muscat d'Alsace, to sweet golden Muscat de Beaumes-de-Venise and rich dessert Black and Orange Muscats from California and Australia.

MUSIGNY   *France, Burgundy, AOC, R, W*   Côte de Nuits *Grand Cru,* in the commune of Chambolle-Musigny, whose site and soil produce some of Burgundy's greatest, most refined and subtle R wines. There is also a rare W wine. Leading producers include: Ch de Chambolle-Musigny, Dom Georges Roumier, Dom Comte Georges de Vogüé.

MUSKAT-SILVANER   German/Austrian synonym of **SAUVIGNON BLANC**.

MYRAT, CH DE   *France, Bordeaux, Barsac, 2ème Cru Classé, W*   For 15 years there were no vines here, but they were replanted in 1988. The first vintage released was the 1991. With young vines, the wine cannot yet match its neighbours.

N

NAHE *Germany, Anbaugebiet, W* Region of vineyards along the Nahe and its tributaries, south of the Mosel and west of the Rhine. Good, even great Riesling Ws from **BAD KREUZNACH**, **SCHLOSSBÖCKELHEIM**, **TRAISEN** etc.

NAIRAC, CH *France, Bordeaux, Barsac, 2ème Cru Classé, W* The winemaking here is perfectionist, though the wine is always marked by new oak, excessively for some tastes. The 1990 is a classic Barsac.

NAOUSSA *Greece, R* The Xynomavro grape dominates in this norrthern wine area, producing hefty R wines which have been wood-aged. Leading producers include: Boutari.

NAPA *USA, California, VA* Napa County – as distinct from the Napa Valley which the county includes – has a VA usable by every vineyard there, including some well outside the actual Valley and its watershed. Labels may carry the Napa name or that of a sub-VA such as **STAGS LEAP DISTRICT**, **RUTHERFORD** or **LOS CARNEROS**.

NAPOLÉON, GRAND CHAMPAGNE *France, Champagne* Family-owned, this is the least-known of the **GRANDES MARQUES**, and one of the smallest. The wines, however, are of top quality, especially the vintage champagnes.

NAUDIN, CLOS *France, Loire, Vouvray, W, Sp* The Foreau family owns 12ha of vineyard, all on the high ground above the village of Vouvray, and makes the usual range of Vouvray wines, from Sp through all sweetness levels of still wine.

NAVARRA *Spain, Navarra, DO, W, P, R* This northern province, which adjoins **RIOJA**, has been making wine for centuries. The big, powerful *rosados* are among the world's best P wines but the Rs are steadily improving in quality. Research into grapes and microclimates has boosted quality. Leading producers include: **BODEGAS JULIÁN CHIVITE**, **BODEGAS IRACHE**, Vinícola Navarra, Bodegas Principe de Viana.

NAVARRO *USA, California, Mendocino, W, R* In the cool quiet of remote **ANDERSON VALLEY** the Navarro winery make crisp, dry Chardonnays, supple Pinot Noirs and sweet W botrytized Riesling and Gewürztraminer.

NÉAC See **LALANDE DE POMEROL**.

NEBBIOLO Classic red grape from Piedmont in northern Italy. Its wine is high in acidity, needing wood-ageing and then many years in bottle to soften the tannins. Makes Barolo, Barbaresco and other northern Italian wines such as Gattinara and Valtellina. Nebbiolo is sometimes grown under other names, such as Spanna and Chiavennasca.

NEDERBURG *South Africa, Paarl, R, W* Home to the annual Nederburg Auction, this huge winery produces an astonishing array, but is most famous for its dessert wines like the Special and Noble Late Harvests and Edelkeur, the latter from Chenin Blanc.

NÉGOCIANT *France* Merchant who buys grapes or wine from growers to mature it and/or sell it to wholesalers or foreign importers.

NELSON *New Zealand, South Island* Small north-coast wine area enjoying a good climate. Mainly W wines are produced, from Chardonnay and Riesling. Leading producers include: Neudorf, Seifried/Redwood Valley.

NEMEA *Greece, Peloponnese, R* St George is the grape variety used in this area near Corinth for making fruity R wines.

NENIN, CH *France, Bordeaux, Pomerol, R* This large estate was until recently making rather old-fashioned wine, lacking the concentration and richness of the top Pomerols. The wine has much improved following investment.

NEUSIEDLERSEE *Austria, Burgenland* Wine zone, split into two districts, around the shores of the wide, shallow Neusiedlersee lake. Almost 20% of Austria's grapes are grown here. Vast quantities of botrytized wines (of mixed quality; some excellent) are produced in the south. Over in Neusiedlersee-Hügelland, on the eastern shore, superb botrytized wines are made. Rust, on the west bank, is its most famous village and Ruster *Ausbruch*, a style of wine generally less sweet than *Beerenauslese*, has been made here for centuries. R wines are increasingly made, from Blauburgunder and Cabernet Sauvignon, among other grapes. Leading producers include: Anton Kollwentz, Alois Kracher, Willi Opitz, Heidi Schröck, Josef Umathum.

NEW HAMPSHIRE *USA* Harsh winters have killed off attempts to make wine from classic grapes, though hybrids are successful.

NEW JERSEY *USA* Some encouraging wines in European styles come from the small producers in the "Garden State" such as RENAULT and Tewksbury.

NEW MEXICO *USA* The Rio Grande Valley offers a relatively cool climate: grapes were first grown here in 1580. Today wineries in three VAs offer good Cabernet Sauvignon and the record for Sp W wines is impressive. Leading producers include: ANDERSON VALLEY VINEYARDS, Gruet.

NEW SOUTH WALES *Australia* The first Australian state to cultivate grapevines. There are three main regions – HUNTER VALLEY, MUDGEE and MURRUMBIDGEE – Hunter being the best known, especially for Shiraz (R) and Sémillon (W). Vines are also grown at COWRA, noted for Sp and W wines, at MURRUMBIDGEE and elsewhere in the state.

NEW YORK   *USA*   America's second wine state (after California) with wine zones The FINGER LAKES, HUDSON RIVER VALLEY and LONG ISLAND. The first two have track-record of a century or more for both quality and bulk wine, while Long Island is a new zone profiting from the mild ocean climate. New York's wines were mostly from native American (LABRUSCA) grapes until the 1980s, when classic *vinifera* and hybrid vines began to be popular. For producers see named zones mentioned above.

NEW ZEALAND   Wine has nearly two centuries of history here, but only in the 1970s did true quality become the norm. A fast-moving industry incessantly explores new wine zones, grapes and styles. Many vineyards are new, and maturity will boost the quality, particularly of R wines. A cool and variable climate leads to character and finesse but can mean small crops. The Ws are established stars: from Sauvignon Blanc, particularly from MARLBOROUGH, Chardonnay, Riesling and others. Rs are less successful – so far, though there are increasing numbers of interesting ones – but Sp wines are very good. Other wine zones include AUCKLAND, HAWKE'S BAY, NELSON, CENTRAL OTAGO.

NICOLAS FEUILLATTE   *France, Champagne, AOC, Sp*   This Epernay house is owned by 85 cooperatives with some 4,000 members and 1,600ha of vines. Their best wine is the prestige *cuvée*, Palmes d'Or.

NICOLAY, PETER   *Germany, Mosel, W, R*   See PAULY-BERGWEILER.

NIEDERHAUSEN   *Germany, Nahe, W*   Wine town and centre of quality wine in the Nahe, home of the State Domain (STAATSDOMÄNE) and with top vineyards such as Hermanshölle and Hermannsberg.

NIERSTEIN   *Germany, Rheinhessen, Bereich, W*   Wide and thus diverse zone west and south of Nierstein on the Rhine. Wine with the *bereich* label ("Bereich Nierstein") will be soft, everyday W, usually from Müller-Thurgau grapes. Nierstein the town has excellent vineyards (including Bruderberg, Hipping, Pettenthal) along the RHEINTERRASSE: know wines from these vineyards by the prefix "Niersteiner" in their names, but beware Niersteiner Gutes Domtal, a GROSSLAGE which covers a large area, only 2% of which is within Nierstein, and which is mostly lower-quality vineyards. Leading producers in Nierstein itself include: Anton Balbach Erben, Heyl zu Herrnhausern.

NOBILO VINTNERS   *New Zealand, North Island, W, R, Sp*   This large, family-owned firm uses grapes from both North and South Islands to make mainly Chardonnay, but also a full range of other single variety wines – including a rare for New Zealand planting of South Africa's Pinotage R.

NOBLET, DOM GILLES *France, Burgundy, Mâconnais, W* Very fine producer of rich, generous Pouilly-Fuissé, worthy of bottle-age in good vintages.

NOË, CH DE LA *France, Loire, Muscadet, W* The Comte de Malestroit's historic estate makes Muscadet of good structure, worth keeping for 2–3 years. Curiously, the wine is not bottled *sur lie*.

NOËLLE, LES VIGNERONS DE LA *France, Loire, Muscadet, W, R, P* One of the biggest cooperatives in the Loire, based at Ancenis. Makes COTEAUX D'ANCENIS (W, R, P), Muscadet des Coteaux de Loire and *vin de pays*; also an excellent GROS PLANT. Labels used include Domaine des Hautes Noëlles for Muscadet.

NORTH CAROLINA *USA* The extravagent CHÂTEAU BILTMORE leads a clutch of wineries in a state best known as the home of the native Scuppernong grape, which makes highly individual wines.

NORTH COAST *USA, California, VA* Wine zone taking in Napa, Sonoma and other coastal counties north of San Francisco: the quality heart of California wine.

NOUVEAU *France* Wine of the most recent vintage: after 31 August of the following year, wines can no longer claim this appellation. Beaujolais Nouveau is the most famous.

NOVA SCOTIA *Canada* Three wineries in this cool zone grow hybrid vines, and there are experiments with new kinds of grapes from Russia.

NOVAL, QUINTA DO *Portugal, port* The two vintage ports under this name are from the beautiful *quinta* vineyards: the sweet and fruity regular vintage, a classic Portuguese style; and the Naçional, made in tiny (and expensive) quantities from ungrafted vines. The rest of the range, made from estate and bought-in grapes, is of good quality, from the Late Bottled Noval to the aged tawnies.

NOVELLO *Italy* New wine: see NOUVEAU.

NOZET, CH DE *France, Loire, Pouilly-Fumée, W, R* The most famous and most important Pouilly estate, owned by the de Ladoucette family. The top wine from the 52-ha vineyard is Baron de L, which is made only in best years and which commands high prices. Other wines are made from bought-in grapes.

NUITS/NUITS-ST-GEORGES *France, Burgundy, AOC, R* This important wine centre at the heart of Burgundy's Côte d'Or has around 40 *Premiers Crus*. The wines vary in style from scented and opulent to earthy and robust; most are best drunk at 5–8 years. Leading producers include: Dom Georges & Michel Chevillon, Dom Jean-Jacques Confuron, Dom Henri Gouges, Dom Jean Grivot, Dom Jean Gros, Henri Jayer, Dom Mongeard-Mugneret.

NV Non-vintage; often applied to champagne.

OAK, OAK-AGEING Shorthand terms for the use of oak casks in winemaking and ageing. *See* BARRELS.

OAKVILLE *USA, California, VA* Small settlement, the southern neighbour of RUTHERFORD, and like Rutherford also a wine zone within Napa, growing Cabernet Sauvignon and other vines on "bench" – gravel terrace – soils. Leading producers include: Far Niente, Heitz, Robert Mondavi.

OC, VIN DE PAYS D' *France, Vin de Pays, R, P, W* This name can be used for *vins de pays* from the entire southern sweep of France, from the Rhône to Spain. Most wines using the name are from named varieties: grapes for Rs and Ps include Cabernet Sauvignon, Merlot and Syrah; for Ws Chardonnay, Sauvignon, Chenin and others. Many successful producers; most of the wine is exported.

OHIO *USA* In the 19th century Ohio was a major wine state, and now has 40 producers, most on a small scale. Most vines are along the Lake Erie shore, though the Ohio River VA revives a century-old tradition. Leading producers include: Chalet Debonne, FIRELANDS.

OISLY ET THÉSÉE, LA CONFRÉRIE DES VIGNERONS DE *France, Loire, Touraine, W, R* Large cooperative with 52 members and 275ha of vines, producing a high-quality range of Touraine wines. Brand name Baronnie d'Aignan is used for R and W blends. The Sauvignon de Touraine (W) has been very successful.

OLASZRIESLING See WELSCHRIESLING.

OLIVIER, CH *France, Bordeaux, Pessac-Léognan, Cru Classé, R, W* The château is a splendid medieval moated castle, but the wines are not as sensational, though improving.

OLOROSO *Spain* Style of sherry that never developed *flor*. True oloroso is dry and rich, but many so-labelled are quite sweet.

OLT, LES CÔTES D' *France, South-West, Cahors, R* This co-op makes one bottle in three of Cahors. Styles range from the soft and fruity to more structured wines, eg Ch les Bouysses and Impernal, which are aged in *barriques*.

OLTREPO-PAVESE *Italy, Lombardy, DOC, R, W, Sp* Lombardy's most productive DOC. The R is from Bonard and Barbera, a lively blackberry-coloured wine with a bitter cherry flavour. Leading producers include: Castello di Luzzano, Tenuta Mazzolino.

ONTARIO *Canada* Main wine province of Canada, with 85% of the country's vineyards, exploiting moderate climate conditions along the shores of Lakes Erie and Ontario. Wines include successful Cabernet Sauvignon and Cabernet-Merlot Rs, Ws from Chardonnay and Riesling and ice wine (see **EISWEIN**). Wines labelled "product of Ontario" come entirely from the state; others may contain imported wine. Leading producers include: Cave Spring, Ch des Charmes, Henry of Pelham, Hillebrand, Inniskillin, Konzelmann, Marynissen, Pelee Island, Reif, Southbrook, Stony Ridge, Vineland.

OPITZ, WILLI *Austria, Neusiedlersee W, R* Great inventor of new and highly original wine styles and Austria's king of sweet wines, both R and W. Quality across the estate's range is outstanding and some of his more esoteric offerings include a Trockenbeerenauslese from Grüner Veltliner and a R Blauburger *Eiswein* with delicious toffee flavours.

OPPENHEIM *Germany, Rheinhessen, W* Neighbour to **NIERSTEIN**, with its own excellent vineyard the Sackträger. Like Nierstein, Oppenheim has a *grosslage*: a large tract of lesser vines, named Krötenbrunnen, which is allowed to use its name. Leading producers in Oppenheim itself: Guntrum, State cellars (Staatsweingut Domäne Oppenheim).

OREGON *USA* State in the Northwest with a cool climate akin to that of Europe's best wine zones. Wine areas include **WILLIAMETTE VALLEY** and **UMPQUA VALLEY**, from which come good Pinot Noir Rs, and Ws from Chardonnay and Riesling. Leading producers include: Adelsheim, Amity, Domaine Drouhin, Eyrie, Knudsen Erath, Ponzi, Tualatin.

ORLANDO *Australia, South Australia, Barossa R, W* Owned by Pernod-Ricard, Orlando's wide range of wines under a variety of labels includes the world-famous Jacob's Creek brand.

ORLÉANAIS, VIN DE L' *France, Loire, VDQS, R, P, W* Wines made in small amounts on the upper Loire near Orléans. Light Rs and Ps from Pinot Noir and Pinot Meunier, Ws from Pinot Blanc and Chardonnay.

ORMES DE PEZ, CH LES *France, Bordeaux, St-Estèphe, Cru Bourgeois, R* Owned by the Cazes family of Ch **LYNCH-BAGES**, this estate makes easy to enjoy, modern-style wines.

ORNELLAIA *Italy, Tuscany, R, W* This top estate gives its name to the long-lived R wine based on Cabernet Sauvignon with some Merlot and Cabernet Franc. Poggio alle Gazze (W), from Sauvignon Blanc, is also praised.

ORSCHWIHR *France, Alsace* This village has a reputation for Ws from Riesling and Pinot Gris, especially from *Grand Cru* Pfingstberg. Leading producers include: Albrecht, Théo Cattin.

ORTENAU   *Germany, Baden, Bereich, R, W, P*   Zone south of Baden-Baden (the famous spa town) with a good name for Ws from Riesling, and Rs from Spätburgunder. Important villages include DURBACH and Ortenberg; leading producers Freiherr von Nevau, Wolf-Metternich, Schloss Staufenberg.

ORVIETO   *Italy, Umbria, DOC, W*   This well-known wine is currently undergoing a renaissance in quality. The main variety is Procanico and the wine should be fresh, dry and quite concentrated. The best come from the *classico* zone. Semi-sweet (*amabile*) and sweet (*dolce*) versions are also made. Leading producers include: Antinori, Bigi.

OSBORNE   *Spain, sherry, Portugal, port*   Quintessential Puerto de Santa Mariá sherries, soft, elegant and light, come from this famous firm, still family-owned. The firm's large size, modernity and experimentation seem to have done no harm to their Fino Quinta, the dry amontillado Coquerino, or the dry oloroso Bailen. The Osborne port firm was set up in 1967: it makes a full range of ports, most of them exported to western European countries.

OTT, DOMAINES   *France, Provence, Côtes de Provence, W, R, P*   The Ott family's wines command high prices with high standards. R,W and P wines come from the 41-ha Ch de Selle estate, and one top-quality W from the Clos Mireille, based on sandy soils by the coast.

OUDINOT   *France, Champagne*   A wide range of reliable quality wines, with an attractively accessible, fruity style.

P

PAARL *South Africa, WO*　Major wine district, home to the KWV and the annual Nederburg wine auction. Mainly Ws, including Chenin Blanc, Sauvignon Blanc and Chardonnay, but also successful Rs from Cabernet Sauvignon and Pinotage. Leading producers include: Fairview, Glen Carlou, Nederburg, Villiera.

PACHERENC DU VIC-BILH *France, South-West, AOC, W*　Dry, delicate, perfumed Ws from local grapes such as Gros and Petit Manseng, Courbu and Arrufiat (or Ruffiac), grown in the same vineyard area as the Rs of Madiran. Leading producers include: Ch d'Aydie, Ch Bouscassé, Dom du Crampilh, Dom Laffitte-Teston, Ch Montus, Dom Moureou, Union Plaimont.

PADTHAWAY *Australia, South Australia*　Close to Coonawarra, although with a slightly warmer climate, this wine region yields high-quality Ws, especially Chardonnay, Riesling and Sauvignon Blanc. Leading producers include: Padthaway Estate.

PAGLIARESE *Italy, Tuscany, Chianti, R*　On this traditional estate the Sanguinetti family produce an elegant Chianti Classico. They also make the *barrique*-aged Camerlengo R from Sangiovese grapes grown in Montalcino.

PAILLARD, BRUNO *France, Champagne*　Recently founded, Paillard has quickly established a good reputation. A stickler for quality, the date of disgorgement is on every bottle and some wood fermentation is being introduced.

PALETTE *France, Provence, AOC, R, P, W*　Small area just east of Aix-en-Provence making Rs from Grenache, Mourvèdre, Cinsaut; Ws from local Clairette, Sémillon and Muscat. Producers are: Dom de la Crémade, Ch Simone.

PALLIÈRES, DOM DES *France, Rhône, Gigondas, R*　Long-lasting, traditionally made wines with warmth and vigour: good value.

PALMER *France, Champagne*　The 170 members of this highly-regarded co-op own several *Grand Cru* vineyards in the Montagne de Reims. The vintage wines age well.

PALMER, CH *France, Bordeaux, Médoc, Margaux, 3ème Cru Classé, R*　Palmer made better wine than neighbouring Ch Margaux for several vintages in the '60s and '70s. Today Margaux has reasserted itself, but Palmer still makes superb wine, the fruit of a fine site on the same gravel bank as Ch Margaux, plus long fermentation and careful selection. There is 40% Merlot, which shows in the style, but the wines can be very long-lived. 2nd wine: Réserve du Général.

PALMER VINEYARDS   *USA, New York, Long Island, R, W*   Founded in 1983, great strides have been made with Gewürztraminer W and Merlot R. Also makes Cabernet Sauvignon and Chardonnay.

PALO CORTADO   *Spain*   A sherry that started life as a FINO, but has the flavour of an OLOROSO.

PALOMINO   *Fortified Wines, sherry*   This high-yielding white grape is used primarily for sherry (and for sherry-style wines in Australia and New Zealand), but is also grown elsewhere in Spain (and Argentina) for everyday W wines.

PALOMINO & VERGARA   *Fortified Wines, sherry*   Tio Mateo, the top fino from this firm, is dry and full. It is well known throughout Spain as one of the best made.

PAPE-CLÉMENT, CH   *France, Bordeaux, Pessac-Léognan, Cru Classé, R, W*   Bordeaux's oldest surviving vineyard, dating from the 14th century. Rich, lush R wine, full-flavoured, with impressive length in the mouth. A tiny but increasing amount of W.

PARDUCCI   *USA, California, Mendocino, R, W*   John Parducci makes sound affordable wines such as his Petite Sirah (R), with its plum and berry spice flavours.

PARRAS VALLEY   *Mexico, Central America, W, R*   North of Mexico City, this area is possibly the cradle of American wine, with Bodegas de San Lorenzo, the second-oldest winery in America (founded 1626). The best vineyards are at 1,500m (5,000ft), where the climate is suitable for fine wine production.

PARSAC ST-EMILION   *France, Bordeaux, AOC, R*   This AOC is no longer seen: its wines use the MONTAGNE ST-EMILION name.

PASADA   *Spain*   A MANZANILLA sherry that has been aged: it will be dry but full in taste.

PASO ROBLES   *USA, California, San Luis Obispo, VA*   The largest wine zone in San Luis Obispo County, known for its fruity, soft, accessible Cabernet Sauvignons and its peppercorn-fruited R Zinfandels. Leading producers include: Eberle, Meridian, Ridge.

PATERNINA, BODEGAS FEDERICO   *Spain, Rioja, R, W, P*   Known as a large-scale producer of good everyday wines; but the W Federico Paternina can be very good as can the R *reservas* and *gran reservas*, which age very well in bottle.

PATRAS   *Greece, Peloponnese, W, R*   Some W wine is produced here from the pink-skinned Rhoditis grape, but the best-known wine of the area is Mavrodaphne, a fortified R wine of about 15°, matured in oak.

PATRIACHE PÈRE & FILS   *France, Burgundy, Côte d'Or, R, W*   Beaune-based *négociant* on a very large scale, making mid-rank wines of many Burgundy and other appellations. Patriache also owns the Château de Meursault domaine, whose wines are very good.

PATRIMONIO *France, Corsica, AOC, R, P, W*   This serious Corsican appellation has Rs (and Ps) made mainly from the native Nielluccio grape, dry Ws from Vermentino, and sweet Ws from Muscat. Leading producers include: Dom Gentile, Dom Leccia.

PAUILLAC *France, Bordeaux, AOC, R*   Clarets from this famed Haut-Médoc commune include 18 classed growths, three of them Firsts. Cabernet Sauvignon dominates, giving a powerful, long-lived wine that smells and tastes of blackcurrants and cedarwood; top wines may need up to 30 years to rise to their full stature, though mid-rank ones can be superb at 8-12. Leading producers include: Ch Lafite-Rothschild, Ch Latour, Ch Mouton Rothschild, Ch Pichon-Longueville Baron, Ch Pichon-Longueville Comtesse de Lalande.

PAULY-BERGWEILER, WEINGUT DR *Germany, Mosel, W, R*   This important owner of middle-Mosel vineyards makes fresh, balanced Rieslings using modern techniques. Also owns the estate of Peter Nicolay: similar wines.

PAVIE, CH *France, Bordeaux, St-Emilion, 1er Grand Cru Classé, R*   This, the largest of all the St-Emilion *1ers Grands Crus Classés*, with 15,000 cases a year, is owned by the Valette family. Pavie has made a noticeable improvement since 1979: consistently high-quality wines.

PAVIE-DECESSE, CH *France, Bordeaux, St-Emilion, Grand Cru Classé, R*   Owned by Jean-Paul Valette, whose family owns **PAVIE**. His wine is quite powerful and noticeably tannic in youth, but starts to mature after 3 years in bottle.

PAVIE-MACQUIN, CH *France, Bordeaux, St-Emilion, Grand Cru Classé, R*   Potentially one of the future stars, this well-placed-château made a distinct leap forward in the 1988 vintage, and adopted BIODYNAMIC viticulture in 1990.

PAVILLON ROUGE DU CHATEAU MARGAUX *France, Bordeaux, Médoc, Margaux*   2nd wine of Ch Margaux. Pavillon Blanc is Margaux's unusual Sauvignon white.

PÉCHARMANT *France, South-West, AOC, R*   Wines from a BERGERAC enclave. Superior soils, Malbec grapes added to the usual Cabernets and Merlot and longer ageing give the wines more structure and potential than AOC Bergerac. Leading producer: Ch de Tiregard.

PÉDESCLAUX, CH *France, Bordeaux, Médoc, Pauillac, 5ème Cru Classé, R*   This château is small and little-known, but the wines have been reliable in recent vintages.

PEDRONCELLI *USA, California, Sonoma, R, W, P*   Prices at this winery remain reasonable and the following strong. Popular wines include Ws from Chardonnay, Sauvignon and Chenin Blanc; R from Cabernet Sauvignon, and Zinfandel which comes as pale blush, P and R.

PENAFLOR *Argentina, R, W* Argentina's largest producer, with several *bodegas*. The best-known label is Trapiche, including a solid Reserve Cabernet Sauvignon, Malbec (R) and Chardonnay. Other labels include Andean Vineyards and Fond de Cave. The latter is exceptional.

PEÑALBA LÓPEZ, BODEGAS *Spain, Castilla-León, Ribera del Duero, R, P* The latest winemaking technology here produces above-average R and P wines. Their best appear under the Torremilanos label.

PENEDÈS *Spain, Catalonia, DO, W, P, R, Sp* The most important Catalonian wine region, south of Barcelona, producing CAVA Sp wines, a large range of impressive W wines and some good Rs. Leading producers include: Masia BACH, RENÉ BARBIER, Cooperativa Vinícola del Penedès, JEAN LÉON, TORRES.

PENFOLDS *Australia, South Australia, Barossa R, W* Australia's giant of giants. R wines are its strongest suit, with the brilliant Grange, a long-lived Shiraz-based wine, as its ace. Penfolds has made Ws since 1990.

PENNSYLVANIA *USA* Vines are grown in the state's south-east, with classic *vinifera* grapes joining native (LABRUSCA) vines. Leading producers include: Allegro, CHADDSFORD, Naylor.

PERALDI, DOM *France, Corsica, Ajaccio, W, R, P* One of the best-known Corsican estates, owned by the Comte de Poix. The Clos du Cardinal (R) is aged in oak barrels.

PERNAND-VERGELESSES *France, Burgundy, AOC, R, W* Parts of the *Grands Crus* of CORTON and CORTON-CHARLEMAGNE lie within this Côte de Beaune village. Rs (around 80% of production) need 5–15 years in bottle. Leading producers include: Bonneau du Martray, Marius Delarche, P Dubreuil-Fontaine.

PERRIER, JOSEPH *France, Champagne* The NV Cuvée Royale from this GRANDE MARQUE has been somewhat inconsistent in the past. The best wine is the Cuvée Josephine, an almost equal blend of Pinot Noir and Chardonnay.

PERRIER-JOUET *France, Champagne* One of the oldest champagne houses, now owned by Seagram. Chardonnay is the dominant grape and the wines are consistently elegant with lots of finesse. Their finest wine is Belle Epoque *blanc de blancs* with its distinctive *art nouveau* bottle.

PERRIÈRES, LES *France, Burgundy, Côte de Beaune, 1er Cru, W* One of the best vineyards in Meursault, abutting neighbouring Puligny-Montrachet to the south. Its wines are distinctly classy, displaying lovely buttery character, with an elegance and steeliness behind. Leading producers include: Robert Ampeau, Coche-Dury, Comtes Lafon, Albert Grivault, J & P Matrot, Guy Roulot.

PERU *South America* With less than 250,000 cases annually, Peru is one of South America's lesser producers. However, vines have been grown in the main region, south of Lima, for more than 400 years. The Moquega Valley, near the Chilean border, is another region. Most production goes into brandy.

PESSAC-LÉOGNAN *France, Bordeaux, AOC, R, W* Appellation covering 10 communes in the northern (superior) part of the Graves; all the Graves classed growths are here. Around 75% of the wine is R, to be drunk at 10 years or so. Cabernet Sauvignon is the dominant R grape, blended with Merlot, Cabernet Franc, Petit Verdot and Cot (Malbec). Ws are from Sauvignon Blanc and Sémillon; the best (which are expensive) demand at least 5 years in bottle. Leading producers include: Ch Bouscaut, Dom de Chevalier, Ch'x Couhins-Lurton, de Fieuzal, La Garde, Haut-Bailly, Haut-Brion, Larrivet-Haut-Brion, Laville-Haut-Brion, La Louvière, Malartic-Lagravière, La Mission-Haut-Brion, Pape-Clément, Smith-Haut-Lafitte, La Tour Martillac.

PETALUMA *Australia, South Australia, Adelaide Hills, W, Sp* Famed winemaker Brian Croser makes top-quality wines here, including a fine Sp wine, Croser, good Cabernet Sauvignon and a most interesting Riesling W. Bridgewater Mill is their 2nd label.

PÉTILLANT *France* Term meaning slightly sparkling.

PETIT CHABLIS *France, Burgundy, AOC, W* An appellation within the Chablis district. Seldom seen on a label, as the land in the delimited area is mostly unplanted.

PETIT CHÂTEAU *France* Bordeaux term for an unclassified wine château. It has no official status and is not seen on labels.

PETIT VILLAGE, CH *France, Bordeaux, Pomerol, R* Owned by insurance firm AXA, and managed by Jean-Michel Cazes of Ch Lynch-Bages in Pauillac, this is an estate to watch. Its big, voluptuous style of wine can match some of the best estates in Pomerol. In the finest years the wines will last 20 years or more.

PETIT-FAURIE-DE-SOUTARD, CH *France, Bordeaux, St-Emilion, Grand Cru Classé, R* The Capdemourlin family who own this château also own **BALESTARD-LA-TONNELLE**. This little-known estate produces St-Emilion in a fairly exotic style.

PETITE SIRAH Red grape from California, no relation to the Rhône's **SYRAH**, although it is possibly the same grape as the Durif of southern France. Used in generic blends and as a dark, tannic varietal.

PÉTRUS, CH *France, Bordeaux, Pomerol, R* Very old vines on pure clay, brilliant winemaking and no expense spared make one of the world's most expensive, and best, R wines. Pétrus is virtually pure Merlot. Seductive young, it can age for decades. The estate is part-owned and managed by **J-P MOUIEX**.

PEYMARTIN, CH *France, Bordeaux, Médoc, St-Julien, R* 2nd wine of Ch Gloria.

PEYRASSOL, COMMANDERIE DE *France, Provence, Côtes de Provence, R, P* Françoise and Yves Rigord have made this estate near Flassans one of the best in the *appellation*. There are good Ps, a standard R, Cuvée Eperon, and the top-quality R Cuvée Marie-Estelle, an unusual blend of Cabernet Sauvignon, Grenache and Syrah, which is oak-aged.

PEZ, CH DE *France, Bordeaux, St-Estèphe, Cru Bourgeois, R* The senior *cru bourgeois* of the appellation, very traditional in techniques and in the austere, tannic, spicy style of its wine. The wines need, but reward, patience.

PEZA *Greece, Crete, R, W* Local varieties such as Kotsifali, Liatiko and Vilana are used to produce quite rich and powerful R and W wines in this zone.

PEZINOK *Slovakia* Winery in the Little Carpathians region, making a variety of sound wines under Western supervision.

PFAFFENHEIM *France, Alsace* Wine village with a *Grand Cru*, Steinert, and a growing name for Ws from Pinot Blanc and Pinot Gris.

PFALZ *Germany, Anbaugebiet, W, R* Formerly known as the Rheinpfalz, this southern region makes good W and (increasingly) R wines in a solid, flavoursome style. The best zone is MITTEL-HAARDT, but the Südpfalz or SÜDLICHE WEINSTRASSE makes growing amounts of good wine.

PFEFFINGEN, WEINGUT *Germany, Pfalz, W* Family estate in the heart of the Pfalz specializing in dry, fruity Riesling wines.

PHEASANT RIDGE *USA, Texas, R, W* The winery, in Lubbock, is inconsistent but with flashes of greatness. Owner Bobby Cox produces Ws from Chardonnay, Sauvignon, Chenin Blanc and, most promising of all, R Cabernet Sauvignon.

PHÉLAN-SÉGUR, CH *France, Bordeaux, St-Estèphe, Cru Bourgeois, R* Large and well-known estate, on good form since 1986 and especially in 1990.

PHELPS, JOSEPH *USA, California, Napa, R, W* This winery produces Rhône-style wines, from rose-petal-scented Syrah and delicately spiced Grenache Rs to a tangy W based on Viognier grapes.

PHILLIPPONNAT *France, Champagne* A small house, best known for its fine, weighty, single-vineyard Clos des Goisses.

PHYLLOXERA The *phylloxera vastatrix* aphid, which attacks the roots of the vine, devastated European vineyards in the 19th century after its accidental introduction from America. The only cure was found to be grafting vines onto roots from American vines. Phylloxera, in a slightly different form or biotype, is currently a problem in the USA: US vines are resistant, but not the European varieties they have imported. Failure to graft onto resistant rootstocks has given the pest a chance. Many vines in California and elsewhere are being grubbed up and burnt, to be replaced with vines growing on the correct rootstocks.

PIBARNON, CH DE *France, Provence, Bandol W, R, P* The wines from Comte Henri de Saint-Victor's estate regularly receive awards and taste most attractive, thanks to new wood and a high proportion of Mourvèdre. The P is fruity and fresh, the W crisp and lightly acidic.

PIBRAN, CH *France, Bordeaux, Médoc, Pauillac, Cru Bourgeois* This small estate is under the same ownership as Ch **PICHON-BARON**: the French insurance concern AXA. Jean-Michel Cazes is making deep-coloured wine in a fruity yet muscular style.

PICHON-LONGUEVILLE BARON, CH *France, Bordeaux, Médoc, Pauillac, 2ème Cru Classé, R* The two Pichons glare at each other across the D2 road south of Pauillac. Pichon-Baron's restored château and controversial new *chai* show the investment by insurance giant AXA. Jean-Michel Cazes (owner of Ch **LYNCH-BAGES**) runs the property for AXA, making much-improved, very ripe and solid wine, a worthy contrast to the other Pichon. A good 1993.

PICHON-LONGUEVILLE COMTESSE DE LALANDE, CH *France, Bordeaux, Médoc, Pauillac, 2ème Cru Classé, R* Mme May-Eliane de Lencquesaing has stamped her demanding personality on the wines, and the image, of her estate. The results have been spectacular. A high 35% of Merlot makes the wine softer and more opulent than most Pauillacs. A good 1993, but a small crop. The 2nd wine is Réserve de la Comtesse which, thanks to rigorous selection, contains excellent material and is well-regarded in its own right.

PICQUE-CAILLOU, CH *France, Bordeaux, Pessac-Léognan R* This supple, soundly-made wine is relatively quick to evolve.

PIÈCE *France, Burgundy* Cask of 228 litres, traditional for ageing wine. See also **BARRIQUE**.

PIED D'ALOUE *France, Burgundy, Chablis, 1er Cru* See **MONTÉE DE TONNERRE**.

PIEDMONT *Italy* Together with Tuscany, Italy's most important quality wine area, centred around Turin in the north-west. Long-lived Barolo and Barbaresco are the top DOCG R wines, both made from the Nebbiolo grape. Also produces a wide range of lighter R wines, from Barbera and Dolcetto grapes, and attractive W and Sp wines.

PIEMONTE *Italy* See **PIEDMONT**.

PIEROPAN *Italy, Veneto, W* Prestigious estate which pioneered single-vineyard Soaves. The range now includes single-vineyard Calvarino and the sweet Recioto di Soave Le Colombare.

PIESPORT *Germany, Mosel, Bereich, W* Famous village of the Mittelmosel, with some of its steepest vineyards. Piesport makes top-class wines from Riesling which combine a touch of spiciness with underlying steel. Wines from top producers age very well. The best vineyard is the large Goldtröpfchen. Leading producers here include Bischöflichen Weingüter and Vereinigte Hospitien, both of which are charities, and von Kesselstatt. Much of Piesport's reputation has been lost by Piesporter Michelsberg, a *grosslage* taking in wide tracts of flat north-facing land, producing large quantities of indifferent wine.

PIN, CH LE *France, Bordeaux, Pomerol, R* Tiny amounts of prohibitively priced and reportedly superb wine are made here.

PINDAR VINEYARDS *USA, New York, Long Island, W, R* Long Island's largest winery, with 85ha planted at North Fork. The wide range is gaining an international name with its Merlot and Mythology, a R bordeaux-style blend. Chardonnay has also been impressive.

PINOT BLANC White grape that can make delicately aromatic wines, particularly in Alsace, and makes a good base for sparkling wines. Known as Weissburgunder in Germany and Austria, Pinot Bianco in Italy. Pinot Blanc is increasingly popular in California.

PINOT GRIS Grape variety that may be red or white; its wine is usually a deep-coloured, full-bodied dry white. Known as Tokay d'Alsace in France, Rülander or Grauburgunder in Germany, Pinot Grigio in Italy, Szürkebarát in Hungary; it is also grown in Romania and Oregon. Pinot Gris is becoming better known as winemakers seek alternatives to the ubiquitous Chardonnay.

PINOT NOIR The classic grape of red burgundy. Pinot Noir can be difficult to grow and yields must be low to make quality wine. As growers worldwide have found to their frustration, much of the taste of the resulting wine depends upon *terroir* and winemaking. Pinot Noir grown in Oregon, Australia, Italy or eastern Europe can be great – or disappointing. It is also used in Champagne (blended with Pinot Meunier and Chardonnay).

PIPER-HEIDSIECK *France, Champagne* Owned by Rémy Cointreau who also own Charles Heidsieck. The overall style is fairly light and fruity, but the dry Brut Sauvage is one of the finest non-*dosage* (very dry) champagnes and the prestige *cuveé*, Rare, is extremely elegant.

PLAYA, LA *Chile, R, W* Wine estate in the MAIPO VALLEY, owned by the Pavone family. La Playa produces Rs from Cabernet Sauvignon and Merlot, plus Ws from Chardonnay and Sauvignon Blanc. All but the Chardonnay are estate-grown.

PLETTENBERG, WEINGUT REICHSGRAF VON *Germany, Nahe, W* This estate's dry wines, made for the German domestic market, where food-wines are the fashion, complement their beautiful naturally sweet ones, which sell abroad.

POCHON, ETIENNE *France, Rhône, Crozes-Hermitage, R, W* This estate makes quality R wine, with fruit, concentration and plenty of flavour, from an AOC which can be variable. A little W is also made under the same appellation.

PODRAVSKI *Slovenia* Also known as the Drava Valley region, in the north-east near Austria, this zone produces the country's best wines. It has a sub-region, LJUTOMER-ORMOZ. The W wines are at their best reminiscent of Germany and Austria: good Pinot Gris, Rhein Riesling and Traminer, pungent Sauvignon Blanc and *botrytis*-affected dessert wines.

POGGIO ANTICO *Italy, Tuscany, Brunello di Montalcino, R* Maker of modern-style Brunellos designed for earlier drinking. Brunello grapes are also used to make Altero, a R *vino da tavola*.

POINT DU JOUR, DOM DU *France, Burgundy, Beaujolais, R* Elegant feminine Fleurie is produced at this leading Beaujolais estate.

POJER & SANDRI *Italy, Trentino, W, R, Sp* Makers of an innovative range of varietal *vini da tavola* from grapes such as Chardonnay and Pinot Noir, plus *metodo classico* Sp wines, and Essenzia, a sweet late-harvest W.

POL ROGER *France, Champagne* Traditional, family firm whose wines are of consistently high quality. The Cuvée Sir Winston Churchill, whose favourite champagne it was, is all elegance and finesse; the special *cuvée*, PR, is richer with greater body.

POMEROL *France, Bordeaux, AOC, R* Superb wine from a small area north-west of St-Emilion. Merlot is the dominant grape, followed by Cabernet Franc and a small amount of Cabernet Sauvignon. Generally the wines are ready at 4–6 years, with a plummy appeal and fullish, well-rounded palate. The finest are richer and more concentrated, and can mature for 40 years or more, taking on a gamey character. Leading producers include: Ch'x Le Bon Pasteur, Bonalgue, Certan de May, Clinet, La Conseillante, L'Evangile, La Fleur-de-Gay, La Fleur-Pétrus, Lafleur, Latour à Pomerol, Petit Village, Petrus, Trotanoy; Vieux-Ch-Certan.

POMINO *Italy, Tuscany, DOC, R, W* High-quality DOC which owes much to the Frescobaldi family. Cabernet and Merlot are combined with Sangiovese for the R wine. Pinot Bianco, Chardonnay and Trebbiano are used for the W. Leading producers include: Frescobaldi.

POMMARD *France, Burgundy, AOC, R* Burgundies of deep colour, intense aroma, concentrated flavours, full body and complex structure that can improve in bottle for 10 years, especially from the best *Premiers Crus* (Epenots, Rugiens, Clos de la Commeraine). Leading producers include: Robert Ampeau, Dom Jean-Marc Boillot, Dom de Courcel, Dom Bernard Glantenay, Dom de Montille, Ch de Pommard.

POMMERY & GRENO *France, Champagne* Owned by the LVMH group, this **GRANDE MARQUE** has 300ha of vines. There has been some inconsistency in the NV, but both the Louise Pommery Brut and Rosé are outstanding.

PONIATOWSKI, PRINCE *France, Loire, Vouvray, W, Sp* The family has owned Le Clos Baudoin since 1910. The 22-ha vineyard is the source of traditional Vouvray, with emphasis on dry and Sp wines, sold under the name Aigle d'Or, with sweet wines made only in exceptional years.

PONTET-CANET, CH *France, Bordeaux, Médoc, Pauillac, 5ème Cru Classé, R* A large and well-placed vineyard, just south of Mouton's, promises more than the wine has always delivered. However a slow process of improvements has showed results, especially since 1989.

PONZI *USA, Oregon, W, R* Racy Riesling Ws and taut, richly built Pinot Noir Rs (tasting notes cite black cherry, mushroom, clove) are well regarded. Chardonnay is barrel-fermented in Allier oak, stressing the wine's sweet lime fruit.

PORTO *Portugal, DOC* One of the world's great fortified wines, from the Douro Valley of northern Portugal. Essentially R, although a tiny quantity of W is also made. R port comes in a variety of styles but is always sweet. Cask ageing is a critical aspect of most port production., with lesser wines like Ruby and Vintage Character spending several years in wood. Aged tawnies can spend up to 40 years or more in wood. Vintage and Single Quinta ports, however, are bottled after two years and mature in bottle (for at least 15 years and up to 50). Leading producers include: Croft, Delaforce, Dow, Ferreira, Fonseca Guimaraens, Quinta do Noval, Sandeman, Smith Woodhouse, Taylor Fladgate & Yeatman, Warre.

POUGET, CH *France, Bordeaux, Médoc, Margaux, 4ème Cru Classé, R* Little-known classed growth making good wine.

POUILLY-FUISSÉ *France, Burgundy, AOC, W* Five southern Mâconnais villages share land well suited to growing Chardonnay. Old vines and new oak can make this W burgundy a rich, long-lived and serious wine. Other wines, especially from *négociants*, are made to be drunk young. Not all Pouilly-Fuissé lives up to its reputation. Leading producers include: Dom Coursin, Dom Jeanne Ferret, Dom Michel Forest, Ch de Fuissé, Dom Gilles Noblet, Dom Guffens-Heynen, Dom Roger Saumaize.

POUILLY FUMÉ *France, Loire, AOC, W* World-famous dry W wine from Sauvignon Blanc grapes; fuller and longer-lasting than **SANCERRE** on the opposite bank of the Loire. The name "fumé" encapsulates the typically smoky flavour of the grape, which reaches perfection on Pouilly's flint and chalk soils. Leading producers include: Didier Dagueneau, Masson-Blondelet, Ch du Nozet, Ch de Tracy.

POUILLY-LOCHÉ   *France, Burgundy, AOC, W*   This village east of POUILLY-FUISSÉ makes similar but usually cheaper W wines, also from Chardonnay grapes.

POUILLY-SUR-LOIRE   *France, Loire, AOC, W*   Wines made from Chasselas grapes; a declining appellation. Do not confuse with the Sauvignon-based POUILLY FUMÉ which is made in the same area. Leading producers include: Bernard Blanchet, Patrick Coulbois, Jean-Claude Dagueneau.

POUILLY-VINZELLES   *France, Burgundy, AOC, W*   Chardonnay W wines, made in a village neighbouring POUILLY-FUISSÉ.

POUJEAUX, CH   *France, Bordeaux, Moulis, Cru Bourgeois, R*   This large château contends with Maucaillou and Chasse-Spleen as the best in the commune. Good traditional claret: dark, flavoursome and long-lived.

POUSSE D'OR, DOM DE LA   *France, Burgundy, Côte d'Or, R*   Leading Volnay estate, producing balanced and elegant red burgundies which age well. Also makes good Pommard and Santenay.

PREDICATO   *Italy*   Term for Tuscan quality wines, R and W, meeting certain local criteria.

PREMIER CRU   *France*   Officially-defined vineyard or estate in a ranking system. Definitions vary; the term is used in Bordeaux, Burgundy and elsewhere. In Burgundy it signifies a vineyard below *Grand Cru* in status.

PREMIERES CÔTES DE BLAYE   See CÔTES DE BLAYE.

PREMIERES CÔTES DE BORDEAUX   *France, Bordeaux, AOC, R, W*   Good R wines and sweet Ws from hillside vineyards on the north bank of the Garonne River. Leading producers include: Ch'x Brethous, Gourran, de Haux, du Juge, Lagarosse, Mestrepeyrot, Ch de Plassan, Reynon, Tanesse.

PRESTON   *USA, California, Sonoma, R, W*   Sauvignon W and Zinfandel R are this winery's mainstays, but the latest wines are from Rhône varieties such as W Marsanne and Viognier, and R Carignane, Syrah, Mourvèdre, Grenache and Cinsaut; there is also a particularly tasty R Barbera.

PREUSES   *France, Burgundy, Chablis, Grand Cru*   Vineyard making wine considered to be more feminine and elegant than LES CLOS. It shares LA MOUTONNE with VAUDÉSIR.

PRIEUR, DOM JACQUES   *France, Burgundy, Côte d'Or, R, W*   Dynamic domaine with an impressive array of *Grand* and *Premier Cru* vineyards throughout the Côte d'Or, including land in Montrachet and Chambertin. Rising quality.

PRIEURE-LICHINE, CH   *France, Bordeaux, Médoc, Margaux, 4ème Cru Classé, R*   Alexis Lichine (*see* Ch LASCOMBES) built up this estate, which consists of widely scattered plots, and it is now run by his son Sacha. The wine is a good monument to the estate's creator.

PRIMEUR   *France*   Wines made to be drunk very young; they are marketed from 21 November of the year they are made till 31 January of the following year. (Not to be confused with *en primeur*.)

PRIMORSKI   *Slovenia*   One of Slovenia's three major wine zones, on the Adriatic coast, influenced in wine styles and grapes by Italy's proximity. Primorski has good Rs from Merlot and Cabernet Sauvignon, and often excellent Ws from Pinot Gris and Blanc, Chardonnay and Malvasia. The local speciality is Refosk (R), dark and acidic.

PRIORATO   *Spain, Catalonia, DO, W, R*   One of eight Catalonian wine zones, with mountain vineyards producing a range of light *joven* W to heavy, powerful R. Leading producers include: DE MULLER, Cellers Scala-Dei.

PRISSÉ, CAVE COOPERATIVE DE   *France, Burgundy, Mâconnais, R, W*   Good, reliable producer of R and W Mâconnais wines.

PROSECCO DI CONEGLIANO-VALDOBBIADENE   *Italy, Veneto, DOC, Sp*   Wine zone to the north of Venice, home of a Sp wine with a slightly almondy flavour, crisp acidity and lowish alcohol.

PRULIERS, LES   *France, Burgundy, Côte de Nuits, 1er Cru, R*   One of the top Nuits-St-Georges vineyards. The wines are densely coloured, very aromatic, well-structured with a good tannic backbone. Leading producers include: Henri Gouges, Jean Grivot.

PRÜM, J J   *Germany, Mosel, W*   This leading middle-Mosel estate owns superb plots in Wehlener Sonnenuhr and other vineyards. The wines are classics, especially the AUSLESEN. Lesser (QBA) wine use the Dr M Prüm label.

PRÜM ERBEN, S A   *Germany, Mosel, W*   Estate with a traditional approach making cask-aged, classic Mosels from fine vineyards in Graach, Wehlen etc.

PRUNOTTO, ALFREDO   *Italy, Piedmont, R*   One of the leading *négociants* of the wine town of Alba, producing single-vineyard Barolo Bussia and Cannubi, Barbaresco Montestefano, Barbera d'Alba Pian Romualdo and Nebbiolo d'Alba Occhetti.

PUCELLES, LES   *France, Burgundy, Côte de Beaune, 1er Cru, W*   One of the best Puligny-Montrachet vineyards, making lovely, elegant wines with a nice steely acidity which age very well. Leading producers include: Leflaive, Henri de Villamont.

PUISSEGUIN ST-EMILION   *France, Bordeaux, AOC, R*   Among the "satellite" zones to the north-east of St-Emilion. It can equal St-Emilion in quality and offers good value. Leading producers include: Ch'x l'Abbaye, Durand, Guibeau, Laplagne, des Laurets, de Roques, Teillac, Teyssier.

PULIGNY-MONTRACHET   *France, Burgundy, AOC, W*   Côte de Beaune village which concentrates on great W wines from its four *Grands Crus* – MONTRACHET, CHEVALIER-MONTRACHET, BIENVENUES-BÂTARD-MONTRACHET and BÂTARD-MONTRACHET – and a clutch of excellent *Premiers Crus*. Vineyards are ideally sited and the wine is often the best W burgundy – and expensive. The *Grand Cru* wines reach their best in 10 years, as do some of the elegant *Premiers Crus*. Village Puligny-Montrachet is less special, although still expensive. Leading producers include: Adrien Belland, Dom Henri Clerc, Dom Leflaive, Olivier Leflaive Frères, Dom Michelot-Buisson, Dom Jean Monnier & Fils, Dom Etienne Sauzet.

PUYGUERAUD, CH *France, Bordeaux, Côtes de Francs, R* The Thienponts of Pomerol own this château as well as nearby Ch **LACLAVERIE** and have given the appellation a boost. The wine is dark and solid, showing the potential of the area.

PYRENEES *Australia, Victoria* This region enjoys a temperate climate ideally suited to full-bodied, textured R wines from Shiraz and Cabernet Sauvignon.

PYRÉNÉES-ORIENTALES, DES *France, Vin de Pays, R, P, W* Wines from the hilly country close to the Pyrenees: solid, powerful Rs are in the majority.

Q

QBA *Germany* See QUALITÄTSWEIN EINES BESTIMMTEN ANBAU-GEBIETES.

QMP *Germany* See QUALITÄTSWEIN MIT PRÄDIKAT.

QUADY *USA, California* Andrew Quady's winery makes a fascinating range of sweet wines, including Muscats both orange and black and a port-style wine which he calls Starboard.

QUALITÄTSWEIN EINES BESTIMMTEN ANBAUGEBIETES (QBA) *Germany* Quality wine from a defined region. The lower of two bands into which all German quality wine is divided.

QUALITÄTSWEIN MIT PRÄDIKAT (QMP) *Germany* Quality wine with distinction. The higher of the two bands for German quality wine. QmPs are made from grapes sweet enough to need no added sugar. Each QmP wine falls into one of six levels, in ascending order of sweetness: KABINETT, SPÄTLESE, AUSLESE, BEERENAUSLESE, TROCKENBEERENAUSLESE, EISWEIN.

QUARTS-DE-CHAUME *France, Loire, AOC, W* Luscious sweet W wines from Chenin Blanc grapes are produced from this enclave within the Coteaux du Layon zone. Leading producer: Jacques Lalanne/Ch de Belle Rive.

QUEBEC *Canada* A small area 50 miles south of Montreal manages to make wine, mostly Ws from Seyval Blanc, in this cold-winter province.

QUEENSLAND *Australia* State in the north-east corner of Australia which has a small area in the south under vine, but serious wines have been made only since 1970. Sémillon (W) and Shiraz (R) do well here, though Cabernet Sauvignon and Chardonnay are also planted.

QUÉNARD, RAYMOND *France, Savoie, R* Leading maker of the rare R of Chignin, in the Alps.

QUINCY *France, Loire, AOC, W* Dry W wines from Sauvignon Blanc, produced on the south bank of the Cher not far from Sancerre. Can be good value. Leading producers include: Joseph Mellot, Dom Sorbe.

QUINTA *Portugal* Farm, estate or vineyard.

QUINTARELLI *Italy, Veneto, R, W* Estate with a range of rich, complex wines include a *ripasso* Valpolicella and Recioto Amarone. *Vini da tavola* include *passito* Amabile del Cerè (W), Alzero (R) and Molinara (R).

R

RABASSE-CHARAVIN, DOM *France, Rhône, Côtes du Rhône-Villages,* *R* Excellent Syrah-based R wine made to age, plus a good W.

RABAUD-PROMIS, CH *France, Bordeaux, Sauternes, 1er Cru Classé, W* Since 1983 this estate has made some of the most delicious wines in the region: not too oaky, with charm not power and, in top years, a delectable freshness and raciness.

RAIMAT *Spain, Catalonia, Costers del Segre, R, W,* *P, Sp* Extremely well-run, large and innovative winery, using both French and Spanish grape varieties. Their Sp Chardonnay is excellent. The blended Clos Abadia (R) and the single-variety R wines are also very good.

RAMONET, DOM ANDRÉ *France, Burgundy, Côte d'Or, R, W* Top quality W burgundies, including some Le Montrachet, emerge from this leading estate based in Chassagne-Montrachet.

RANCIO A pungent taste found in old, maderized, fortified wine.

RANDERSACKER *Germany, Franken, W* This village just upstream from Würzburg has a good cooperative cellar and some good estates, including Weingut Robert Schmitt. The Pfulben vineyard includes some of the best sites in Franken, suited to Riesling, Müller-Thurgau and Silvaner.

RASTEAU *France, Rhône, AOC, R, P, W, VDN* Grenache-based dessert wine (*vin doux naturel*); most is sweet W, but the R is generally better. Rasteau village also produces hearty R wine under the Côtes du Rhône-Villages appellation. Leading VDN producer: Dom de la Soumade.

RATTI-ANTICHE, RENATO *Italy, Piedmont, R* The late Renato Ratti was a leading maker of Barolo. His family now run the estate, which makes a range including Barolo Marcenasco, Barbera, Dolcetto and Nebbiolo d'Alba.

RAUENTHAL *Germany, Rheingau, W* In the hills above the Rheingau, this village makes good wines in warm years. The Baiken vineyard is noted for fine Riesling Ws.

RAUSAN-SÉGLA, CH *France, Bordeaux, Médoc, Margaux, 2ème Cru Classé, R* An example of the dramatic improvements in the Médoc in the 1980s: new stainless steel, better vines, a new team – and the estate is back where it was last century, a true 2nd Growth. A good 1993, and in 1994 David Orr, ex-head of Latour, took over for new owners Chanel.

RAUZAN-GASSIES *France, Bordeaux, Médoc, Margaux, 2ème Cru Classé, R*   Less in the limelight than the other half of the old Rausan estate *(see* RAUSAN-SÉGLA*)*, and less consistent.

RAUTENTRAUCH'SCHE WEINGUTSVERWALTUNG *Germany, Ruwer, W*   Estate which is a source of some of the best Ruwer wines: Rieslings of restrained but long-lived elegance.

RAVENEAU, FRANÇOIS AND JEAN-MARIE *France, Burgundy, Chablis, W*   Small estate making some of Chablis's finest *Premiers* and *Grands Crus*: wines with great weight, nerve and flintiness, developing complexity with age.

RAVENSWOOD *USA, California, Sonoma, R, W*   Joel Peterson's intense, berry-laden Zinfandel R makes up over half the production at his winery. A Merlot R and a Meursault-like Chardonnay, both intense, are also made.

RAYAS, CH *France, Rhône, Châteauneuf-du-Pape, R, W*   Many feel this is the top wine of the appellation. Low yields, 100% Grenache vines and superb winemaking contribute: sadly, the estate is so small there is little of it. Also excellent white Châteauneuf and Ch de Fonsalette, a Côtes du Rhône far better than the modest appellation would suggest.

RAYMOND-LAFON, CH *France, Bordeaux, Sauternes, W*   Meticulous winemaking yields sumptuous sweet wines that require long ageing. By harvesting as late as possible, excellent wine is made even in modest years. Raymond-Lafon is the most expensive Sauternes after Yquem and Fargues, but superb and well worth the price.

RAYNE-VIGNEAU, CH DE *France, Bordeaux, Sauternes, 1er Cru Classé, W*   Standards have greatly improved here recently, and Rayne-Vigneau is once again a reliable source of some fine Sauternes. The wines of the late 1980s and 1991 were very good.

REAL COMPANHIA VINÍCOLA DO NORTE DO PORTUGAL *Portugal, W, R*   Table wine arm of the port house Royal Oporto. Evel brand R and W wines are generally good value.

REBHOLZ, WEINGUT *Germany, Pfalz, W, R*   This estate is at Siebeldingen in the up-and-coming southern part of the Pfalz, the SÜDLICHE WEINSTRASSE. Rebholz makes good Rs, plus Ws such as well-made dry but powerful Rieslings and excellent Müller-Thurgaus.

RECIOTO *Italy*   Sweet red wine from grapes that have been left to dry for a time after picking, to concentrate their juice. High in alcohol and velvety in texture, it is akin to port.

REDDE, MICHEL ET FILS *France, Loire, Pouilly-Fumé, W*   Important producers, with a large estate of 27ha. They make a straight *cuvée*, and in the best years a deluxe wine, Cuvée Majorum. Winemaking equipment is modern and these wines are designed for early drinking.

REGALEALI *Italy, Sicily, W, R, P* The island's premier estate, producing high-quality *vini da tavola* in all three colours. The top W, Nozze d'Oro, contains Sauvignon Blanc; the Rosso del Conte R is aged in new wood.

RÉGNIÉ *France, Burgundy, AOC, R* Beaujolais *cru*: the 10th and most recent to be delineated. The wines reflect their location: in the north the *cru* adjoins **MORGON**; in the south **BROUILLY**. In general Regnie is a light and elegant wine for a *cru* Beaujolais, but with a pronounced and pleasant aroma. Leading producers include: Dom de Bel Air, Caveau des Deux Clochers, Georges Duboeuf.

REINE-PÉDAUQUE, LA *France, Burgundy, Côte d'Or, R, W* This firm is a *négociant* and landowner, with the same owners as **PIERRE ANDRÉ**, with fine sites, mostly around Corton.

REINHARTSHAUSEN, SCHLOSS *Germany, Rheingau, W, R* The Prince of Prussia owns this large estate, which has Riesling in some top Rheingau vineyards and Chardonnay on an island in the Rhine. Most wines are dry, though there are traditional sweet wines too.

REMOISSENET, PERE & FILS *France, Burgundy, Côte d'Or, R, W* Beaune is the headquarters of the *négociant* and vineyard owner. The Ws are extremely good, the Rs less reliable.

RENAULT WINERY *USA, New Jersey, Sp, W, R* One of the oldest and most successful wineries in the state, located in Egg Harbor City, producing some 25,000 cases of assorted wines. Sp wines, such as Spumante, head the list.

RENOU, RENÉ *France, Loire, Bonnezeaux, W, R* One of the great advocates of the wines of the Layon Valley and président of the Syndicat des Vins de Bonnezeaux, M Renou makes Bonnezeaux and R wines from his 18ha in Thouarcé.

RESERVA *Spain* Red wines that must spend three years in the *bodega*, of which at least one must be in *barricas* (**BARRIQUES**). W and R *reservas* must spend two years in the *bodega*, of which six months must be in *barricas*.

RESERVE *France* Term used for special *cuvées* put aside for ageing and future use.

RÉSERVE DE LA COMTESSE *France, Bordeaux, Médoc, Pauillac, R* 2nd wine of Ch Pichon-Lalande.

RESS, BALTHASAR *Germany, Rheingau, W, R* This leading Rheingau estate has good vineyards at Rüdesheim and elsewhere. Ress is a member of **CHARTA** and a specialist in dry wines.

RETSINA *Greece, W* Greek speciality, dating from Classical times, which is now made like other W wines, except that small pieces of resin from the Alep pine are added to the must and removed at the first racking of the young wine. Retsina should be drunk very cold. Leading producers include: Boutari.

REUILLY *France, Loire, AOC, R, P, W* Dry Ws from Sauvignon Blanc, and Rs and Ps from Pinot Noir and Pinot Gris, made in the Upper Loire region near Bourges.

REVERCHON, WEINGUT *Germany, Saar, W, R* Harmonious and elegant are words used of the Reverchon estate's Saar Rieslings, which though light show the concentration of low yields from fine vineyard sites.

REVERDY, JEAN, ET FILS *France, Loire, Sancerre, W, R, P* One of the traditional names of Sancerre since the 17th century, Reverdy makes Ws from Clos de la Reine Blanche in Verdigny; also R and P Sancerre from a 2-ha plot.

REYNON, CH *France, Bordeaux, 1er Côtes de Bordeaux, R, W* Prof Dubourdieu of Bordeaux University here practices what he preaches: good Rs, well above the status of the appellation, and a W under the Bordeaux AOC.

RHEINGAU *Germany, Anbaugebiet, W, R* Generally reckoned Germany's top wine region, a band of mostly south-facing vineyards overlooking the Rhine west of Weisbaden. Riesling is the classic grape, for W wines traditionally sweet (Auslese etc.) and increasingly dry (see CHARTA). Some Rs are made at the western end of the region, around Assmanshausen. Important villages include ELTVILLE, GEISENHEIM, HOCHHEIM, JOHANNISBERG, RÜDESHEIM etc. Leading producers include: Becker, Breuer, Eser, Schloss Groenesteyn, Prinz von Hessen, Schloss Johannisberg, von Mumm, Schloss Reinhartshausen, Balthasar Ress, Schloss Schönborn, Staatsweingut Eltville, Schloss Vollrads.

RHEINHESSEN *Germany, Anbaugebiet, W, R* Large region of flat vineyards making mostly everyday wines, including large amounbts of LIEBFRAUMILCH. There are islands of high quality at BINGEN and the RHEINTERRASSE around NIERSTEIN.

RHEINTERRASSE *Germany, Rheinhessen, W, R* Long slope overlooking the Rhein, providing good vineyard sites which produce the finest wines of the region. Famous villages here include NACKENHEIM, NIERSTEIN and OPPENHEIM, although two Grosslagen, Niersteiner Gutes Domtal and Oppenheimer Krotenbrunnen, are best known for mass production wines. Leading producers include: Anton Balbach Erben, Gunderloch, Louis Guntrum, Kühling-Gillot, and Heyl zu Herrnsheim.

RHODE ISLAND *USA* This small state with a moderate climate has a handful of producers and some good wines from classic varieties. Leading producer: SAKONNET.

RÍAS BAIXAS *Spain, Galicia, DO, W* The newest wine zone of Galicia, in north-west Spain, is investing in modern technology and makes excellent W wine from the Albariño grape. Albariño is rich but dry wine which is among the best Ws in Spain. Leading producers include: Granxa Fillaboa, Bodegas Morgadío-Agromiño.

RIBEAUVILLÉ   *France, Alsace*   Overlooked by three castles, this village makes splendid wines from *Grands Crus* Geisberg, Kirchberg de Ribeauvillé and Osterberg. The Rieslings produced are among the best in Alsace. Leading producers include: Trimbach, Faller.

RIBEIRO   *Spain, Galicia, DO, W, R*   Galician wine zone, producing light, fresh *joven* R and W, and *enverado* from under-ripe grapes. New investment is under way and great potential is apparent. Leading producers include: **BODEGAS LAPATENA**, Cooperativa Vitivinícola del Ribeiro.

RIBERA DEL DUERO   *Spain, Castilla-León, DO, P, R*   The most important wine zone in Castilla-León and one of the best in Spain for R wines. It takes in part of the upper Duero Valley, which has limestone soils and a cool climate. The zone makes high-quality *rosado* and R wines, mostly *crianzas*, with some superb *reservas* and *gran reservas*. The sole grape is Tinta Fino – the Tempranillo of Rioja. Leading producers include: **ALEJANDRO FERNÁNDEZ, BODEGAS PEÑALBA LÓPEZ, BODEGAS RIBERA-DUERO, BODEGAS VEGA SICILIA.**

RIBERA-DUERO, BODEGAS   *Spain, Castilla-León, Ribera del Duero, R, P*   The oldest cooperative in the area, producing reliable quality wines from cellars at Peñafiel. It also uses the labels Peñafiel and Protos (for its best wine).

RICASOLI   *Italy, Tuscany, Chianti, R, W*   The Ricasoli family were the creators of modern-style Chianti in the 19th century. Their Chianti Classico, Riserva del Barone, which is aged for five years, is very reliable. Barrique-ageing helps shape the R *vino da tavola*, San Ripolo. Ricasoli is also the largest maker of **VIN SANTO** in Tuscany.

RICAUD, CH DE   *France, Bordeaux, Loupiac, W, Bordeaux, R*   The long-lived, complex sweet W from this château is better than the appellation would suggest. Also makes AOC Bordeaux R.

RICCADONA   *Italy, Piedmont, W, Sp*   Large producer of vermouth, Asti and *metodo classico* Conte Balduino Extra Brut and Riserva Privata Angelo Riccadona.

RICEYS, ROSÉ DES   *France, Champagne, AOC, P*   Rare Pinot Noir still P wines from a small AOC in the Aube. Leading producers include: Alexandre Bonnet, Morel Père & Fils.

RICHEAUME, DOM DE   *France, Provence, Côtes de Provence, R, W, P*   Henning Hoesch produces excellent local R wines, practising strict organic techniques. Of three styles of R, the best is Cuvée Tradition, and there is also a little P and W. The wines spend up to 18 months in small wooden barrels.

RICHEBOURG   See ROMANÉE.

RICHOTEY, CH *France, Bordeaux, Fronsac, R* Estate with a good reputation for solid, well-flavoured wines.

RICHTER, MAX-FERDINAND *Germany, Mosel, W* Producer of a range of high-class Mosels, the best being cask-aged, including regular supplies of Eiswein.

RIDGE *USA, California, Bay Area, R* One of the best names in California. Based at Cupertino, this winery is now Japanese-owned. Veteran R specialist Paul Draper produces great Cabernet Sauvignons and distinctive Zinfandel R from disparate vineyards (Sonoma, Paso Robles, Amador). A collectors' favourite is the dense, almost black York Creek (Napa) Petite Sirah.

RIESLING Classic white grape from Germany, which in careful hands makes dry or superb sweet wines that perfectly balance acidity and sweetness, for early drinking or to age for decades. Grown in the best vineyards of the Mosel and Rhine valleys, in Austria, northern Italy and Alsace, where its wine is typically higher in alcohol and drier than in Germany. It also does well in California (sometimes called Johannisberg or White Riesling), New Zealand and Australia (Rhine Riesling).

RIESLING ITALICO See WELSCHRIESLING.

RIEUSSEC, CH *France, Bordeaux, Sauternes, 1er Cru Classé, W* Owned since 1984 by the Rothschilds of Lafite, Rieussec has recaptured its reputation as one of the great Sauternes: powerful and rich, though balanced.

RIO NEGRO *South America, Argentina, Sp, W* Argentina's southernmost wine region, and one of the coolest, its grapes mainly used for Sp wines.

RIOJA *Spain, La Rioja, DOC, R, W, P* Spain's best-known wine region, subdivided into Rioja Alavesa, Rioja Alta and Rioja Baja. Many large-scale bodegas, or wineries, produce a vast range of good to outstanding wines, in all three colours, by a process which stresses cask-ageing. W wines are from Viura grapes, and the majority are made to be fresh and light. P wines too are for drinking young. Traditional oak-aged W Rioja – still made by some bodegas – has some Malvasía to add weight to the Viura. R grapes are Tempranillo, Garnacha and Graciano. Styles of R are *joven* – sold without wood-ageing; *crianza* – with at least a year in cask; *reserva* – at least 4 years old; and *gran reserva* – at least 6 years old. Most Rioja is ready to drink when sold, though the top Rs will gain from extra bottle-age. Leading producers include: BODEGAS CAMPO VIEJO, CVNE, BODEGAS MUGA, MARQUÉS DE MURRIETA, BODEGAS FEDERICO PATERNINA, BODEGAS LA RIOJA ALTA.

RIOJA ALTA, BODEGAS LA *Spain, Rioja, R, W* One of the very top names for quality in the Rioja region, concentrating mainly on *reservas* and *gran reservas*. Viña Ardanza is an elegant and well-balanced R and the Reserva 904 is a bigger, more concentrated R wine.

RION, DOM DANIEL   *France, Burgundy, Côte d'Or, R*   Estate with widespread vineyard holdings in the Côte de Nuits making wines in a modern, fruit-dominated style.

RIQUEWIHR   *France, Alsace*   Ancient and lovely village that includes two *Grands Crus* – Schoenenbourg and Sporen – known for Ws from Riesling, Gewürztraminer and Muscat. Leading producers include: Deiss, Dopff Au Mouiin, Hugel.

RISCAL, MARQUÉS DE   *Spain, Rioja, R, P, W*   Quality has been somewhat patchy at this *bodega* in the past, but recent investment means that wines from the late 1980s onwards are much improved. Riscal also produces wines in Rueda, from French varieties including Sauvignon Blanc as well as Spanish staples.

RISERVA   *Italy*   DOC or DOCG wines with additional ageing in cask or bottle or both.

RIVENDELL WINERY   *USA, New York, Hudson River Valley, W, R*   The high reputation of Rivendell is built upon Ws such as Chardonnay, barrel-fermented Seyval Blanc and Vidal Blanc, Rs including Cabernet Sauvignon and blends.

RIVERA   *Italy, Southern Italy, Apulia, W, R, P*   The leading producer of the Castel del Monte DOC, making R, W and P wines. Il Falcone is a *riserva* R. The Terre al Monte range includes an interesting Aglianico *rosato*.

RIVERINA   *Australia, New South Wales*   A vast inland area encompassing the Murrumbidgee region. Production is mainly bulk Ws, especially Sémillon and Trebbiano. Rs are mainly Shiraz.

RIVESALTES   *France, Midi, AOC, VDN*   This name covers a wide range of *vins doux naturels*: Ws (*blanc* or *doré*) tend to darken, and Rs become lighter, with age. Best is the RANCIO style, achieved by ageing for at least 9 months with some exposure to oxygen; such wine is often sold as Vieux Rivesaltes. The W Muscat de Rivesaltes, on the other hand, should be drunk within 1-2 years: it may have a lemony, honeyed flavour, or a fuller, richer, orangey taste. Leading producers include: Dom Cazes, Ch de Corneilla, Mont Tauch co-op, Dom Sarda-Malet.

RIVIÈRE, CH DE LA   *France, Bordeaux, Fronsac, R*   The largest Fronsac estate: a splendid château with ancient cellars and long-lived, opulent wines.

ROBERTSON   *South Africa, WO*   In the Breede River Valley, this region enjoys a hot, arid climate tempered by sea breezes from the Indian Ocean. Its estates and co-ops produce good Chardonnay and Shiraz, as well as Sp wines. Leading producers include: Graham Beck, Van Loveren, Weltevrede, De Wetshof.

ROBOLA   *Greece, Islands, W*   A big dry W wine from the island of Cephalonia from the native Robola grape.

ROC DES CAMBES, CH *France, Bordeaux, Côte de Bourg, R* François Mitjavile's St-Emilion, **LE TERTRE RÔTEBOEUF**, is well known: this, his second estate, makes equally uncompromising and (for the AOC) costly wine in a rich, heady style.

ROCAILLES, DOM DU *France, Savoie, W, R* Leading maker of Ws from the best Savoie villages (*crus*), Abymes and Apremont, as well as R Vin de Savoie.

ROCCA DELLE MACIE *Italy, Tuscany, Chianti, R, W* Maker of a good-value range of fruity wines. The basic Chianti Classico and the *riserva* are designed for relatively early drinking. The *vino da tavola* Ser Gioveto (R) needs age.

ROCHEMORIN, CH DE *France, Bordeaux, Pessac-Léognan R, W* Large estate with a fine fleshy R and sound W, both enjoyable young; medium-priced and very good value.

RODERN *France, Alsace* Known historically for R from Pinot Noir, this village now produces Gewürztraminer and Pinot Gris Ws, and includes most of *Grand Cru* Gloeckelberg. Leading producers include: Gassmann, J Sipp.

RODET, ANTONIN *France, Burgundy, Chalonnais, R, W* An important *négociant* firm, producing wines from the whole of Burgundy and also making an excellent Mercurey from the Château de Chamirey vineyards.

ROEDERER *USA, California, Mendocino, Sp* Champagne house Louis Roederer started making classic Sp in California in 1985. The goal is 100,000 cases from almost 162ha of vines. The oak-aged Estate Brut is elegant, with lemon and bread-dough aromas.

ROEDERER, LOUIS *France, Champagne* Founded over 200 years ago, this family-owned **GRANDE MARQUE** makes some of the greatest champagnes. Reserve wines and long ageing before sale are two keys to the consistent quality of the NV Brut Premier. The prestige *cuvée*, Cristal, created for a Tsar, is one of the great luxury champagnes.

ROLET PÈRE ET FILS *France, Jura, R, W, P, Sp* Estate which concentrates on single-variety wines, including a P (Poulsard), Rs (Pinot Noir and Trousseau) and Ws from Chardonnay (including an oak-aged *cuvée*) and Savagnin. Sp, **VIN JAUNE** and Macvin complete the range.

ROMANÉE, LA *France, Burgundy, AOC, R* The five *Grands Crus* of La Romanée, **ROMANÉE CONTI**, Romanée-St-Vivant, **RICHEBOURG** and **LA TÂCHE** form a block on the hillside above the Côte de Nuits village of Vosne-Romanée. Their wines are known for their phenomenal cost as well for their spicy opulence and capacity to age for 10–15 years or more. Leading producers include: Bouchard Père et Fils, Alain Hudelot-Noéllat, Domaine de la Romanée-Conti, Ch de Vosne-Romanée.

ROMANÉE CONTI See ROMANÉE (La).

ROMANEE-CONTI, DOM DE LA *France, Burgundy, Côte d'Or, R, W* Sole owners of Romanée-Conti and La Tâche and major owners of other top *Grands Crus*. These are the wines by which all other red burgundies are judged. Rich, heady and incredibly deep in taste, they are destined for a long life. Greatly sought after, their very limited production on occasion ensures ridiculously high prices. Have been known to disappoint.

ROMANÉE-ST-VIVANT *See* ROMANÉE (LA).

ROPITEAU FRÈRES *France, Burgundy, Côte d'Or, R, W* Estate owner and *négociant*, whose Ws are generally better than Rs. Their best wines are the Meursaults.

ROSADO *Spain* Rosé or pink wine.

ROSATO *Italy* Rosé or pink wine.

ROSEMOUNT ESTATE *Australia, New South Wales, Hunter Valley W, R* Rosemount, founded in 1969, produces remarkably consistent wines. Chardonnays are rich and fruity, R wines enjoyable and with character. Roxburgh Chardonnay and Show Reserve wines are the flagships.

ROSETTE *France, South-West, AOC, W* Tiny enclave within the Bergerac zone which offers a name for local sweet W wine. Often these are sold as Côtes de Bergerac.

ROSSO CONERO *Italy, Marches, DOC, R* This coastal zone near Ancona is increasingly promising, yielding flavoursome meaty wines from the Montepulciano grape. Leading producers include: Fazi-Battaglia, Garofoli, Monte Schiavo, Umani Ronchi.

ROSSO DI MONTALCINO *Italy, Tuscany, DOC, R* Little brother to Brunello di Montalcino. May be sold after one year's ageing, so much less tannic than the Brunello. Leading producers include: Tenuta Caparzo, Col d'Orcia, Villa Banfi.

ROSSO PICENO *Italy, Marches, DOC, R* Broad DOC whose best wines come from the *superiore* zone. Mainly Sangiovese with some Montepulciano. Leading producers include: Fazi-Battaglia, La Torraccia, Villa Pigna, Villamagna.

ROT, NOBLE *See* BOTRYTIS CINEREA.

ROTHBURY ESTATE *Australia, New South Wales, Hunter Valley W, R* Created by wine guru Len Evans, this estate is now a public company. Its annual 250,000 cases include buttery Chardonnays, dense Shiraz Rs and fine Sémillon Ws.

RÔTI *France* Literally "roasted". A characteristic of sweet wines with aromas of dried grapes resulting from noble rot (BOTRYTIS CINEREA.)

ROTY, JOSEPH *France, Burgundy, Côte d'Or, R* Leading producer in Gevrey-Chambertin, making densely concentrated, fruity, oaky, long-lived R wines.

ROUDIER, CH *France, Bordeaux, Montagne St-Emilion, R* A top estate of the St-Emilion "satellites" making rich, solid wine worth a few years' cellaring.

ROUFFACH *France, Alsace* This village's vineyards encompass the *Grand Cru* Vorbourg, which includes the noted Clos St-Landelin. Pinot Noir (for Rs), Riesling and Pinot Gris (Ws) all do well. Leading producers include: Dopff and Irion, Schlumberger.

ROUMANIA Although it has a long winemaking history, most wine is drunk locally. The best wines come from four main regions: Tîrnave, Cotnari, Dealul Mare and Murfatlar. W wines with good aromas and firm acidity are made from a wide range of grapes including Muscat Ottonel, Sauvignon Blanc and Pinot Gris. For Rs, Pinot Noir, Cabernet Sauvignon and Merlot do well in Dealul Mare. The best Cabernet Sauvignon comes from the warmest region, Murfatlar. Cotnari is known for its pale, honeyed sweet wine which gained fame alongside Hungarian Tokaji.

ROUSSEAU, DOM ARMAND *France, Burgundy, Côte d'Or, R* Estate with vineyards in Morey-St-Denis and Gevrey-Chambertin. Traditional, benchmark wines.

ROYAL OPORTO WINE COMPANY *Portugal, port* Originally set up in 1756 by the Portuguese government as the controlling body for the port trade, today it is by far the largest producer of port. The wines are mainly very commercial and often appear in supermarkets as own-label wines.

ROZAY, CH DU *France, Rhône, Condrieu, W* Quality wines, from old vines, that can be among the appellation's best.

RUCHOTTES-CHAMBERTIN *See* CHAMBERTIN.

RÜDESHEIM *Germany, Rheingau, W* Town situated below its famous vine-covered hill, the Rüdesheimer Berg. The steep Berg Schlossberg vineyard yields Riesling Ws with a distinctive flavour from the slaty soil. Leading producers include: Dr. Heinrich Nägler, Bernard Breuer, Balthasar Ress.

RÜDESHEIM *Germany, Nahe, W* Village (as opposed to the town of the same name in the Rheingau) which is the centre of the *grosslage* Rosengarten. The district produces pleasant, everyday wine.

RUEDA *Spain, Castilla-León, DO, W, Sp* One of the fine wine zones of Castilla-León, owing its modern prominence to the Marqués de Riscal brand, and now producing many styles of wine including W DO Rueda Superior and new Sp wine DO Rueda Espumoso. W Rueda is usually crisp, dry and fresh – very much a modern W wine. There are plans to extend the DO to include R and *rosados*. Leading producers include: Castilla la Vieja, Marques de Griñon, Marqués de Riscal, Vinos Blancos de Castilla.

RUFFINO   *Italy, Tuscany, Chianti, R, W*   One of Chianti's giants with some of its best *riservas*, such as Riserva Ducale. The firm was instrumental in creating Predicato wines. Nero del Tondo is a R from Pinot Nero; their prestige W wine is called Libaio.

RUGIENS, LES   *France, Burgundy, Côte de Beaune, 1er Cru, R*   This Pommard vineyard is divided into Rugiens Bas and Rugiens Haut, the former in particular producing wines of exceptional quality with great ageing potential. Leading producers include: J-M Boillot, de Courcel, Michel Gaunoux, de Montille, Pothier-Rieusset.

RUINART   *France, Champagne*   This relatively unknown small GRANDE MARQUE was founded in 1729 and is now owned by the LVMH group. Very well-made, elegant and flowery; and good value: especially the *blanc de blancs* prestige *cuvée*, Dom Ruinart.

RULÄNDER   See PINOT GRIS.

RULLY   *France, Burgundy, AOC, R, W*   Village in the CÔTE CHALONNAIS district. Rully makes elegant, spice-accented Chardonnay Ws and clear, pleasing Pinot Noir Rs. Some, but not all, of the best vineyards are *Premier Cru*. Leading producers include: Dom Belleville, Jean-Claude Brelière, Chartron & Trébuchet, Pierre Cogny, André Delorme, Dom de la Folie, Dom de la Hermitage, Paul & Henri Jacqueson, Dom de la Renarde, Ch de Rully/Antonin Rodet.

RUPPERTSBERG   *Germany, Pfalz, W, R*   Wine village in the central or Mittelhaardt zone of the Pfalz region. Produces fine W Riesling, Silvaner and Scheurebe from the Hoheburg and Linsenbusch vineyards.

RUSSIAN REPUBLIC   W and Sp wines are made in the south and east of the republic from varieties including Muscatel (for dessert wines), Silvaner, Riesling, Aligoté and the ubiquitous Rkatsiteli. R wines are made in the south and east. The greatest potential is for Rs from Cabernet Sauvignon.

RUSSIAN RIVER VALLEY   *USA, California, Sonoma, VA*   In Sonoma County, a cool climate wine zone producing interesting Rs from Pinot Noir, Ws from Chardonnay, flinty White Riesling and nutmeg-spiced W Gewürztraminer. Also some crisp Sp wines. Leading producers include: Gary Farrell, Korbel, Piper Sonoma, Sonoma Cutrer.

RUSSIZ SUPERIORE   *Italy, Friuli-Venezia-Giulia, Collio and Colli Orientali, W*   Estate producing some very stylish varietal wines. Two *vini da tavola*, Roncuz (W) and a sweet wine Verduzzo (W), have received acclaim.

RUST-EN-VREDE   *South Africa, Stellenbosch, R*   This R-only estate is owned by former Springbok Jannie Englebrecht. His Shiraz, with its rich, roasted quality, is distinctly reminiscent of the northern Rhône. Shiraz also appears in the estate's best wine, a blend of R grapes called Rust-en-Vrede.

RUSTENBERG ESTATE *South Africa, Stellenbosch, R, W* Outstandingly beautiful, and one of the Cape's oldest estates, Rustenberg has a fine reputation notably for its Rs, including a fairly restrained Cabernet Sauvignon and a good bordeaux blend, Rustenberg Gold.

RUTHERFORD *USA, California, VA* In the heart of the Napa Valley, this area, sometimes called the Rutherford Bench, is the wide, flat, low terrace along the side of the valley. Rutherford is famous for its distinctive Cabernet Sauvignons with firm, tannic structure and somewhat herbaceous flavours. Leading producers include: Beaulieu, Caymus, Grgich Hills, Heitz Cellars, Inglenook.

RUTHERGLEN *Australia, Victoria* Vines were first planted here in Victoria's north-east in the mid-19th century. This region now enjoys an excellent reputation for liqueur Muscats. Leading producers include: Baileys, Morris.

RYMAN, HUGH A name appearing on millions of wine labels. An Australian-trained oenologist, son of Nick Ryman, formerly of Ch Jaubertie in Bergerac, Ryman works in Eastern Europe, Spain, southern France and elsewhere, conjuring good modern wines out of backward areas by use of straightforward modern techniques.

S

SAALE-UNSTRUT *Germany, Anbaugebiet, W* Region in the east of Germany, around Leipzig, making mostly dry W wines. The former monastic estate now called the Staatsweingut (state cellars) Naumberg is the main producer, along with the Freyburg/Unstrut co-op.

SAAR-RUWER *Germany, Mosel-Saar-Ruwer, Bereich, W* Zone along two small rivers, the Saar and Ruwer, tributaries of the Mosel. Top-class Riesling Ws are made in warm years. Ordinary wines carry the **WILTINGER SCHARZBERG** name. Leading producers include: Karthäuserhof, von Schubert (both Ruwer); Bischöfliche Weingüter, Egon Müller-Scharzhof, von Hövel, Reverchon, Bert Simon, Vereinigte Hospitien.

SAARSTEIN, SCHLOSS *Germany, Saar, W* Rieslings with pronounced acidity, balanced by fruit, are the aim of this Saar estate.

SABLES DU GOLFE DU LION *France, Vin de Pays, P, R, W* This is the *vin de pays* for the sandy coastal plain where the Listel firm (*see* SALINS DU MIDI) have a successful venture making P wines from Grenache, plus Rs (Cabernets, Syrah, Cinsaut etc), and Ws from Sauvignon and Muscat as well as local grapes.

SACHSEN *Germany, Anbaugebiet, W* Region in eastern Germany around Dresden and Meissen, making dry W wines. Leading producers: Meissen co-op, Schloss Wackerbarth.

SAGET, GUY *France, Loire, Pouilly-Fumé, W* Familiar throughout the Loire Valley as *négociants*, the Sagets started in Pouilly, where they still farm. Their wines, especially the Pouilly-Fumé, can be attractive and age well.

SAINT-GEORGES, LES *France, Burgundy, Côte de Nuits, 1er Cru, R* Leading vineyard in the Nuits-St-Georges appellation, with great bouquet and a full, satisfying palate. Leading producers include: Robert Chevillon, Henri Gouges.

SAINTSBURY *USA, California, Napa, R, W* In the heart of the Carneros district, this estate grows R Pinot Noir and W Chardonnay. Garnet is a lighter, fresher Pinot Noir R bursting with cherry fruit.

SAKONNET VINEYARDS *USA, Rhode Island, W, R* The 17.5-ha vineyard provides Ws from Vidal Blanc, Chardonnay and Gewürztraminer and Rs from Pinot Noir and Cabernet Franc. The best-selling wines are two blends, America's Cup White and Spinnaker White.

SALES, CH DE *France, Bordeaux, Pomerol, R* Pomerol's biggest estate and the only real château in the region: not great wine, but enjoyable and early-maturing.

SALINS DU MIDI, LES *France, Midi, Gard, R, W, P* Enormous enterprise with three estates on the Carmargue sand dunes, and two in Provence, at the forefront of new developments, including organic viticulture. The flagship wine, a Vin de Pays des Sables du Golfe du Lion, is a delicate P using the Listel name.

SALON *France, Champagne* Owned by Laurent-Perrier, this miniscule **GRANDE MARQUE** has just one hectare of vines in the Côte des Blancs. Its sole vintage wine, expensive and extremely sought after, ages beautifully.

SALWEY, WEINGUT B *Germany, Baden, R,W, P* This estate is a specialist in Rs, ageing all wines in oak. A dry Weissherbst P is another speciality.

SAMOS *Greece, Islands, W, VDN* The Aegean island of Samos produces sweet wines from the Muscat grape. They can be *vin de liqueur*, *vin doux naturel* or Samos Nectar, a very sweet W from sun-dried grapes, capable of long wood-ageing. Leading producers include: Cambas.

SAN FELICE *Italy, Tuscany, Chianti, R, W, P* Estate making good basic Chianti Classico and single-vineyard Pogio Rosso and Villa la Pagliaia *riserva* Chiantis. San Felice is also known for fresh, young Bianco Val d'Arbia (DOC, W), fruity Rosé di Canaiolo *vino da tavola* and blended Vigorello (R).

SAN JUAN DEL RIO *Mexico, Central America, R, W, Sp* Recently developed, this vineyard region is 160km (100 miles) north of Mexico City. Most plantings are at a cool 1,800m (6,000ft). Some Cabernet Sauvignon and Pinot Noir Rs are made, also Sp wines.

SAN PEDRO *Chile, R, W* Based in the **MAULE VALLEY**, this is one of Chile's oldest wineries, founded in 1865. San Pedro is one of the country's largest producers with roughly 770,000 cases a year. It is best known for its good-value Gato Nero and Gato Blanco wines which account for 50% of exports. Other labels include Castillo de Molina and Santa Helena.

SAN VALERO *Spain, Aragón, Cariñena, R, W, P* The largest cooperative in this wine zone, producing wines from everyday young Rs and Ws to prizewinning *gran reservas*.

SANCERRE *France, Loire, AOC, W, R, P* Dry W wine with vibrant acidity, grassy bouquet and gooseberry or blackcurrant flavours; a model Sauvignon Blanc wine now emulated around the world. It tends to be lighter and earlier-drinking than its twin, **POUILLY FUMÉ**. Rs and P are from Pinot Noir. Leading producers include: J-F Bailly, J-M Bourgeoise, Lucien Crochet, Gitton, Alphonse Mellot, Clos de la Poussie, Prieur, Reverdy, J-M Roger, J-L Vacheron, A Vatan.

SANDEMAN *Portugal, port, Spain, sherry* George Sandeman began in London in 1790, with initial capital of £300. Today his firm is owned by Seagram but still family-run and is one of the largest port producers. Much of the range, eg Founder's Reserve, is standard commercial port, but there are also fine wines, from attractively fruity 10-year-old Royal Tawny to soft, relatively fast-maturing vintage wines. House of Sandeman sherry has seen a considerable increase in quality of brands such as Don Fino, and wines like Royal Ambrosante amontillado and Imperial Corregidor oloroso, based on long-established *soleras*.

SANFORD *USA, California, Santa Barbara & Southern California, R, W, P* From vines on the bank of the Santa Ynez River, Rich Sanford makes butter- and grapefruit-tasting Chardonnay, black cherry-rich Pinot Noir R, herbaceous Sauvignon W which ages well, and tangy orange-peel and rose-petal Pinot Noir Vin Gris P.

SANGIOVESE The main red grape for Chianti. Clones are found all over Italy, making wines of varying quality.

SANTA CAROLINA *Chile, South America, R, W* Established in 1875 in the MAIPO VALLEY, one of the first wineries to develop vineyards in the new CASABLANCA area. The firm enjoys a good reputation for Cabernet Sauvignon, Sauvignon Blanc and Sémillon, especially for the Special Reserve versions of the first two.

SANTA MONICA *Chile, South America, R, W* Owned by well-known winemaker Emilio de Solminihac and his wife, Monica, this firm produces export wines only from Cabernet Sauvignon and Merlot (Rs), Chardonnay, Sauvignon Blanc, Sémillon and Riesling (Ws).

SANTA RITA *Chile, South America, R, W* Chile's leading exporter to both the UK and North America. Founded in 1880, it has recently developed vineyards in the new CASABLANCA region. Santa Rita sells under three different labels, the best of which is Medalla Real, headed by Cabernet Sauvignon and Chardonnay.

SANTA YNEZ VALLEY *USA, California, Santa Barbara, VA* Wine zone in Santa Barbara County, where Chardonnay and particularly Pinot Noir seem perfectly suited. Also Sauvignon Blanc and Merlot. Leading producers include: Firestone, Sanford.

SANTENAY *France, Burgundy, AOC, R, W* Here R wine reasserts itself in this village south of the famous W-wine vineyards of Montrachet. There are several *Premiers Crus*, and some good wines are made in a rather tough, earthy style. Try them at 5–8 years. Leading producers include: Adrien Belland, Ch de la Charrière, Fleurot-Larose, Mestre Père & Fils, Piieur-Brunet, Roussot.

SANTENOTS, LES *France, Burgundy, Côte de Beaune, 1er Cru, R, W* The R wines from this vineyard are under the appellation Volnay-Santenots and combine breeding and elegance. The Ws appear as Meursault-Santenots and are full-bodied with a long finish. Leading producers include: Marquis d'Angerville, Comtes Lafon.

SANTORINI *Greece, Islands, W* The volcanic soil here produces a powerful dry W wine from the Assyrtiko grape, in addition to a sweet wine called Vissanto.

SARDINIA *Italy* This Mediterranean island continues to make wines from native varieties such as R Cannonau and Girò and W Nuragus and Torbato in addition to more modern styles. Leading producer Sella & Mosca is a driving force.

SARGET DE GRUAUD-LAROSE *France, Bordeaux, Médoc, St-Julien, R* 2nd wine of Ch Gruaud-Larose.

SARTRE, CH LE *France, Bordeaux, Pessac-Léognan, R, W* With the same owners as Ch Carbonnieux, this small Léognan estate offers the Carbonnieux style at half the price. The R here is better than the W.

SASSICAIA *Italy, Tuscany, DOC, R* Legendary wine, the brainchild of Mario Incisa della Rochetta, first made in 1968. It is from 75% Cabernet Sauvignon and 25% Cabernet Franc, *barrique*-aged. Superb and very long-lived.

SAUMUR *France, Loire, AOC, R, W, P, Sp* The basic AOC is for R and W still wines from the Cabernets (Franc and Sauvignon) and Chenin Blanc grapes, made around Saumur on the south bank of the Loire. Also crisp, Sp (*mousseux* or *pétillant*) W wines. Saumur-Champigny (from Cabernet grapes) is one of France's most fashionable light R wines, from nine communes east of Saumur. Leading producers include: Ackerman-Laurence, Bouvet-Ladubay, Ch de Chaintre, Paul Filliatreau, Gratien Meyer Seydoux, Ch de Targé, Philippe et Georges Vatan.

SAUSSIGNAC *France, South-West, AOC, W* Enclave within Bergerac for medium-sweet or rich sweet W wine. Often sold as Côtes de Bergerac. Leading producers include: Pierre Sadoux.

SAUTEJEAU, MARCEL *France, Loire, Muscadet, W* Firm based at Dom de l'Hyvernière near Le Pallet, which, along with Dom de la Botinière at Vallet, is the source of their Muscadet. Its turnover of more than a million cases a year includes wines from Anjou, Saumur and Vouvray.

SAUTERNES *France, Bordeaux, AOC, W* World-famous, luscious sweet W wine from the southern Graves region. The most common blend of grapes is 80% Sémillon, 20% Sauvignon Blanc. Great Sauternes – rich, viscous, honeyed wine that retains a dash of acidity that helps it improve for decades – is made only from grapes that have been attacked by **BOTRYTIS CINEREA** ("noble rot"). The châteaux were classified in 1855, into *Premier Cru supérieur* (of which there is only one, Ch d'Yquem), *Premiers Crus* (11 châteaux) and *Deuxièmes Crus* (14 châteaux). Leading producers include: Ch Filhot, Ch Guiraud, Ch Lafaurie-Peyraguey, Ch Rieussec, Ch de Suduiraut, Ch d'Yquem.

SAUVIGNON BLANC   White grape used in Bordeaux blends for both dry and sweet wines, and for dry whites such as Sancerre and Pouilly Fumé in the upper Loire. Most are designed to be drunk young, in the fresh, acidic and assertive yet fruity style of the Loire wines: New Zealand Sauvignon Blancs are often excellent. A short period of oak-ageing emphasizes the smokiness of the grape, and has led to its alternative name, Fumé Blanc, being widely used in California. Also grown in Chile, Austria, Slovenia and Bulgaria.

SAUVION   *France, Loire, Muscadet, W, R, P*   One of the most dynamic *négociants* in the region, based at the Ch du Cléray in Vallet. Brands include Sauvion du Cléray, Cardinal Richard and Carte d'Or. Despite buying 80% of its grapes from growers, it ensures quality by basing purchases on tastings, selling some wines as *cuvées*, known as Découvertes.

SAUZET, DOM ETIENNE   *France, Burgundy, Côte d'Or, W*   Together with Domaine Leflaive, Sauzet is the top producer in Puligny-Montrachet, making classic W burgundies in the *Grands* and *Premiers Crus*.

SAVENNIÈRES   *France, Loire, AOC, W*   Bone-dry Ws from Chenin Blanc, made on the north bank of the Loire. There are two high-quality single-vineyard appellations: COULÉE-DE-SERRANT and ROCHE-AUX-MOINES. Leading producers include: Dom des Baumard, Clos de la Coulée de Serrant, Dom Mme Laroche, Pierre et Yves Soulez.

SAVIGNY/SAVIGNY-LES-BEAUNE   *France, Burgundy, AOC, R, W*   For Côte d'Or burgundies, these are very reasonably priced R wines. The *Premiers Crus* are notable for their appealing scent and clean, fruity taste; they are best drunk between 4–10 years old. Some Ws are also made. Leading producers include: Dom Simon Bize & Fils, Dom Pierre Guillemot, Dom Antonin Guyon, Dom Rapet Père & Fils, Dom Seguin.

SAVOIE, VIN DE   *France, Savoie, AOC, R, P, W, Sp*   Still or Sp (*mousseux* and *pétillant*) dry W wines, and some Rs and Ps, from large mountainous area. 17 villages or *crus* can use their name on the label: the most important are Abymes, Apremont, Arbin, Ayze, Chautagne, Chignin and Jongieux. The W grape Roussette has its own AOC, in which it may be used alone or blended with Chardonnay. Other local W-wine grapes are Jacquère, Gringet, Chasselas and high-acid Molette, which is used for Sp wine. The characteristic R-wine grape of Savoie is Mondeuse; Gamay and Pinot Noir are more recent arrivals. Leading producers include: Louis Magnin, Raymond Quénard, Ch de Ripaille, Dom des Rocailles, Le Vignerons Savoyard.

SAVOYE, DOM RENÉ   *France, Burgundy, Beaujolais, R*   One of the top producer of Chiroubles, the most fragrant of the Beaujolais Crus and best drunk young.

SCHARFFENBERGER *USA, California, Mendocino, Sp, W, P*
Champagne firms Pommery and Lanson are partners with John
Scharffenberger in this Sp wine producer at Philo. The Sp W leans
towards the austere, though the Brut P has rich, fruity aromas,
and plum and strawberry tastes.

SCHEUREBE White grape (Silvaner x Riesling) from Germany,
making good-quality wine, especially in the Pfalz, where the
strong bouquet and high acidity can result in characterful wine
for long-term keeping. Also grown in England.

SCHLOSS BÖCKELHEIM *Germany, Nahe, Bereich, W* Zone covering the southern half of the Nahe, including fine vineyards at
TRAISEN, NIEDERHAUSEN and SCHLOSSBÖCKELHEIM and rather
ordinary ones elsewhere. Mostly W, the best from Riesling,
which can from good sites be concentrated and long-lived.
Leading producers include: Paul Anheuser, Crusius, Dönhoff,
Staatliche Weinbaudömane.

SCHLOSS STAUFENBERG, MARKGRÄFLICH BADISCHES WEINGUT
Germany, Baden, R, W, P Fruity, intense Rieslings and Rs of high
quality keep up the reputation of this old estate.

SCHLUMBERGER, DOM *France, Alsace, W, R* This family firm has
amassed many vineyard plots over the years and now has the
largest holding in Alsace and one of the most important in France.
It includes steeply terraced plots which are expensive to cultivate,
but the *terroirs* are worth it. Their Gewürztraminers made their
name – especially Cuvée Christine (now defined as a *vendange
tardive*) and Cuvée Anne, a *sélection des grains nobles*. Also of top
quality are Pinot Gris and Rieslings from *Grands Crus* Kitterlé and
Saering.

SCHMITT, ROBERT WEINGUT *Germany, Franken, W* This estate
stresses natural viticulture and winemaking, yielding well-
balanced, long-lived wines in the traditional Franken style.

SCHOLTZ HERMANOS *Spain, Málaga* Probably the best málaga
producer; certainly the most familiar in export markets, and also
the oldest (founded 1805). Its most famous brand is Solera 1885:
essentially a dry wine, although with considerable richness.
Moscatel Palido is very sweet; Seco Añejo is intensely dry, like an
old amontillado sherry. Dulce Negro is very dark, concentrated
and sweet.

SCHÖNBORN, SCHLOSS *Germany, Rheingau, W, R* Estate producing classic Rheingau Rieslings, with well-balanced acidity and
fruit, and *barrique*-aged Rs.

SCHRAMSBERG *USA, California, Napa, Sp, W* Jack Davies and
his wife Jamie founded this specialist Sp wine estate in 1965 on
an old Calistoga winery. Their Blanc de Blancs, with lemon and
bread-dough aromas, and Blanc de Noirs, with flinty, berry
flavours, both age beautifully.

SCHRÖCK, HEIDI   *Austria, Neusiedlersee-Hügelland, W, R*   One of a small coterie of female winemakers, based in Rust, Schröck produces a wide range of wines, including Welschriesling and Weissburgunder (Ws), a grippy P from Cabernet Sauvignon and the rare Ausbruch (sweet W). One of her best wines is the R Blaufränkisch with its fine, ripe, silky-fruit palate.

SCHUBERT, WEINGUT VON   *Germany, Ruwer, W*   The estate's beautiful labels stress the name of the Maximin Grünhaus vineyard, all three parts of which it owns. Superb, long-lived Rieslings with balance and style.

SCHUSTER, EDUARD WEINGUT   *Germany, Pfalz, W*   Traditional maker of Rieslings and other Ws, which show all the Pfalz fullness and character.

SEBASTIANI   *USA, California, Sonoma, W, R*   Once a bulk producer, the stress has switched to high quality, notably the flinty, floral dry W from the rare vine Green Hungarian.

SEC   *France,*   **SECO**   *Spain and Portugal,*   **SECCO**   *Italy*   All mean dry. In champagne, however, sec means medium-dry.

SECOND VIN   The second wine of a château, as opposed to its *grand vin*. Often made from young-vine fruit.

SEGONZAC, CH   *France, Bordeaux, 1er Côtes de Blaye, R*   One of the top châteaux of Blaye: large amounts of well-made claret.

SEKT   *Germany*   Sparkling wine, made by a variety of methods. "Deutscher (German) Sekt" is despite the name usually made from non-German base wine, and is medium-dry and bland. Better-quality Sekt is labelled *brut* and has a district name on the label: the best are made from Riesling or Weissburgunder and will say so, while Winzersekt is made by a grower or estate.

SÉLECTION DE GRAINS NOBLES   *France*   Luscious, sweet wines with a natural concentration of sugars from late-picked **BOTRYTIZED** grapes or from grapes which have begun to dry on the vine. Term used particularly in Alsace; also Sauternes, Monbazillac and Coteaux du Layon.

SELVAPIANA   *Italy, Tuscany, Chianti, W, R*   Chianti Rufina estate known for its long-lived wines: normal, *riserva* and *cru*, Vigneto Bucerchiale (R), plus Borro Lastricato (W).

SÉMILLON   Useful but unfashionable white grape, best known for its partnership with Sauvignon Blanc in great sweet wines such as Sauternes. Sémillon is particularly prone to rot – good news if the rot is "noble" **BOTRYTIS CINEREA**, bad if it is grey rot. Sémillon is also blended with Sauvignon Blanc in dry Bordeaux whites, and alone has made some superb, long-maturing dry wines in Australia's Hunter Valley. Also grown in Chile, Argentina and South Africa.

SÉNARD, DOM DANIEL   *France, Burgundy, Côte d'Or, R*   Now a follower of Guy ACCAD's style of vinification, this domaine produces top-quality red Cortons.

SETÚBAL   *Portugal, DOC*   Peninsula in southern Portugal known for Moscatel de Setúbal, a sweet, fortified wine, but also for exciting new styles of R and W wine. Leading producers include: J P Vinhos.

SEYSSEL   *France, Savoie, AOC, W, Sp*   The best-known wine of this appellation is the Sp Seyssel Mousseux, made mainly from Molette grapes, but usually with a little Roussette for finesse, made as in Champagne. Leading producers include: Maison Mollex, Varichon & Clerc.

SEYVAL BLANC   Hybrid white grape with high acidity, making dry wine with neutral or grapefruity character in England, New York State and Canada.

SHIRAZ   Synonym for the Syrah grape grown in Australia and South Africa.

SHOMRON   *Israel, R, W, P*   One of Israel's main wine-production areas using grapes produced in the Carmel Valley. Leading producers include: Carmel.

SIAURAC, CH   *France, Bordeaux, Lalande-de-Pomerol, R*   The leading estate of the appellation; quite large, with delicious, early-maturing wine.

SICHEL, H   *Germany, Rheinhessen, W, R*   Large merchant house, known for its Blue Nun Liebfraumilch brand and for a range of good wines from all German regions.

SICILY   *Italy*   The Mediterranean's largest island is paying increasing attention to quality. Although some international varieties have infiltrated, native grapes such as Grillo and Inzolia remain important for the mainly W wine production. Also home to one of the world's great fortified wines, MARSALA.

SIEGRIST, THOMAS   *Germany, Pfalz, R, W*   Red-wine specialist, noted for his *barrique*-aged Spätburgunder and Dornfelder, and also Ws from Weiss- and Grauburgunder.

SIERRA FOOTHILLS   *USA, California, VA*   Wine zone along the eastern edge of the Central Valley, producing densely-fruited R wines from Zinfandel and Cabernet Sauvignon, plus Ws from Chardonnay and Sauvignon, and some fortified and dessert wines. Leading producers include: Boeger, Monteviña, Renaissance.

SIGALAS-RABAUD, CH   *France, Bordeaux, Sauternes, 1er Cru Classé, W*   Not much new oak is used here, and bottled young, Sigalas is delicious: intensely fruity and racily elegant. Drink at 8-10 years old. Bought in 1994 by Cordier: standards should further improve.

SIGOLSHEIM *France, Alsace* Wine village long known for its Riesling, Muscat and Gewürztraminer; the latter especially in *Grand Cru* Mambourg. Leading producers include: Sick-Dreyer, Pierre Sparr.

SILVANER/SYLVANER White grape making wine high in acidity, low in aroma, except from good producers in Alsace and Franken in Germany. Useful in blends.

SILVER OAK *USA, California, Napa, R* This Oakville winery makes just Cabernet Sauvignon. The Napa Valley, Alexander Valley (Sonoma) and Bonny's Vineyard Cabernets are all powerful and violet-scented.

SIMI *USA, California, Sonoma, W, R* The Healdsburg winery built in 1890 was refurbished by Russ Green and Moët-Hennessy of France. Chardonnays feature ripe clove, apple and anise flavours, the Cabernet Sauvignons are round and soft with violet scents and Sendal, a new W Sémillon/Sauvignon blend, is fleshy with ripe fig and honeydew-melon fruit.

SIMMERN, LANGWERTH VON *Germany, Rheingau, W, R* Traditional-style Rheingau Rieslings which respond beautifully to bottle-age.

SIMONE, CH *France, Provence, Palette, W, R* The leading producer in this small AOC, with very old vines (Grenache, Mourvèdre, Cinsaut for Rs; Clairette, Sémillon, Muscat for Ws). Traditional methods, and wine that can age for many years.

SIN CRIANZA *Spain* Wines that have spent no time in oak, or less than the legal minimum for *crianza* wines.

SIRAN, CH *France, Bordeaux, Margaux, Cru Bourgeois, R* This showplace château makes smooth silky wines that can age well.

SLOVAKIA The country has 28,000ha under vine, representing two-thirds of the former Czechoslovakia's vineyards. Mainly makes W wines from a wide number of varieties, including the native, aromatic Irsay Oliver, which at their best can be very attractive, with good fruit, very ripe and crisp. Of the small amount of R wine made, Pinot Noir stands out.

SLOVENIA There are 21,500ha under vine, divided into three major regions: PRIMORSKI; PODRAVSKI (the best) in the northeast which includes the Ljutomer sub-region; and (less important) Posavski. Production is fairly evenly divided between Ws (including Pinot Gris, Traminer, Sauvignon Blanc and Laski Rizling) and Rs (good Merlot and Cabernet Sauvignon and the local Refosk).

SMITH-HAUT-LAFITTE, CH *France, Bordeaux, Pessac-Léognan, Cru Classé, R, W* This large estate changed hands in 1990, with much money spent since. The first vintages under the new régime show the results. The W in particular, an all-Sauvignon Blanc wine, shows real concentration and breed. The (R) 2nd wine is Hauts de Smith.

SOAVE *Italy, Veneto, DOC, W* Well-known W from north Italy. Pale straw in colour, it has crisp acidity balanced by delicate fruit flavours that hint of toasted almonds. The main variety is Garganega. The best wines come from the *classico* zone. Recioto di Soave is sweet. Leading producers include: Anselmi, Bolla, Masi, Pieropan.

SOCIONDO-MALLET, CH *France, Bordeaux, Haut-Médoc, Cru Bourgeois, R* Serious, long-lived wine with the structure to repay patience. A good 1993.

SOGRAPE *Portugal, W, R* Portugal's largest winemaker, based at Vila Real, produces balanced R and W wines including Gazela, one of the best W Vinhos Verdes, and the whistle-dry Chello.

SOLERA *Spain* The system of blending sherry, across years as well as between casks. The aim is to maintain consistency and character. A solera may carry a date: its year of foundation.

SOMANTANO *Spain, Aragón, DO, W, P, R* Aragón wine zone, with up-to-date equipment and exciting prospects, producing highly individual R and light, fruity W and *rosados*. Both French and Spanish grape varieties are grown. Leading producers include: COVISA (COMPAÑÍA VITIVINÍCOLA DE SOMANTANO), Cooperativa Comarcal Somontano de Sobrarbe.

SONOMA *USA, California* County north of San Francisco, between Napa and the coast. Essentially a cool-climate zone, it has eight major viticultural areas (VAs): LOS CARNEROS, SONOMA VALLEY, SONOMA MOUNTAIN, RUSSIAN RIVER VALLEY, GREEN VALLEY, CHALK HILL, SONOMA COAST, KNIGHTS VALLEY, ALEXANDER VALLEY and DRY CREEK VALLEY. Together with Napa, Sonoma is California's major quality-wine region, well suited to growing a wide variety of grapes.

SONOMA COAST *USA, California, Sonoma, VA* At its best a wine zone where cool conditions make for intense, vine-matured fruit flavours. Something of a political creation, however, and the areas within it are linked only by their contact with the seashore. Wide range of varieties including Cabernet Sauvignon, Chardonnay, Merlot and Sauvignon Blanc.

SONOMA MOUNTAIN *USA, California, Sonoma, VA* Small subzone at the north-western end of Sonoma Valley. Best suited to Cabernet Sauvignon, Zinfandel and Sauvignon Blanc.

SONOMA VALLEY *USA, California, Sonoma, VA* About 2,450ha are mainly devoted to Cabernet Sauvignon, Merlot and Sauvignon Blanc on the valley floor, whereas the upper slopes are home to radiant, raspberry-fruited Zinfandel.

SOPRON *Hungary* North of Lake Balaton, this zone enjoys a more temperate climate than the rest of Hungary. Mainly R wines from Kékfrankos, with some Pinot Noir and Cabernet and Ws from Zöldveltelini, Tramini and Leányka.

SOUMADE, DOM DE LA *France, Rhône, Côtes du Rhône-Villages R, VDN* Good Syrah-dominated Rs and an excellent Vin Doux Naturel come from this Rasteau estate.

SOUTARD, CH *France, Bordeaux, St-Emilion, Grand Cru Classé, R* One of St-Emilion's oldest estates, run organically along traditional lines. Wines are dark, quite tannic when young and of very fine quality: the best will last more than 20 years.

SOUTH AUSTRALIA *Australia* Quality R, W and Sp wines are made in this state which boasts some of the country's finest regions, including BAROSSA VALLEY – birthplace of Australia's great R wine, Grange – the ADELAIDE HILLS, MCLAREN VALE, COONAWARRA and PADTHAWAY.

SOUTH CAROLINA *USA* A big wine region in pre-Revolutionary days, wine is being revived here by a few growers.

SOUTH-WEST COASTAL *Australia, Western Australia* This narrow coastal strip, 250km long by 20km wide, is noted for its unusual soil, a fine Tuart sand. Wine styles are diverse. Leading producers include: Capel Vale.

SOUVERAIN, CH *USA, California, Sonoma, R, W* Now part of Nestlé, Souverain produces fine Sonoma wines that are undervalued and hence underrated. Winemaker Tom Peterson's wines include spicy Zinfandel R, supple Pinot Noir R and silky Chardonnay.

SPARR, PIERRE *France, Alsace, W* Wines have a rich fruit flavour, sometimes with a hint of sweetness, with Pinot Gris, Riesling and Gewürztraminer the best. There are also some top-quality blends, such as Kaefferkopf (Gewürztraminer/Pinot Gris) and Symphonie (Riesling/Pinot Gris/Pinot Blanc/Gewürztraminer), as well as sparkling wine.

SPÄTBURGUNDER German synonym for PINOT NOIR.

SPÄTLESE *Germany* Literally, late-picked. QMP wine from riper grapes than *Kabinett*. *Spätlese* can be sweet, but is increasingly the basis for drier wines.

SPRING MOUNTAIN *USA, California, Napa, VA* Wine zone of Napa Valley, on the hills west of St. Helena where old vineyards yield densely-flavoured fruit. Main varieties include Cabernet Sauvignon, Merlot (R) and Johannisberg Riesling (W). Leading producers include: Cain Cellars, Robert Keenan, Smith-Madrone.

SPUMANTE *Italy* Term meaning sparkling.

ST AMOUR, CH DE *France, Burgundy, Beaujolais, R* One of the leading estates in St-Amour, making delicately fruity wines which also age well in bottle.

ST HALLETT *Australia, South Australia, Barossa, W, R* Top-quality winery with a meticulous eye for detail. The superb Old Block Shiraz R is from vines at least 60 years old and the wine is aged in

American oak. Other stars include Poachers White, a tangy Sémillon/Chardonnay/Sauvignon Blanc blend.

ST HUBERTS *Australia, Victoria, Yarra Valley, W, R* The first of the Yarra Valley revivalists, and now owned by ROTHBURY ESTATE (of the Hunter Valley), St Huberts makes excellent Chardonnay and Cabernet Sauvignon.

ST JEAN, CH *USA, California, Sonoma, W, R* Chardonnay accounts for 70% of the 225,000-case output: the Robert Young Vineyard wine is creamy and toasty, that from the Belle Terre Vineyard toasty and pear-like. Rs include an earthy, meaty Pinot Noir; Ws a honeyed, botrytized Riesling and Gewürztraminer.

ST JULIAN WINE CO *USA, Michigan, W* Founded in 1921 in the Paw Paw region, the company has success with a wide range of wines including Sp from hybrid grapes.

ST-AMAND, CH *France, Bordeaux, Sauternes, W* Charming, traditionally-made Sauternes; never very concentrated, but elegant: good value for money.

ST-AMOUR *France, Burgundy, AOC, R* Most northerly of the Beaujolais *crus* (strictly speaking, it is part of Mâconnais), and one of the smallest, St-Amour makes light, delicately fruity Gamay Rs. For drinking young, or after 2–3 years in bottle. Thanks to the atractive name, they can be expensive. Leading producers include: Jean-Paul Ducoté, Dom des Ducs, Dom Dufour, Dom de la Cave Lamartine/Paul Spay, Dom du Paradis, Dom Jean Pâtissier, Ch de St-Amour/Pierre Siraudin.

ST-AUBIN *France, Burgundy, AOC, W, R* Tucked behind the Côte de Beaune, this village's well-sited, south-facing vineyards make light, fresh, delicious and good-value W and R wines. Leading producers include: Jean-Claude Bachelet, Gérard Thomas.

ST-BRIS, SAUVIGNON DE *France, Burgundy, VDQS, W* Dry W wine made from the only Sauvignon Blanc grown in Burgundy, south-west of Chablis. Leading producers include: Caves de Bailly, Dom Bersan, Luc Sorin.

ST-CHINIAN *France, Midi, AOC, R* Large area of the COTEAUX DU LANGUEDOC in the Cévennes foothills. Its varied soils and micro-climates makes light, fruity Rs for early drinking and more substantial ones that gain from ageing. Grenache, Syrah, Mourvèdre are the main grapes, with Carignan which can provide acidity and backbone as well as perfumed fruit. Leading producers include: Berlou co-op, Ch Cazal-Viel, Ch Coujan, Dom des Jougla.

ST-EMILION *France, Bordeaux, AOC, R* Important Bordeaux region making enjoyable, sometimes splendid, Rs from Merlot, Cabernet Franc and some Cabernet Sauvignon. Typical St-Emilion has youthful appeal after 3–6 years, with supple plummy fruit. Top wines can easily last 15 years or more, depending on the vintage. The best châteaux are classified into 11 *Premiers Grands Crus Classés* and 64 *Grands Crus Classés*, though this is reviewed every 10 years. Lesser châteaux are awarded *Grand Cru* status. To the north are the "satellite" villages of LUSSAC, MONTAGNE, PUISSEGUIN and ST-GEORGES.

ST-ESTÈPHE   *France, Bordeaux, AOC, R*   Haut-Médoc commune north of Pauillac; with five classed growths and many other châteaux: wines are generally less prestigious than Pauillac. Top châteaux may be slow to mature, but much wine is now made in a faster-maturing style with more Merlot in the blend.

ST-ESTÈVE, CH DE   *France, Rhône, Côtes du Rhône, R, W, P*   Experimental attitudes here produce a range of unusual, characterful wines, including a Viognier W, two Rs and a P.

ST-GAYAN, DOM   *France, Rhône, Gigondas, R*   Big, sometimes agressively tannic wines which age well.

ST-GEORGES ST-EMILION   *France, Bordeaux, AOC, R*   Wine from this small St-Emilion satellite may also be sold as MONTAGNE ST-EMILION. Leading producers include: Ch'x Belair St-Georges, Calon, Macquin St-Georges, St-André Corbin, St-Georges, Tours du Pas St-Georges.

ST-GEORGES, CH   *France, Bordeaux, St-Georges St-Emilion, R*   Large and beautiful château and a well-placed vineyard: quality wine well up to St-Emilion standards and worth ageing.

ST-JEAN-DE-MINERVOIS, MUSCAT DE   *France, Midi, AOC, VDN*   This *vin doux naturel* is from 100% Muscat Blanc à Petits Grains (the best Muscat variety), picked when almost overripe; thus with high potential alcohol. Producers aim for a delicate grapey Muscat flavour. Leading producers include: Dom Barroubio, Dom Sigé, St-Jean-de-Minervois co-op.

ST-JOSEPH   *France, Rhône, AOC, R, W*   Northern Rhône district across the river from Hermitage and Crozes-Hermitage. Rs are from Syrah, Ws from Marsanne, Roussanne or both. Variable in quality, but the best wines are good value. Leading producers include: Clos de l'Arbalestrier, Courbis, Jean-Louis Grippat.

ST-JULIEN   *France, Bordeaux, AOC, R*   Smallest of the great Médoc communes, with 11 classed growths. Ch Talbot makes a rare W ; the rest are all R, dominated by Cabernet Sauvignon: consistent, concentrated wine. Leading producers include: Ch'x Ducru Beaucaillou, Léoville Barton, Léoville Las-Cases, Léoville Poyferré.

ST-NICOLAS-DE-BOURGUEIL   *See* BOURGUEIL.

ST-PÉRAY   *France, Rhône, AOC, W*   Still or Sp W from Marsanne or (rather better) Roussanne grape, or a blend of both. The best still St-Péray is like a good, minor W Hermitage. Leading producers include: Bernard Gripa, Jean Lionnet, Alain Voge.

ST-PIERRE, CH *France, Bordeaux, Médoc, St-Julien, 4ème Cru Classé,
R* Small estate with the same owners as Ch GLORIA. The wine
is solid, dark and flavoursome and can take a long time to mature.
The 1986 is superb, the 1993 good.

ST-POURÇAIN *France, Loire, VDQS, R, P, W* Zone between the
Loire and Burgundy making wine from Burgundian grapes: Tres-
sallier, Chardonnay, Aligoté (and Sauvignon Blanc) for Ws, Pinot
Noir and Gamay for Rs and Ps.

ST-ROMAIN *France, Burgundy, AOC, R, W* Fresh crisp W wines
and firm, cherry-flavoured Rs come from this village on the edge
of Hautes Côtes de Beaune. Leading producers include: Bernard
Fèvre, Maison Jean Germain, Alain Gras, René Gras Broisson,
Louis Latour, Leroy, René Thévenin, Charles Viénot.

ST-SAPHORIN *Switzerland, Vaud, Lavaux, W, R* Leading wine-
producing village to the east of Lausanne whose steep vineyards
produce easy-drinking W wine from Chasselas and appealing R
from Pinot Noir.

ST-VERAN *France, Burgundy, AOC, W* Chardonnay W, grown in
south Mâconnais, which overlaps with Beaujolais: the wine can
also be called Beaujolais Blanc. Cheaper than Pouilly-Fuissé, St-
Véran can easily equal it in quality. Leading producers include:
Dom des Deux Roches, Prissé co-op, Dom Vincent.

**STAATLICHE WEINBAUDOMÄNE NIEDERHAUSEN-SCHLOSSBÖCK-
ELHEIM** *Germany, Nahe, W* The State Domain of the Nahe, a
famous maker of Rieslings, concentrated and long-lived wines
from the famous Kupfergrube vineyard and light, elegant and
fresh ones from Niederhausen and Schlossböckelheim.

STAATSWEINGUT ELTVILLE *Germany, Rheingau, W, R* The State
Domain, based in Eltville, inherited monastic vineyards and owns
the famous Steinberg and many others, including R-wine plots at
Assmanshausen. High standards, with the stress on typicity from
the various sites. Eiswein is a speciality.

STAGS LEAP DISTRICT *USA, California, Napa, VA* Wine zone of
Napa Valley, east of Yountville, known for the "iron-fist-in-vel-
vet-glove" style of Cabernet Sauvignon, whose herbal, violet and
black pepper flavours surround a sturdy core of fruit. Leading
producers include: Clos Du Val, Shafer, Pine Ridge, Silverado,
Stag's Leap Wine Cellars, Stags' Leap Vineyard.

STAG'S LEAP WINE CELLARS *USA, California, Napa, W, R* Warren Winiarski makes Chardonnays that are neither over-oaked
nor flabby with ultra-ripe fruit, and Cabernet Sauvignons with a
firm tannin backbone underlying a silky, olive-pepper cloak.
World-class wines.

STE MICHELLE, CH *USA, Washington State, R, W, Sp* The Yakima
Valley winery makes a range of varietal wines (Riesling and
Cabernet Sauvignon) and Domaine Michelle Sp.

STE-ANNE, DOM *France, Rhône, Côtes du Rhône-Villages, R, W* The R wines from here, made from Syrah and Mourvèdre grapes, have inspired a generation of local winemakers with their structure and ageing ability. The Viognier W is also very good.

STE-CROIX-DU-MONT *France, Bordeaux, AOC, W* Sweet W wine from zone opposite Sauternes on the north bank of the Garonne. Leading producers include: Ch'x La Grave, Loubens, La Rame.

STE-EULALIE, DOM *France, Midi, Minervois, R* This abandoned estate in La Livinière was bought in 1979 by Gérard Blanc. He replanted and re-equipped; the favoured technique is *macération carbonique*, and there is also some oak ageing.

STE-FOY BORDEAUX *France, Bordeaux, AOC, R, W* These wines from the far east of the region are often sold under the more widely-known AOC Bordeaux.

STEEN South African synonym for CHENIN BLANC.

STEIERMARK *Austria* For wine Styria is split into three unequal parts: Süd (south), Süd-Ost (south-east) and West Steiermark. The Süd makes the finest wines. In quality and price its Ws equal those of the Wachau, although different in style: delicate in structure and high in acidity. Many grapes are grown, including Weissburgunder (Pinot Blanc), Riesling and Morillon (Chardonnay). Weststeiermark is known for a rare P, Schilcher, from the indigenous Blauer Wildbacher grape, it can be refreshing if the acidity is not too high. The Süd-Ost is very small. Leading producers include: Alois Gross, Erich Kuntner, Manfred Platzer, Manfred Tement.

STEINBERG *Germany, Rheingau, W* Famous walled, ex-monastic vineyard owned by the Staatsweingut, the state domain of the Rheingau.

STELLENBOSCH *South Africa, WO* The most important area of South Africa. Many of its top wines are blended Rs, from the two Cabernets, Merlot and Shiraz, often aged in oak. The best Pinotage comes from here. Also good Ws from Chardonnay and Sauvignon. Leading producers include: Meerlust, Mulderbosch, Rustenberg, Rust-en-Vrede, Vriesenhof, Warwick.

STERLING *USA, California, Napa, R, W* Perched atop its Calistoga hilltop, Sterling makes an exquisite Merlot R, dense and focused Diamond Mountain Ranch Cabernet Sauvignons and Chardonnays, and the lush, supple Winery Lake Pinot Noir R.

STIGLER, WEINGUT RUDOLF *Germany, Baden, R, W* Quality estate making both the traditional Ws of Baden – dry, fruity and characterful – and good Rs.

STONE HILL WINE CO *USA, Missouri, W, R* Produces a wide range of wines, apart from its own 25-ha vineyard. Catawba and

Norton (*labrusca* wines) remain popular, while respectable hybrids include Seyval Blanc, Vidal and Vignoles, among Ws, Villard Noir among Rs.

SUAU, CH *France, Bordeaux, 1er Côtes de Bordeaux, R* The large vineyard, equally Merlot, Cabernet Sauvignon and Cabernet Franc, plus intelligent winemaking yields claret worth ageing. Also a W, fresh and soft.

SUCHOTS, LES *France, Burgundy, Côte de Nuits, 1er Cru, R* This large vineyard in the commune of Vosne-Romanée yields full, elegant, supple wines with a touch of spice. They develop very well in bottle. Leading producers include: Robert Arnoux, Jean Grivot, Hudelot-Noëllat, Mongeard-Mugneret.

SÜDLICHE WEINSTRASSE *Germany, Pfalz, Bereich, W, R* The southern part of the Pfalz, just north of the French border. Here mass-produced wines are the norm, but good, estate-bottled Ws (from Weissburgunder, especially) and *barrique*-aged Rs are on the increase. Leading producers (apart from co-ops) include Becker, Hohenberg, Rebholz, Siegrist.

SUDUIRAUT, CH DE *France, Bordeaux, Sauternes, 1er Cru Classé, W* A byword for power and opulence, it can also be coarse and unpredictable: 1983 and 1986 were disappointing, 1990 magnificent. No wine was made under the château label in 1991, '92 & '93 due to bad weather. Now owned by AXA and run by Jean-Michel Cazes, Suduiraut's standards should be maintained.

SULFITES *See* SULPHUR DIOXIDE.

SULPHUR DIOXIDE Used as a disinfectant in winemaking. Too much produces a smell of rotten eggs in the wine, and induces headaches. EU wines may have no more than fixed maximum levels of the product. *See* Tasting Wine p242.

SUMAC RIDGE *Canada, British Columbia, W, R* Specialist in Ws with high-quality Pinot Blanc, Gewürztraminer and Riesling.

SUPERIORE *Italy* Describes wine that has a higher alcohol content (or a little extra ageing) than the standard DOC wine.

SUR LIE *France* On the lees (unracked). Used of wines (especially Muscadet) bottled without being racked.

SUTTER HOME *USA, California, Napa W, R* In the last decade Sutter Home has grown from a 50,000-case Zinfandel-only winery to one making nearly five million cases, including the enormously popular White Zinfandel, the light, fruity R Soleo, and new alcohol-free wines.

SWAN VALLEY *Australia, Western Australia* Pioneer region of the West: hot and dry in summer, but the deep alluvial soils have very good water-holding capacity. It has undergone a recent decline in production as new areas have emerged. Leading producers include: Haughton, Sandalford.

SYMINGTON *Portugal, port* The Symingtons sell the single-quinta vintage Quinta do Vesuvio under their own name, but this family firm also own a host of other familiar port houses: GRAHAM'S, DOW'S, WARRE'S, Gould Campbell, Smith Woodhouse.

SYRAH Red grape from the Rhône, making deep-coloured, smoky, peppery, complex, long-lived wines such as Hermitage and Côte Rôtie. Australians call it Shiraz, and often blend it with Cabernet Sauvignon to make a relatively soft, accessible wine. Used alone and to add interest to blends in Provence and the Midi, and also grown in varying amounts in Italy, Spain, New Zealand and California.

T

TÂCHE, LA *France, Burgundy, Côte de Nuits, Grand Cru, R* Top R-wine vineyard in the group headed by La **ROMANÉE**. La Tâche is owned by Domaine de la **ROMANÉE-CONTI**.

TACORONTE-ACENTEJO *Spain, Canary Islands, DO, R, P, W* The vineyards of this zone, situated in north-west Tenerife, in the Canary Islands, enjoy a sub-tropical climate. Most production is R in the *joven* style, and there is some W and *rosado*.

TAFELWEIN *Germany* Table wine. The lowest grade of German wine. The prefix Deutscher or German means the wine is actually grown in Germany. Some modern wines of high quality are sold as *Tafelwein* because their producers do not submit them for official testing.

TAHBILK, CH *Australia, Victoria, Goulburn Valley, R, W* Family-owned, historic winery with some Shiraz vines dating from 1862 which still produce. Wines include elegant W Marsanne and long-lived, sometimes tannic but always concentrated Shiraz and Cabernet Sauvignon Rs.

TAILLEFER, CH *France, Bordeaux, Pomerol, R* Large (for the area) property which makes a light, early-maturing style of Pomerol.

TAITTINGER *France, Champagne* This is a **GRANDE MARQUE** whose style stresses delicacy and elegance, although the wines become richer and weightier after several years in bottle. The NV *brut* reserve is mainly Chardonnay and the luxury *cuvée*, Comtes de Champagne, is 100% Chardonnay.

TALBOT, CH *France, Bordeaux, Médoc, St-Julien, 4ème Cru Classé, R, W* Large estate owned by the Cordier family and run with great attention to detail. The wine, soft, full and rich, has many friends. In great vintages it can age well; in minor ones it is reliable. A good 1993. 2nd wine: Connétable de Talbot. Also, unusually, a white: Caillou Blanc, made from Sauvignon Blanc grapes grown in St-Julien.

TARGÉ, CH DE *France, Loire, Saumur-Champigny, R* Edouard Pisani-Ferry makes one of the best wines of the AOC in his spectacular caves and modern cellars. His only wine is a blend of Cabernet Franc with a little Cabernet Sauvignon. It ages well.

TARRAGONA *Spain, Catalonia, DO, W, P, R* One of eight wine zones in Catalonia, formerly known for sweet R fortified wine, but now producing mainly light wines in all colours, mostly in *joven* style, but also some heavier R. Main producers include: DE MULLER, Pedro Rovira.

TASMANIA *Australia* A small island off the south-east coast, with a tiny wine production. Its cool climate ensures that Pinot Noir for Rs does well, and some very good Chardonnay is also made. Sp wines are another speciality.

TAURASI *Italy, Campania, DOCG, R* Campania's best R wine, and some of Italy's best value: tannic when young but after many years evolves into a fine, rich wine with pruney fruit. Leading producers include: Mastroberardino.

TAVEL *France, Rhône, AOC, P* Big, alcoholic P from southern Rhône, with a high proportion of Grenache Noir in the blend. Leading producer: Ch d'Aquéria.

TAYAC, CH *France, Bordeaux, Côtes de Bourg, R* Several *cuvées* are made: the top one, "Prestige" is mostly Cabernet Sauvignon. Not typical of the AOC, but good (if expensive) claret.

TAYAC, CH *France, Bordeaux, Margaux, Cru Bourgeois, R* This large vineyard yields solid, traditional wine.

TAYLOR FLADGATE & YEATMAN *Portugal, port* For many the epitome of vintage port. Taylor (known as Taylor Fladgate in the USA) was founded in 1692 and is still a family-controlled partnership. Grapes are still trod at Quinta de Vargellas: next door to computerized stainless steel. The range goes from the classic vintages (among the finest), through the single-quinta Quinta de Vargellas, excellent aged tawnies (especially the 20-year-old) and the first (and the best-selling) Late Bottled Vintage. Quinta de Terra Feita has recently been released as a single-quinta wine. Basic wines are never less than well made.

TE MATA *New Zealand, North Island, W, R, P* The oldest New Zealand winery, and among the most prestigious. Top wines are the Coleraine Cabernet Sauvignon/Merlot R blend, and the rich Elston Chardonnay. Also good-value P and dry W blends.

TELMONT, DE *France, Champagne* Good value, well-made champagnes from a family-owned producer.

TEMECULA *USA, California, VA* Sited north of San Diego, this is a wine zone whose sandy soil is well suited to Chardonnay for both still and Sp wine. Leading producers include: Callaway, Thornton.

TEMPIER, DOM *France, Provence, Bandol, R, P* Lucien Peyraud of Tempier is an influential local figure. Traditional techniques rule; the wines possess huge tannins and fruit, and can age for many years. The two Rs are a normal *cuvée* and a Cuvée Spéciale.

TEMPRANILLO Red grape used in Spain's best red wines, including Rioja, Ribera del Duero, Navarra and Penedès. Aromatic and subtly flavoured, with an affinity for oak-ageing, it goes under many names in Spain (Ull de Llebre, Cencibel) and Portugal (Aragonez, Tinta Roriz).

TENNESSEE *USA* Fifteen producers, most of them along the Tennessee valley, combat a tough climate to make wine here.

TENNESSEE VALLEY WINERY *USA, Tennessee, W* Loudon County winery using native American varieties, hybrids and classic vines. The best wines are Aurora (W), de Chaunac (R) and Maréchal Foch (R). Chardonnay and Sauvignon Blanc have been erratic in quality.

TENUTA IL POGGIONE *Italy, Tuscany, Brunello di Montalcino, R, W* Estate making a large range of wines include Brunello and Rosso di Montalcino DOC, Moscadello, Vin Santo and Bianco di Sant'Angelo (W).

TENUTA *Italy* Wine estate; holding.

TERLANO *Italy, Trentino-Alto Adige, DOC, W, Sp* This wine zone enjoys a good reputation for its fine, still varietal Ws. Dry Sp wine is also produced, predominantly from Pinot Bianco. Leading producers include: Alois Lageder, Castel Schwanburg.

TERRA ALTA *Spain, Catalonia, DO, W, R* The highest and most southerly wine zone in Catalonia, bordering Aragón, producing the traditional sweet, oak-aged *rancio* Rs, but also lighter, fresher wines. Experimental plantings of French grapes. Leading producers include: Pedro Rovira.

TERRES BLANCHES, DOM *France, Provence, Coteaux d'Aix-en-Provence Les Baux, W, R, P* Noël Michelin uses no herbicides or insecticides on his vines and few chemicals in the *chai*. He makes a W, an attractive P and a R of elegance after a few years' bottle-ageing.

TERROIR *France* The winegrowing environment, covering soil, site and local climate.

TERTRE DAUGAY, CH *France, Bordeaux, St-Emilion, Grand Cru Classé, R* Comte Léo de Malet-Roquefort also owns LA GAFFE-LIÈRE. This estate's somewhat chequered history is now behind it: worth seeking out.

TERTRE, CH DU *France, Bordeaux, Médoc, Margaux, 5ème Cru Classé, R* This estate has a large amount of Cabernet Sauvignon on its inland outcrop of gravel. The wines have improved markedly over the last few years.

TESCH, WEINGUT ERBHOF *Germany, Nahe, W* This estate has a good name for dry wines from Riesling and other varieties.

TESSIER, PHILIPPE *France, Loire, Cheverny, W, R* Run by the Tessiers for three generations, this estate makes R and (better) W wines, with a soft spot for the local Romorantin grape, which here produces a crisp, rather than piercingly acidic, W wine.

TETRE-ROTEBOEUF, CH LE *France, Bordeaux, St-Emilion, Grand Cru, R* This superb small property makes roughly 2,000 cases a year. Meticulous vineyard management and winemaking by François

Mitjavile results in an almost pure Merlot wine with wonderful depth and longevity. ROC DES CAMBES (Côte de Bourg) has the same owner.

TEXAS   *USA*   New vineyards on a grand scale make Texas the fourth US wine state. Most vines are in three cool-climate zones: on the High Plains near Lubbock, the Hill Country (VA) west of Austin, and in West Texas. Good wines from Cabernet Sauvignon and other French varieties show the potential. Leading producers include: Cap Rock, FALL CREEK, LLANO ESTACADO, PHEASANT RIDGE.

THANISCH, DR   *Germany, Mosel, W*   Two famous estates, with the same name, each own part of the great Doctor vineyard at Bernkastel, plus other fine Riesling vineyards. Those who can afford the wines will know them apart.

THANN   *France, Alsace*   The southernmost wine village of Alsace has been renowned for wine since the 12th century. Looming above is the famous *Grand Cru* Rangen. Steep, south-facing slopes produce Pinot Gris, Riesling and Gewürztraminer. Leading producers include: Zind-Humbrecht.

THELEMA MOUNTAIN VINEYARDS   *South Africa, Stellenbosch, R, W*   Gyles Webb is one of the Cape's top winemakers. Elegance and balance sum up his wines, from his Cabernet Sauvignon, easily the best in the Cape, to the citrussy, classy Chardonnay.

THERMENREGION   *Austria, Niederösterreich*   Region south of Vienna. Production is small, but the area is famous for the village of Gumpoldskirchen, much of whose wine is made from two local grapes, Zierfandler (or Spätrot) and Rotgipfler. W wine is rich, broad and spicy, usually semi-sweet and strong. R wines are also gaining a reputation, notably from St-Laurent and Zweigelt.

THEUILEY, CH   *France, Bordeaux, Entre-Deux-Mers W, Bordeaux R*   Good-value fruity light R and increasingly impressive Sauvignon Blanc W.

THIVIN, CH   *France, Burgundy, Beaujolais, R*   Delicious Côte de Brouilly is produced at this property, rich, weighty and round with lovely fruit and finesse.

THOUARSAIS, VIN DU   *France, Loire, VDQS, R, P, W*   This small Loire zone south of Anjou produces Rs and Ps from Cabernet Franc, Cabernet Sauvignon or Gamay, Ws from Chenin Blanc.

TICINO   *Switzerland*   Italian-speaking canton in southern Switzerland, especially well known for its soft, easy-drinking R wine from the Merlot grape. Some Cabernet Sauvignon has been recently introduced and there is a little W and P too. Leading producers include: Delea, Tamborini.

TIEFENBRUNNER   *Italy, Alto Adige, W, R*   Estate with fine Alto Adige Pinot Nero, notable Gewürztraminer W and excellent *vini da tavola*: Goldmuskateller, Feldmarschall and Linticlarus (R, W).

TINHOF, ERWIN *Austria, Neusiedlersee-Hügelland, W, R* Young producer who studied in France and achieves elegance and balance in all his wines, from a classy, steely Muskat Ottonel W, through a superb almost Viognier-like Neuburger W (called Fuchsenriegl) fermented and partly aged in new oak to a delicious, red-fruited Blaufränkisch R.

TINTA RORIZ See TEMPRANILLO.

TINTO *Spain and Portugal* Red.

TIO MATEO *Spain, sherry* Palomino & Vergara's top fino, Tio Mateo, is known throughout Spain: a classic Jerez fino, dry and full.

TIREGAND, CH DE *France, Southwest, Bergerac, R, W* Classic Pécharmant Rs, one from young vines, and a *grand vin* from Merlot, both Cabernets and a little Malbec, are aged in a proportion of new oak.

TOKAJI *Hungary* This region in the north-east of the country produces Hungary's most famous wine, hailed by Louis XIV of France as the king of wines. Botrytis-affected grapes are added to a dry white wine and the mixture begins to referment very slowly, resulting in an intense sweet wine with highish alcohol, rich in both extract and glycerol. The more *puttonyos* (maximum six) on the label the sweeter the wine. Main grape varieties are Furmint, Hárslevelü and Sárga Muskotály (Muscat Lunel). Also a dry version (Dry Szamorodni) and extremely sweet Aszú Eszencia. Single-variety Furmint is a good dry wine. Currently undergoing a renaissance, thanks to foreign investment and expertise.

TOKAY D'ALSACE See PINOT GRIS.

TOLLOT-BEAUT ET FILS *France, Burgundy, Côte d'Or, R* Large family-owned estate around Corton and Beaune, producing robust, long-lived R wines.

TONDONIA *Spain, Rioja, R, W, P* Probably the most traditionalist of all Rioja producers. Wines – R and W– are full and oaky and can age well. The best is Tondonia but Bosonia and Cubillo are also very good.

TONNERRE *France, Burgundy, Chablis, 1er Cru* See FOURCHAUME.

TORGIANO *Italy, Umbria, DOC, W, R* Much is owed to the LUNGAROTTI family for raising the quality levels of this DOC. It offers well-balanced W from Trebbiano and Grechetto; while the R is mainly Sangiovese. The *riserva* has DOCG status. Leading producers include: Cantine Lungarotti.

TORO *Spain, Castilla-León, DO, R, W, P* One of the Castilla-León wine zones, producing Toro, a heavy, heady R wine, mainly from the Tinta Toro grape, R *crianza* wines and a small quantity of *rosado* and W wines. Leading producers include: Bodegas Fariña, Bodegas José-María Fermoselle.

TORRACCIA, DOM DE   *France, Corsica, Porto-Vecchio, R*   Experimentation and traditional varieties (Syrah, Mourvèdre and Corsican R grapes) combine to make interesting wines reflecting the island's true character.

TORRE QUARTO   *Italy, Southern Italy, Apulia, R*   Renowned for its Malbec and Uva de Troia-based wine (R). Malbec is now replaced by Montepulciano grapes.

TORRES, MIGUEL   *Spain, Catalonia, Penedès, R, W*   Brilliant, innovative winemaker who took over the family bodega in the early 1960s and subsequently put Catalonia firmly on the international map. He uses Spanish and French grapes to great effect, notably with Vina Sol (W), Sangre de Toro (R) and full-bodied Gran Coronas (R) – especially the Black Label. Also active in Chile: *see* MIGUEL TORRES.

TOUCHAIS, LES VINS   *France, Loire, Anjou, W, R, P*   Large *négociant* and estate based at Doué-la-Fontaine. The sweet Layon wines, sold as Anjou Blanc Moulin Touchais, can be extraordinary, showing the ageing ability of Chenin Blanc. But most sales are of straightforward Rs and Ps.

TOUR BLANCHE, CH LA   *France, Bordeaux, Sauternes, 1er Cru Classé, W*   The wines of the 1970s and early 1980s were dire, but happily standards have risen: since 1988 again worthy of its *Premier Cru* status.

TOUR-CARNET, LA   *France, Bordeaux, Haut-Médoc, 4ème Cru Classé, R*   Sited in St-Laurent, the commune inland from St-Julien, this château used to make wine in a rather rustic, tough style. Recent vintages here have been softer, though still well-structured.

TOUR DU BIEF, DOM DE LA   *France, Burgundy, Beaujolais, R*   One of the finest producers of Moulin-à-Vent, the most powerful of the Beaujolais Crus, with a powerful structure that ages well.

TOUR MARTILLAC, CH LA   *France, Bordeaux, Pessac-Léognan, Cru Classé, R, W*   Consistent maker of plump, fleshy yet elegant Rs, and impeccably balanced Ws that are oaky but retain their youthful fruitiness for many years.

TOUR-DE-MONS, CH LA   *France, Bordeaux, Margaux, Cru Bourgeois, R*   Well-known property making reliable, smooth, enjoyable wine from, almost equally, Merlot and Cabernet Sauvignon.

TOUR-DU-PIN-FIGEAC (MOUEIX), CH   *France, Bordeaux, St-Emilion, Grand Cru Classé, R*   Much better than the other property of the same name. Fairly full-bodied, with lots of fruit.

TOURAINE   *France, Loire, AOC, R, P, W, Sp*   Large appellation south of Tours for W (still or Sp), R and P wines. The best wines are from three village appellations: Touraine-Amboise, Touraine-Azay-le-Rideau and Touraine-Mesland. Some varietal appellations are grouped under the Touraine AOC: Sauvignon for Ws, Gamay for Rs. Leading producers include: Paul Chainier, Ch de

Chenonceau, Dom de la Gabillière, Jacky Marteau, J M Monmousseau, Vignerons de Oisly et Thésée co-op, Jacky Preys.

TOURELLES DE LONGUEVILLE, LES *France, Bordeaux, Médoc, Pauillac, R* 2nd wine of Ch Pichon-Baron.

TRACY, CH DE *France, Loire, Pouilly-Fumé, W* The Comte d'Estutt d'Assay's family has been here since the 16th century. Recent modernization of the cellars has produced some very fine Pouilly-Fumé from their 24ha.

TRAISEN *Germany, Nahe, W* Village in the heart of the Nahe. The most famous vineyard, planted exclusively with Riesling, is the Bastei, whose W wines are full of character and incredibly intense in flavour and bouquet. Riesling from the larger Rotenfels is almost as good. Leading producers include: Crusius, Staatliche Weinbaudomäne.

TREBBIANO White grape of central Italy: prolific, acidic, often characterless, widely planted throughout the world, and used for blending and distilling. Grown as Ugni Blanc in France, particularly in Cognac.

TREFETHEN *USA, Napa* The fine wooden Eshcol winery just north of Napa city is one of the valley's oldest. It now makes good Chardonnay and Cabernet and a popular, good-value pair of blended wines, Eshcol R and W.

TRENTINO *Italy, Trentino-Alto Adige, DOC, R, W, Sp* This DOC covers a wide range of wines. W varieties include Nosiola, Chardonnay and Pinot Bianco. Rs are Marzemino and Teroldego. Fine sweet Vin Santo is also made. Leading producers include: Concilio Vini, Ferrari, Pojer & Sandri, De Tarczal.

TRENTINO-ALTO ADIGE *Italy* Mountainous region of north-east Italy combining two distinct areas. Alto Adige is particularly well known for its fine dry W wines from French and German varieties. In lower-lying Trentino the wines tend to be mellower and broader in flavour.

TRÉVALLON, DOM DE *France, Provence, Coteaux d'Aix-en-Provence Les Baux, R* Acclaimed as the finest estate in Les Baux, and one of the top few in Provence. All methods are organic. Eloi Durrbach's one wine is 60% Cabernet Sauvignon; it needs at least 5 years in bottle, then develops gradually.

TRIGUEDINA, CH *France, Southwest, Cahors, R* Prince Probus, the top *cuvée* from this old family estate, is among the best-known Cahors. A quarter of the vines are Merlot, which are felt to add suppleness to the traditional Auxerrois (Malbec).

TRIMBACH, F E *France, Alsace, W, R* With Hugel, Trimbach has done more than anyone to promote Alsace. Wines include W Gewürztraminer (especially Cuvée des Seigneurs de Ribeaupierre) and Pinot Gris; but the Rieslings are undoubtedly the best of the region. Cuvée Frédéric-Emile, from *Grand Cru* Osterberg, is bettered only by Clos Ste-Hune, their vineyard (for the last 200 years) within *Grand Cru* Rosacker. A world-class wine (though not legally *Grand Cru*), Clos Ste-Hune epitomizes Riesling and is considered by many to be the best wine in Alsace.

TRITTENHEIM *Germany, Mosel, W* Famous town in the Mittelmosel, whose Riesling Ws can have much finesse and breeding, The most noted vineyard is Trittenheimer Apotheke.

TROCKEN *Germany* Dry wine. Do not confuse with TROCKEN-BEERENAUSLESE.

TROCKENBEERENAUSLESE *Germany* The top QMP grade. As with *Beerenauslese*, it is made from individually selected grapes, which are always overripe and thus very sweet; in this case the grapes are shrivelled and dry, their juice concentrated from the action of noble rot.

TRONQUOY-LALANDE, CH *France, Bordeaux, St-Estèphe, Cru Bourgeois, R* A familiar wine in export markets, made in the solid St-Estèphe style. The late-1980s' vintages were very good, though these wines always need patience.

TROPLONG-MONDOT, CH *France, Bordeaux, St-Emilion, Grand Cru Classé, R* Beautiful property, and one of St-Emilion's largest. Run by Christine Valette since 1980: a superb run of vintages in 1988, 1989, 1990. A future star.

TROTANOY, CH *France, Bordeaux, Pomerol, R* Ranks as one of Pomerol's top dozen estates and in its finest years the wine can be almost as dense as Pétrus, with virtually the same potential lifespan at a fraction of the price.

TROTTEVIEILLE, CH *France, Bordeaux, St-Emilion, 1er Grand Cru Classé, R* There has been noticeable improvement here since the mid-1980s. Before, wines lacked concentration and aged too quickly, but are now much more serious. Medium rather than long-term drinking.

TUALATIN *USA, Oregon, W, R* The 34-ha estate in the tiny town of Forest Grove produces flinty, apricot Riesling W, smoky-clove Pinot Noir R and toasty, clear clove Chardonnay; also Ws from Sauvignon, Gewürztraminer, Flora (a Sémillon/Gewürztraminer crossing) and Müller-Thurgau.

TUNISIA *North Africa, R, W, P* Tunisia's vineyards are concentrated in the north-east sector of the country, around the capital of Tunis. Her best wines are Ws from the Muscat grape which can be sweet or dry. Also makes fairly reliable R and P wine. A system of AOC control is similar to that of France.

TURCKHEIM *France, Alsace* Village with a name for some of the best Pinots Noir Rs in Alsace. *Grand Cru* Brand yields Ws from Pinot Gris, Riesling and Gewürztraminer. Leading producers include: Dopff Au Moulin, Meyer, Zind-Humbrecht.

TURKEY   The vast country has an extremely long winemaking history, but since most of the population is Muslim, only 2% of the produce of its 600,000ha of vines is turned into wine. 40% of production is state controlled. Production is split almost equally between R and W, with only a very little P.

TURSAN   *France, South-West, VDQS, R, P, W*   The W wine is from Baroque grapes, with Sauvignon Blanc, Gros and Petit Manseng and Sémillon to provide flavour and vitality. R Tursan, from Tannat, Cabernet Sauvignon and Cab Franc, tends to be rustic in flavour.

TURSAN, LES VIGNERONS DE   *France, South-West, Tursan, W, R*   Leading maker of these obscure but tasty W and R wines from the Landes.

TUSCANY   *Italy*   Together with Piedmont, Italy's leading region for quality wine production. Sangiovese is the great Tuscan grape for R wine and the mainstay of CHIANTI, Italy's best-known wine. It is here that the renaissance in Italian winemaking has made its greatest mark with wines like SASSICAIA and Ornellaia. Tuscany also has some fine traditional wines like BRUNELLO DI MONTALCINO (R), VINO NOBILE DI MONTEPULCIANO (R) and VIN SANTO.

TXAKOLI (CHIACOLÍ)   *Spain, Basque Country, DO, W, R*   Spain's northernmost wine region, in the Basque country, produces light, dry W and light R, both in the *joven* style. Leading producers include: Txakoli Eizaguirre, Txomin Etxaniz.

TYRRELLS   *Australia, New South Wales, Hunter Valley, R, W*   One of the great Hunter names, where tradition and commerce are intelligently balanced. Excellent Sémillon and Chardonnay Ws.

U

UGNI BLANC   French synonym for TREBBIANO.

UKRAINE   The speciality here is W and Sp wine, the latter especially in the Crimea (which once had a quality wine industry, and could do again). Principal varieties are Rkatsiteli and Aligoté, with some Rhein Riesling and Sauvignon Blanc. Quality is fairly indifferent. Sp wine may be made by the champagne method, *cuve close* or the Russian "continuous" system.

ULL DE LLEBRE   See TEMPRANILLO.

UMANI RONCHI   *Italy, Central Italy, Marches, W, R*   Large, innovative private producer. Ws include Verdicchio dei Castelli di Jesi, fine single-vineyard Verdicchios and Le Busche, a barrel-fermented Verdicchio. Rosso Conèro wines are Casal di Serra, San Lorenzo and top-quality Cùmaro.

UMATHUM, JOSEF   *Austria, Neusiedlersee, W, R*   Producer of very attractive W wines including a Welschriesling with lees-ageing and a good, spicy Ruländer fermented and partly aged in new oak. He uses new oak for his Rs too, including a delicious St-Laurent with attractive strawberry fruit and his top R wine, a heady blend of Zweigelt, Cabernet Sauvignon and Blaufränkisch.

UMBRIA   *Italy*   This small, landlocked region in the very centre of Italy is most famous for its W wines, notably Orvieto DOC. Its best known R wine is Torgiano from the LUNGAROTTI stable.

UMPQUA VALLEY   *USA, Oregon, VA*   One of Oregon's three wine zones, to the south of the Willamette Valley. Varieties which do well here include Pinot Noir and Chardonnay.

UNDURRAGA   *Chile, R, W*   One of the first Chilean producers to export, it also dominates the domestic market. The firm produces more than one million cases a year, of which exports are 40%, mainly Chardonnay and Sauvignon Blanc Ws. Merlot and Pinot Noir are recent additions to the list.

UNGSTEIN   *Germany, Pfalz, W, R*   Village in the MITTELHAART. Rich, fruity and fiery are among terms used for Ungstein's wine. R is quite important, but the best wines are Riesling Ws. Leading producers include: Pfeffingen.

UNION PLAIMONT   *France, Southwest, Côtes de St-Mont, W, R*   This co-op dominates the area, using the latest techniques to make three ranges with increasing amounts of oak-ageing: Tradition, Privilège and Collection. Also makes lots of good-value Vin de Pays des Côtes de Gascogne (R, W and P).

URUGUAY   *South America*   The fourth-largest wine producer in South America, with 14,000ha of vines in the south and west of the country. More than half the vineyard area is classic vines. Production totals eight million cases.

URZIG   *Germany, Mosel, W*   Town on a bend in the river in the MITTELMOSEL zone, where the top vineyards begin. Noted vineyards here are Prälat and Treppchen. Urzig's Würzgarten ("spice garden") is known for the spicy notes in its wine. Leading producers include: Dr Loosen, Mönchhof-Robert Eymnael and Dr Pauly-Bergweiler.

UTIEL-REQUENA   *Spain, Levante, DO, W, R*   Hilly wine zone of Valencia, producing W and R wines characteristic of the province. Leading producers include: C. Augusto Egli.

V

VACHERON, DOM JEAN-LOUIS *France, Loire, Sancerre, W, R* This firm specializes in R Sancerre, of which it makes fine examples, some matured in new wood. The 30-ha domaine produces Les Cailleries (R), Les Romains (P) and Le Paradis (W).

VACQUEYRAS *France, Rhône, AOC, R* Southern Rhône grapes (eg Grenache, Syrah) make Rs with good depth of colour and flavour. Leading producers include: Dom Le Couralou, Dom la Fourmone.

VAL JOANIS *France, Rhône, Côtes du Luberon, R, W* Reliable and large estate making good, fresh Ws for drinking young, and a fruity, flavoursome R.

VALAIS *Switzerland* The most important wine-producing canton of Switzerland with 5,000ha under vine, much of it at extremely high altitudes. Fendant (the local name for the Chasselas grape) is the main W wine and Dôle, a blend of Pinot Noir and other varieties the most important R. Leading producers include: Charles Bonvin, Simon Maye, Rouvinez.

VALDEORRAS *Spain, Galicia, DO, R, W* The easternmost wine zone of Galicia, contiguous with Bierzo, making similar light, fresh *joven* style R and W wines. Leading producers include: Bodega Cooperativa Jesús Nazareno.

VALDEPEÑAS *Spain, Castilla-La Mancha, DO, W, R* Of the four wine zones of Castilla-La Mancha, this has consistently produced good-quality wines from its hilly, south-facing vineyards. W wines are in *joven* style, but better Rs are made up to *gran reserva* level. Leading producers include: Bodegas Los Llanos.

VALDESPINO *Spain, sherry* Not the best-known or biggest firm; but for many, the small, high-quality Valdespino range of sherries is the very best. Their finest, the full but elegant fino Inocente, comes (uniquely for Jerez) from just one ancestral vineyard. Valdespino is also known for the dry, nutty amontillado Tio Diego, the sweet but not overwhelming 1842 Oloroso – and for fine sherry vinegar.

VALENÇAY *France, Loire, VDQS, R, P, W* Wines from the edge of Touraine, seldom found outside the area. Ws are from Menu Pineau (or Arbois), Sauvignon Blanc, Chardonnay, Chenin Blanc and Romorantin, a local high-acid variety. Rs and Ps are from Cabernets Sauvignon and Franc, Gamay and Pineau d'Aunis (a Loire original, also known as Chenin Noir).

VALENCIA *Spain, Levante, DO, W, P, R* East coast province which has vineyards from sea level up to more than 800m, producing a wide range of wines in all colours, from everyday blends to some reasonably impressive *crianza* and *reserva* Rs, as well as sweet wines. Leading producers include: C Augusto Egli, Bodegas Levantinas-Españolas, Bodegas ViniVal.

VALLE D'AOSTA *Italy* A very small and relatively unimportant wine producing region in Italy's north-west mountains. Most of the wine is drunk locally.

VALLÉE DU PARADIS, DE LA *France, Vin de Pays, R* The attractive name of this *vin de pays* ensures wide sales of the attractive Rs from the hills of Roussillon, in the far south of France.

VALMUR *France, Burgundy, Chablis, Grand Cru* One of the lighter *Grand Cru* wines, for drinking earlier than Les Clos.

VALPOLICELLA *Italy, Veneto, DOC, R* Mainly from Corvina, Rondinella and Molinara, a zesty, light ruby-R wine, with an appealing grapey flavour. Also made as the richer, darker *ripasso*, sweet *recioto* and dry *amarone*. Leading producers include: Allegrini, Bolla, Masi, Quintarelli.

VALTELLINA *Italy, Lombardy, DOC, R* Mountain-valley wine from the Nebbiolo grape, known locally as Chiavennasca. Garnet in colour with floral and herbal fragrances. For early drinking, although the *superiore* version is best at 5–10 years. Leading producers include: Enologica Valtellinese, Nino Negri.

VARICHON ET CLERC *France, Savoie, Seyssel, W, Sp* Leading maker of Sp Seyssel, using the classic method aided by modern equipment. Their top Sp is Royal Seyssel. They also make a still W under the Roussette de Savoie AOC.

VARIETAL Term for a wine made from a single variety of grape.

VAROILLE, DOM DE *France, Burgundy, Côte d'Or, R* Both *négociant* and vineyard owner, the estate wines of this domaine are very serious indeed, with lots of ageing potential.

VASCOS, LOS *Chile, R, W* Famous vineyard dating from 1750, now part-owned by Ch Lafite-Rothschild. Cabernet Sauvignon makes up more than half the production. Some Chardonnay and Sauvignon Blanc.

VATAN, PHILIPPE ET GEORGES *France, Loire, Saumur, W, R* Philippe Vatan makes one of the best wines in Saumur-Champigny as well as a memorable Saumur Blanc. Also a standard Saumur-Champigny, a Vieilles Vignes and a rare sweet Saumur Moelleux (W).

VAUCRAINS, LES *France, Burgundy, Côte de Nuits, 1er Cru, R* Nuits-St-Georges vineyard, which produces richly-coloured, highly-structured wines which require long bottle ageing. Leading producers include: Robert Chevillon, Henri Gouges.

VAUD *Switzerland* After Valais, Switzerland's most important wine-producing canton, with 3,700ha under vine, divided into five districts. Main grape varieties are Chasselas for W and Pinot Noir for R. The wines produced make attractive, easy drinking, and are best consumed young. Leading producers include: Badoux, Chevalley, J & P Testuz.

VAUDÉSIR *France, Burgundy, Chablis, Grand Cru* Solid, long-lived and lively wines. Vaudésir includes part of La Moutonne, a vineyard on the *Grands Crus* slope, but without the status of a *Grand Cru*: a 2.3-ha parcel within Vaudésir and Preuses that once belonged to the nearby Cistercian abbey of Pontigny. LONG-DEPAQUIT are the principal producers, making a stylish wine of considerable finesse.

VAULORENT *France, Burgundy, Chablis, 1er Cru* See FOUR-CHAUME.

VDN *France* See VIN DOUX NATUREL.

VDP *Germany* The Verband Deutscher Prädikatsweingüter, an association of top wine estates: the VDP seal is a good sign of quality.

VDQS *France* See VIN DÉLIMITÉ DE QUALITÉ SUPÉRIEURE.

VECCHIO *Italy* Wine that has been aged for a longer period than most in cask and/or bottle.

VEGA SICILIA, BODEGAS *Spain, Castilla-León, Ribera del Duero, R* Established in 1864, and at the time a lone pioneer of quality winemaking in the Duero Valley. Meticulous care and traditional methods combine to produce carefully crafted wines which age supremely well, from the Valbuena (R) to Vega Sicilia Unico (R) which may have spent up to 10 years in oak.

VENDANGE *France* Vintage time. *Vendange tardive*, late harvest, refers mainly to sweet Alsace wine.

VENEGAZZÙ *Italy, Veneto, R* The first famous Venegazzù from this estate was a classic bordeaux-style blend needing long ageing. These wines now come in a range of styles.

VENETO *Italy* The most geographically diverse of all Italy's regions, offering a broad range of styles. Best-known wines include Soave (DOC, W), Valpolicella and Bardolino, both of which DOCs make R.

VENOGE, DE *France, Champagne* Good value and quality from this old firm whose luxury *cuvée* Des Princes is well regarded.

VERDICCHIO DEI CASTELLI DI JESI *Italy, Marches, DOC, W, Sp* Verdicchio is the main W grape of the Marches, producing light, lemony wines which go well with seafood. Can be Sp. Leading producers include: Fazi-Battaglia, Fratelli Bucci, Monte Schiavo, Umani Ronchi.

VEREINIGTE HOSPITIEN   *Germany, Mosel, W*   Centuries old, this charity, equivalent in status and intent with the **HOSPICES DE BEAUNE**, owns former monastic vineyards in the Middle Mosel and Saar Valleys where it makes fine traditional Rieslings.

VERGELESSES, ILE DE   *France, Burgundy, Côte de Beaune, 1er Cru, R, W*   Vineyard in the commune of Pernand-Vergelesses. The W wines are aromatic and quite delicate and the Rs have lovely supple, strawberry fruit. Leading producers include: Dubreuil-Fontaine, Laleure-Piot, Louis Latour.

VERNACCIA DI SAN GIMIGNANO   *Italy, Tuscany, DOC, W*   From vineyards near the medieval town of San Gimignano, the Vernaccia grape produces a slightly honeyed wine with just a hint of crisp acidity. Leading producers include: Castello de Montauto, Fattoria di Cusona, Montenidoli.

VERNAY, GEORGES   *France, Rhône, Condrieu, W*   The leading maker of this rare and fashionable W: several grades of wine, all excellent.

VEUVE CLICQUOT PONSARDIN   *France, Champagne*   One of the top **GRANDS MARQUES**. The NV blend, with its distinctive yellow label, is consistently good and the flagship wine, La Grande Dame, is a rich, weighty blend of Pinot Noir and Chardonnay.

VICCHIOMAGGIO, CASTELLO   *Italy, Tuscany, Chianti, R, W*   Estate making mainly Chianti Classico (labels are San Jacopo, Vigna Petri and La Prima); and also a Chardonnay-based *vino da tavola* (Ripa delle Mimose, W) and a Sangiovese/Cabernet blend (Ripa delle More, R).

VICTORIA   *Australia*   The most southerly state of mainland Australia. Produces an enormous variety of wines and, increasingly, some of very high quality.

VIDAL BLANC   Hybrid white grape derived from **TREBBIANO**, used in a range of reasonable wines, including ice wines (**EISWEIN**), in north-eastern USA and Canada.

VIDAL WINE PRODUCERS   *New Zealand, North Island, W, R*   This Hawke's Bay winery makes good-quality, classy wines.

VIDAL-FLEURY   *France, Rhône, R, W*   This respected grower of Côte Rôtie Rs is also a *négociant* making a range of wines: the R and W Côtes du Rhônes stand out.

VIEILLE FERME   *France, Rhône, Côtes du Ventoux, R*   The same ownership as Ch **BEAUCASTEL**, which lends class to this large-scale maker of easy-to-enjoy Rs.

VIEUX TÉLÉGRAPHE, DOM DU   *France, Rhône, Châteauneuf-du-Pape, R, W*   Noted estate in Châteauneuf: reliable, quality wine. The R is mosly Grenache, with some Syrah and Mourvèdre.

VIEUX-CHATEAU-CERTAN *France, Bordeaux, Pomerol, R* Once considered Pomerol's finest wine, now eclipsed by PÉTRUS. The largest of the top properties in the appellation. The Cabernet Franc and Cabernet Sauvignon in the blend can make it taste quite Médoc-like.

VIGNA, VIGNETO *Italy* Vineyard.

VIGNELAURE *France, Provence, Coteaux d'Aix-en-Provence, R, W, P* George Brunet's estate remains the best in the appellation. The R, in a bordeaux style, is 60% Cabernet Sauvignon, 30 Syrah and 10 Grenache, with long ageing in Hungarian oak. A second wine, La Page de Vignelaure, continues the bordeaux parallel.

VIGNERON *France* A wine-grower or vineyard worker.

VIGNOBLE *France* Vineyard, which can be just one plot or an entire region, as in "the Bordeaux *vignoble*".

VIGOUROUX *France, Southwest, Cahors, R* This *négociant* firm owns four Cahors estates, including Ch de Haut-Serre, on the plateau land where Cahors gained its reputation, which they helped revive. Vigouroux make good use of oak-ageing.

VILLA BANFI *Italy, Tuscany, Brunello di Montalcino, R, W* Spectacular modern winery producing Brunello, Rosso di Montalcino DOC, a R blend, Castello Banfi, a pure Cabernet Sauvignon, and two varietal W wines.

VILLA MARIA ESTATE *New Zealand, North Island, W, R* New Zealand's third-largest producer makes a full range of R and W wines, including botrytized Riesling W.

VILLA SACHSEN, WEINGUT *Germany, Rheinhessen, W* Based at Bingen, on the Rhine, this estate offers well-made, cask-matured wines, mostly Riesling.

VILLAINE, A & P DE *France, Burgundy, Chalonnais, R, W, P* Aubert de Villaine is part-owner of Dom de la ROMANÉE-CONTI, but at his estate in the Côte Chalonnaise he makes excellent Aligoté from old vines.

VILLÁNY-SIKLÓS *Hungary* To the west of the Great Plain, this is Hungary's southernmost wine district, making plummy, earthy Merlot and Cabernet Sauvignon Rs for export. Local specialities are the (R) Kékfrankos and Kékoportó grapes. Siklós is known for Ws.

VILLARS, CH *France, Bordeaux, Fronsac, R* Leading estate of Fronsac with a good record in the 1980s and especially 1990 for fruity, well-structured wine.

VILMART *France, Champagne* A small, top-quality grower with 11ha at Rilly-la-Montagne making all its wine in oak. Weighty, rich champagne.

VIN DE L'ANNÉE   *France*   Wine of the most recent vintage.

VIN DE PAILLE   *France*   Literally, straw wine. Sweet wine made from grapes dried on straw mats.

VIN DE PAYS   *France*   Country wine: A superior grade of *vin de table* produced according to regulations concerning grape varieties, yields and localities.

VIN DE TABLE   *France*   The lowest grade of wine defined in French law. It cannot claim a specific origin and is usually sold under a brand name.

VIN DÉLIMITÉ DE QUALITÉ SUPÉRIEURE (VDQS)   *France*   The grade of French quality wine below AOC.

VIN DOUX NATUREL (VDN)   *France*   Literally, naturally sweet wine. Wines that are rich in natural sweetness are fortified to preserve residual sugar.

VIN GRIS   *France*   A pale P wine made as W wine, but from R grapes.

VIN JAUNE   *France*   Wine made in the Jura which is affected by FLOR.

VIN ORDINAIRE   *France*   Everyday wine that is included in the classification *vin de table*.

VIN SANTO   *Italy*   A wine made from dried grapes, aged in small barrels. Can be sweet or dry.

VIÑA DE VERO   *Spain, Aragón, Somontano, R, W, P*   Name used by a relatively new company producing good-quality wines from both Spanish and French varieties, including Pinot Noir and Gewürztraminer.

VINCENT, DOM   *France, Burgundy, Mâconnais, W*   Maker of very fine St-Véran, in quite an opulent style.

VINCOR INTERNATIONAL   *Canada, Ontario & British Columbia, W, R*   North America's eight-largest winery, also owning Brights, Cartier and Innisskillin. A vast portfolio of wines from imported blends to single-vineyard bottlings.

VINELAND ESTATES   *Canada, Ontario, W, R*   Riesling specialist, with a range from bone-dry wines to Late Harvest and Icewine (EISWEIN).

VINHO VERDE   *Portugal, DOC, W, R*   The term means "green wine" but Vinho Verde can be either W or R (the R is rarely exported). It is so named because it is made to be drunk young and fresh, retaining a slight *pétillance* or sparkle. It should be low in alcohol and high in natural acidity. Leading producers include: Quinta da Aveleda, Borges & Irmão, Palácio de Brejoeira.

VINHOS, J P   *Portugal, W, R*   Look for fresh, grapey João Pires Dry Muscat and ripe-tasting R Tinto da Anfora from this firm.

VINIFERA   Vines of the species *vitis vinifera* – the classic grape vine of Europe – are sometimes so-named in the USA and Canada to distinguish them from hybrid or LABRUSCA vines.

VINO DA TAVOLA   *Italy*   Table wine. Much of it is ordinary, but some *vini da tavola* are superior wines made in DOC areas but not according to DOC rules.

VINO DE CRIANZA   *Spain*   Literally, wine of breeding. Quality wine that must have two full years' storage (one for W and P *crianzas*), with a minimum of six months in barrel.

VINO DE LA TIERRA (VDT)   *Spain*   Country wine (like the French *vin de pays*) from one of 28 areas that have shown their own character.

VINO NOBILE DI MONTEPULCIANO   *Italy, Tuscany, DOCG, R*   Mainly made from Prugnolo, a local Sangiovese clone, softened by Canaiolo Nero and lent fragrance by Mammolo. This wine must be aged in wood for two years. It can be lean, but the best have hints of spice and sandalwood. Leading producers include: Avignonesi, Boscarelli, Tenuta Trerose.

VINOS DE MADRID   *Spain, Madrid, DO, W, P, R*   The vineyards of this zone produce good, everyday wines for the capital, mostly in *joven* style but also some *crianza* R. Leading producers include: Bodegas Orusco.

VINTAGE   Originally the grape harvest; as there is only one per year, the term has come to refer to the wine made from the harvest of a particular year.

VIOGNIER   White grape of the northern Rhône, fabulously scented, often tasting of sweet, ripe peaches and apricots, it reaches perfection in the Condrieu and Château Grillet AOCs. Also grown in the Midi and California.

VIRÉ, CAVE COOPÉRATIVE DE   *France, Burgundy, Mâconnais, R, W, Sp*   One of south Burgundy's best- run cooperatives, producing wines of consistently reliable quality.

VIRGINIA   *USA*   Winemaking here started in 1609, and Thomas Jefferson's Monticello estate had vines in the 1770s. Today there are 50 wineries, and 7 VAs, the most important the Blue Ridge Mountains and Monticello. Leading producers include: MEREDYTH, Montdomaine (Chardonnay, and Bordeaux-style Rs from Monticello), Piedmont Vineyards (good Ws), Prince Michel (Chardonnay).

VOARICK, DOM MICHEL   *France, Burgundy, Côte d'Or, R*   Domaine based in Aloxe-Corton: low yields and fine Corton vineyards combine to produce concentrated wines for long ageing.

VOGE, ALAIN   *France, Rhône, St-Péray W, Sp; Cornas, R*   An important grower of long-lived, massive Cornas, in three *cuvées*, and a maker of good, dry Sp St-Péray.

229

VOGÜÉ, DOM COMTE GEORGES DE   *France, Burgundy, Côte d'Or, R*
Major owner of *Grands* and *Premiers Crus*, mostly in Chambolle-Musigny. Top-class wines.

VOLKACH   *Germany, Franken, W*   Town in the
Steigerwald zone to the east of the region. The
Escherndorfer Lump vineyard, immediately
south of Volkach, is one of the few known outside Franken. Good Riesling, Müller-Thurgau
and Traminer Ws are produced at one of the
good smaller co-ops at nearby Nordheim.
Leading producers include: Schloss Halburg.

VOLLRADS, SCHLOSS   *Germany, Rheingau, W*   Ancient aristocratic
estate with its vineyard set high above the Rheingau, yielding
Riesling wine in a balanced, racy style.

VOLNAY   *France, Burgundy, AOC, R*   Côte de Beaune R, from Pinot
Noir. The appellation's hallmark is delicate, silky, violet- and
strawberry-scented wines from *Premiers Crus* such as Caillerets,
Champans, Clos des Chênes and Clos des Ducs. Drink from 4–5
years old, though they can age much longer. Leading producers
include: Marquis d'Angerville, Jean-Marc Bouley, Joseph
Drouhin, Dom Lafarge, Hubert de Montille, Dom de la Pousse
d'Or, Joseph Voillot.

VOLPAIA, CASTELLO DI   *Italy, Tuscany, Chianti, R, W*   Maker of elegant, perfumed, long-lived Chianti Classico; also Bianco Val d'Arbia (DOC, W), the W oak-aged Torniello, and two *vini da tavola*:
Coltassala and Balifico (R).

VON MUMM, G H   *Germany, Rheingau, W, R*   Important vineyard
owner in Johannisberg, making classic Rieslings which are dry
but solid and full of character.

VOSNE-ROMANÉE   *France, Burgundy, AOC, R*   Côte de Nuits village, with five *Grands Crus* and a clutch of excellent *Premiers Crus*:
(Aux Malconsorts, Les Suchots, Les Chaumes Aux Brûlées, Les
Beaux Monts), which produce outstandingly opulent wines that
can age for 10–15 years. The village AOC also produces elegant,
reliable wines.

VOUGEOT   *France, Burgundy, AOC, R*   Besides the famous *Grand
Cru* Clos de Vougeot, other Vougeot wines include some *Premiers
Crus* and village wines: some divided from the *Grand Cru* only by
the Clos wall. Leading producers include: Domaine Bertagna.

VOUVRAY   *France, Loire, AOC, W, Sp*   High-quality Ws, dry,
medium and sweet; still or Sp, from east of Tours, on the north
bank of the Loire. Styles vary from vintage to vintage: in a warm
year, most wines will be sweet; if the weather is not so good,
drier wines will result. Good sweet wines can age very well.
Leading producers include: Philippe Brisebarre, Dom Bourillon
d'Orléans, Gaston Huet, Ch Moncontour, Clos Naudin, Prince
Poniatowski.

VRANKEN *France, Champagne* Large house with 153ha of vines. The wines stress Chardonnay and are light and elegant. Brands include Charles Lafitte, Sacotte and Demoiselle.

VRAYE CROIX-DE-GAY, CH *France, Bordeaux, Pomerol, R* Small but well-placed vineyard making long-lived and well-regarded wines.

W

WACHAU *Austria, Niederösterreich* Vineyards along the Danube gorge form one of the smallest Austrian regions, but the source of the best W wines. Grüner Veltliner and Riesling dominate. Wachau has its own quality categories which appear on the label; lightest is *Steinfeder*; richest are *Smaragd*; *Ried* on the label denotes a vineyard of singular merit. Leading producers include: Franz Hirtzberger, Emmerich Knoll, Nikolaihof, F X Pichler, Franz Prager.

WACHENHEIM *Germany, Pfalz, W* Fine-wine village in the MITT-ELHAARDT, with famous vineyards such as Gerümpel and Altenberg. Solid-long-lasting W wine is the local tradition. Some estates also make drier wines in a modern style. Leading producers include: Bürklin-Wolf.

WAGNER VINEYARDS *USA, New York, Finger Lakes, W* Premier maker of Chardonnay. All wines are estate-grown; about half of 20,000-case annual production is of classic-grape wines, including Pinot Noir R and Riesling and Gewürztraminer Ws. Also makes barrel-fermented Seyval Blanc and Reserve White.

WAIKATO *New Zealand, North Island* South of Auckland, this area is noted for Müller-Thurgau, Sauvignon Blanc and Chardonnay. Leading producers include: De Redcliffe.

WAIRARAPA *New Zealand, North Island* Small, recently-planted area internationally renowned for its Rs from Pinot Noir. Also grows some W varieties. Leading producers include: Ata Rangi, Dry River, Palliser, Te Kairanga.

WALKER BAY *South Africa, WO* Cool-climate coastal area benefitting from Atlantic breezes, ideal for Pinot Noir and Chardonnay in a subtle, Burgundian style. The potential here is very exciting. Leading producers include: Bouchard-Finlayson, Hamilton Russell.

WALLHAUSEN, SCHLOSS, PRINZ ZU SALM-DALBERG'SCHES WEIN-GUT *Germany, Nahe, W* Modern-minded, though aristocratic, this estate does not use vineyard names except for a few top ones, the rest of the wine being blended as one *cuvée*.

WALNUT CREST *Chile, R, W, Sp* Highly ambitious company founded in 1986 by several major shareholders of Concha y Toro in partnership with Banfi Vintners. Produces about one million cases a year, including a Sp wine. Best wines include Merlot, Cabernet Sauvignon and Sauvignon Blanc.

WARRE *Portugal, port* Wines of immense power from the oldest of the British port houses, founded 1670. A Symington became a partner in 1892, and they still own it.

WARREN-BLACKWOOD *Australia, Western Australia* A very new wine region better known by its two sub-regions Manjimup and Pemberton. Thought to have great potential, especially for Pinot Noir and Chardonnay. Leading producers include: Donnelly River, Gloucester Ridge, Mounford, Piano Gully, Smithbrook, Warren.

WARWICK ESTATE *South Africa, Stellenbosch, R, W* Essentially an R-only estate with a particular penchant for Cabernet Franc, produced as a rich, grassy single varietal and also included in the outstanding bordeaux blend, Trilogy.

WASHINGTON *USA* Major grape-growing state, though most grapes end up as juice, not wine. The wine zones, which include the COLUMBIA VALLEY and YAKIMA VALLEY, are east of the Cascade Mountains and thus dry (meaning irrigation), warm in summer and cold in winter. Crisp, fresh Ws from Chardonnay and Riesling are the mainstays; with soft, fruity Rs from Merlot and Cabernet Sauvignon. Leading producers include: ARBOR CREST, COLUMBIA, COVEY RUN, HOGUE, STE-MICHELLE, WOODWARD CANYON.

WEGELER-DEINHARD *Germany, Rheingau & Mosel, W* Owner of part of the Bernkasteler Doctor and other fine vineyards, making classic Mosels that age well in bottle, and a large estate in the Rheingau making good-value, characterful Rieslings, many dry. Increasingly, the Rheingau wines are sold by village, not vineyard, name.

WEHLEN *Germany, Mosel, W* Town in the MITTELMOSEL, whose most famous vineyard, Wehlener Sonnenuhr, meaning sundial, enjoys a superb, southwest-facing site. Leading producers include: J A Prüm, S A Prüm and Max-Ferdinand Richter.

WEIL, ROBERT *Germany, Rheingau, W* Estate making very fine Rieslings from top Rheingau vineyards, both dry ones to partner food and superb sweet ones for sipping alone.

WEINVIERTEL *Austria, Niederösterreich* Largest of the Austrian wine regions, north and north-west of Vienna, accounting for 31% of total production. Most wines are in a light, easy-to-drink style although some producers concentrate on *eiswein*. Leading producers include: Richard Luckner, Roman Pfaffl, Fritz Rieder.

WEISSBURGUNDER See PINOT BLANC.

WELSCHRIESLING White grape, unrelated to Riesling, which makes light, aromatic dry and sweet wines of variable quality in Austria, northern Italy (Riesling Italico), and throughout southeast Europe (where its synonyms include Laski Rizling and Olaszriesling).

WENTE   *USA, California, Bay Area, W, Sp, R*   The Wentes started winegrowing in the Livermore Valley in 1883 and the estate remains family-owned, the former Cresta Blanca winery now remodelled into a restaurant and Sp wine centre. Wente's Sémillon W has lovely melon-fig fruitiness.

WERNER'SCHES WEINGUT, DOMDECHANT   *Germany, Rheingau, W*   Fine, elegant traditional Riesling Ws from an old family estate at Hochheim. These are wines worth bottle-age.

WEST VIRGINIA   *USA*   Promising wines are being made in the east of the state, close to the expanding areas of Virginia.

WESTERN AUSTRALIA   *Australia*   The country's newest wine state has already an exciting reputation for quality. The cool-climate areas of MARGARET RIVER and MOUNT BARKER-FRANKLAND produce an excellent range of Rs and Ws, though the hot, dry SWAN VALLEY has undergone a recent decline.

WESTHALTEN   *France, Alsace*   Distinctive Pinot Blanc and Pinot Gris Ws come from this village, which includes the *Grands Crus* Vorbourg and Zinnkoepflé. Leading producers include: Frick.

WETSHOF ESTATE, DE   *South Africa, Robertson, W*   Chardonnay specialist Dannie de Wet produces a wide range of very good-quality Ws under both the De Wetshof and Dannie de Wet labels. The main difference is the amount of oak influence, from the fresh lemony Finesse, with just a touch of oak, to the bigger, more full-flavoured Chardonnay d'Honneur.

WIEDERKEHR VINEYARDS   *USA, Arkansas, W, R*   Founded in Altus by the Swiss Wiederkehr family in 1880, now one of the largest producers east of the Rockies. With two-thirds of the 263-ha vineyard containing classic varieties, the company produces a wide range, the list topped by Riesling W and several Muscat-based Ws.

WIEN   *Austria*   The capital (Vienna in English) is surrounded by 700ha of vines and almost all the wine is drunk locally. Around Vienna are dozens of *Heurigen*, inns where growers sell their own wines; mainly light, racy W wine from the last vintage. Grüner Veltliner is the most popular grape, also excellent Riesling and Weissburgunder (Pinot Blanc). Leading producers include: Fuhrgassl-Huber, Franz Mayer, Herbert Schilling.

WILLAMETTE VALLEY   *USA, Oregon, VA*   Oregon's most important wine zone, extending south and west from Portland to Eugene. A cool-climate area, providing up to three-quarters of the state's wine-grapes. This is home to extremely elegant Pinot Noir Rs (accounting for nearly half of the land under vine) and Ws from Chardonnay, Riesling and Pinot Gris. Leading producers include: Knudsen Erath, Oak Knoll, Ponzi.

WILTINGEN   *Germany, Mosel-Saar-Ruwer, W*   Town in the Saar, surrounded by vineyards. Cheaper Saar QbA wine is sold under the *grosslage* name Wiltinger Scharzberg, but much wine with a high level of acidity finds its way to the makers of Sekt, Germany's sparkling wine. The best vineyard site is Scharzhofberg, not to be confused with the *grosslage*. Leading producers include: Egon Müller-Scharzhof.

WINKEL   *Germany, Rheingau, W*   Top Rieslings, marked by a pronounced fruity-acid style, are produced in this village. The best vineyard is Winkeler Hasensprung and the most famous producer is Schloss Vollrads.

WINNINGEN   *Germany, Mosel, W*   One of the largest wine villages on the Mosel. Shares the top-quality terraced vineyard Winninger Uhlen with its neighbour, Kobern. Winningen is known for its characterful, strongly-flavoured Riesling wines. Leading producers include: von Heddesdorff, Richard Richter, von Schleinitz.

WINTZENHEIM   *France, Alsace*   This village has one of the most famous vineyards, *Grand Cru* Hengst, which produces Ws from Gewürztraminer plus Pinot Gris and Riesling. Leading producers include: Meyer, Zind-Humbrecht.

WIRSCHING, WEINGUT   *Germany, Franken, W*   Characterful dry wines, much appreciated with food, come from good vineyards at Iphofen.

WISCONSIN   *USA*   Wine is made here in commercial quantities, with Riesling and Pinot Noir among the successful varieties. Leading producers include: Wollersheim.

WOODWARD CANYON   *USA, Washington State, R, W*   At his winery in Walla Walla Valley, Rick Small specializes in R from Cabernet Sauvignon (blackcurrant and dill flavours) and Merlot (coffee and tobacco), but also makes a W Burgundian-style Chardonnay (clove and butter). His Meritage (bordeaux-style) R is called Chabonneau.

WORCESTER DISTRICT   *South Africa, WO*   District of highly efficient cooperatives making 25% of country's total output, including good Ws from Riesling, Sauvignon Blanc and Colombard. Also important for brandy production. Leading producers include: Nuy Cooperative.

WÜRTTEMBERG   *Germany, Anbaugebiet, R, W, P*   Region around Stuttgart and Heilbronn in the Neckar Valley, specializing in soft, sweet R wines, all drunk locally. Ws from Riesling, and modern-style, sometimes *barrique*-aged, Rs, are more in the international taste. Leading producers include: Graf Adelmann, Robert Bauer, von Neipperg.

WÜRZBURG   *Germany, Franken, W*   The capital of Franken, containing its three greatest wine estates: the Bürgerspital, noted for its intense Trockeenbeerenauslesen; the Juliusspital, regarded as best at the moment; and the Staatlicher Hofkeller with its prime sites in the Stein vineyard.

WÜRZBURG STAATLICHER HOFKELLER *Germany, Franken, W, R* Great estate whose cellars beneath the Residenz in Würzburg are as famous as the wines, which are made in classic Franken style.

WYNNS COONAWARRA ESTATE *Australia, S Australia, Coonawarra, R, W* Possibly the most famous, certainly the most successful, producer in this southernmost area. Very good, reliable quality – and some outstanding wines under the John Riddoch and Michael labels.

Y

YAKIMA VALLEY *USA, Washington State, VA* Sub-zone of the Columbia Valley, growing varieties like Riesling and Chardonnay for Ws; Merlot and Cabernet Sauvignon for Rs.

YALUMBA *Australia, S Australia, Barossa, R, W* This family firm is best known for its Sp wine, Angas Brut, the Oxford Landing range and its well-priced brands.

YARRA VALLEY *Australia, Victoria* A beautiful, cool-climate area of Victoria, noted especially for top-quality Pinot Noir R in a style to challenge Burgundy. Also makes very good Chardonnay, Shiraz (R), Merlot and Cabernet Sauvignon. Leading producers include: de Bortoli, Domaine Chandon, Coldstream Hills, St Huberts, Yarra Yering.

YECLA *Spain, DO, Levante, W, P, R* One of two wine zones in Murcia, inland from Alicante, recently investing in new technology to make a wider range of distinctive wines to attract new markets. Leading producers include: Bodegas Castaño.

YORK MOUNTAIN *USA, California, VA* In San Luis Obispo County, and a mere 12ha in size, this is the exclusive domain of York Mountain Winery, founded in 1882.

YQUEM, CH D' *France, Bordeaux, Sauternes, 1er Cru Supérieur, W* For many years the only Sauternes château to follow the highest standards, Yquem still leads with its hand-crafted, long-lived, enormously complex (and costly) wine.

Z

ZELL/MOSEL *Germany, Mosel-Saar-Ruwer, Bereich, W* Also called the Lower Mosel, a zone rather in the shadow of the Mittelmosel (*see* **BERNKASTEL**) but making good-value W wines.

ZELTINGEN *Germany, Mosel, W* Village in the Mittelmosel, opposite Wehlen, with some superb, south-west facing vineyards, the famous vineyards being Himmelreich, Schlossberg and Sonnenuhr.

ZIND HUMBRECHT *France, Alsace, W* Leonard Humbrecht has campaigned tirelessly for lower yields. His 30ha are extremely well sited and include four *Grand Cru* holdings. Methods are natural and traditional; Pinot Gris and Gewürztraminer excel.

ZINFANDEL Versatile red grape from California, probably related to southern Italy's Primitivo. Can make long-lived, complex, deep red wines, but also very pale P or "blush" wines.

ZÜRICH *Switzerland* This important wine-producing canton in German-speaking Switzerland makes W wines mainly from Riesling-Sylvaner (Müller-Thurgau) and R from Blauburgunder (Pinot Noir, also known as Clevner or Beerli). Most production is handled by two large local cooperatives although a few very small estates do exist.

TASTING
WINE

DESCRIBING A TASTE

WINETASTING IS NOT DIFFICULT: it only needs concentration in order to make full use of the memory, which is our main tasting tool. The words used to describe a taste – or a smell – are those which trigger the memory.

The process of tasting has a few simple steps. First, pour a little wine into a clean glass. Look at the colour, against a white background if possible. Is the wine dark or pale, dense or light? Is it clear and bright, or muddy and dull? Clear your mind, concentrate hard. Then sniff: what does the wine's smell remind you of? Maybe another wine, or something quite different. Finally, take a good taste and hold the wine in your mouth, letting it coat the palate and tongue. The mouth is less subtle than the nose: look for weight, acidity, sweetness, astringency and texture.

The key to learning – if that, rather than appreciation, is the aim – is to make notes straight away.

TASTING TERMS

This is a basic glossary of words for describing wine. Words that describe the principal components of wine – acid, alcohol and tannin (in **CAPITALS**) – are grouped under their respective entries.

Acetic   *See* Volatile.
ACID/ACIDITY   Gives life and freshness. Also helps define and prolong wine flavours. Words for acidity (from too little to too much) include: flat, flabby, soft, supple, fresh, lively, crisp, firm, hard, sharp, green, tart, acid.
ALCOHOL   Gives wine its characteristic "weight". Described as (from inadequate to excess): watery, thin, light, medium-bodied, full-bodied, ample, generous, heady, heavy, alcoholic, hot.
Aroma   Smells that come from the grape rather than from ageing in barrel or bottle, or from vinification. *See also* Bouquet.
Aromatic   Wines from grapes with a particularly pronounced aroma (eg Gewürztraminer, Muscat, Sauvignon Blanc, Cabernet Sauvignon).
Astringent   The drying, gripping sensation on the gums produced by tannin (*qv*).
Austere   Hard, unyielding impression given by wine with high tannin or acid, which needs time to soften.
Backward   Not ready to drink; needs more bottle-age to mellow.
Balanced   Wine whose component parts "balance" each other nicely, so that no element appears lacking or obtrusive for its type.
Blackcurrant   The smell and taste usually associated with Cabernet Sauvignon wines .
Body   Combined impression of weight and consistency,

due mainly, but not solely, to the level of alcohol.

Botrytis   *See* Noble rot.

Bouquet   General term to describe the smell of wine, but particularly used for smells deriving from vinification and barrel- or bottle-age. *See also* aroma.

Buttery   A smell and taste often associated with rich, oaked Chardonnay.

Cedary   Cedar-wood smell found in wines aged in new French oak.

Closed   Muted but promising bouquet or flavour.

Cloying   Sweetness that is "sticky" because it is not balanced by enough acidity.

Coarse   Used to describe texture, tannin in particular. Also describes a harsh mousse in sparkling wines.

Complex   Indicates quality: variety and subtlety in both flavour and bouquet.

Corked wine   Smell of damp and mould completely dominates the bouquet and flavour of the wine. Nothing to do with harmless fragments of cork in the glass.

Drying out   Mature wines that are losing their flavour, so allowing their acid, alcohol or tannin to appear obtrusive.

Dumb   *See* Closed.

Earthy   Usually a positive term; recalling damp earth on nose and palate.

Elegant   Finesse, harmony, no harsh impressions.

Fierce   Harshness, from high levels of alcohol and/or acidity.

Fine   High-quality wine.

Finish   Tastes and aromas that linger on after the wine has been swallowed. *See also* Length, Short.

Fleshy   Rich in flavour, supple in texture. Refers mainly to reds.

Flinty   Mineral taste in crisp dry white wines, such as Chablis and Sancerre.

Fruity   Many wines smell or taste of a specific fruit (eg peach, apple, blackcurrant, cherry); others have a pleasant general "juiciness" of aroma and flavour. A term difficult to avoid, easy to over-use.

Gooseberry   A taste and smell mostly associated with Sauvignon Blanc.

Grapey   Used to suggest a taste of fresh grape juice. Muscats are almost the only wines to smell and taste just like the fresh grape.

Green   Unripe, young. Also refers to acidity.

Grip   A firm, dry feel on the gums; produced by tannin in red wine.

Harsh   Refers to texture.

Herbaceous   A smell reminiscent of green plants, or freshly cut grass.

Hollow   Empty of flavour and noticeably short.

Lean   Used critically, means a lack of ripe fruit.

Length/Long   The hallmark of a high-quality wine. *See also* Finish.

Maderized   *See* Oxidized wines

Mature   Ready to drink.

Mellow   With a soft, agreeable texture.

Noble rot *Botrytis cinerea*, the rot on ripe grapes that concentrates natural flavours. Tasters spot this intensity and a honey-and-lemon character.

Nutty A smell and taste often found in mature white burgundy, good-quality dry marsala, amontillado sherry.

Oaky Smells (vanilla, cedar wood, caramel, toast) and sometimes slight dryness of texture that derive from ageing in new oak barrels.

Oxidized wines So-called because excess contact with oxygen has spoiled their taste. White wines look dull, with a darker colour than normal for age/type: lacklustre straw to brown. Flat, stale smell; dull, sharp taste. Also called maderized. Red wines too have a dull appearance, browner than normal for age/type. Flat, stale nose with a "sweet and sour" or caramelly smell and taste.

Peppery Smell of ground black pepper, in port and Rhône wines especially.

Pétillant Lightly sparkling.

Petrolly Agreeable petroleum smell in mature Rieslings.

Raw Harsh impressions from alcohol, acid and tannin in immature wine.

Reduced *See* Sulphur-related faults.

Rich Describes flavour and texture.

Ripe A sweetness of flavour in wines made from very ripe grapes.

Rustic Coarse; a result of primitive or careless winemaking techniques.

Short Lacking in persistence of flavour on the finish. *See also* length.

Smoky Smell and/or taste; eg in white Sancerre and northern Rhône reds.

Stewed Like tea brewed too long: dull, vegetal smell; coarse, astringent.

Sulphur-related faults The pungent, acrid, suffocating smell of sulphur dioxide: like a safety match on being lit; shows as a sharp, dry prickling sensation in throat on tasting. The smell of Hydrogen sulphide is bad eggs, rubber, garlic, rotting vegetation, with tastes to match. Also called reduced.

Supple Soft and gentle, without being flabby.

TANNIN Substance from grape skins that gives red wine its dry, mouth-puckering feel. Described as (from a little to a lot): fine-grained, soft, matt, dry, rich, firm, tough, coarse, vegetal, stemmy, astringent.

Thin Dilute and meagre in flavour.

Tired Lacking freshness.

Vanilla The smell and taste most often associated with wines that have been aged in new oak barrels.

Volatile wines Have a noticeable sour vinegar smell from the "volatile" acid: acetic acid, ie vinegar. Thin, sharp, sour taste.

Wet wool Smell in unoaked Chardonnay (Chablis) and Sémillon (Sauternes). Also found in wines with too much sulphur.

VALUE
AND
VINTAGES

VALUE-FOR-MONEY WINES

WHICH WINES TODAY OFFER the best *rapport qualité:prix*, in the expressive French phrase? They may be new areas, striving for recognition, or classic ones unjustly overlooked. Here are some suggestions, grouped by wine style, for wines which offer both quality at their various levels, and good value.

VALUE DRY WHITES

Here the value-hunter has to search hardest, for while the world's winemakers vie to make look-alike Chardonnays, wines with real interest are harder to find.

CÔTE CHALONNAIS
White wines from the village appellations Rully, Montagny and Givry offer real burgundy flavours, and quite a lot of finesse, at sensible prices. Wines come from the excellent local cooperatives and from private estates.

RHONE WHITES
Rhône reds get the limelight, but skilled winemakers can conjure excellent whites from the sunny valley: Condrieu is expanding, and its Viognier-grape wine is better value; White Crozes-Hermitage can be well made and good value. White Hermitage and Châteauneuf are serious and age-worthy wines yet far cheaper than burgundies of equivalent stature.

VIN DE PAYS D'OC
This French "country wine" name covers the whole of the Midi and is used on some good, modern wines such as Chablis expert Domaine Laroche's whites from Sauvignon, Chardonnay (oak-aged) and Viognier; the Fortant de France range; and the wines made by Australian wine giants Penfolds, working with Midi cooperatives.

RIESLING FROM AUSTRALIA
The obsession with Chardonnay is wearing off, and Australia's better winemakers are trying their skills on Riesling, another classic white grape. Styles tend to be fruity yet acidic, clean and with a touch of sugar on the finish. Good young, but can age well.

IRSAY OLIVIER

This grape variety, native to Hungary and Slovakia, is being taken seriously by western- (and Australian-) trained winemakers working in these Danube countries. It produces extremely fresh, flowery, perfumed white wines with an attractive appealing palate.

BADEN WHITES

Wines with more weight and flavour than most white Germans are found in the relatively warm zone of Baden. They range from soft and refreshing everyday wines, often labelled just Baden, to solid, dry Grauburgunders (Pinot Blanc) from individual estates. And – unlike the more usual German wine styles – all are good with food.

VALUE REDS

Red wine is less troublesome to make than white, and thus value is easier to find. Character, and that imponderable called personality, are more apparent in the following wines than in the average reds at mid-market prices.

PÉCHARMANT

This superior sub-zone within Bergerac in South-West France makes good Bordeaux-like reds with substance and structure, worth bottle-age. They are a little more fruity, and less austere, than clarets of similar stature.

CÔTES DU RHÔNE-VILLAGES

Wines from this southern French appellation offer much more flavour and character than straight Côtes du Rhône for a moderate amount more. The best villages are Séguret, Rochegude, Cairanne.

MONTEPULCIANO D'ABRUZZO

Rich, soft and enjoyable, these R wines from one of Italy's wildest mountain areas are pleasant drunk young yet can improve with a year or two in bottle.

TEMPRANILLO

Rioja's main grape also makes interesting, age-worthy reds (under the name Tinto Fino) in Ribera del Duero; and is also starting to appear as a varietal wine from other parts of Spain.

DOURO

From the port country of northern Portugal, these red table wines were once the exclusive meal-time drink of the port shippers – before they started on the port. Now more widely available, they are dark, solid yet fruity.

SHIRAZ

Wines from Australia's Shiraz grape (France's Syrah), either alone or blended with Cabernet Sauvignon, offer flavourful yet soft reds akin to Bordeaux from a hot vintage. Everyday examples are excellent value: spend some more and real character can be found.

CABERNET FROM CHILE

Cabernet Sauvignon thrives in Chile, and in recent years winemaking techniques have improved to take advantage of it. Everyday wines are black-cherry-red, fruity and good slightly chilled. Most producers also offer more serious age-worthy wines akin to mid-rank Médocs.

VALUE SWEET WHITES

Sweet wines at moderate prices are fast shaking off their headachy image as modern winemakers take control of the process. These suggestions cover a wide range of styles. All should be served well chilled, and all are enjoyable with or without food.

SAUTERNES ALTERNATIVES

Bordeaux and its surrounding areas produce some extremely good, value-for-money, lesser sweet wines, which may or may not be *botrytis*-affected. Cérons is the best known, followed by Loupiac, St-Croix-du-Mont, Monbazillac and Saussignac.

VENDANGE TARDIVE

Alsace has refined this traditional wine which uses very ripe grapes, usually picked after the main harvest. It is normally sweet, but can be dry. These are top-quality wines from either Gewürztraminer, Pinot Gris, Riesling or Muscat, and they are never cheap, but they are unusual, intense and clean in taste, thus good value.

JURANÇON

In the vineyards of the Pyrenees, grapes are allowed to dry on the vine until well into the autumn to concentrate sweetness, and the wine is then oak-aged. The result is like fine Sauternes, although developing greater complexity with bottle-age.

TOKAJI

Hungary's classic zone (also called Tokay) is reviving. The technique is complex: the result is a rich, heady mix of extract, alcohol and glycerol. The more "puttonyos" on the label (maximum 6), the sweeter the wine. As Tokaji is still regaining prestige and thus price, it is currently good value.

RECIOTO DI SOAVE

This northern Italian speciality is made from semi-dried grapes, and is much richer in taste and texture than dry Soave, with a higher alcohol content.

EISWEIN (ICE WINE) FROM CANADA

A well-kept secret, Canada's Ontario vineyards are the largest producer of rare, sweet white Eiswein, made from Riesling and the hybrid Vidal. The late-harvest grapes are frozen solid by the cold, and the resulting wine has wonderfully intense flavours.

MUSCAT

One of the world's most adaptable and appealing vine varieties, immediately recognizable for its grapiness. Muscat wines offer refreshing pleasure from the lighter style of Valencia in southern Spain and France's Midi, to the more exotic Orange and Black Muscats of California and Australia's even richer Rutherglen Liqueur Muscats.

DESSERT WINES FROM ENGLAND

Not fully exploited yet, but England has very good potential for producing lusciously sweet, botrytized wines, with a fine balance of flavours. Leading producers include: Chiltern Valley Vineyards, Denbies, Northbrook Spring, Pilton Manor, Westholme.

VALUE SPARKLING WINES

It will never be cheap to make sparkling wine, as getting the bubbles in means more work than leaving the wine still. Industrial-scale methods allow fizz of a sort to be made quite cheaply, but these use very ordinary base wine, and can rarely offer much in the way of flavour to go with the froth. Champagne is the benchmark, and for occasions when only champagne will do there are some suggestions below. As for the rest, look for sparklers made in the champagne method, or the Charmat technique, and look widely: the whole world seems to be trying to gain a slice of the celebration market.

CRÉMANT

The name used for French sparkling wines made outside Champagne by the same method: mainly in the Loire, Burgundy, Alsace and Bordeaux (labels say Crémant de Loire, d'Alsace, etc). Quality can be extremely good.

CHAMPAGNE'S SOUTHERN ZONES

Previously little-heard-of areas in the south of the Champagne region are beginning to forge an identity for themselves as producers of well-made, good-value champagnes. Mainly Chardonnay is grown in the Côte de Sézanne, ripening very well and making rich, slightly exotic wines. Over in the Aube Pinot Noir dominates, giving wines of finesse and staying power. These zones offer the magic name Champagne on the label, plus some real character and flavour: qualities that really cheap champagnes may lack.

CAVA

Spain's premium sparkling wine, Cava is made from native grape varieties like Macabeo (Viura) and Parellada, and offers high standards, broad fruit flavours and low acidity. Some of the premium *marques* have Chardonnay in the blend.

ASTI SPUMANTE

Famous but sadly maligned. If well-made, Asti from Northern Italy these days offers a deliciously refreshing soft grapey mouthful of flavours, combined with low alcohol. Look also for Moscato d'Asti, with even lower alcohol and an unusual Muscat-grape flavour.

PROSECCO DI CONEGLIANO-VALDOBBIADENE

This wine, usually called just Prosecco, is from near Venice. Clean but fairly neutral, with a slightly almondy flavour, it has snappy acidity and lowish alcohol. Unpretentious, for drinking young.

SPARKLING WINE FROM NEW ZEALAND

With its cool European-style climate, New Zealand produces some seriously good champagne alternatives made by the same method and with the same grape varieties, resulting in rich, weighty flavours balanced by good acidity.

SPARKLING WINE FROM AUSTRALIA

With a wide range of prices and qualities, from basic party fizz (Angas Brut, Seaview, Yalumba) to some serious classic-method wines, often made by companies linked with champagne houses (Domaine Chandon's Green Point, Petaluma's Croser), Australia has plenty of value. All offer fair value, plenty of fruit and an interesting alternative to European sparklers. Look for classic grapes (Pinot Noir, Chardonnay) on labels for more European-style wines.

VALUE FORTIFIED WINES

Fortified wines take time, skill and money to make. Success demands that the maker hold large stocks of slowly maturing wine: a challenging task financially. Areas with long traditions – port, sherry, South Africa – have the reserves of blending wine and the skills to offer interesting fortified wines, especially if the obvious names are bypassed.

SINGLE QUINTA PORTS

These are ports from a single estate made by some of the leading shippers, sometimes using just one or two of the top port grape varieties. Bottled two years after the vintage, they always bear a vintage date, age very well in bottle and represent an excellent alternative to vintage port.

MANZANILLA

This style of dry sherry can only be made on the coast at Sanlúcar de Barrameda, where moist conditions ensure that *flor* grows all year round. Manzanilla has a deliciously salty tang. The best is like a fine Fino, but less expensive.

AUSTRALIAN LIQUEUR MUSCATS

Fermentation is stopped almost before it has begun by the addition of spirit, ensuring that the finished wine retains wonderfully fresh, grapey aromas and flavours.

CAPE FORTIFIEDS

The South African tradition of making wines in the style of sherry and port has left a legacy: cellars full of superb old wines at value-for-money prices. Some are blends: Muscat styles, some like rather sweet chocolaty port, others like sherries. Fifteen-year-old wines can be had at very reasonable prices.

VINTAGE CHARTS

VINTAGE CHARTS MADE MORE SENSE when there were fewer wines: now, nothing can be that simple. However most wines are designed to be drunk young: it is the exceptions which are discussed below.

Ratings (the first figure) are out of 10. D means drink now; (D) means probably past its best; K means drink now, but can be kept; L means lay down for the future: the figure (eg L 10+) gives an estimate of likely time to maturity from the vintage.

RED BORDEAUX

Ordinary Bordeaux AC red will be good at 2 years old, *petits châteaux* of the Médoc and other areas at 2–5 years, though in great vintages they can surprise by lasting longer. Ratings are for classed growths or their equivalent; other wines will mature sooner. Recent vintages are proving to be attractive earlier than is traditionally the case, but good years will still have a long life.

1994	**8**	**L 5 +**

Rain in September again dashed the highest hopes, but wines promise well: first tastings show dark, solid wines, especially where careful selection has weeded out poor vats

1993	**7**	**L 4 +**

September rain spoilt prospects, in St-Emilion most of all, but still fair to good: early-maturing wines

1992	**6**	**K**

Large crop; best wines from Pauillac and St-Estèphe, light and simple wines elsewhere

1991	**5**	**D**

Poor weather – frost and rain – ended the run of good years

1990	**10**	**L 8 +**

Another hot, dry vintage: the best wines ripe and superb

1989	**9**	**L 8 +**

Large, ripe, opulent vintage: elegant and consistent wines

1988	9	L 10 +

Wines with structure and balance for long life

1987	6	D

Poor weather, moderate wines, best in St-Emilion/Pomerol

1986	8	K

Fine wines; the best are for keeping: Médoc better than St-Emilion/Pomerol

1985	7	K

Ripe, delicious, early-maturing wines

1984	5	D

Tough Cabernet-based wines in the Médoc and Graves: almost total failure across the river in St-Emilion

1983	8	D

High quality, elegant wines, especially from Médoc

1982	10	K

Magnificent and ripe from all areas

1981	7	D

Good wines in 1982's shadow, diluted by rain at harvest

Older fine vintages: 1978, 1970, 1975 (in Pomerol especially), 1966, 1961

RED BURGUNDY

The most difficult of wines to generalize about: the myriad growers and *négociants* make markedly different wines, and weather can cause big local variations. Comments are based on Côte d'Or *Premiers Crus*. Chalonnais wines follow the same pattern but do not keep so long. Village and appellation Bourgogne wines rarely mature beyond 4–5 years.

1994	6	K

Fair to good, but variable as growers battled with patchy weather

1993	7	K

Variable owing to weather problems: some fine wines

1992	7	K

Good but not for long keeping

1991	6	K
Weather problems		
1990	10	L 8+
Third great year in a row: fine, rich but balanced wines		
1989	9	L 8+
A hot year: good, perhaps great, wines		
1988	9	K
Solid, rich wines, especially in the Côte de Nuits		
1987	7	D
Good if light, despite September rain		
1986	6	D
Variable due to rot but many good wines		
1985	8	D
Good, ripe, balanced wines, some very fine		
1984	4	–
A poor, cold year		
1983	8	D
Hail and rot in places spoilt high hopes		
1982	6	(D)
Large crop of sometimes dilute wines		

WHITE BURGUNDY

Côte de Beaune wines, at *Premier Cru* level, form the basis of these ratings. Chablis vintages are broadly comparable, but see also notes at the foot of the chart. Chalonnais and Mâconnais wines: follow the chart, but enjoy them young: few wines except the best Chalonnais and some Pouilly-Fuissé will keep beyond 5–7 years.

1994	7	K
Better than '93, and than '94 reds		
1993	6	K
Less good than the reds		
1992	8	L 5+
Fine, typical wines, worth ageing		

1991	7	D
Lighter, more balanced wines than 1990		
1990	8	K
The third in a run of fine vintages: rich, full wines		
1989	9	D
A hot year; fine, full, complex wines, but not for keeping		
1988	8	D
A large crop, with some wines too light, but on the whole a good vintage		
1987	5	(D)
Vintage-time rain dashed hopes		
1986	7	D
More acidity and balance than 1985		
1985	8	D
Rich, fat wines which sometimes lack balance		
1984	4	(D)
A cool year; light wines		
1983	8	D
Hot year making rich, powerful wines, some unbalanced		

CHABLIS

1993 and 1994 were better than in the Côte de Beaune, but not exceptional.

1992: large crop of full, fat wines.

1991: hard-hit by frost, small crop; top wines can be good.

1990: very good for top wines, others soft.

1989: very good but fat: drink soon.

1988: balanced and typical: drink soon.

Older vintages of Premiers and Grands Crus: 1986, 1985 and 1983 were all good.

CHAMPAGNE

For most champagnes the vintage is irrelevant: makers blend wines of different vintages for consistency. Vintage-labelled wines are produced by the top champagne houses only in very good years. Not every house will "declare" every vintage. Vintage champagne from a *grande marque* house needs a decade in bottle to reach its best. Recent vintage years have been the trio of 1988, '89 and '90 (best of the three), with 1990 perhaps the best; 1986, '85, '83, '82, '79, '76.

ALSACE

Most everyday Alsace wines can be drunk at 1–4 years old; *Vendange Tardive* and *Sélection de Grains Nobles* wines can have a longer life.

In 1994, rain spoilt a potentially superb vintage, but good wines were still made.

1993 was a smaller crop, better than 1992; but Rieslings and late-harvest wines were patchy.

1992 saw a large crop of soft enjoyable wines.

1990, '89, '86 and '85 were superb.

LOIRE

The dry wines of Pouilly and Sancerre, from Sauvignon Blanc, are at their best under 5 years old, with rare exceptions.

Sweet whites of Anjou and Touraine from Chenin Blanc can, in the rare great years (1990, '89, '88 – though '94 had some good ones), last for decades.

Red wines for ageing are made only in warm years: 1990 was the last real one, but some good reds in 1993.

RHÔNE

North and South Rhône conditions can vary. Wines for keeping are the longer-lived, Syrah-based wines of the northern areas– Côte Rôtie, Hermitage – and wines such as Châteauneuf and Gigondas in the south.

1994 was good in the south.

1991, '92 and '93 moderate to poor everywhere.

1990, '89 and '88 all great.

Straight Côtes du Rhône is for drinking young, though some Côtes du Rhône-Villages wines gain from age.

Rhône whites, with rare exceptions such as Hermitage, are best at 2–4 years old.

GERMANY

Vintages here differ not just in quality but in style: traditionally, the best years are warm ones – those yielding lots of sweet (Auslese and above) wine. Cooler years, such as 1991 and 1984, with good Kabinett wines, are not to be despised. Spätlese and above wines in great vintages can keep for decades, and even Kabinett wines can, in the right years, improve for 8–10 years. Rheingau wines are perhaps the longest-lived, though well-balanced Mosels can last well too.

Great sweet wines were made in 1990, '89 and '88. 1993 was good in Baden and Pfalz, and 1994 is very promising.

The more southerly regions, such as the Pfalz and Baden, make wines which mature faster.

No-one is quite sure how modern German reds will age: do not keep them too long.

ITALY

Tuscany: the best recent vintages are 1990, 1988 and 1985.

Simpler Chianti does not need more than 2–4 years' ageing. Chianti Classico and Rufino are at their best at 4–8 years old. Brunello di Montalcino and Vino Nobile di Montepulciono, plus the growing legion of "super" *vini da tavola*, are at their best at 10+ years old.

Piedmont: Barolo and Barbaresco reds demand bottle-age, though the more modern style of winemaking favoured by some producers means faster-maturing wines. Old-fashioned Barolo from good vintages may take 10 years to become approachable, and will last in bottle for 20 years. Barbaresco starts to become accessible in 4–5 years.

Few Italian whites are designed to age; the exceptions are modern-style Chardonnays.

CALIFORNIA

The enormous size of the California vineyards, and their great variation in conditions, grapes and winemakers' intentions, make useful vintage judgements hard to come by. Most California wines are enjoyable young, though a limited number of top reds, especially Cabernet Sauvignon and Meritage, and Chardonnay whites, are designed for bottle-ageing. Prestige Chardonnays can gain from 5 years or more in bottle.

Good recent vintages: 1994, 1991, 1990.

AUSTRALIA

The great variety of Australia's regions and wines make generalizations impossible. Contrary to myth, conditions can and do vary: drought, floods, bush fires and heat waves add to the confusion.

In general terms, Australian red wines such as Cabernet Sauvignon, Pinot Noir and Shiraz are ready sooner than their northern hemisphere equivalents.

White wines for ageing include Rieslings and Semillons which can last 20 years; Chardonnays are mostly made to drink young. However wines from the same grape, and area, will differ in their ageing potential according to the maker's methods and intentions.

Mass-produced wines here are far less subject to vintage variation than more expensive ones, and are made to be drunk as soon as they are released for sale. Some vintage wines are aged by their makers and only released when ready: back labels will say so. Remember that harvest in Australia is in February–April, so all wines are six months older than northern hemisphere wines with the same vintage date on the label.

Good recent vintages are:

1992, which was cool and unsuccessful in the Hunter; better in South Australia. Some good solid reds were made.

1991 saw a small crop, from which came some good reds which could improve further

1990 had some good reds, mostly now past their best

NEW ZEALAND

Very new vineyard areas, and a variable climate, make vintage reports on New Zealand hard to compile.

1995 saw a large vintage after several small ones. Rain at harvest-time affected some of the cooler regions, such as Marlborough, but overall quality is good.

1994 was a very good vintage, especially for Marlborough area whites.